AMERICAN PREMIUM GUIDE TO

ELECTRIC TRAINS

by Richard O'Brien
with Richard MacNary,
Steven and Catherine Hintze,
Terry Amadon, Frank Ferrara

ISBN-0-89689-052-X

BOOKS AMERICANA
INC

To Ray Funk
for his unfailing generosity and helpfulness

ACKNOWLEDGMENTS

Like the first edition, this volume is heavily indebted to the work of many hands other than mine.

Thanks to Thomas W. Sefton and Jerry Wagner for again helping out on the pricing of the Buddy L line, to Steve Hintze for wholesale revisions to the Lionel section, and the same to Richard MacNary for his work on Marx, as well as for his corrections and additions to several other sections.

Newcomers Terry Amadon and Frank Ferrara jumped in feet first with completely revised listings on, respectively, Ives and American Flyer S Gauge, and Herman Lotstein pitched in with considerable help on Dorfan, for all of which I'm exceedingly grateful.

Heinz Mueller of Continental Hobby House was stunningly generous in his contribution of photographs and general expertise, Mr. and Mrs. Stacy Feller volunteered their expertise on Auburn with photos, listings and price information, J. McAuliffe helped out with the Dorfan listing, and Charles M. Vessell did the same for American Flyer. Gramercy, all!

TABLE OF CONTENTS

HISTORIES OF MANUFACTURERS

DEFINITION OF TERMS

Gauge is the measurement between the inside of the rails:
- 2-7/8" — 2-7/8"
- Standard — 2-1/8"
- No. 2 — 2"
- No. 1 — 1-¾"
- No. 0 — 1¼"
- S — 7/8"
- HO — 5/8"

Condition in this book is given for Good, Very Good, Excellent (in the case of Lionel trains) and Mint. The following is an indication of what the terms suggest:

GOOD: All complete and original, well used, with scratches and perhaps small dents, perhaps dirty, but not broken.

VERY GOOD: Relatively clean, few scratches, no dents or rust, complete and original.

EXCELLENT: Extremely clean, minute scratches, no discoloration, no dents or rust, all complete and original.

MINT: Appears as it did when it was manufactured. No blemishes at all, never track run. In the opinion of many collectors, original carton, inserts, instructions, etc., must accompany to qualify it as true mint. Add 20 to 25% over the Excellent value for any mint trains.

Bulbs: The prices for bulbs are for working bulbs only.

2-4-2, 0-4-0, etc., refers to the number of wheels under each section of the unit.

All prices on Lionel engines include the accompanying tender, where applicable.

LIONEL
By Steven W. Hintze

Lionel is indisputably the foremost name in the field of toy trains. The company was founded in 1900 by Joshua Lionel Cowen at the age of twenty-one, after which he went on to manufacture many of the world's most coveted collectors' pieces. Starting out with a crude 2-7/8" gauge battery-powered flat car, he kept up with his already well-established competitor (Ives) by introducing and successfully marketing a "Standard Gauge" line in 1906. Rather primitive in appearance, but mechanically sound, these larger-scale trains actually were quite true to the real operating prototypes of this period. This era is known as the "Early Period" of standard gauge (1906 - 1923). Lionel published his first black and white catalogue in 1903, and a color supplement by 1912. By then he had established himself as a competitor to be taken seriously. Because of the large area needed to set up standard gauge, Lionel introduced a smaller size (0 gauge) in 1915. The public took to it instantly. Much of what was being produced in the larger standardized gauge was made available in 0 gauge. This new size went on to establish itself as the industry's standard for many years to come. World War I stopped toy production for little more than a year, and in 1918 Lionel incorporated and became "The Lionel Corporation". With sales showing consistent gains, the period which follows (known as the Classic Period, 1923 - 1940) has left us with many valuable

STEVEN W. HINTZE is a roofing and siding mechanic working out of the Hudson and Bergen County areas of New Jersey. A relatively new name in the train world, he has compiled a very fine post-war Lionel collection that has propelled him into the ranks of many other leading collectors and dealers. The knowledge and experience he has gained over these years have played a very instrumental part in attempting to set a realistic market value on many of the Lionel trains listed in this book. Until recently, he had considered himself primarily a collector, but with his son, Steven Jr., "coming of age", the project of constructing an operating layout has begun. "Trains should be used for what they were originally intended . . . and that is to have fun watching them run." Residents of Leonia, New Jersey, he and his wife, Catherine (who compiled this book's American Flyer history), have taken toy trains very seriously. They also boast an extensive collection of old Christmas ornaments which they treat just as seriously. They have a little girl, Samantha, who will also know the "Lionel Tradition".

1

and prized collector's items, such as the 400E steamer (Standard Gauge, 1931-40), 381 Electric (Standard Gauge 1928-29), 408E Electric (Standard Gauge 1927-36), 9U Electric (Standard Gauge 1928-29), 700E Steamer (0 Gauge, 1937-42) and an extensive line of special sets. In 1928, the Ives corporation was bought out by Lionel, with limited production of "Ives" trains continued for several years, until they were completely phased out. During this "transition" period, many items were marketed with remaining Ives inventory using Lionel markings and trim, which has resulted in many sought-out variations.

With the financial collapse of 1929 crippling the nation, all sales were off drastically and Lionel was on the brink of going under. The introduction and successful marketing of the No. 1101 "Mickey Mouse Handcar" for $1.00 in 1934 helped turn the company around. As the economy gradually recovered, sales continued to grow and Lionel experienced a success of unprecedented proportion. This was suddenly halted as the war efforts in 1942 forced shutdowns and changeovers to meet the demand of government contracts.

Later, as the war was winding down, Lionel prepared to embark on a media blitz second to none. In the November 23, 1946 edition of Liberty Magazine (circulation 3,500,000), a 16-page Lionel catalogue was included in each issue. Standard Gauge, though still available for years through dealers' surplus inventories, was discontinued in 1940 with Lionel concentrating all its efforts on 0 and 027 gauge.

Bakelite and other plastics were now playing an important part in the assembly of these post-War trains and many new innovations followed . . . the knuckle-type coupler replaced the pre-War latch-and-box coupler (1945), smoke units were part of the better streamliners (1946), the pre-War whistle units with remote control continued, along with the introduction of a battery-powered diesel horn (1948) and the addition of "Magnetraction" (magnetized wheels and axles for greater pulling power) in 1950.

Their only serious competition at this time was American Flyer, under the leadership of A. C. Gilbert, though Lionel generally remained one step ahead throughout this competitive era. Many fine 0 gauge items were produced during this period, such as the 773 Hudson (1950), 2332 GGI single motor (1947-49), F-3 Diesels (under twelve different road names, 1948-1966), 2340 GGI double motor (1955), FM Trainmasters (1954 - 1966), 2360 GGI double motor (1956 - 63), many fine passenger and freight cars (both operating and non-operating) along with an extensive line of operating accessories.

2

This heyday period is known as the "Golden Years" (and rightly so!). In 1955, the Lionel Corporation was ranked as the largest toy company in the world. This was also the turning point, not only for Lionel but for toy trains in general. Due to the changing attitudes and interests of the public, train sales began to show a progressive decline. The competition from other toy manufacturers was great, cutting deeply into projected train sale profits. The lessening quality and diversification into other fields contributed to further declines in sales. By the mid-sixties all that remained was stocked inventory and a handful of smaller 0-27 sets (some being manufactured abroad).

Joshua Lionel Cowen died September 8, 1965 at the age of 85. He, sadly enough, was witness to the downfall of this once-mighty empire he had spent a lifetime to build. In 1969, Lionel was purchased by General Mills and an agreement was reached permitting the manufacture of trains once again. The Lionel name was retained as part of this pact. After moving the entire operation to Mount Clemons, Michigan, by 1971 trains were being produced in limited numbers. As each year's line was offered, a steady increase in quality and sales followed suit. Today these better sets can be purchased once again from leading Lionel dealers across the country. On these pages, Lionel listed up to 1971.

	G	VG	E
1 Trolley, Motor Car, (Powered) Std GA 4 wheel (1906-1910) "No. 1 Electric-Rapid Transit No. 1"			
A. Creme body, orange roof 1200.00		1800.00	2400.00
B. White body, blue roof 1100.00		1700.00	2200.00
C. Creme body, blue roof 1000.00		1500.00	2000.00
D. Blue body, blue roof 1000.00		1500.00	2000.00
E. Creme body, blue roof 1200.00		1800.00	2500.00
"No. 1 Curtis Bay No. 1"			
1 Trolley, Trailer, (non-powered), Std GA (1907)			
A. White body & blue roof 900.00		1500.00	2000.00
B. Creme body & blue roof 900.00		1500.00	2000.00
1 Bild-A-Motor — 0 (1928) 75.00		100.00	150.00
1 Bild-A-Motor (1928), small 37.50		56.25	75.00
00-1 Loco, steam – (1938-42) Either 001T Tender without whistle or 001W Tender with whistle, full scale, 3-rail, BK 4-6-4 Hudson 90.00		140.00	200.00

3

USMC "Land, Sea and Air" Set
Top left to right: 45 loco, 6640 rocket launcher
Middle: 3429 flat with helicopter
Bottom left to right: 3820 flat with submarine, 6824 caboose
Courtesy Richard MacNary

	G	VG	E
2 Trolley Motor Car, (powered), 4 wheel, Std GA (1906-1915) "No. 2 Electric-Rapid Transit No. 2"			
A. Red body, creme windows & doors	1000.00	1500.00	2000.00
B. Creme body, red windows & doors	1000.00	1500.00	2000.00
2 Trolley, Trailer, (non-powered), Std. GA (1906-1915)			
A. Red body, creme windows & doors	800.00	1200.00	1500.00
B. Creme body, red windows & doors	800.00	1200.00	1500.00
2 Bild-A-Motor — 0 (1928), large	100.00	150.00	200.00
00-2 Loco, steam — 00 (1939-1942) Bk 4-6-4 Hudson, semi-scale, 3 rail, with either 002T Tender (without whistle)	80.00	150.00	175.00
002W Tender (with whistle)	80.00	150.00	175.00
3 Trolley, Motor Car, (powered), 8 wheel, Std GA (1906-1909) "No. 3 Electric-Rapid Transit No. 3"			
A. Lt. orange body dk. orange roof	1500.00	2000.00	2500.00
B. Creme body, orange roof	1500.00	2000.00	2500.00
C. Dk green body and roof	1600.00	2200.00	2700.00

4

Lionel No. 6 loco and tender (circa 1911-1923)
T. W. Sefton Collection

Lionel No. 7 (Brass & Nickel) (circa 1912-22) Standard Gauge
T. W. Sefton Collection

Lionel No. 42 Locomotive "The Classic early locomotive", circa 1915-1924
T. W. Sefton Collection

"No 3 Bay Shore No. 3"

	G	VG	E
3 Trolley, Trailer, (non-powered), 8 wheel, lt. orange body, dk orange roof, St. Ga. (1906-09)	1400.00	1900.00	2300.00
00-3 Loco, steam — 00 (1939-42), Bk 4-6-4, Hudson, full scale (2 rail) with either 003T Tender (without whistle)	110.00	160.00	225.00
or 003W with whistle	120.00	175.00	250.00

5

	G	**VG**	**E**
4 Trolley, Motor Car, (powered), 8 wheel, double motor, Std GA (1908-1910)			
"No. 4 Electric-Rapid Transit No 4"			
A. Green body & green roof	2200.00	3000.00	5500.00
B. Creme body & green roof	2200.00	3000.00	5500.00
4 Loco, Electric 0-4-0 0-ga (1928-32)			
A. Grey	300.00	500.00	700.00
B. Orange	250.00	400.00	600.00
4U Loco Electric 0-4-0 oga. 1928 "You Build It" Orange (only) (unassembled, and complete with instructions in original box)	300.00	500.00	800.00
00-4 Loco, steam — 00, (1939-1942,) Bk 4-6-4, Hudson, semi-scale, 2 rail, with either 004T tender (without whistle)	110.00	160.00	225.00
or 004W tender (with whistle)	120.00	175.00	250.00
5 Loco, steam 0-4-0, (no tender), Std ga (1906-1926) Bk cab and boiler, red window trim			
A. "Pennsylvania	800.00	1200.00	1500.00
B. "B.&O.R.R."	600.00	900.00	1200.00
C. "N.Y.C. & H.R.R.R."	700.00	1000.00	1400.00
5 Special loco steam, no tender, 0-4-0 Std. Ga. BK cab and boiler, red window trim with tender	600.00	900.00	1200.00
6 Loco steam (with tender) 4-4-0 Std. g (1906-1923) BK cab and boiler, red window trim			
A. "Pennsylvania"	500.00	700.00	1000.00
B. "B.&O.R.R."	500.00	700.00	1000.00
C. "N.Y.C.&H.R.R.R."	400.00	600.00	800.00
6 Special loco, steam 4-4-0 with tender Std. ga (1908-1909) BK cab and boiler, red window trim (non-lettered)	800.00	1200.00	1500.00
7 Loco, steam 4-4-0 Std. ga (1910-1923) brass boiler, nickel cab and tender	1400.00	1800.00	2200.00
8 Trolley, motor car, (powered), Std. ga 8 wheel, (1908-1909) "No. 8 Pay As You Enter No. 8" cream or dk green	2000.00	2500.00	3000.00

	G	VG	E
8 Loco, electric, 0-4-0 Std. ga (1925-32)			
A. Maroon	60.00	85.00	125.00
B. Olive	50.00	75.00	110.00
C. Red	60.00	85.00	125.00
D. Mojave	60.00	85.00	125.00
E. Peacock	75.00	125.00	150.00
8E Loco, electric 0-4-0 Std. ga (1926-32)			
A. Olive	65.00	90.00	140.00
B. Red	65.00	90.00	140.00
C. Peacock	80.00	120.00	175.00
D. Pea green, cream stripe (Macys)	100.00	150.00	225.00
E. Mojave	75.00	120.00	150.00
9 Trolley, motor car, (powered), 8 wheel, Std. ga (1909) "No. 9 Pay As You Enter No. 9" cream or dark green	2500.00	3200.00	4000.00
9 Loco, elec. — Std. (1929), dark green	600.00	800.00	1000.00
9 Special set with 9 loco — Std. (uncat 1928), must have box, orange, green	800.00	1200.00	1500.00
9E Loco, elec. (0-4-0) — Std. (1928), 242, 2-tone green	600.00	800.00	1200.00
9E Loco, elec. (2-4-2) — Std. (1931), grey	400.00	600.00	900.00
9E Special set with 9E loco — Std. (uncat 1928-30), 428, 429, 490, orange	1500.00	2000.00	2500.00
9E Special set with 9E loco — Std. (uncat 1936), grey, 309, 310, 312, two tone green	900.00	1350.00	1800.00
9U Loco, elec. — Std. (1928), orange, assembled	800.00	1000.00	1200.00
9U Special set with 9U loco — Std. (1929), kit form with original box, orange (unassembled)	1000.00	1400.00	1800.00
10 Interurban, motor car (powered) Std. ga (1910) "Interurban" and "New York Central Lines"			
A. Maroon or dk green	500.00	800.00	1200.00
B. Lettered "10 W.B.&A. 10" & "Interurban"	1600.00	2100.00	2500.00
10 Loco, elec. — Std. (1925-29), 0-4-0, peacock blue, mojave, grey	60.00	90.00	120.00

US Army Attack Set
Top left to right: 44 loco, 6844 flat with missiles
Middle: 3419 flat with helicopter
Bottom left to right: 6823 flat with rockets, 6814 caboose
Courtesy Richard MacNary

Top left to right: 3927 track cleaner, 65 hand car
Middle left to right: 60 trolley, 68 inspection auto
Bottom left to right: 520 loco, 50 gang car
Courtesy Richard MacNary

	G	VG	E
10 Macy loco, elec. — Std. (uncat 1930), 0-4-0, red	125.00	175.00	250.00
10 Macy Special set with 10 loco — Std. (uncat 1931), 337, 334, 341, red .	250.00	375.00	600.00

	G	VG	E
10E Loco, elec. — Std. (1926-30), 0-4-0, brown (green frame)	150.00	225.00	300.00
Peacock or grey	50.00	75.00	110.00
Peacock or red, with Bild-a-Loco Motor	125.00	175.00	225.00
10E Macy Loco, elec. — Std. (uncat 1930), 0-4-0, peacock with orange stripe	150.00	200.00	250.00
11 Flat — Std. (1906-26)	20.00	30.00	40.00
0-11 Switches, electric, nonderailing - 0 (1933), pair	10.00	15.00	20.00
0-11-11 Fiber pins — 0 (1937)	1.00	1.50	2.00
12 Gondola — Std. (1906)	20.00	30.00	40.00
0-12 Switches, electric — 0 (1927) ..	10.00	15.00	20.00
13 Cattle — Std. (1906)	30.00	40.00	50.00
0-13 Switches and panel board set — 0 (1929)	10.00	15.00	20.00
14 Box — Std. (1906-26)	30.00	40.00	50.00
14 Harmony Creamery Special Boxcar — Std. (uncat 1920)	90.00	130.00	175.00
00-14 Box — 00 (1938), yellow, tuscan	20.00	30.00	40.00
15 Oil — Std. (1906-26)	30.00	40.00	50.00
00-15 Tank — 00 (1938)	20.00	40.00	60.00
16 Ballast — Std. (1906-26), dark green	40.00	60.00	80.00
00-16 Hopper — 00 (1938)	20.00	30.00	40.00
17 Caboose — Std. (1906-26)	20.00	40.00	60.00
00-17 Caboose — 00 (1938)	20.00	30.00	40.00
18 Pullman Std. ga (1906-1927)			
A. Dark olive "Parlor Car" and "New York Central Lines" (1918-23)	60.00	90.00	120.00
B. Light orange "18 Pullman 18" and "New York Central Lines" 1916-17 .	150.00	225.00	300.00
C. Dk olive "18 Pullman 18" and "New York Central Lines" (1906-10)	300.00	400.00	500.00
19 Combine Std. ga (1906-1927)			
A. Match above			
B. Match above			
C. Match above			
190 Observation Std. ga (1907-1927)			
A. Match above			
B. Match			
C. Match above			

9

	G	VG	E
20 Direct current shunt resistor (1906)	1.00	2.00	3.00
20 90° Crossing — Std. (1909)	2.00	3.00	4.00
0-20 90° Crossing — 0 (1915)	1.00	2.00	3.00
0-20X 45° Crossing — 0 (1915)	1.00	2.00	3.00
21 Crossing — Std. (1906)	2.00	3.00	4.00
0-21 Switch with light — 0 (1915)	10.00	15.00	20.00
0-22 Switches, electric — 0 (1946-49)	20.00	30.00	40.00
23 Bumper — Std. (1906), red or black	3.00	6.00	9.00
0-23 Bumper — 0 (1915)	2.00	3.00	4.00
24 Station — Std. (1906)	175.00	250.00	375.00
24 Bulb, 8 volt (1915)	fifty cents		
00-24 Box — 00 (1939)	20.00	30.00	40.00
25 Station — Std. (1906)	175.00	250.00	375.00
25 Bulb, 3½ volt DC (1911)	fifty cents		
25 Bulb, pear shaped (1924)	fifty cents		
25 Bumper — Std. (1928), cream or black	3.00	6.00	9.00
0-25 Bumper — 0 (1928)	5.00	7.50	10.00
00-25 Tank — 00 (1939)	20.00	30.00	40.00
26 Passenger foot bridge (1906)	40.00	65.00	100.00
26 Bulb, 14 volt AC (1911)	fifty cents		
26 Bumper — 0 (1948), red	2.00	3.00	4.00
Grey	4.00	6.00	10.00
27 Station — Std. (1909)	200.00	250.00	300.00
27 Lighting set for cars — Std. (1911)	20.00	30.00	40.00
27 Bulb, 12 volt - red, green or clear (1927)	fifty cents		
27-3 Bulb, 14 volt - clear (1950)	fifty cents		
27-6 Bulb, 12 volts - clear (1940) ...	fifty cents		
0-27-C1 Track clip - 027 (1949)	.50	.75	1.00
00-27 Caboose — 00 (1939)	15.00	25.00	30.00
28 Two stations and dome — Std. (1909), IVES	300.00	500.00	700.00
28 Bulb, 18 volt - red, green, amber or clear (1927)	fifty cents		
28-3 Bulb, 18 volt - clear (1939)	fifty cents		
28-6 Bulb, 18 volt - red (1939)	fifty cents		
29 Day Coach — Std. (1909), dark olive	300.00	400.00	500.00
Same as above, maroon	500.00	600.00	750.00
29 Bulb, 3½ volt (1915)	fifty cents		
29-3 Bulb, 18 volt - yellow (1932) ...	fifty cents		

	G	VG	E
30 Bulb, 14 volt (1915)	fifty cents		
30 Curved rubber roadbed — Std. (1931)	1.00	1.50	2.00
30 Water tank 1947-50			
A. Grey support structure	20.00	30.00	45.00
B. Black support structure	25.00	40.00	65.00
0-30 Curved rubber roadbed - (1931)	1.00	1.50	2.00
31 Combine — Std. (1921), orange, green, maroon	30.00	50.00	75.00
31 Straight rubber roadbed — Std. (1931)	1.00	1.50	2.00
31 Curved track - Super 0 (1957) ...	.50	.75	1.00
0-31 Straight rubber roadbed — 0 (1931)	1.00	1.50	2.00
00-31 Curved track, 2 rail — 00 (1939)	.75	1.00	1.25
32 Set of twelve miniature figures — Std. (1910)	30.00	60.00	90.00
32 Baggage — Std. (1921), maroon, dark olive, brown, orange	30.00	50.00	75.00
32 Rubber roadbed, 90° crossing — Std. (1931)	1.00	1.50	2.00
32 Straight track — Super 0 (1931) .	.50	.75	1.00
0-32 Rubber roadbed, 90° crossing — 0 (1931)	1.00	1.50	2.00
00-32 Straight track, 2 rail — 00 (1939)	.75	2.00	3.00
33 Set — Std. (1912), 0-6-0, dark green	300.00	450.00	600.00
33 Loco, elec. (0-6-0) (1913), engine only, dark green	200.00	275.00	375.00
33 Loco, elec. (0-4-0) — Std. (1913-24), dark olive or black	40.00	60.00	90.00
As above, in maroon	90.00	150.00	175.00
As above, in red	150.00	225.00	300.00
As above, in peacock	90.00	140.00	200.00
As above, in grey	40.00	60.00	90.00
33 Montgomery Ward Special set with 33 loco — Std. (uncat 1913), dark blue	600.00	800.00	1200.00
33 Rubber roadbed, 45° crossing — Std. (1931)	1.00	1.50	2.00
33 Half curve track - Super 0 (1957)	.50	.75	1.00

11

	G	VG	E
0-33 Rubber roadbed, 45° crossing — Std. -0 (1931)	1.00	1.50	2.00
0-33 Rubber roadbed, 45° crossing — Std. -0 (1931)	1.00	1.50	2.00
34 Set — Std. (1920) 33-35-35-36, all dark olive	300.00	450.00	600.00
34 Loco, elec. (0-6-0) — Std. (1912), dark green	300.00	400.00	500.00
34 Loco elec. (0-4-0) — Std. (uncat 1913), dark green	125.00	175.00	225.00
34 Rubber roadbed, switch — Std. (1913)	1.00	2.00	3.00
34 Half straight track - Super 0 (1957)	.50	.75	1.00
0-34 Rubber roadbed, switch — 0 (1931)	1.00	1.50	2.00
00-34 Curved track connection — 00 (1939)	1.00	1.50	2.00
35 Lamp Post (1940), grey or silver	12.50	18.75	25.00
35 Pullman — Std. (1915), dark olive, maroon or brown	15.00	20.00	35.00
Same as above, in orange	25.00	40.00	60.00
36 Observation — Std. (1912), dark olive, maroon or brown	15.00	20.00	35.00
Same as above, in orange	25.00	40.00	60.00
36RM Controller — Std. (1937)	.50	.75	1.00
37 Uncoupling track - Super 0 (1957)	1.00	1.50	2.00
38 Loco, elec. — Std. (1913-24), 0-4-0, black or gray	40.00	60.00	80.00
Same as above, in pea green	150.00	225.00	300.00
Same as above, in red	200.00	300.00	400.00
Same as above, in brown	150.00	225.00	300.00
38 Water tower (1946-47), Red roof	75.00	140.00	225.00
Brown roof	65.00	125.00	200.00
38 Accessory adapter - Super 0 (1957)	.50	.75	1.00
39 Bulb, 12 volt - frosted (1927)	fifty cents		
39-3 Bulb, 12 volt - frosted (1939)	fifty cents		
39-5 Operating Unit set - Super 0 (1957)	1.00	1.50	2.00
39-25 Operating and Uncoupling set - Super 0 (1960)	1.00	1.50	2.00
HO-039 Track cleaning car - HO (1961)	20.00	30.00	40.00

LIONEL Standard Gauge 408E Locomotive,
Courtesy PB Eighty-Four, New York

LIONEL "Blue Comet" Standard Gauge
Train set,
Courtesy PB Eighty-Four New York

	G	VG	E
40 Bulb, 18 volt (1927)	fifty cents		
40-3 Bulb, 8 volt (1939)	fifty cents		
40-25 Four conductor cable and reel (1950)	.75	1.00	1.25
40-50 Three conductor cable and reel (1960)	.50	.75	1.00

13

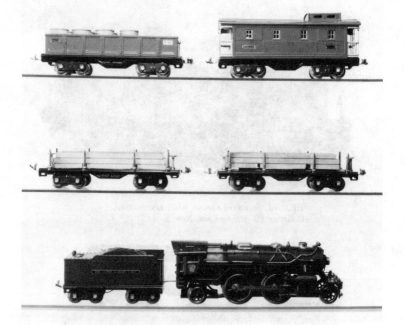

LIONEL Standard Gauge 500 series six-piece Freight Train set,
with 385E grey locomotive.
Courtesy PB Eighty-Four New York

Lionel 52 Fire Car,
0/027 ga. 1958-61,
small motorized unit.
Photo by Steve
Hintze

	G	VG	E
41 Accessory contractor (1936)	.50	.75	1.00
41 Loco, Army switcher — 027 (1955), black shell sm motorized unit	30.00	40.00	60.00
42 Loco, electric (square body) Std. ga 0-4-4-0 (1912), dark green	600.00	800.00	1000.00
42 Loco, electric Std. ga (1913-1923)			
A. Dk green, grey black	250.00	375.00	450.00
B. Peacock or mojave	300.00	400.00	500.00
C. Maroon	400.00	500.00	600.00

14

	G	VG	E
42 Loco, Picatinny Arsenal switcher — 027 (1957), olive shell, small motorized unit	75.00	125.00	175.00
0-42 Switch, manual — 0 (1938), single	5.00	7.00	9.00
43 Set — Std. (1919) 51-29-29 Loco black, cars dark olive	600.00	750.00	1000.00
43 Bild-A-Motor gear set — Std. (1929)	30.00	60.00	75.00
43 Pleasure boat 1933-36, 1939-41 cream, red, and white	100.00	175.00	250.00
43 Power track - Super 0 (1957)	.50	.75	1.25
0-43 Bild-A-Motor gear set — 0 (1929)	20.00	30.00	40.00
44 Race boat, 1935-1936, green, white, and dark brown	125.00	200.00	300.00
44 Set — Std. (1920) 42-29-29 Loco black, cars dark olive	600.00	750.00	1000.00
blue shell	40.00	60.00	80.00
44-80 Four missiles - Super 0 (1959-62)	two dollars		
00-44 Box — 00 (1939)	20.00	30.00	40.00
00-44K Kit, original box — 00 (1939)	50.00	75.00	100.00
45 Set — Std. (1921) 38-31-32-35-36, Loco black, cars dark olive	170.00	225.00	340.00
45/45N/045 Automatic gateman (1935-1936) (1937-1942) green base creme house, red roof with creme chimney	10.00	15.00	25.00
45 Loco, U.S. Marine Missile Launcher - Super 0 (1960-62), olive shell with white missiles	50.00	75.00	100.00
00-45 Tank — 00 (1939)	20.00	30.00	40.00
00-45K Kit, tank — 00 (1939)	50.00	75.00	100.00
46 Bulb, 8 volt (1936)	fifty cents		
46 Single arm crossing gate (1939-42), creme and green base, lantern on tip of gate	20.00	40.00	60.00
00-46 Hopper — 00 (1939)	20.00	30.00	40.00
00-46K Kit, hopper — 00 (1939)	50.00	75.00	100.00
47 Bulb, 6 volt (1916)	fifty cents		
47 Double arm crossing gates (1937-42), same as #46 but with two crossing gates on each side	40.00	60.00	80.00

	G	VG	E
47-40 Bulb, 18 volt - red (1937)	fifty cents		
47-73 Bulb, 12 volt (1942)	fifty cents		
00-47 Caboose — 00 (1939)	15.00	20.00	30.00
00-47K Kit, caboose — 00 (1939) ...	50.00	75.00	100.00
48 Bulb, 21 volt (1936)	fifty cents		
48 Insulated straight track - Super 0 (1958)	.50	.75	1.00
48W Whistle station (1937-42), lithographed building, red base housing whistle	10.00	15.00	20.00
49 Lionel Airport 1937-39 printed cardboard base for center control and airplane	30.00	60.00	90.00
49 Insulated curved track - Super 0 (1958)	.50	.75	1.00
50 Set — Std. (1920), 51-181-180-182 Loco black, cars maroon	400.00	600.00	800.00
50 Loco, elec. — Std. (1924), gray, 0-4-0	60.00	90.00	120.00
Same as above, maroon	90.00	120.00	175.00
Same as above, dark green	60.00	90.00	120.00
Same as above, mojave	90.00	120.00	175.00
50 Airplane (1936) with controls ...	60.00	90.00	120.00
50 Paper train set (uncat 1943)	60.00	90.00	140.00
50 Gang Car - 027 (1954)	10.00	15.00	25.00
HO-050 Gang Car - HO (1959)	5.00	10.00	15.00
51 Loco, steam — Std. (1912-23), "5 Special", 4-4	400.00	550.00	750.00
51 Airport (1936-39), printed cardboard base for center control and airplane	30.00	60.00	90.00
51 Loco, Navy switcher - 027 (1956-57) blue shell (small motorized unit)	25.00	30.00	45.00
00-51 Curved track, 3 rail — 00 (1939)	.75	1.00	2.00
52 Set — Std. (1915) 53-180-182 All maroon	350.00	525.00	700.00
52 Lamp post (1933), aluminum	15.00	20.00	30.00
52 Fire fighting car — 027 (1958-61), red shell with man	40.00	75.00	110.00
00-52 Straight track, 3 rail — 00 (1939)	.75	1.00	2.00

16

	G	VG	E
53 Loco, elec. (0-4-0) — Std. (1912-14), mojave, maroon, dark olive	500.00	700.00	900.00
53 Loco, elec. (0-4-0) — Std. (1920) similar to above	200.00	300.00	400.00
53 Lamp post (1931), gray, alum, mojave	10.00	15.00	20.00
53 Snow plow, D.R.G. — 027 (1957), Rio Grande, black and yellow,			
A. In Grande backwards	75.00	125.00	175.00
A. Grande correct	75.00	150.00	200.00
53-8 bulb, 18 volt (1932)	fifty cents		
54 Loco, elec. - square body — Std. (1912), brass, 0-4-4-0	2000.00	2500.00	3000.00
54 Loco, elec. — Std. (1913-23), 0-4-4-0, brass, single or double motor	1500.00	1800.00	2200.00
54 Lamp post (1929), double light, dark green	15.00	20.00	30.00
54 Ballast tamper — 027 (1957), yellow shell, small motorized unit, with track trips	45.00	75.00	100.00
00-54 Curved track connection — 00 (1939)	75.00	100.00	200.00
55 Bulb, 14 volt (1924)	fifty cents		
55 Airplane (1937-1939), red and silver with control	100.00	140.00	200.00
55 TieEjector — 027 (1957-1961), red shell with wooden track ties (small motorized unit) and track trips	30.00	60.00	90.00
HO-055 Loco, M. & St. L. switcher — HO (1961)	10.00	15.00	20.00
55-150 Set of twenty-four ties — 027 (1957)	two dollars		
56 Lamp post (1925-49), gray, green, mojave	10.00	15.00	25.00
56 Loco, M. & St. L. Mining — 027 (1958), red shell, small motorized unit	90.00	130.00	175.00
HO-056 Loco, A.E.C. Switcher — HO (1959)	9.00	13.50	18.00
57 Lamp post (1924-1942),			
A. Orange "Broadway & Main"	15.00	25.00	40.00
B. Orange "Broadway & Fifth Ave."	15.00	25.00	40.00
C. Yellow "Broadway & Main"	20.00	40.00	60.00
D. Orange "Broadway & 42nd Street"	20.00	40.00	60.00

	G	VG	E
57 Loco, A.E.C. switcher — 027 (1959-60), cream-red shell, small motorized unit	125.00	200.00	275.00
HO-057 Loco, U.P. switcher — HO (1959)	10.00	15.00	20.00
58 Lamp post (1922-50), green, maroon, cream	8.00	15.00	20.00
58 Loco, Rotary snow plow — 027 (1959-61), green shell, white cab	150.00	225.00	325.00
HO-058 Loco, R.I. switcher (1960)	8.00	12.00	16.00
59 Lamp post (1920-36), green	6.00	9.00	12.00
Olive	10.00	15.00	20.00
59 Loco, U.S. Air Force switcher — 027 (1962), Minute Man, white shell 1963	125.00	200.00	275.00
HO-059 Loco, U.S. Air Force switcher — HO (1960)	10.00	15.00	20.00
60 Automatic trip reverse — Std. (1906)	1.00	2.00	3.00
60 Loco elec.—F.A.O. Schwarz Special — Std. (0-4-0) (uncat 1913)	450.00	700.00	900.00
60 Telegraph pole — Std. (1920), set of 6	20.00	30.00	40.00
60 Trolley — 027 (1955-58), yellow with red roof			
A. Blue lettering	30.00	45.00	65.00
B. Black lettering	40.00	60.00	90.00
C. Moving silhouettes (motor man in front with direction of movement)	60.00	100.00	160.00
0-60 Telegraph pole — 0 (1929), set of 6	20.00	30.00	40.00
61 Loco, elec. - F.A.O. Schwarz Special — Std. (0-4-4-0) (uncat 1913)	600.00	900.00	1200.00
61 Lamp post (1914-36), dark green, maroon, mojave, olive	15.00	20.00	25.00
61 Ground lockon - Super 0 (1957)	.50	.75	1.00
00-61 Curved track, 3 rail — 00 (1938)	.75	1.00	2.00
62 Loco, elec. - F.A.O. Schwarz Special — Std. (0-4-0) (uncat 1913)	400.00	600.00	800.00
62 Automatic reversing trip — Std. (1914)	1.00	2.00	3.00
62 Semaphore (1920-32)	20.00	25.00	30.00
00-62 Straight track, 3 rail — 00 (1939)	.75	1.00	2.00

18

"0" General Set — The 5 Star General
Top left to right: 1872 loco, 1872T tender
Middle left to right: 1877 horse car, 1876 baggage
Bottom left to right: 1875 coach, 1875W coach
Courtesy Richard MacNary

Lionel 258, steam (late), 0, 2-4-2, with tender.
Courtesy H. A. Mueller, Continental Hobby House

Lionel 450 Macy Special loco, 1930
Courtesy H. A. Mueller, Continental Hobby House

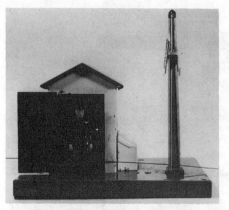

Lionel (45) Automatic Gateman
Courtesy H. A. Mueller
Continental Hobby House

Lionel 71 Lamp Post and 151
Semaphore.
Courtesy H. A. Mueller
Continental Hobby House

Lionel 125 Whistle Station
Courtesy H. A. Mueller
Continental Hobby House

	G	VG	E
63 Semaphore (1915-21)	20.00	25.00	30.00
63 Lamp post (1933-42), double globe, silver	20.00	25.00	30.00
63-10 Opal globe (1933)	1.00	2.00	3.00
63-11 Bulb, 18 volt - opal (1935) ...	fifty cents		
00-63 Half curve track, 3 rail — 00 (1939)	.75	1.00	2.00
64 Semaphore (1915-21)	20.00	25.00	30.00
64 Lamp post (1940-42), green	10.00	15.00	20.00
64-15 Bulb, 12 volt - clear (1940) ...	fifty cents		
64-26 Bulb, 12 volt - opal (1941) ...	fifty cents		
00-64 Curved track connection, 3 rail — 00 (1939)	.75	1.00	2.00
65 Semaphore (1915-26)	20.00	25.00	30.00

Lionel 128 Animated Newsstand
Courtesy H. A. Mueller, Continental Hobby House

Lionel 145 Automatic Gateman
Courtesy H. A. Mueller
Continental Hobby House

	G	VG	E
65 Whistle Controller (1935)	1.00	2.00	3.00
65 Motorized hand car — 027 (1962), yellow, two rubber men, small motorized unit lt yellow or dk yellow	100.00	140.00	175.00
00-65 Half straight track, 3 rail — 00 (1939)	.75	1.00	2.00
66 Semaphore (1915-26)	25.00	30.00	35.00
66 Whistle and reversing controller (1936)	1.00	2.00	3.00
00-66 5/6 straight track, 3 rail — 00 (1939)	.75	1.00	2.00
67 Lamp post (1915-26)	20.00	25.00	30.00
67 Whistle and reversing controller (1936)	1.00	2.00	3.00
68 Warning signal — Std. (1926-39) non-operative	2.00	3.00	4.00
68 Executive inspection car (1958-61), red DeSoto, small motorized unit ...	40.00	60.00	90.00

21

	G	VG	E
0-68 Warning signal — 0 (1926-42) .	2.00	3.0	4.00
0-68 Warning signal, Ives — 0 (Ives 1931)	2.00	3.00	4.00
HO-068 Inspection car — HO (1961)	8.00	12.00	20.00
69 Warning bell — Std. (1921-35) ...	12.00	18.00	25.00
69 Motorized maintenance car — 027 (1960-62), gray platform, black frame, with blue man and red "Danger" sign	60.00	90.00	140.00
69-7 Fiber track pins (1933)	.50	.75	1.00
69N Warning bell — Std./0 (1936-42)	12.00	18.00	25.00
0-69 Warning bell — 0 (1921-35) ...	12.00	18.00	25.00
70 Accessory set (1921)	37.50	56.25	75.00
Consists of 2 #62			
1 #68			
1 #59			
70 Lamp post (1949-50), yard light .	10.00	15.00	20.00
00-70 90° crossing, 3 rail — 00 (1939)	2.00	4.00	6.00
71 Set of six telegraph poles (1921), green	20.00	30.00	40.00
71 Lamp post (1949-59), crackle gray	3.00	6.00	9.00
071 Telegraph Poles (six) (1929), 0-Gauge	20.00	30.00	40.00
072 "T-Rail" curved track, per section	2.00	4.00	6.00
00-72 Switches, electric, 3 rail — 00 (1939), pair	60.00	90.00	140.00
00-72-70 Bulb, 12 volt - yellow — 0 (1939)	fifty cents		
00-74 Box, 2 rail — 00 (1939)	20.00	30.00	40.00
75 Low bridge sign (1921)	15.00	25.00	35.00
75 Bulb, 12 volt (1924)	fifty cents		
75 Lamp set, two (1961-1969), black plastic	2.00	4.00	6.00
00-75 Tank, 2 rail — 00 (1939)	20.00	30.00	40.00
76 Block signal — Std. (1923)	15.00	20.00	25.00
76 Warning bell and shanty (1939-42) red base, orange roof, black bell fastened to cross gate sign post (similar in appearance to #45 gateman, no watch man bell inside shanty)	25.00	50.00	75.00
76 Set of 3 Boulevard lights, green plastic, (1959-69)	1.00	2.00	3.00

	G	VG	E
77 Automatic crossing gate — Std. (1923-39)	8.00	12.00	15.00
77N Automatic crossing gate — Std. /0 (1936-39)	8.00	12.00	15.00
0-77 Automatic crossing gate — 0 (1923-39)	8.00	12.00	15.99
00-77 Caboose, 2 rail — 00 (1939)	20.00	30.00	40.00
78 Train control block signal — Std. (1924), red base, orange base	15.00	25.00	40.00
0-78 Train control block signal — 0 (1924) red or orange base	15.00	25.00	40.00
79 Flashing signal (1928-42), cream or aluminum	15.00	25.00	40.00
79-23 Bulb, 12 volt - red (1939)	fifty cents		
80 Semaphore — Std. (1926-35)	10.00	15.00	20.00
80N Semaphore	10.00	15.00	20.00
0-80 Semaphore — 0 (1926-35)	10.00	15.00	20.00
80/81 Race car set (1912-1916) set consists of car, driver, 8 sections of curve track	400.00	600.00	900.00
81 Rheostat (1927)	1.00	1.50	2.00
00-81 or KW Kit, loco and tend, 3 rail — 00 (1938)	300.00	400.00	500.00
82 Train control semaphore — Std. yellow and green (1927-35)	30.00	40.00	60.00
82N Train control semaphore — Std./0 (1936-42)	30.00	40.00	60.00
0-82 Train control semaphore — 0 (1927-35)	30.00	40.00	60.00
83 Traffic crossing signal			
A. Red base 35-42	30.00	40.00	65.00
B. Tan base 27-34	30.00	40.00	65.00
00-83 or W. Loco and tender, 3 rail — 00 (1939-42)	125.00	175.00	250.00
84 Set of racing cars (1912)	800.00	1200.00	1800.00
84 Semaphore — Std. (1927-32)	20.00	35.00	60.00
0-84 Semaphore — 0 (1928-32)	20.00	35.00	60.00
85 Set of racing cars (1912)	800.00	1200.00	1800.00
85 Telegraph pole — Std. (1929-42) orange	3.00	6.00	9.00
86 Set of six telegraph poles — Std. (1932) inc. orig. box	35.00	50.00	75.00

Top left to right: 56 loco "MSTL", 57 loco "AEC"
Bottom left to right: 58 loco, Great Northern snowplow, 59 loco "US Air Force"
Courtesy Richard MacNary

USMC Set #1
Top left to right: 6804 flat with two trucks, 6803 flat with tank and truck
Middle; 6806 flat with two trucks
Bottom left to right: 212 loco, 601750 caboose
Courtesy Richard MacNary

	G	VG	E
87 Crossing signal (1927), orange or green base	25.00	40.00	65.00
88 Battery rheostat (1915)	1.00	1.50	2.00
88 Direction controller (1933)	1.00	1.50	2.00
89 Flagstaff and flag (1923-34)	20.00	30.00	40.00
89 Flag pole (1956-58)	15.00	25.00	35.00

	G	VG	E
90 Flagstaff and flag (1927-42), with round grass plot	25.00	40.00	65.00
91 Automatic circuit breaker (1930-42), brown with red light bulb	6.00	9.00	12.00
91 Circuit breaker (1957-60), brown with red light	3.00	4.00	6.00
00-91 or W Loco and tender, 2 rail — 00 (1939)	125.00	175.00	250.00
92 Floodlight tower (1931), terra cotta/green	60.00	90.00	125.00
Same as above, red/silver	60.00	90.00	125.00
92 Circuit breaker with controller (1959)	.50	.75	1.00
93 Water tower — 0 (1932), green ...	8.00	12.00	15.00
Same as above, silver	10.00	15.00	20.00
90-93 or W Loco and tender, 2 rail — 00 (1939)	125.00	175.00	250.00
94 High tension tower (1932), gray/ terra cotta, silver/red	75.00	140.00	175.00
95 Rheostat (1934)	1.00	1.50	2.00
96 Coal elevator, manual control (1938-40)	40.00	60.00	75.00
97 Coal elevator, electric (1938-42) and (1946-50)	50.00	65.00	90.00
97C Contractor (1938)	.50	.75	1.00
0-97 Telegraph pole set — 0 (1934) .	20.00	35.00	60.00
99 Train control block signal — Std. (1932), red or black base	40.00	60.00	80.00
99N Train control block signal — Std./0 (1936), red or black base	40.00	60.00	80.00
0-99 Train control block signal — 0 (1930), red or black base	40.00	60.00	80.00
100 Loco - 2⅞" (1901)	EXTREMELY RARE		
100 Trolley, motor car — Std. (1910), blue or red, "100 Electric Rapid Transit 100"	1200.00	1600.00	2000.00
100 Bridge approaches — Std. (1920)	10.00	15.00	20.00
100 Ives bridge approaches — Std. (Ives 1931)	10.00	15.00	20.00
HO-100 Power Pack — HO (1961) .	1.00	2.00	3.00
101 Summer trolley, motor car — Std. (1910), "101 Electric Rapid Transit 101", blue or red	800.00	1200.00	1400.00

	G	VG	E
101 3 section bridge — Std. (1920), cream and green	15.00	20.00	25.00
101 Ives 3 section bridge — Std. (Ives 1931)	15.00	20.00	25.00
HO-101 Power pack — HO (1961) ..	1.00	2.00	3.00
102 4 section bridge — Std. (1920) ..	20.00	25.00	30.00
103 5 section bridge — Std. (1913) ..	25.00	30.00	35.00
HO-103 Power pack — HO (1959) ..	1.00	2.00	3.00
HO-103-800 Power pack — HO (1961)	1.00	2.00	3.00
104 Tunnel — Std. (1909-1914)	20.00	30.00	40.00
104 Bridge, center span — Std. (1920)	3.00	7.00	10.00
104 Ives bridge, center span — Std. (Ives 1931)	3.00	7.00	10.00
HO-104 Power pack — HO (1961) ..	1.00	2.00	3.00
105 5 section bridge — Std. (1911) ..	20.00	30.00	40.00
105 3 section bridge — Std. (1913) ..	15.00	20.00	25.00
105 Bridge approaches — 0 (1920) .	5.00	10.00	15.00
105 Ives bridge approaches — 0 (Ives 1931)	5.00	10.00	15.00
106 AC current reducer, 110 or 120 volts (1911)	1.00	1.50	2.00
106 3 section bridge — 0 (1920)	15.00	20.00	25.00
106 Ives 3 section bridge — 0 (Ives 1931)	15.00	20.00	25.00
107 DC current reducer, 110 volts (1911)	3.00	5.00	7.00
107 DC current reducer, 220 volts (1911)	3.00	5.00	7.00
108 Battery Rheostat (1912)	1.00	1.50	2.00
108 4 section bridge — 0 (1920)	20.00	25.00	30.00
109 Tunnel — Std. (1913)	15.00	20.00	30.00
109 5 section bridge — 0 (1920)	20.00	30.00	40.00
110 Bridge center span — 0 (1920) .	3.00	7.00	10.00
110 Ives bridge, center span — 0 (Ives 1931)	3.00	7.00	10.00
110 Trestle set — 0 (1955-69), 24 pieces	2.00	3.00	4.00
HO-110 Trestle set — HO (1958) ...	3.00	4.50	6.00
111 Trolley, trailer — Std. (1910) ...	800.00	1200.00	1400.00
111 Light bulb set (1920)	three dollars		
111 Trestle set — 0 (1956-69), 10 pieces	2.00	3.00	4.00
111-100 2 Piers — 0 (1960-63), 2 pieces	1.00	2.00	3.00
HO-111 Trestle set — HO (1959) ...	1.00	1.50	2.00

Lionel No. 211 Flat with Lumber, Std., 1926-40.
Photo by Steve Hintze

Lionel 212 Gondola with barrels, Std., 1926-40
Photo by Steve Hintze

Lionel 213 Cattle Car, Std., 1926-40
Photo by Steve Hintze

Lionel 214 Box Car, double door, Std., 1926-40.
Photo by Steve Hintze

Lionel 215 Tank Car, Std., 1926-40.
Photo by Steve Hintze

Lionel 218 Dump Car, double bin, Std., 1926-40.
Photo by Steve Hintze

Lionel 217 Caboose, Std., 1926-40.
Photo by Steve Hintze

Lionel 219 Crane Car, Std., 1926-40.
Photo by Steve Hintze

	G	VG	E
112 Gondola, 7″—Std.(1910)	25.00	40.00	60.00
112 Gondola, 9½″—Std.(1913)	15.00	30.00	40.00
112 Station—Std.(1931-35), cream .	60.00	90.00	125.00
112 Switch — Super 0 (1957-60), pr. with controls	20.00	30.00	40.00
113 Cattle — Std. (1912-26)	20.00	30.00	40.00
113 Station — Std. (1931-34) creme .	60.00	90.00	125.00
114 Box — Std. (1912)	20.00	30.00	40.00
114 Station — Std. (1931-34), cream	400.00	650.00	900.00
114 Newstand with horn — 0 (1957-59)................................	20.00	30.00	45.00
HO-114 Engine house with horn — HO (1958).........................	10.00	15.00	20.00
115 Station (1935), cream, red or green trim	60.00	100.00	140.00
115 Station (1949), cream, red or green trim	60.00	100.00	140.00
HO-115 Kit, engine house — HO (1961)	2.00	3.00	4.00
116 Ballast — Std. (1910)	20.00	30.00	40.00
116 Station (1935), cream	400.00	650.00	900.00
117 Caboose — Std. (1912-26)	20.00	30.00	40.00
117 Station (1936-42)	60.00	100.00	140.00
Same as above, no outside lights ...	60.00	100.00	140.00
HO-117 Engine house — HO (1959)	3.00	4.50	6.00
118 Tunnel — 0 (1915-1920)	15.00	25.00	40.00
118 Newstand with whistle — 0 (1958)	20.00	30.00	50.00
118L Tunnel, lighted — 0 (1927) ...	20.00	30.00	40.00
HO-118 Engine house with whistle — HO (1958)	4.00	8.00	12.00
119 Tunnel — Std./0 (1915)	20.00	30.00	40.00
119 Tunnel — 0 (1957)	4.00	8.00	12.00
119L Tunnel, lighted — Std./0 (1927)	20.00	30.00	45.00
HO-119 Tunnel — HO (1959)	2.00	3.00	4.00
120 Tunnel — Std./0 (1915)	15.00	20.00	25.00
120 90° crossing — Super 0 (1957) .	1.00	2.00	3.00
120L Tunnel, lighted — Std./0 (1927)	20.00	30.00	40.00
121 Tunnel — 0 (1959-66)	6.00	9.00	15.00
121 SPECIAL Station — Std. (1909)	125.00	175.00	250.00
121x Station with lights — Std. (1917)................................	125.00	175.00	250.00
122 Station — Std. (1920)	60.00	90.00	120.00

	G	VG	E
123 Station — Std. (1920)	60.00	90.00	120.00
123 Curved tunnel — 0 (1933)	30.00	40.00	60.00
124 Station — Std. (1920)	60.00	90.00	140.00
124 Station — Std. (1933)	60.00	90.00	140.00
125 Station — Std. (1923)	75.00	125.00	175.00
125 Track template — 72 (1938)	1.00	2.00	3.00
125 Whistle station (1950-55), grey or green base	10.00	15.00	20.00
126 Station — Std. (1923-36)	40.00	65.00	90.00
127 Station (1923-36)	40.00	60.00	90.00
128 Tunnel, lighted — 0 (1920)	30.00	45.00	60.00
128 Animated Newsstand (1957-60)	30.00	45.00	75.00
129 Station and Terrace — Std. (1929-40)	300.00	650.00	1000.00
129 Tunnel, lighted — Std./0 (1920)	30.00	45.00	60.00
129 Terrace — Std. (1928)	200.00	400.00	800.00
130 Tunnel — 0 (1920)	60.00	90.00	150.00
130 60° crossing — Super 0 (1957) .	1.00	2.00	3.00
130L Tunnel, lighted — 0 (1927) ...	60.00	90.00	150.00
131 Corner elevation (1924-28)	150.00	225.00	300.00
131 Curved tunnel — 0 (1959-66) ...	2.00	5.00	10.00
132 Corner grass plot (1924-28)	150.00	225.00	300.00
132 Station — 0 (1949-55)	10.00	15.00	25.00
133 Heart shape grass plot (1924-28)	150.00	225.00	300.00
133 Station — 0 (1957-66)	10.00	15.00	25.00
134 Oval grass plot large (1924-28) .	150.00	225.00	300.00
134 Stop station (1937-42), brown, red roof	90.00	140.00	225.00
135 Oval grass plot, small (1924-28)	150.00	225.00	300.00
136 Stop station, lighted (1937-42) .	30.00	60.00	90.00
137 Stop station, lighted (1937-42) .	30.00	60.00	90.00
138 Water tank, operating (1953-57)	20.00	30.00	40.00
140 Banjo signal — 0 (1954-66)	4.00	8.00	12.00
140L Tunnel, lighted — Std. (1927-32)	200.00	300.00	400.00
HO-140 Banjo signal — HO (1962)	1.00	2.00	3.00
142 Switches, pair, manual — Super 0 (1957)	9.00	12.00	15.00
144 Set — 0 (1931)	160.00	240.00	320.00
145 Automatic Gateman — 0 (1950-66)	5.00	10.00	15.00
145C Contractor — 0 (1950)	.50	.75	1.00

	G	VG	E
HO-145 Automatic Gateman — HO (1959)	2.00	3.00	4.00
HO-245-200 Contractor — HO (1960)	1.00	1.50	2.00
147 Whistle controller — 0 (1961)	.50	.75	1.00
148 Dwarf signal — 0 (1957)	7.00	15.00	25.00
148-100 Double pole switch (1957)	1.00	2.00	3.00
150 Loco, elec. — 0 (1918-25), 0-4-0, dark green	30.00	45.00	60.00
150 Set of 6 telegraph poles — 0 (1947-50)	3.00	6.00	9.00
HO-150 Rectifier - HO (1958)	.50	.75	1.00
151 Semaphore — 0 (1947-69)	4.00	6.00	8.00
151-51 Bulb, 14 volt - clear (1950)	fifty cents		
152 Loco, elec. — 0 (1917-27), dark gray or dark green	75.00	125.00	200.00
Same as above, light gray	100.00	150.00	250.00
Same as above, peacock or mojave	125.00	175.00	325.00
152 Crossing gate — 0 (1945-48)	4.00	8.00	12.00
152-33 Bulb, 12 volt - red — 0 (1940)	fifty cents		
153 Loco, elec. — 0 (1924), mojave	125.00	225.00	300.00
Same as above, dark green	65.00	100.00	150.00
Same as above, gray	75.00	125.00	200.00
153 Block signal — 0 (1945-69)	4.00	8.00	12.00
153C Contractor — 0 (1940)	1.00	2.00	3.00
153-23 Bulb, 6 volt - red (1940)	fifty cents		
153-24 Bulb, 6 volt - green (1940)	fifty cents		
153-48 Bulb, 14 volt - green (1940)	fifty cents		
153-50 Bulb, 14 volt - red (1940)	fifty cents		
154 Loco, elec. — 0 (1917-23), 0-4-0, dark green	5.00	125.00	175.00
154 Highway signal — 0 (1940-42)	6.00	9.00	12.00
154C Contractor — 0 (1940)	1.00	2.00	3.00
154-18 Bulb, 12 volt - red (1942)	fifty cents		
155 Freight shed (1930-39), (1940-42)	65.00	100.00	150.00
A. Yellow base maroon roof	100.00	150.00	200.00
B. Ivory base grey roof	125.00	175.00	250.00
155 Signal light (1955-57) W.M Bell	10.00	15.00	20.00
156 Loco, elec. — 0 (1917-23), 4-4-4, gray, olive, maroon	200.00	300.00	450.00
156 Station platform — 0 (1939-40), (1946-51)	10.00	15.00	25.00

Lionel #115 Station (1946-49) with Barclay civilians
Photo Courtesy Steven W. Hintze

Lionel No. 115 Station, circa 1932.
T. W. Sefton Collection

	G	VG	E
156X Loco, elec. — 0 (1923-24), same as 156, but without pilot trucks	200.00	300.00	450.00
156-13 Bulb, 18 volt - clear (1939) . .	fifty cents		
157 Hand truck — Std. (1930-32), red	15.00	20.00	25.00
157 Station platform — 0 (1952-59) .	9.00	12.00	15.00

	G	VG	E
158 Loco, elec. — 0 (1919-23), 0-4-0, gray	100.00	125.00	175.00
Same as above, in black	125.00	150.00	200.00
158 Platform set, lighted (1940-42), two 156 platforms and one 136 station, includes original box	50.00	75.00	125.00
159C Block signal contractor (1940)	1.00	2.00	3.00
160 Unloading bin (1938)	.50	.75	1.00
161 Baggage truck — Std. (1930-32), green	20.00	30.00	40.00
161 Mail pickup set — 0 (1961-63)	20.00	30.00	45.00
162 Dump truck — Std. (1930-32), red or grey	20.00	30.00	40.00
163 Freight accessory set (1930), includes 2 #157 handtrak, 1 #161 baggage cart 1# dump bin, includes original box	75.00	100.00	150.00
163 Block signal, single target — 0 (1961-63)	3.00	6.00	9.00
164 Lumber loader (1940-42), (1946-50) red or gr roof	45.00	90.00	145.00
164-64 Set of five logs (1952)	one dollar		
165 Magnetic crane (1940-42)	45.00	75.00	125.00
165-53 Bulb, 18 volt - red (1940)	fifty cents		
165C Controller (1940)	3.00	5.00	8.00
166 Controller, 3 button (1938)	1.00	3.00	5.00
167 Whistle and reverse controller — 0 (1945)	1.00	3.00	5.00
167X Whistle controller — 00 (1940)	1.00	3.00	5.00
168 Controller (1940)	1.00	3.00	5.00
169 Uncoupling and reversing controller (1940)	1.00	2.00	3.00
170 DC current reducer, 220 volts (1914)	2.00	3.00	5.00
171 Inverter, DC to AC (1936)	2.00	3.00	5.00
172 Inverter, DC to AC - 220 volts (1937)	2.00	3.00	5.00
175 Rocket launcher — 0 (1958-60)	35.00	75.00	100.00
175-50 Extra rockets — 0 (1958)	1.00	3.00	5.00
180 Pullman — Std. (1911), maroon, brown, orange	40.00	60.00	90.00
180 Trailer truck — Std. (1915)	500.00	800.00	1400.00
181 Combine — Std. (1911), maroon, brown, orange	40.00	60.00	90.00

Lionel 911 Country Estate, 0/Std., 1932-42, illum., early colors.
Photo by Steve Hintze

Lionel 912 Suburban Home, 0/Std., 1932-42, illum.
Photo by Steve Hintze

Lionel 911 Country Estate, 0/Std., 1932-42, illum., late colors.
Photo by Steve Hintze

34

Lionel #123 Tunnel (1933-42)
#1101 Mickey Mouse (1934-37)
Photo Courtesy Steven W. Hintze

Lionel Mickey Mouse Circus Train Set (partial), Number 1536.
Courtesy PD Eighty-Four New York

	G	VG	E
HO-181 Cab control — HO (1958)	3.00	5.00	7.00
182 Observation — Std. (1911), maroon, brown, orange	40.00	60.00	90.00
182 Magnet crane (1946-49), with 165C controller	30.00	50.00	80.00
184 Bungalow, lighted (1923)	15.00	20.00	25.00
185 Bungalow, no lights (1923)	15.00	20.00	25.00
186 Bungalow set (1923), five (185) bungalows	75.00	125.00	175.00
186 Log loading outfit (1940), log loader, car, bin, uncoupler	75.00	125.00	175.00
187 Bungalow set (1923), five (185) bungalows	75.00	125.00	175.00

35

	G	VG	E
188 Coal elevator outfit (1938)	75.00	125.00	175.00
189 Villa, lighted (1923)	40.00	60.00	90.00
190 Same as numbers 18 and 19			
191 Villa, lighted (1923)	40.00	60.00	90.00
192 Railroad control tower (1959-60)	40.00	60.00	90.00
193 Automatic accessory set — 0 (1927-29), consists of: 1 #69, 1 #76, 1 #78, 1 #77, 1 #80	125.00	175.00	250.00
193 Water tower (1953-55)	20.00	30.00	45.00
194 Automatic accessory set — Std. (1927-29) (same as #193 set)	125.00	175.00	250.00
195 Terrace — Std. (1927), includes 1 (191) villa, 1 (189) villa, 1 (184) bungalow, 1 (90) flagpole, 2 (56) lamp posts	300.00	450.00	600.00
195 Floodlight tower (1957-69)	9.00	12.00	15.00
195-75 Spare tower head (1957), add lights and holder for (195) floodlight tower	1.00	3.00	5.00
196 Accessory set — Std./0 (1927), includes (127) station, 6 (60) telegraph poles, (62) semaphore, (68) warning signal, 2 (58) lamp posts includes original box	75.00	125.00	175.00
196 Smoke pellets (1946), 100 pellets in bottle/package	six	dollars if	complete
197 Radar antenna – 0 (1957-59) gray gray base or orange	20.00	30.00	45.00
197-75 Replacement radar head (1958)	3.00	6.00	9.00
HO-197 Radar antenna — HO (1958)	3.00	4.50	6.00
199 Scenic railway set — Std. (1924)	75.00	125.00	175.00
199 Microwave tower (1958-59)	10.00	15.00	25.00
200 Gondola, motorized — 2⅞"	EXTREMELY RARE		
200 Trolley, trailer — Std. (1910), non-powered	1200.00	1800.00	2400.00
200 Turntable — Std. (1928), 17" green and tan	45.00	75.00	120.00
201 Loco, steam — 0 (1940), switcher (0-6-0, with 2201 B bell tender	150.00	200.00	250.00
Same as above, with 2201 T no bell tender	140.00	185.00	225.00

	G	VG	E
202 Summer trolley, motor car — Std. (1910), "202 Electric Rapid Transit 202"	1200.00	1600.00	2200.00
202 Loco, Alco A diesel, U.P. — 027 (1957), orange with black lettering ..	10.00	15.00	20.00
203 Loco, steam — 0 (1940), switcher, 0-6-0, no bell (similar to 201)	200.00	225.00	275.00
203 Loco, armored — 0 (1917), 0-4-0 cannon, only prewar war-oriented locomotive produced by Lionel	300.00	500.00	800.00
204 Loco, steam — 0 (uncat 1940-41) 2-4-2 black	20.00	30.00	40.00
Same as above, gunmetal gray	20.00	30.00	45.00
204 Loco, Alco Diesel AA, A.T.S.F. — 027 (1957)	20.00	30.00	45.00
205 L.C.L. Merchandise Containers — Std. (1930-38), price per one, dk. green	30.00	45.00	60.00
205 Loco, Alco Diesel, AA, M.P. — 027 (1957)	20.00	30.00	45.00
208 Tool Set 1934-42			
Grey box	30.00	45.00	60.00
Silver box	25.00	40.00	50.00
includes tools - sledge hammer, pick, rake, shovel, axe			
208 Loco, Alco Diesel AA, A.T.S.F. — 027 (1958)	20.00	30.00	45.00
209 Barrels — Std. (1934-42), wooden, four (open two-piece)	1.00	2.00	3.00
209 Loco, Alco Diesel, AA, N.H. — 027 (1958)	15.00	20.00	35.00
0-209 Barrels — 0 (1934-42), wooden, set of six	2.00	3.00	4.00
210 Switch, automatic, Std. (1926), pair	10.00	15.00	20.00
210 Loco, Alco Diesel AA, Texas Spec. — 027 (1958)	20.00	30.00	45.00
211 Flat — Std. (1926-40) with wooden load	30.00	45.00	75.00
211 Loco, Alco Diesel AA, Texas Spec — 027 (1962)	20.00	30.00	45.00
212 Gondola — Std. (1926-40), green, maroon	30.00	45.00	75.00
Same as above in gray	40.00	60.00	90.00

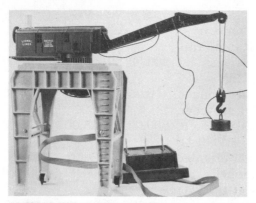

Lionel 282 Gantry Crane
Courtesy H. A. Mueller,
Continental Hobby House

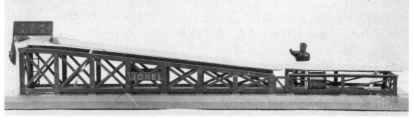

Lionel 362 Barrel Loader
Courtesy H. A. Mueller, Continental Hobby House

Lionel 3656 Operating Cattle Car
Courtesy H. A. Mueller, Continental Hobby House

Lionel 3462P, Milk Car Platform
Courtesy H. A. Mueller, Continental Hobby House

Lionel 943 Exploding Ammo
Dump
Courtesy H. A. Mueller,
Continental Hobby House

Lionel 465 Sound Dispatching Station
Courtesy H. A. Mueller, Continental Hobby House

Lionel 460 Piggyback Terminal
Courtesy H. A. Mueller, Continental Hobby House

	G	VG	E
212 Loco, Alco Diesel AA, Marine — 027 (1958)	15.00	25.00	40.00
212 Loco, Alco Diesel AA, A.T.S.F. — 027 (1964)	15.00	20.00	30.00
213 Cattle — Std. (1926-40), orange body, green roof	40.00	60.00	75.00
Same as above, mojave body, maroon roof................................	75.00	125.00	175.00
213 Cattle — Std, rarer Ivory/maroon	90.00	145.00	190.00
213 Cattle — Std. ivory/maroon nickel trim with blue stripes, indicating it is 1937 factory control piece. One item was held from each run to use as a sample for the next year's production run	500.00	750.00	1000.00
213 Loco, Alco Diesel AA, M & St. L. — 027 (1964)	15.00	25.00	45.00
214 Box — Std., (1926-40)	75.00	125.00	175.00
214 Box — Std., rarer yellow/brown	90.00	140.00	200.00
214 Girder bridge — 0 (1953-69) light or dark gray	2.00	3.00	4.00
HO-214 Girder bridge — HO (1958)	1.00	1.50	2.00
214R Refrigerator — Std. (1929) ...	200.00	250.00	325.00
214R Refrigerator — Std., rarer white/blue	250.00	350.00	450.00
215 Tank — Std. (1926-40), silver (Sunoco)	75.00	125.00	175.00
Same as above, green	60.00	100.00	160.00
Same as above, cream or white	75.00	125.00	175.00
216 Hopper — Std. (1926-40), Dk green	75.00	125.00	175.00
216 Loco, Alco Diesel A, Burlington — 027 (1958)	15.00	25.00	45.00
Same, Minneapolis & St. Louis	20.00	35.00	60.00
217 Lighting set for cars, 8 volts — Std. (1914)	20.00	30.00	40.00
217 Caboose — Std. (1926-40), red/peacock	75.00	125.00	175.00
Same, orange and maroon	100.00	150.00	200.00
217 Loco, Alco Diesel AB, B & M — 027 (1959)	150.00	250.00	300.00
218 Dump — Std. (1926-40), mojave	75.00	125.00	175.00

	G	VG	E
218 Loco, Alco Diesel AA, A.T.S.F. —027 (1959)	20.00	30.00	45.00
218 Loco, Alco Diesel AB, A.T.S.F. — 027 (1961)	20.00	30.00	45.00
218C Loco, Alco Diesel B.A.T.S.F. — 027 (1961), B unit dummy	10.00	15.00	20.00
219 Crane — Std. (1926), peacock cab	75.00	125.00	175.00
Same, yellow cab	125.00	175.00	250.00
Same, white, ivory cab	150.00	225.00	300.00
220 Floodlight — Std. (1931), terra cotta base	75.00	125.00	175.00
Same, green base	90.00	140.00	200.00
220 Loco, Alco Diesel A, A.T.S.F. — 027 (1961)	15.00	20.00	30.00
221 Loco, steam — 027 (1946), gray	25.00	35.00	45.00
Same as above, black	20.00	30.00	40.00
221 Loco, Alco Diesel A, D & RGW — 027 (1963)	15.00	20.00	30.00
221 Loco, Alco Diesel A, A.T.S.F. — 027 (uncat 1963)	15.00	25.00	40.00
221 Loco, Alco Diesel A. Marine — 027 (uncat 1963)	15.00	25.00	40.00
HO-226 Truss bridge — HO (1961)	2.00	3.00	4.00
222 Switches — Std. (1926), pair	10.00	15.00	25.00
HO-222 Deck bridge — HO (1961)	3.00	4.50	6.00.
223 Switches, non-derailing — Std. (1932), pair	10.00	15.00	25.00
223-50 Loco, Alco Diesel A.B. A.T.S.F. — 027 (1963)	**15.00**	**20.00**	**35.00**
224/224E Loco steam 2-6-2 ga. 1938-42			
A. BK with 2224 die cast tender	75.00	100.00	125.00
B. BK with plastic tender	60.00	90.00	110.00
C. Gunmetal grey with 2224 diecast tender	150.00	200.00	250.00
D. Gunmetal grey with 2689 sheet-metal tender	75.00	100.00	125.00
224 Loco, steam — Paper train (uncat 1943), complete, including original box	60.00	90.00	125.00

41

	G	VG	E
224 Paper Train Set, includes 224 loco, 2224 tender, 2812 red gondola, 61100 yellow box with brown roof, 47618 red caboose, crossing signal, crossing gate, three figures, baggage, paper track	100.00	200.00	300.00
224 Loco, Alco Diesel AB, Navy — 027 (1960)	15.00	25.00	40.00
HO-224 Girder bridge — HO (1961)	2.00	3.00	4.00
225/225 E Loco steam — 0 (1939-40), 2-6-2, black 2235, 2265, 2225, 2245 tenders	75.00	100.00	125.00
Same as above, in gun metal gray tenders	85.00	110.00	140.00
225 Loco, Alco Diesel A, C&O — 027 (1960)	15.00	20.00	30.00
226E Loco, Steam — 0 (1938-41), 2-6-4 2226 tender	125.00	175.00	250.00
227 Loco, steam — 0 (1939), #8976 under cab window, 0-6-0 switcher (scale), with tender 2227T (no bell) .	400.00	600.00	900.00
Same as above, with tender 2227B (bell)	450.00	700.00	1000.00
227 Loco, Alco Diesel A, C.N. — 027 (uncat 1960), Canadian market distribution	20.00	30.00	45.00
228 Loco, steam — 0 (1939), 0-6-0 switcher scale (similar to 227), tender 2228T (no bell)	300.00	375.00	450.00
Same as above, tender 2228B (bell) ..	325.00	400.00	475.00
228 Loco, Alco Diesel A, C.N. — 027 (uncat 1961), Canadian market distribution	20.00	30.00	45.00
229 Loco, Alco Diesel A, M&ST. L. — 027 (1961)	15.00	25.00	40.00
229C Loco, Alco Diesel B, M&St.L — 027 (1962), B Unit (dummy)	10.00	15.00	20.00
229/229E Loco Steam — 0 (1939), 2-4-2, black	15.00	20.00	30.00
Same as above, gun metal gray	15.00	25.00	40.00

	G	VG	E
229P Loco, Alco Diesel A, M & St. L. — 027 (1962)	15.00	25.00	40.00
230 Loco, Alco Diesel A, C&D — 027 (1961)	10.00	15.00	25.00
230 Steam, 0-6-0 (1939), switcher (scale)	400.00	600.00	900.00
231 Loco, steam — 0 (1939), 0-6-0, switcher (scale)	400.00	600.00	900.00
231 Loco, Alco Diesel A, R.I. — 027 (1961)	15.00	25.00	40.00
232 Loco, steam — 0 (1940), 0-6-0 switcher (scale)	400.00	600.00	900.00
232 Loco, Alco Diesel A, N.H. — 027 (1962)	15.00	25.00	40.00
233 Loco, steam — 0 (1940), 0-6-0 switcher (scale), "8976" under cab window	400.00	600.00	900.00
233 Loco, steam — 027 (1961), 2-4-2 with 233W tender	10.00	15.00	20.00
235 Loco, steam — 027 (uncat 1962), 2-4-2	10.00	15.00	20.00
236 Loco, steam – 027 (1961), 2-4-2	10.00	15.00	20.00
237 Loco, steam — 027 (1963)	10.00	15.00	20.00
238 or E Loco Steam — 0 (1936-40), BK or gun metal gray, P.R.R. torpedo type, tenders 2225T, 2225W or 265W	75.00	125.00	175.00
238 Loco, steam — 027 (1963), 2-4-2.	10.00	15.00	20.00
239 Loco, steam — 027 (1965), 2-4-2.	10.00	15.00	20.00
241 Loco, steam — 027 (uncat 1963), 2-4-2	10.00	15.00	20.00
242 Loco, steam — 027 (1962), 2-4-2.	10.00	15.00	20.00
243 Loco, steam — 027 (1960), 2-4-2.	10.00	15.00	20.00
244 Loco, steam — 027 (1960), 2-4-2	10.00	15.00	20.00
245 Loco, steam — 027 (1959), 2-4-2.	10.00	15.00	20.00
246 Loco, steam — 027 (1959), 2-4-2.	10.00	15.00	20.00
247 Loco, steam, B&O — 027 (1959, 2-4-2	10.00	15.00	25.00
248 Loco, elec — 0 (1926-32), red, orange, dark green, olive	40.00	60.00	90.00
249 or E Loco Steam — 0 (1936), gun metal gray	50.00	90.00	125.00
Same as above, in black	60.00	100.00	140.00
249 Loco, steam, P.R.R. — 027 (1958), 2-4-2	10.00	15.00	20.00

	G	VG	E
250 Loco, elec. — 0 (1926), 0-4-0, N.Y.C., dark green, peacock, orange	75.00	125.00	175.00
250 Loco, elec. — 0 (uncat 1934), 0-4-0, orange, terra cotta...........................	65.00	75.00	100.00
250 Loco, steam, P.R.R. — 027 (1957), 2-4-2..	10.00	15.00	20.00
250E Loco, steam Hiawatha — 0 (1935), tenders 250W, 250WX, 2250W	350.00	450.00	600.00
251 Loco, elec. — 0 (1925), 0-4-0, NYC box cab, gray or red cabs........	125.00	175.00	225.00
251E Loco, elec — 0 (1927), 0-4-0, NYC box cab, gray or red cabs........	125.00	175.00	225.00
252 Loco, elec — 0 (1926), 0-4-0, NYC, peacock, olive, dark green	45.00	60.00	75.00
Same as above terra cotta, orange...	60.00	75.00	100.00
Same as above, maroon (Macy's Special)...	75.00	125.00	175.00
252 Crossing gate — 0 (1950-62)	5.00	7.00	9.00
252E Loco, elec. — 0 (1933-35), 0-4-0, terra cotta or orange	60.00	90.00	125.00
HO-252 Crossing gate — HO (1959)	2.50	3.75	5.00
253 Loco, elec. — 0 (1924), 0-4-0, peacock, mojave, dark green	60.00	75.00	100.00
Same as above, maroon	150.00	200.00	250.00
Same as above, terra cotta	100.00	140.00	200.00
Same as above, red.........................	125.00	175.00	225.00
253 Automatic block signal — 0 (1956)...	3.00	5.00	10.00
253E Loco, elec — 0 (1931), 0-4-0, green	60.00	90.00	140.00
Same as above, terra cotta	100.00	140.00	225.00
254 Loco, elec — 0 (1924), 0-4-0, mojave, olive, dark, pea green	60.00	90.00	125.00
Same as above, apple green	125.00	175.00	225.00
Same as above, red.........................	150.00	200.00	300.00
254E Loco, elec — 0 (1927), 0-4-0, olive green	60.00	90.00	125.00
Same as above, apple green	100.00	150.00	225.00
255E Loco, steam — 0 (1935), 2-4-2, gunmetal gray with 263W tender.....	175.00	250.00	325.00
256 Loco, elec — 0 (1924), 0-4-4-0	250.00	350.00	500.00
256 Freight shed (1950-53)..............	5.00	10.00	15.00
257 Loco, steam — 0 (1930), 0-4-0, 257T or 259T tender.......................	50.00	85.00	125.00

	G	VG	E
257 Ives loco, steam — 0 (Ives 1931)	50.00	85.00	125.00
257 Freight station with horn (1956-57)	15.00	20.00	30.00
258 Loco, steam (early) — 0 (1930), 2-4-0	50.00	75.00	100.00
258 Ives loco, steam — 0 (Ives 1931)	50.00	75.00	100.00
258 Loco, steam (late) — 0 (uncat 1941), 2-4-2, with 1689T tender	25.00	45.00	65.00
259 Loco, steam — 0 (1932), 2-4-2	20.00	30.00	50.00
259E Loco, steam — 0 (1933), black	20.00	30.00	50.00
Same as above, gun metal gray	25.00	35.00	60.00
260 Bumper — 0 (1952)	2.00	3.00	5.00
260E Loco, steam — 0 (1930), black, 260T	250.00	350.00	450.00
Same as above, gun metal gray, 263 tender	275.00	375.00	475.00
261 Loco, steam — 0 (1931), 2-4-2, 257T tender	40.00	65.00	90.00
261E Loco, steam — 0 (1935), 261T .	60.00	85.00	125.00
262 Loco, steam — 0 (1931), 2-4-2, 262T	60.00	90.00	125.00
262 Crossing gate — 0 (1962)	5.00	7.00	10.00
262E Loco, steam — 0 (1933), 2-4-2, 262T or 265T	50.00	75.00	100.00
263E Loco, steam — 0 (1936), 2-4-2, gun metal gray	200.00	300.00	400.00
263T Blue (Blue Comet)	225.00	350.00	475.00
264 Operating Forklift Platform Assembly	30.00	60.00	90.00
264-150 Set of 12 boards (1957)	2.00	3.00	4.00
264E Loco, steam — 0 (1935), 2-4-2, streamlined, red (Red Comet)	125.00	175.00	250.00
Same as above, black	75.00	125.00	175.00
264E Streamliner set with 264E — 0 (uncat 1936), Red Comet set, 264E, two 603 Pullmans, one 604 Observation (red matching set)	250.00	350.00	450.00
265E Loco, Steam — 0 (1935), 2-4-2, streamlined, black	60.00	90.00	125.00
Same as above, gun metal gray	50.00	75.00	100.00
Same as above, blue (Blue Streak) ...	150.00	200.00	250.00
265E Streamliner set with 265E loco — 0 (1936), Blue Streak set (matching			

	G	VG	E
blue set), 265E, 619 Baggage, 617 coach, 618 observation	250.00	350.00	450.00
270 Lighting set for 2 cars, 3½ volt — Std. (1915)	20.00	30.00	40.00
270 Bridge — 0 (1931) maroon, or red	10.00	15.00	20.00
271 Lighting set for 2 cars, 8 volt — Std. (1915)	10.00	20.00	30.00
271 Bridge, 2 span — 0 (1931)	15.00	20.00	30.00
272 Bridge 3 span — 0 (1931)	20.00	30.00	60.00
280 Bridge — Std. (1931)	10.00	15.00	20.00
281 Bridge, 2 span — Std. (1931)	15.00	20.00	25.00
282 Bridge, 3 span — Std. (1931)	20.00	25.00	30.00
282 Gantry crane — 0 (1954)	40.00	60.00	90.00
289E Loco, steam — 0 (uncat 1937), 2-4-2, streamlined, 1689 tender, black	20.00	30.00	40.00
Same as above, gunmetal gray	25.00	35.00	50.00
299 Code transmitter set (1961-63)	15.00	25.00	40.00
300 Trolley 2⅞″ (1901), "City Hall Park 175"	EXTREMELY RARE		
300 Trolley, trailer — Std. (1910), powered	1200.00	1600.00	2200.00
300 Bridge — "HELLGATE" Std./0 (1928), ivory/green, orange base	400.00	600.00	800.00
Same, white/silver red base, (largest single span bridge Lionel ever made.)	600.00	900.00	1200.00
HO-300 Operating lumber car — HO (1960)	3.00	4.50	6.00
HO-301 Operating dump car — HO (1960)	3.00	4.50	6.00
HO-301-16 Cargo bin — HO (1960)	1.00	1.50	2.00
303 Summer trolley, motor car — Std. (1910), "303 Electric Rapid Transit 303"	1400.00	2000.00	2600.00
306 Ives lamp post (Ives 1931)	10.00	20.00	30.00
307 Ives double lamp post (Ives 1931)	15.00	20.00	30.00
308 Metal sign set — 0 (1945-49), five-piece	2.00	4.00	6.00
309 Trolley, trailer 2⅞″ (1901)	EXTREMELY RARE		
309 Pullman — Std. (1926), blue, apple green, pea green, maroon, light brown, mojave	30.00	45.00	75.00
309 Plastic sign set (1950-59), nine-piece	2.00	3.00	4.00

Top: Lionel 341 observation car, 339 pullman car
Bottom: 10E loco, 332 railway mail car
Courtesy PB Eighty-Four New York

	G	VG	E
310 Track 2⅞″ (1903)	2.00	5.00	7.00
310 Baggage — Std. (1924-29), colors same as 309 Pullman......................	30.00	45.00	75.00
310 Billboard set — 0 (1950-68) billboard and five different inserts	1.00	2.00	3.00
310R Billboard set, racing — 0 (1963)	1.00	2.00	3.00
310 Baggage — Std. (1926), same colors as 309 Pullman......................	30.00	45.00	75.00
312 Observation — Std. (1926), same colors as 309 Pullman......................	30.00	45.00	75.00
313 Bascule bridge — 0 (1940-42), grey...	125.00	175.00	250.00
Postwar (1946-49), silver	100.00	150.00	225.00
314 Girder bridge — 0 (1946-50), grey	2.00	4.00	6.00
315 Trestle, bridge - 0 (1946-47), illuminated silver	15.00	20.00	30.00
315-20 Bulb, 12 volt - clear (1940)...	fifty cents		
318 Loco, elec. — Std. (1924), 0-4-0, mojave, pea green, gray..................	100.00	135.00	200.00
Same as above, state brown	150.00	200.00	300.00
318E Loco, elec. — Std. (1926), 0-4-0, pea green, mojave, gray	100.00	135.00	185.00

Lionel Standard Gauge 358E Work Train Set
Top left to right: 217 red caboose, 219 work crane
Middle left to right: 212 gondola with barrels, 220 floodlight car, 208 chest of tools
Bottom left to right: 400E engine, 400T tender
Courtesy PB Eighty-Four New York

	G	VG	E
Same as above, state brown	150.00	200.00	250.00
Same as above, black	200.00	300.00	400.00
319 Pullman — Std. (1924)	40.00	60.00	80.00
HO-319 Oper, helicopter car — HO (1960)......................................	6.00	9.00	12.00
HO-319-125 Oper, helicopter car — HO (1962).......................................	7.00	10.00	15.00
320 Switch 2⅞″ (1903)	10.00	15.00	20.00
320 Baggage — Std. (1925)	40.00	60.00	90.00

48

	G	VG	E
321 Trestle bridge — 0 (1958)..........	4.00	6.00	8.00
322 Observation — Std. (1924)........	40.00	60.00	90.00
330 90° Crossing 2⅞″ (1903)	4.00	6.00	8.00
330 Ives block signal — Std. (Ives 1931)...	15.00	20.00	30.00
330-0 Ives block signal — 0 (Ives 1931)...	15.00	20.00	30.00
332 Baggage — Std. (1926), gray, red, peacock, olive	20.00	30.00	50.00
Same as above, beige body, maroon roof...	60.00	90.00	125.00
332 Macy baggage — Std. (uncat 1930)...	30.00	60.00	90.00
332 Ives baggage — Std. (Ives 1931), transition car	60.00	95.00	120.00
332 Arch bridge — 0 (1959-66), grey	9.00	15.00	22.00
334 Operating dispatching board — 0 (1957-60)..	30.00	45.00	70.00
337 Pullman — Std. (1925), pea green, olive, red, mojave	20.00	30.00	50.00
337 Macy Special Set, pullman — Std. (uncat 1930), red	75.00	112.50	150.00
HO-337 Operating giraffe car — HO (1961)...	3.00	4.50	6.00
338 Observation — Std. (1925), pea green, olive, red, mojave	20.00	30.00	45.00
338 Macy special set, observation — Std. (uncat 1930)............................	45.00	67.50	90.00
339 Pullman — Std. (1925), peacock, brown, gray	20.00	30.00	45.00
Same as above, beige body, maroon roof...	60.00	90.00	125.00
339 Macy special set, pullman — Std. (uncat 1930)	50.00	75.00	100.00
339 Ives pullman — Std. (Ives 1931) transition car	50.00	75.00	100.00
340 Bridge 2⅞″ (1903)	90.00	140.00	175.00
341 Observation — Std. (1925), peacock, brown, gray......................	20.00	30.00	45.00
Same as above, beige body, maroon roof...	60.00	90.00	125.00
341 Macy special set, observation — Std. (uncat 1930)............................	50.00	75.00	100.00

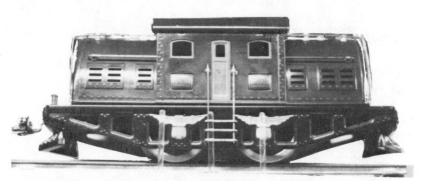

Lionel No. 380E locomotive, dark green, circa 1927-28
T. W. Sefton Collection

Lionel 381E Locomotive, circa 1929-33, very large and heavy.
T. W. Sefton Collection

	G	VG	E
341 Ives observation — Std. (Ives 1931), transition car......................	45.00	67.50	90.00
342 Culvert loader — 0 (1956-58).....	30.00	45.00	75.00
342E Set — Std. (1930) 318E-310-309-312; Loco Light Brown, cars two-tone brown, cream inserts	400.00	600.00	800.00
343 Set — Std. (1925)	500.00	750.00	1000.00
345 Automatic culvert unloader — 0 (1957)..	40.00	60.00	100.00
347 Set — Std. (1931)	110.00	165.00	220.00
347E Set — Std. (1927) 8E-337-338 Loco light olive, cars light olive with maroon inserts	125.00	175.00	250.00
347E Set — Std. (1931) 8-337-338 Loco red; cars red with cream inserts	125.00	200.00	275.00

	G	VG	E
348E Set — Std. (1926), 380E-429-428-430 dark green with maroon car windows	900.00	1350.00	1800.00
348 Manual culvert unloader — 0 (1966)..	15.00	25.00	40.00
349E Set — Std. (1929) 9E-429-428-430 orange with apple green car windows	1000.00	1500.00	2000.00
HO-349 Turbo missile firing car — HO	8.00	12.00	16.00
350 Bumper 2⅞″ (1903)	15.00	22.50	30.00
350 Set — Std. (1925)	80.00	120.00	160.00
350 Transfer table — 0 (1957-60)	40.00	60.00	90.00
350-50 Transfer table - extension — 0 (1957-60)....................................	20.00	30.00	40.00
352 Set — Std. (1925)	140.00	210.00	280.00
352 Ice depot — 0 (1955-57) red or brown base	60.00	75.00	100.00
352-55 Set of 7 ice blocks — 0 (1955)	3.00	4.00	6.00
352-E 10E-332-339-341 (1926) Loco gray; cars gray with maroon inserts	110.00	165.00	220.00
352-E 10E-332-339-341 (1928) Loco peacock; cars peacock with orange inserts	150.00	250.00	350.00
352-E 10E-332-339-341 Loco peacock; cars peacock with orange inserts - red baggage doors	150.00	225.00	300.00
353 Trackside signal — 0 (1960-61) .	3.00	4.00	5.00
356 Freight station — 0 (1952-57) with green & orange cars................	15.00	25.00	40.00
356-25 Set of 2 baggage trucks — 0 (1952)...	4.00	6.00	8.00
HO-357 Cop and hobo car — HO (1962)...	6.00	9.00	12.00
362 Set — Std. (1930) 384-384T-309-312 Loco black, cars rare terra cotta/maroon with yellow inserts	600.00	900.00	1200.00
362 Barrel loader — 0 (1952-57)	15.00	20.00	30.00
362-78 Set of 6 barrels — 0 (1952) ..	1.00	2.00	3.00
364 Lumber loader — 0 (1948-67), smooth gray or crackle gray	15.00	25.00	40.00
364C On-off switch (1959)	one dollar		
365 Dispatching station — 0 (1958-59)	25.00	40.00	60.00

	G	VG	E
HO-365 Missile launching car — HO (1962)	6.00	8.00	10.00
366W Set — Std. (1937) 1835E-1835W-310-309-312, loco black, cars blue and silver	600.00	900.00	1200.00
HO-366 Operating milk car — HO (1961)	5.00	7.50	10.00
367E Set — Std. (1934), 385E-384T Gunmetal CT, 1767-1766-1768 terra cotta/maroon cars BT	1100.00	1650.00	2200.00
367W Set — Std. (1935-39) 1767-1766-1768, red/maroon cars NT	700.00	1050.00	1400.00
HO-370 Sheriff and outlaw car — HO (1962)	6.00	9.00	12.00
375 Turntable, motorized — 0 (1962-64)	50.00	75.00	100.00
380 Elevated pillars 2⅞" (1903), per each	15.00	20.00	30.00
380 Loco, elec. — Std. (1923), 0-4-0, maroon	125.00	200.00	250.00
Same as above, mojave, dark green	175.00	225.00	300.00
380E Loco, elec. — Std. (1926), 0-4-0, maroon	150.00	200.00	250.00
Same as above, mojave or dark green	200.00	250.00	325.00
381 Loco, elec. — Std. (1928), 4-4-4, state green body	1200.00	1600.00	2200.00
381E Loco, elec. — Std. (1928), 4-4-4, state green body and frame	1000.00	1400.00	2000.00
Same as above, state green body, red frame	1200.00	1600.00	2200.00
381U Loco, elec. — Std. (1928), kit includes tools, track and original box	1400.00	1800.00	2400.00
384 Loco, steam — Std. (1930), 2-4-0 with 384T tender	200.00	275.00	400.00
384E Loco, steam — Std. (1930), 2-4-0 with 384T tender	225.00	300.00	425.00
385E Loco, steam — Std. (1933), 2-4-2 with 384T, 385T, 385TW or 385W tender, gunmetal gray	300.00	400.00	600.00
390 Loco, steam — Std. (1929), 2-4-2 with 390T, black	250.00	350.00	550.00
390C Control switch — 0 (1960)	1.00	1.50	2.00
390E Loco, steam — Std. (1929) BK	300.00	400.00	600.00

	G	VG	E
390E Loco, Std. (1930), two-tone blue, with tender	400.00	600.00	800.00
390E two-tone green	600.00	800.00	1000.00
390E Special set 390E — Std. (uncat 1929)...	1500.00	2250.00	3000.00
392E Loco, steam — Std. (1932), 4-4-2, black....................................	400.00	600.00	900.00
Same, in gunmetal gray..................	500.00	700.00	1000.00
394E Set — Std. (1929) 390E-390T-310-309-312; Loco black with orange stripe, cars pea green with orange inserts	450.00	700.00	1000.00
394 Rotary beacon (1949-53), aluminum, red or green tower frame	5.00	7.50	10.00
394-10 Bulb, 14 volt - clear (1951)...	fifty cents		
394-37 Beacon cap (1953)	two dollars		
395 Floodlight tower 1949-56 (4 lights)			
A. Silver tower	9.00	15.00	20.00
B. Green tower	9.00	15.00	20.00
C. Yellow tower	12.00	18.00	25.00
D. Red tower	12.00	18.00	25.00
396E Ste — Std. "Blue Comet", (1931) 400E-400T-421-422, BT	2500.00	3750.00	5000.00
396E Set — Std. "Blue Comet" (1933), as above, cast journals	2800.00	4200.00	5600.00
397 Diesel type coal loader (1948-57), later model, blue diesel motor cover .	20.00	30.00	40.00
Same as above, yellow diesel motor cover	75.00	125.00	175.00
400 Gondola, trailer 2⅞″ (1901).......	600.00	900.00	1200.00
400 Budd RDC Car, Powered – 0 1956-58).......................................	60.00	90.00	125.00
400E Loco, steam — Std. 4-4-4 with 400T tender, black	1000.00	1400.00	1800.00
Same as above, gunmetal gray........	1200.00	1600.00	2000.00
Same as above, blue	1400.00	1600.00	2200.00
402 Loco, elec. — Std. (1923), 0-4-4-0, mojave..	250.00	325.00	425.00
402E Loco, elec. — Std. (1926), 0-4-4-0, mojave..	250.00	325.00	425.00
403 Set — Std. (1923), 402-419-418-490 Loco mojave, cars mojave with maroon inserts and 10 series trucks	600.00	900.00	1200.00

Lionel Standard Gauge 403E
Top: 490 observation car
Middle: 419 pullman baggage, 418 parlor car
Bottom: 402E loco
Courtesy PB Eighty-Four New York

Lionel "State Car" No. 419 Illinois, the largest cars ever made circa 1929-33
T. W. Sefton Collection

	G	VG	E
403E Set — Std. (1926) 402E-419-418-490 loco mojave, with rubber-stamped E on door. Cars mojave with maroon inserts and 6-wheel trucks..............	600.00	900.00	1200.00
403E Set — Std. (1926), like above, only loco has 402E plates................	600.00	900.00	1200.00
404 Summer trolley, motor car — Std. (1910)..	1200.00	1800.00	2400.00
404 Budd RDC Baggage car, powered — 0 (1957-58).................................	75.00	110.00	140.00
408E Loco, elec. — Std. (1927), 0-4-4-0, apple green or mojave.....................	400.00	500.00	600.00
Same as above, state brown	1200.00	1500.00	1800.00
Same as above, state green	1400.00	1700.00	2000.00
408E Special set with 408E pink/ apple green — Std. (uncat 1931-32)................................	3250.00	4875.00	6500.00
409E Set (1927) 408E-419-418-431-490 mojave set with orange inserts in cars	1200.00	1800.00	2400.00
409 Set — Std. (1927)			
409E "The Olympian", state green 381E-412-413-416, lighter green ventilators, apple green windows (Black Dot), 1930......................................	4300.00	6500.00	8600.00
409E Set — "The Olympian" state green 318E-412-413-416, lighter green ventilators, *ivory windows*, brass journals, rivet detail on ends of cars, (1933)...	4000.00	6000.00	8000.00
410 Billboard blinker 1956-58)	5.00	10.00	15.00
HO-410 Suburban ranch house — HO (1959)......................................	3.00	4.00	5.00
411E "Transcontinental Limited", two-tone brown 408E-412-413-414-416 light brown ventilators, cast journals, 1930-31...	7500.00	11,250.	15,000.
411E "Transcontinental Limited", state green 381E-412-413-414-416 lighter green ventilators, apple green windows (Red Dot), (1929)	6,000.	9,000.	12,000.
HO-411 Figure set — HO (1959) ...	2.00	3.00	4.00
412 Pullman — Std. (1929), California (State Car), light green	600.00	800.00	1000.00
Same as above, light brown	650.00	900.00	1100.00

55

Top: Lionel 408E engine
Middle left to right: Lionel 381 Bild-A-Loco Engine, 413 pullman, 412 California pullman
Bottom left to right: Lionel 416 New York observation car and 414 Illinois pullman
Courtesy PB Eighty-Four New York

	G	VG	E
HO-412 Farm set — HO (1959)	3.00	4.50	6.00
413 Pullman — Std. (1929), Colorado (State Car), light green	600.00	800.00	1000.00
Same as above, light brown	650.00	900.00	1100.00
413 Countdown control panel (1962)	5.00	7.00	10.00
HO-413 Railroad structure set — HO (1959)	3.00	4.50	6.00
414 State Car, 1930, Illinois, light green	600.00	800.00	1000.00
Same as above, light brown	650.00	900.00	1100.00
HO-414 Village set — HO (1959) ..	3.00	4.50	6.00
415 Diesel fueling station (1955-67)	30.00	45.00	75.00
416 Observation — Std. (1929), New York state car, light green	600.00	800.00	1000.00
Same as above, light brown	650.00	900.00	1100.00

	G	VG	E
418 Pullman — Std. (1923), mojave	100.00	130.00	175.00
Same as above, apple green	110.00	160.00	200.00
418 Ives pullman — Std. (Ives (1931), transition period	100.00	150.00	200.00
419 Combine — Std. (1923), mojave	100.00	130.00	175.00
419 Combine — Std. (1928-32) apple green	110.00	160.00	200.00
419 Ives combine — Std. (Ives 1931), transition period	100.00	130.00	175.00
419 Heliport (1962), control tower ..	40.00	60.00	90.00
420 Pullman — Std. (1930), "Faye", light blue body, dark blue roof (Blue Comet car)	300.00	450.00	600.00
421 Pullman — Std. (1930), "Westphal" Blue Comet car, light blue body, dark blue roof	300.00	450.00	600.00
422 Observation — Std. (1930), "Tempel", Blue Comet car, light blue body, dark blue roof	300.00	450.00	600.00
424 Pullman — Std. (1931) "Liberty Bell" (Stephen Girard set), light green	300.00	400.00	575.00
425 Pullman — Std. (1932), "Stephen Girard" (Stephen Girard set), light green	300.00	400.00	575.00
HO-425 Figure set — HO (1962) ...	2.00	3.00	4.00
426 Observation — Std. (1931), "Coral Isle", (Stephen Girard set) light green	300.00	400.00	575.00
428 Pullman — Std. (1926), dark green	125.00	175.00	225.00
Same as above, orange	150.00	225.00	300.00
429 Combine — Std. (1926), dark green	125.00	175.00	225.00
Same as above, orange	150.00	225.00	300.00
430 Observation — Std. (1926), dark green	125.00	175.00	225.00
Same as above, orange	150.00	225.00	300.00
HO-430 Tree assortment — HO (1959)	1.00	2.00	3.00
431 Diner — Std. (1927), mojave ...	150.00	225.00	300.00
431 Diner (1928-29) apple green, orange, dark green	200.00	275.00	375.00

	G	VG	E
431 Ives diner — Std. (Ives 1931), transition period	200.00	275.00	375.00
HO-431 Landscape set — HO (1959)	3.00	4.50	6.00
HO-432 Tree assortment — HO (1961)	2.00	3.00	4.00
433E Set "Twentieth Century Limited" 400E-400T-412-414-416 black loco, state green cars with *dark* ventilators, 1931-33	3000.00	4000.00	5000.00
435 Power station (1926)	50.00	75.00	125.00
436 Power station (1926)	75.00	125.00	175.00
437 Signal tower (1926) green roof .	90.00	150.00	250.00
Same as above, peacock roof	95.00	175.00	275.00
Same as above, orange roof	195.00	275.00	350.00
438 Signal tower (1927), orange/red	90.00	150.00	225.00
Same as above, white/red	125.00	200.00	275.00
439 Panel board (1928), maroon	30.00	40.00	50.00
Same as above, red	40.00	50.00	60.00
Same as above, silver (rare)	50.00	75.00	100.00
0440 Signal bridge — Std. (1932) ..	125.00	175.00	225.00
440C Panel Board	25.00	40.00	60.00
440N Signal bridge — 0/Std. (1936)	125.00	175.00	225.00
441 Weighing scale platform (1932-36), Std., green base creme building	250.00	350.00	450.00
442 Diner (1938)	30.00	50.00	75.00
443 Missile launching platform (1960-62).................................	10.00	15.00	22.00
444 Roundhouse section — Std. (1932-35)	800.00	1200.00	1800.00
445 Operating switch tower (1952-57).................................	15.00	20.00	30.00
448 Missile firing range set (1961-63)	20.00	30.00	45.00
450 Macy Special loco, elec. — 0 (uncat 1930), 0-4-0 red with black frame	300.00	450.00	600.00
450 Signal bridge (1952-58) gray or tan base	10.00	15.00	25.00
450L Signal light head (1952)	three dollars		
452 Gantry signal (1961-63)	15.00	25.00	35.00
455 Elec. range (1932-33)	250.00	350.00	500.00
455 Oil derrick (1950-54), red base ..	25.00	40.00	65.00
Same as above, green base	30.00	50.00	75.00
456 Coal ramp and hopper car (1950-55).................................	35.00	60.00	90.00

	G	VG	E
460 Piggyback terminal (1955-57) ..	20.00	30.00	40.00
460-150 Two trailers (1956)	3.00	6.00	10.00
461 Piggyback with truck & trailers, (1957) (most include "Midge Toy Tractor," red)	30.00	50.00	70.00
462 Derrick platform set (1961-62) ..	40.00	60.00	80.00
464 Lumber mill (1956-60)	40.00	60.00	80.00
464-150 Set of 6 boards (1956)	three dollars		
465 Sound dispatching station (1956-57)	25.00	40.00	65.00
470 IRBM missile launch (1959-62) .	15.00	22.00	30.00
HO-470 Missile launching platform — HO (1960)	4.00	6.00	8.00
479-1 Lionel trucks for 6362 (1955) .	two dollars		
480-25 Conversion coupler (1950) ..	two dollars		
HO-480 Missile firing range set — HO (1961)	2.00	3.00	4.00
490 Observation — Std. (1923), mojave	100.00	130.00	175.00
Same as above, apple green	110.00	160.00	200.00
490 Ives observation — Std. (Ives 1931), transition period	100.00	150.00	200.00
494 Rotary beacon (1954), silver, red	10.00	15.00	20.00
497 Coaling station (1953-58)	50.00	75.00	100.00
500 Motorized derrick 2⅞" (1903) ...	EXTREMELY RARE		
511 Flat — Std. (1927), dark green .	18.00	25.00	35.00
Same as above, medium green	25.00	35.00	45.00
512 Gondola — Std. (1927), bright green	25.00	35.00	45.00
Same as above, peacock	18.00	25.00	35.00
513 Cattle — Std. (1927)	18.00	25.00	35.00
Same as above, nickel trim	125.00	175.00	250.00
514 Refrigerator — Std. (1927), Lionel ventilated refrigerator	75.00	125.00	200.00
514 Box — Std. (1929), ivory/brown	50.00	75.00	100.00
Same as above, yellow/brown	75.00	112.50	150.00
514R Refrigerator — Std. (1929), ivory body, peacock roof	30.00	40.00	60.00
Same as above, nickel trim	125.00	175.00	250.00
515 Tank — Std. (1927), terra cotta, ivory (Sunoco), silver (Sunoco)	30.00	40.00	60.00
Same as above, orange (Sehll)	200.00	275.00	375.00

Lionel No. 444 Roundhouse Section, circa 1932-33.
T. W. Sefton Collection

Lionel Standard Gauge
Top left to right: 490 observation car, 431 dining car
Bottom left to right: 419 baggage-pullman car, 418 pullman car
Courtesy PB Eighty-Four New York

Lionel 1686 Baggage
Courtesy H. A. Mueller, Continental Hobby House

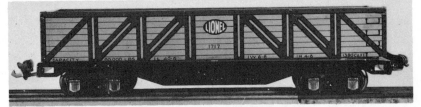

Lionel 1717 Gondola, Yellow, Green, Nickel trim
Courtesy H. A. Mueller, Continental Hobby House

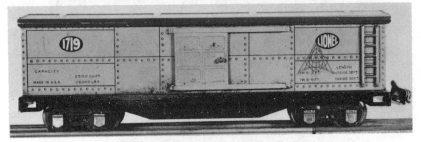

Lionel 1719 Box, 0, Yellow, Green, Black, Nickel trim
Courtesy H. A. Mueller, Continental Hobby House

	G	VG	E
516 Hopper — Std. (1928)	20.00	30.00	40.00
517 Caboose — Std. (1927), red, nickel trim	25.00	40.00	60.00
Same as above, red/black (coal train), nickel trim	40.00	75.00	125.00
Same as above, pea green	20.00	35.00	50.00
520 Search light — Std. (1931), terra cotta platform	30.00	45.00	60.00
Same as above, green platform	40.00	60.00	75.00
520 Loco, diesel 80 ton — 027 (1956), original pantograph must not be broken	20.00	30.00	45.00
529 Pullman — 0 (1926), olive green or terra cotta	10.00	15.00	20.00
530 Observation — 0 (1926), olive green or terra cotta	10.00	15.00	20.00
HO-530 Loco, diesel F-3 powered A, DRGW — HO (1958)	10.00	15.00	20.00
HO-531 Loco, diesel F-3 powered A, C.M.-St.P&P — HO (1958)	10.00	15.00	20.00

Lionel Standard Gauge "Distant Control" 403 E Set
Top: 490 observation car
Middle left to right: 419 pullman-baggage car, 418 pullman car
Bottom:'402E loco
Courtesy PB Eighty-Four New York

	G	VG	E
HO-532 Loco, diesel F-3 powered A, B&O — HO (1958)	10.00	15.00	20.00
HO-533 Loco, diesel F-3 powered A, New Haven — HO (1958)	10.00	15.00	20.00
HO-535 Loco, diesel Alco, AB, Santa FE — HO (1962)	10.00	15.00	20.00
HO-536 Loco, diesel Alco, Sante Fe —HO (1963)	10.00	15.00	20.00
HO-537 Loco, diesel Alco, AB, Santa Fe — HO (1966)	10.00	15.00	20.00
HO-540 Loco, diesel F-3, Dummy B, DRGW — HO (1958)	8.00	12.00	16.00
HO-541 Loco, diesel F-3, Dummy B, CMST P&P — HO (1958)	8.00	12.00	16.00
550 Miniature figures, set of six (1932), includes original box	60.00	90.00	140.00
HO-550 Loco, diesel F-3, Dummy A, DRGW — HO (1958)	8.00	12.00	16.00
551 Miniature figure, engineer (1932)	9.00	12.00	15.00
552 Miniature figure, conductor (1932)	9.00	12.00	15.00

Lionel 1026 "Blue Comet" Standard Gauge Set
Top: 422 observation car
Middle: 421 and 422 "Faye" and "Westphal" pullman cars
Bottom: 400 loco with 400W tender
Courtesy PB Eighty-Four New York

	G	VG	E
553 Miniature figure, porter (1932) .	9.00	12.00	15.00
554 Miniature figure, male passenger (1932)	9.00	12.00	15.00
555 Miniature figure, female, passenger (1932)	9.00	12.00	15.00
HO-555 Loco, diesel F-3 powered A, Santa Fe — HO (1963)	10.00	15.00	20.00
556 Miniature figure, red cap (1932)	9.00	12.00	15.00
HO-561 Rotary snowplow, MSTL — HO (1959)	10.00	20.00	30.00
HO-564 Loco, Diesel Alco, powered A, C&O — HO (1960)	10.00	15.00	20.00
HO-565 Loco, Diesel Alco, powered A, Santa Fe — HO (1959)	10.00	15.00	20.00
HO-566 Loco, Diesel Alco, powered A, Texas special — HO (1959)	10.00	15.00	20.00
HO-567 Loco, Diesel Alco, powered A, Alaska — HO (1959)	10.00	15.00	20.00
HO-568 Loco, Diesel Alco, powered A, Union Pacific — HO (1962)	10.00	15.00	20.00

	G	VG	E
HO-569 Loco, Diesel Alco, powered A, Union Pacific — HO (1963)	10.00	15.00	20.00
HO-571 Loco, Diesel Alco, powered A, PRR — HO (1963)	10.00	15.00	20.00
HO-576 Loco, Diesel F-3, Dummy B, Texas special — HO (1959)	10.00	15.00	20.00
HO-577 Loco, Diesel F-3, Dummy B, Alaska — HO (1959)	10.00	15.00	20.00
HO-581 Loco, rectifier, PRR — HO (1960)	10.00	15.00	20.00
HO-586 Loco, Diesel F-3, Dummy A, Texas special — HO (1959)	8.00	12.00	16.00
HO-587 Loco, Diesel F-3, Dummy A, Alaska — HO (1959)	8.00	12.00	16.00
HO-591 Loco, rectifier, New Haven — HO (1959)	10.00	15.00	20.00
HO-592 Loco, Diesel GP9, Santa Fe — HO (1966)	10.00	15.00	20.00
HO-593 Loco, Diesel GP9, Northern Pacific — HO (1963)	10.00	15.00	20.00
HO-594 Loco, Diesel GP9, Santa Fe — HO (1963)	10.00	15.00	20.00
HO-595 Loco, Diesel F-3, Dummy A, Santa Fe — HO (1959)	8.00	12.00	16.00
HO-596 Loco, Diesel GP9, NYC — HO (1959)	10.00	15.00	20.00
HO-597 Loco, Diesel GP9, Northern Pacific — HO (1960)	10.00	15.00	20.00
HO-598 Loco, Diesel GP7, NYC — HO (1961)	10.00	15.00	20.00
600 Derrick trailer 2⅞" (1903)	EXTREMELY RARE		
600 Pullman 4 wh. 5½" — 0 (1915), maroon, dark green, brown	15.00	20.00	30.00
600 Pullman 8 wh. 9" — 0 (1933), red with red roof	30.00	40.00	60.00
Same as above, light blue with silver roof	35.00	45.00	70.00
Same as above, gray with red roof .	30.00	40.00	65.00
600 Loco, Diesel SW2, MKT — 027 (1955)	20.00	30.00	45.00
601 Pullman, 7" — 0 (1915), dark green	15.00	20.00	30.00

Lionel Standard Gauge
Top left to right: 514 refrigerator car, 517 caboose
Middle left to right: 512 gondola, 515 tank car, 516 hopper
Bottom left to right: 390E loco and tender
Courtesy PB Eighty-Four New York

	G	VG	E
601 Observation 9″ — 0 (1933), red with red roof	30.00	40.00	60.00
Same as above, light blue with silver roof	35.00	45.00	70.00
Same as above, gray with red roof	30.00	40.00	65.00
601 Loco, Diesel SWX, Seaboard — 027 (1956)	20.00	30.00	45.00
602 Baggage, 7″ — 0 (1915), dark green	15.00	20.00	30.00
602 Baggage, 9″ (1933), red with red roof	30.00	40.00	65.00
Same as above, light blue with silver roof	35.00	45.00	75.00
Same as above, gray with red roof	30.00	40.00	65.00
602 Loco, Diesel SW2, Seaboard — 027 (1957)	20.00	30.00	45.00
HO-602 Loco, steam — HO (1960)	8.00	12.00	16.00
603 Pullman, 7″ — 0 (uncat 1921), orange	15.00	25.00	40.00
603 Pullman (later) 6½″ — 0 (1920), orange	20.00	30.00	45.00

Lionel Standard Gauge
Top left to right: 512 gondola with barrels, 517 caboose
Middle: 511 lumber cars
Bottom: 385W tender, 385E loco
Courtesy PB Eighty-Four New York

	G	VG	E
603 Pullman (late) 7½″ — 0 (1931), red, green, orange, maroon	15.00	25.00	40.00
604 Observation (later) 6¼″ — 0 (1920), orange	15.00	25.00	40.00
604 Observation (late) 7½″ — 0 (1931), red, green, orange, maroon	15.00	25.00	40.00
605 Pullman — 0 (1925), 10¼″, gray	40.00	60.00	80.00
Same as above, red	75.00	100.00	125.00
Same as above, orange	75.00	100.00	125.00
Same as above, olive	75.00	100.00	125.00

On three above, add $50.00 in Excellent if marked "Illinois Central"

	G	VG	E
HO-605 Loco, Steam — HO (1959) .	10.00	15.00	20.00
606 Observation — 0 (1925), 10¼", gray	40.00	60.00	80.00
Same as above, orange	75.00	100.00	125.00
Same as above, red	75.00	100.00	125.00
Same as 606, olive	75.00	100.00	125.00
On three above, add $50.00 in Excellent if marked "Illinois Central"			
606 Observation, Macy — 0 (uncat 1930)	40.00	60.00	80.00
607 Pullman — 0 (1926)	20.00	30.00	40.00
607 Pullman, Macy — 0 (uncat 1931)	40.00	60.00	80.00
608 Observation — 0 (1926)	20.00	30.00	40.00
608 Observation, Macy — 0 (uncat 1931)	40.00	60.00	80.00
609 Pullman — 0 (uncat 1937)	20.00	40.00	60.00
610 Pullman (early — 0 (1915)	20.00	30.00	40.00
610 Pullman (late) — 0 (1926)	20.00	40.00	60.00
610 Pullman, Macy — 0 (uncat 1926)	20.00	40.00	60.00
610 Ives Pullman — 0 (Ives 1931) ..	20.00	40.00	60.00
610 Loco, diesel SW2, Erie — 027 (1955)	20.00	30.00	45.00
611 Observation — 0 (uncat 1937) ..	20.00	30.00	40.00
611 Loco, Diesel SW2, CNJ — 027 (1957)	25.00	40.00	60.00
612 Observation (early) — 0 (1915) .	20.00	30.00	40.00
612 Observation (late — 0 (1926) ...	25.00	40.00	60.00
612 Observation, Macy — 0 (1926) .	20.00	40.00	60.00
612 Ives observation — 0 (Ives 1931)	25.00	40.00	60.00
613 Pullman — 0 (1931), terra cotta	150.00	225.00	300.00
Same as above, blue (Blue Comet set)	100.00	150.00	225.00
Same as above, red, aluminum roof	150.00	225.00	300.00
613 Loco, Diesel SW2 UP — 027 (1958)	25.00	40.00	60.00
614 Observation — 0 (1931), terra cotta	150.00	225.00	300.00
Same as above, blue (Blue Comet set)	100.00	150.00	225.00
Same as above, red, aluminum roof	150.00	225.00	300.00
614 Loco, Diesel SW2, Alaska — 027 (1959-60) blue, yellow structure on roof	40.00	60.00	90.00

	G	VG	E
615 Baggage — 0 (1933), terra cotta	150.00	225.00	300.00
Same as 615 blue (Blue Comet set) .	100.00	150.00	225.00
Same as above, red, aluminum roof	150.00	225.00	300.00
616 Loco, Diesel SW2, ATSF — 027 (1961)	20.00	30.00	45.00
616 E or W Diesel Type power car, streamliner — 0 (1935), Flying Yankee, black cast frame, chrome shells	60.00	75.00	90.00
616-13 Bulb, 12V, clear (1935)	fifty cents		
616T Vestibule — 0 (1935)	5.00	10.00	15.00
617 Coach, streamliner — 0 (1935), black and chrome	20.00	30.00	40.00
Same as above, blue and white (Blue Streak)	30.00	40.00	60.00
617 Loco, Diesel SW2, ATSF — 0 (1963), black	20.00	30.00	45.00
618 Observation streamliner — 0 (1935), black and chrome	20.00	30.00	40.00
Same as above, blue and white (Blue Streak)	30.00	40.00	60.00
619 Combine, streamliner — 0 (1935), blue and white (Blue Streak)	60.00	90.00	125.00
620 Set — Std. (1915)	750.00	1125.00	1500.00
620 Floodlight — 0 (1937)	5.00	10.00	15.00
621 Set — Std. (1920), Loco nickel, cars orange	1600.00	2400.00	3200.00
621 Loco, Diesel SW2, CNJ — 027 (1956)	25.00	40.00	60.00
622 Loco, Diesel SW2, Santa Fe (1949), black	60.00	75.00	120.00
623 Loco, Diesel SW2, ATSF — 0 (1952), black	40.00	60.00	75.00
624 Loco, Diesel SW2, C&O — 0 (1952), blue, yellow stripe	40.00	60.00	75.00
625 Loco, Diesel 44 ton, LV — 027 (1957)	60.00	90.00	120.00
HO-625 Loco, steam — HO (1959) .	10.00	15.00	20.00
HO-626 Loco, steam — HO (1963) .	10.00	15.00	20.00
627 Loco, Diesel 44 ton, LV — 027 (1956), red body, white stripe	20.00	30.00	40.00
628 Loco, Diesel 44 ton, NP — 027 (1956), black with yellow stripe	20.00	30.00	45.00

Lionel #736 Berkshire, 2-8-4 (1950-51), 53-66) Photo Courtesy Steven W. Hintze

Lionel #550 Miniature Railroad Figures (1932-36)   Photo Courtesy Steven W. Hintze

Lionel No. 250E loco, used on the "0" gauge scale Hiawatha Set (circa 1937)
T. W. Sefton Collection

	G	VG	E
629 Pullman 4 wh. — 0 (1924)	10.00	15.00	20.00
629 Pullman 8 wh. — 0 (uncat 1934)	20.00	30.00	40.00
629 Loco, Diesel 44 ton, Burlington — 027 (1956), silver, red stripe	30.00	50.00	75.00
630 Observation 4 wh. — 0 (1924) ..	10.00	15.00	20.00
630 Macy observation, 4 wh. — 0 (uncat 1931)	15.00	20.00	30.00
630 Observation, 8 wh. — 0 (uncat (1934)	20.00	30.00	40.00
633 Loco, Diesel SW2, Santa Fe — 0 (1962)	15.00	22.00	30.00

Lionel No. 2332 Pennsylvania, black GG-2 (0-gauge) 1947, single motor, 4-6-6-4 wheel arrangement with an AC vibrator box horn, three position E-unit (reversing unit) protruding from the roof, front and rear pilot with red marker lights, no magne-traction (non magnetic wheels), satin black finish with gold rubber stamped lettering and numbers, five parallel stripes fromend to end, Pennsylvania Keystone decals (red and gold) on each end (front - under headlight) and midway on each side, two adjustable roof-top pantographs designed for overhead catenary operation.

There is much controversy over the authenticity of this piece as very few collectors have actually seen one. The story has it that on one half day's production run (several hundred at best) the orange pigment was not added to the paint blend in sufficient amounts to give the intended color of New Brunswick green as catalogued. As a result the color appeared black. Many a repaint has shown up due to the demand many collectors have shown over the years. Since the rubber stamp striping process Lionel used has not been exactly duplicated, the experienced collector would be readily able to distinguish IT from the ORIGINAL. A true find is one with the gold striping still sharp and complete. (Also known to exist with silver stripes and silver rubber stamped side Keystones.) Photo and caption by Steven W. Hintze.

	G	VG	E
634 Loco, Diesel SW2, Santa Fe — 0 (1962), blue body	15.00	22.00	30.00
HO-635 Loco, steam — HO (1961) .	10.00	15.00	20.00
636W Diesel type power car, streamliner — 0 (1936), yellow and brown, Union Pacific's "City of Denver" ...	50.00	75.00	100.00
636W Streamliner set with 636W — 0 (1936), yellow and brown 636W, two 637 coaches, one 638 observation, Union Pacific's "City of Denver" ...	200.00	275.00	350.00
636W Special streamliner set with 636W — 0 (uncat 1937), two-tone green, 636W, 637 coach, 630 observation, Union Pacific's "City of Denver"	250.00	375.00	500.00
636-13 Bulb, 8 volt - clear (1936) ...	fifty cents		
HO-636 Loco, steam — HO (1963) .	10.00	15.00	20.00
637 Coach, streamliner — 0 (1936), "City of Denver"	40.00	60.00	75.00

Lionel No. 2245 Texas Special, A B units, single motor, 0-27 gauge, 1954-55
Courtesy Kenneth Post

Lionel 2333 "Santa Fe"   Photo by Bill Kaufman   Courtesy Good Old Days Store

	G	VG	E
637 Loco, steam — Super 0 (1959), 2-6-4, 2046W tender or 2040W tender	30.00	40.00	60.00
638 Observation, streamliner — 0 (1936), "City of Denver", yellow and brown	40.00	60.00	75.00
HO-642 Loco, steam — HO (1961) .	10.00	15.00	20.00
HO-643 Loco, steam — HO (1963) .	10.00	15.00	20.00
645 Loco, Diesel SW2, Union Pacific — 027 (1963), yellow body	20.00	30.00	40.00
HO-645 Loco, steam — HO (1962) .	10.00	15.00	20.00
646 Loco, steam — 0 (1954), 4-6-4, 2046W tender	40.00	60.00	80.00
HO-646 Loco, steam — HO (1963) .	10.00	15.00	20.00
HO-647 Loco, steam — HO (1966) .	10.00	15.00	20.00
651 Flat — 0 (1935)	5.00	10.00	15.00
652 Gondola — 0 (1935)	5.00	10.00	15.00
653 Hopper — 0 (1934)	5.00	10.00	15.00
654 Tank — 0 (1934), silver, orange	5.00	10.00	15.00
655 Box — 0 (1934)	5.00	10.00	15.00
656 Cattle — 0 (1935)	5.00	10.00	15.00
657 Caboose — 0 (1934)	5.00	10.00	15.00
659 Dump — 0 (1935)	5.00	10.00	15.00
665 Loco, steam — 0 (1954), 4-6-4, 6026W or 2046W tender	40.00	60.00	80.00
671 Loco, steam — 0 (1946), 6-8-6, 671W tender	40.00	60.00	75.00
Same as above, with 2671 tender ...	60.00	90.00	125.00
671-75 Smoke bulb, 14 volt (1946) .	three dollars		
671 R&R Loco, steam — 0 (1952), 671W tender	40.00	60.00	90.00

71

Lionel #2352 Penn. G.E. EP-5, Tuscan, sprayed gold stripe.
Photo Courtesy Steven W. Hintze

Lionel 2350 New Haven Electric EP-5, 0 ga., 1956-58, (horn unit, double motor).
Photo by Steve Hintze

Lionel No. 58 Great Northern rotary snowplow, 2-4-2, small motorized unit, 1959-61
Courtesy Kenneth Post

Lionel 2360 Pennsylvania Tuscan Red (Single Stripe) GG-1 (0-gauge) 1957-58, 61-63, double motor, (4-6-6-4) wheel arrangement, D size battery operated horn, three position E-unit (reversing unit) protruding from roof, front and rear pilot and red marker lights, magnetraction (magnetic wheels).

Tuscan Red finish with gold heat stamped lettering and numbers, **sprayed** gold single stripe from end to end, Pennsylvania Keystone decals (red & white) on each end (front under headlight) and larger emblems midway on each side, two adjustable roof-top pantographs designed for overhead cantenary operation.

Most later model Tuscan GG-1's had their single stripe rubber stamp applied. Few originals have turned up with the stamp sprayed. As the sixties showed progressive decline in toy trains, Lionel used whatever means possible to cut production costs and use up stock inventory.

As a result several other changes in the GG-1 resulted. In 1963, decaled lettering and numbers, replaced the heat stamped predecessors (decaling being less costly). Also, spray striping (probably in 1961) compared to the rubber stamped method was also tried. I've seen only a handful of these original sprayed stripe versions which leads me to believe that the rubber stamping method was more practical in terms of economics.

Those pieces which are all original with strong, sharp lettering and striping are most sought after by collectors.

Caption and Photo by:
Steven W. Hintze

Lionel 443 Missile Launching Platform
Courtesy H. A. Mueller, Continental Hobby House

Lionel 6804 with "USMC" AA truck, "USMC" Sonar Truck
Photo by Bill Kaufman   Courtesy Good Old Days

Lionel 2321 Lackawanna fm, 0 ga., 1954-56, (horn unit, double motor), gray roof (shown), maroon roof.
Photo by Steve Hintze

	G	VG	E
675 Loco, steam — 0 (1947), 2-6-2, 2466W, 2466WX or 6466WX tender ..	40.00	60.00	75.00
681 Loco, steam — 0 (1950), 6-8-6 2671W tender	40.00	60.00	90.00
682 Loco, steam — 0 (1954), 6-8-6, 2046W 50 tender	95.00	150.00	225.00
685 Loco, steam — 0 (1953), 4-6-4, 6026W tender	40.00	60.00	80.00
700 Window display set 2⅞″ (1904) .	EXTREMELY RARE		
700 Loco, elec. — 0 (1913-16), 0-4-0, dark green NYC Lines	175.00	250.00	325.00
700E Loco, steam and tender — 072 (1937), 4-6-4, black, 700/700W 12 wheel cast tender	1200.00	1800.00	2200.00
700E250 Display stand and track (1938), with Lionel ID plate	200.00	300.00	400.00
700EWX Loco, steam and whistle tender — 072 (1937), black 700/700W 12 wheel cast tender	1200.00	1800.00	2200.00
700K Loco, steam kit — 072 (1939), 4-6-4, gray (kit form), 6 kits all original boxes	1400.00	2200.00	2500.00

	G	**VG**	**E**
700K1 Loco, steam-frame and drive wheels (1939)	All Separate Parts and		
700K2 Loco, steam motor (1939) ...	Tender Kits.		
700K3 Loco, steam-cab and boiler (1939)	Value determined by availability of original		
700K4 Loco, steam trucks and wheels (1939)	pieces and demand.		
700K5 Tender parts (1939)	Most parts and kits were not available to the buy-		
700K6 Whistle parts (1939)	ing public at the time of manufacture.		
700KW Loco, steam and whistle tender kit (1939)			
701 Loco, elec. (1913-16), 0-4-0, dark green	225.00	325.00	400.00
703 Loco, elec. — 0 (1913-16), 4-4-4, dark green	700.00	900.00	1200.00
703-10 Smoke bulb — 0 (1946)	three dollars		
HO-704 Baggage, Texas Special — HO (1959)	3.00	4.50	6.00
HO-705 Pullman, Texas Special — HO (1959)	3.00	4.50	6.00
706 Loco, elec. — 0 (1913-16), 0-4-0, dark green	250.00	375.00	450.00
HO-706 Vista Dome, Texas Special — HO (1959)	4.00	6.00	8.00
HO-707 Observation, Texas Special — HO (1959)	3.00	4.50	6.00
708 Loco, steam, scale switcher — 072 (1939), 0-6-0, "8976" cast in boiler front	800.00	1000.00	1400.00
HO-708 Baggage, Pennsylvania — HO (1960)	3.00	4.50	6.00
HO-709 Vista Dome, Pennsylvania — HO (1960)	4.00	6.00	8.00
710 Pullman — 0 (1924), green, orange	75.00	110.00	140.00
Same as above, red	90.00	125.00	175.00
Same as above, two-tone blue	100.00	140.00	200.00
HO-710 Observation, Pennsylvania — HO (1960)	4.00	5.00	6.00
711 Switches, elec. — 072 (1935), pair	100.00	150.00	200.00
HO-711 Baggage, Pennsylvania — HO (1960)	3.00	4.50	6.00

	G	VG	E
712 Observation — 0 (1924), green, orange	75.00	110.00	140.00
Same as above, red	90.00	125.00	175.00
Same as above, two-tone blue	100.00	140.00	200.00
HO-712 Baggage, Santa Fe — HO (1961)	2.00	4.00	6.00
HO-713 Pullman, Santa Fe — HO (1961)	3.00	4.50	6.00
714 Box — 072 (1940), scale	75.00	155.00	200.00
714K Box, kit — 072 (1940), kit form, new only	Five Hundred Dollars		
HO-714 Vista Dome, Santa Fe — HO (1961)	4.00	6.00	8.00
715 Tank — 072 (1940), scale	75.00	150.00	200.00
715K Tank, kit — 072 (1940), kit form, new only	Five Hundred Dollars		
HO-715 Observation, Santa Fe — HO (1961)	3.00	4.50	6.00
716 Hopper — 072 (1940), scale	75.00	150.00	200.00
716K Hopper, kit — 072 (1940), kit form, new only	Five Hundred Dollars		
717 Caboose — 072 (1940), scale	75.00	150.00	200.00
717K Caboose, kit — 072 (1940), kit form, new only	$275.00		
717-54 Bulb, 18 volt, clear (1940)	fifty cents		
720 90° crossing — 072 (1935)	1.00	3.00	5.00
721 Switches, non-electric — 072 (1935), pair	30.00	45.00	60.00
HO-723 Pullman, Pennsylvania — HO (1963)	3.00	4.50	6.00
HO-725 Observation, Pennsylvania — HO (1963)	3.00	4.50	6.00
726 Loco, steam — 0 (1946), 2-8-4, 2426W tender	125.00	175.00	250.00
Same as above, 2046W tender	60.00	90.00	125.00
730 90° crossing T-rail — 072 (1935)	5.00	10.00	15.00
731 Switches, electric, T-rail — 072 (1935), pair	100.00	150.00	250.00
HO-733 Pullman, Santa Fe — HO (1964)	3.00	4.50	6.00
HO-735 Observation, Santa Fe — HO (1964)	3.00	4.50	6.00
736 Loco, steam — 0 (1950), 2-8-4, 2046W tender	75.00	125.00	175.00

	G	VG	E
746 Loco, steam — 0 (1957), 4-8-4, "Norfolk & Western" 746W tender with short stripe	250.00	350.00	450.00
Same, with long stripe	300.00	400.00	500.00
752E or W Streamliner Power Car — 0 (1934)	175.00	250.00	375.00
752-9 Bulb, 18 volt, clear (1934)		fifty cents	
753 Streamliner coach — 0 (1934) ..	50.00	75.00	100.00
754 Streamliner observation — 0 (1934)	50.00	75.00	100.00-
758W Set streamliner — 072 (1936) .	300.00	450.00	600.00
760 Pack of curved track — 072 (1935), 16 sections	15.00	20.00	35.00
761 Curved track — 072 (1934)	1.00	1.50	2.00
762 Straight track — 072 (1934)	1.00	1.50	2.00
762S Insulated straight track with lock-on — 072 (1934)	1.00	2.00	3.00
763E Loco, steam — 0 (1937), 4-6-4, semi scale Hudson, black, 2226WX tender, or gunmetal gray 263 or 2263W tender	600.00	800.00	1200.00
Same as above, gunmetal gray 2226W or 2226WX tender	800.00	1200.00	1600.00
771 Curved track, T-rail — 072 (1935)	1.00	2.00	3.00
772 Straight track, T-rail — 072 (1935)	1.00	2.00	3.00
772S Insulated straight track, T-rail — 072 (1940)	2.00	3.00	5.00
773 Fish plate set — 072 (1936), 100 bolts, 100 nuts, 50 fishplates and wrench	20.00	25.00	30.00
773 Loco, steam — 0 (1950), 4-6-4 Hudson 2426W tender	400.00	600.00	800.00
Same as above (1964) 4-6-4 Hudson 2046N tender	300.00	450.00	600.00
782 Streamliner front coach — 072 (1935), "The Milwaukee Road", part of articulated Hiawatha set, gray roof, orange sides and maroon underframe	100.00	150.00	225.00
783 Streamliner coach — 072 (1935), "The Milwaukee Road", part of articulated Hiawatha set, gray roof,			

	G	VG	E
orange sides and maroon underframe	100.00	150.00	225.00
784 Streamliner observation — 072 (1935), "The Milwaukee Road", part of articulated Hiawatha set, gray roof, orange sides and maroon underframe	100.00	150.00	225.00
792 Streamliner front coach — 072 (1937), part of Rail Chief set (with 700E loco), "792 Lionel Lines 792", maroon roof, red sides, red underframe	200.00	250.00	350.00
793 Streamliner coach — 072 (1937), part of Rail Chief set, "793 Lionel Lines 793"	200.00	250.00	350.00
794 Streamliner observation — 072 (1937), part of Rail Chief set, "794 Lionel Lines 794", maroon roof, red sides, red underframe	200.00	250.00	350.00
800 Express motor car 2⅞" (1904)	EXTREMELY RARE		
800 Box — 0 (1915)	15.00	25.00	35.00
HO-800 Flat with airplane — HO (1958)	9.00	13.50	18.00
801 Caboose — 0 (1915)	10.00	15.00	20.00
HO-801 Flat with boat — HO (1958)	6.00	9.00	12.00
802 Stock — 0 (1915)	10.00	15.00	20.00
803 Hopper (early) — 0 (1923), dark green	8.00	12.00	16.00
Same as above, peacock	10.00	15.00	20.00
803 Hopper (late) — 0 (1929)	8.00	12.00	16.00
804 Tank (early) — 0 (1923), dark gray	10.00	15.00	20.00
Same as above, terra cotta	10.00	15.00	20.00
Same as above, silver (Sunoco)	7.50	11.25	15.00
804 Tank (late) — 0 (1929)	15.00	22.50	30.00
805 Box — 0 (1927), orange/maroon	15.00	22.50	30.00
Same as above, pea green/orange	12.50	18.75	25.00
HO-805 AEC car with light — HO (1959)	6.00	9.00	12.00
806 Cattle — 0 (1927)	10.00	15.00	20.00
HO-806 Flat car with helicopter — HO (1959)	8.00	12.00	16.00
807 Caboose — 0 (1927)	6.00	9.00	12.00

	G	VG	E
HO-807 Flat car with bulldozer — HO (1959)	7.00	10.50	14.00
HO-808 Flat car with tractor — HO (1959)	7.00	10.50	14.00
809 Dump — 0 (1931)	10.00	15.00	20.00
HO-809 Helium transport car — HO (1961)	6.00	9.00	12.00
810 Crane — 0 (1930-40)	40.00	50.00	60.00
HO-810 Generator transport car — HO (1961)	4.00	6.00	8.00
811 Flat — 0 (1926), maroon	20.00	30.00	40.00
Same as above, in silver	40.00	60.00	80.00
HO-811-25 Flat with stakes — HO (1958)	3.00	4.50	6.00
812 Gondola — 0 (1926)	20.00	30.00	40.00
812T Tool set — 0 (1937)	10.00	15.00	20.00
813 Cattle — 0 (1926)	20.00	30.00	40.00
HO-813 Mercury capsule car — HO (1962)	5.00	7.50	10.00
814 Box — 0 (1926), orange body, brown roof	20.00	30.00	40.00
Same as above, nickel plate	40.00	75.00	100.00
814R Refrigerator — 0 (1929), white body, brown roof	20.00	40.00	60.00
Same as above, with rubber-stamped lettering	300.00	400.00	500.00
HO-814 Auto transport car — HO (1958)	8.00	12.00	16.00
815 Tank — 0 (1926), aluminum (silver)	20.00	30.00	40.00
Same as above, orange (Shell)	40.00	60.00	80.00
HO-815 Tank — HO (1958)	3.00	4.50	6.00
HO-815-50 Tank — HO (1964)	3.00	4.50	6.00
HO-815-75 Tank — HO (1963)	3.00	4.50	6.00
HO-815-85 Tank — HO (1964)	3.00	4.50	6.00
816 Hopper — 0 (1927), red, olive green	20.00	30.00	40.00
Same as 816, black	40.00	60.00	80.00
HO-816 Rocket fuel tank car — HO (1962)	3.00	4.50	6.00
HO-816-50 Rock fuel tank car — HO (1962)	3.00	4.50	6.00

Lionel 1105 Santa Claus Hand Car (with Mickey Mouse) wind-up, 0 ga., 1935-36, red base (shown), green base.
Photo by Steve Hintze

Lionel 2331 Virginian fm, 0 ga., 1955-58, (horn unit, double motor), black roof and black stripe, gold lettering (shown); blue roof and blue stripe, yellow lettering.
Photo by Steve Hintze

	G	VG	E
817 Caboose — 0 (1926)	20.00	30.00	40.00
Same as above, flat red, brown roof, rubber-stamped lettering	40.00	60.00	80.00
HO-817 Caboose — HO (1958)	3.00	4.50	6.00
HO-817-150 Caboose, Santa Fe — HO (1960)	3.00	4.50	6.00
HO-817-200 Caboose, AEC — HO (1959)	3.00	4.50	6.00
HO-817-225 Caboose, Alaska — HO (1959)	3.00	4.50	6.00

Lionel 419 Heliport
Courtesy H. A. Mueller, Continental Hobby House

	G	VG	E
HO-817-250K Caboose, Texas Special — HO (1959)	3.00	4.50	6.00
HO-817-275 Caboose, New Haven — HO (1959)	3.00	4.50	6.00
HO-817-300 Caboose, Southern Pacific — HO (1959)	3.00	4.50	6.00
HO-817-350 Caboose, Rock Island — HO (1960)	3.00	4.50	6.00
HO-819-1 Work Caboose, P.R.R. — HO (1958).........................	4.00	6.00	8.00
HO-819-100 Work caboose, B&M — HO (1958).........................	4.00	6.00	8.00
HO-819-200 Work caboose, B&M — HO (1959).........................	4.00	6.00	8.00
HO-819-225 Work caboose, Santa Fe — HO (1960)	4.00	6.00	8.00
HO-819-250 Work caboose, NP — HO (1960).........................	4.00	6.00	8.00
HO-819-275 Work caboose, C&O — HO (1960).........................	4.00	6.00	8.00
HO-819-285 Work caboose, C&O — HO (1963).........................	4.00	6.00	8.00

	G	VG	E
820 Box — 0 (1915), orange or maroon	20.00	30.00	40.00
Same as 820, dark olive, rubber-stamped ATSF & 48522	50.00	75.00	100.00
820 Floodlight — 0 (1931), terra cotta base	30.00	40.00	50.00
Same as above, green base	40.00	60.00	80.00
821 Cattle — 0 (1915)	20.00	30.00	40.00
HO-821 Pipe car — HO (1960)	3.00	4.50	6.00
HO-821-50 Pipe car — HO (1964) .	3.00	4.50	6.00
HO-821-100 Pipe car — HO (1963)	3.00	4.50	6.00
822 Caboose — 0 (1915)	20.00	30.00	40.00
HO-823 Twin missile car — HO (1960)	9.00	13.50	18.00
HO-824 Flat with two cars — HO (1958)	6.00	9.00	12.00
HO-827 Caboose, Lionel — HO (1961)	3.00	4.50	6.00
HO-827-50 Caboose, AEC — HO (1963)	3.00	4.50	6.00
HO-827-75 Caboose, Lionel — HO (1963)	3.00	4.50	6.00
HO-830 Flat with two vans — HO (1958)	6.00	9.00	12.00
831 Flat — 0 (1927)	5.00	10.00	15.00
HO-834 Poultry car — HO (1959) ..	3.00	4.50	6.00
HO-836 Hopper — HO (1961)	3.00	4.50	6.00
HO-836-60 Hopper, Alaska — HO (1966)	3.00	4.50	6.00
HO-836-100 Hopper, Lionel — HO (1964)	3.00	4.50	6.00
HO-837 Caboose, M&STL — HO (1961)	3.00	4.50	6.00
HO-837-100 Caboose, M&STL — HO (1963)	3.00	4.50	6.00
HO-838 Caboose, Lackawanna — HO (1961)	3.00	4.50	6.00
HO-840 Caboose, NYC — HO (1961)	3.00	4.50	6.00
HO-841 Caboose — HO (1961)	3.00	4.50	6.00
HO-841-50 Caboose, Union Pacific — HO (1962)	3.00	4.50	6.00
HO-841-175 Caboose, Canta Fe — HO (1962)	3.00	4.50	6.00

	G	VG	E
HO-842 Culvert pipe car — HO (1960)	4.00	6.00	8.00
HO-845 Gold bullion car — HO (1962)	5.00	7.50	10.00
HO-847 Exploding target car — HO (1960)	9.00	13.50	18.00
HO-847-100 Exploding target car — HO (1960)	9.00	13.50	18.00
HO-850 Missile launching car — HO (1960)	6.00	9.00	12.00
HO-850-100 Missile launching car — HO (1960)	6.00	9.00	12.00
HO-860 Derrick — HO (1958)	5.00	7.50	10.00
HO-861 Timber transport car — HO (1960)	4.00	6.00	8.00
HO-861-100 Timber transport car — HO (1961)	4.00	6.00	8.00
HO-862-25 Gondola — HO (1958)	3.00	4.50	6.00
HO-863 Rail truck car — HO (1960)	4.00	6.00	8.00
HO-864-1 Box, Seaboard — HO (1958)	3.00	4.50	6.00
HO-864-25 Box, NYC — HO (1958)	3.00	4.50	6.00
HO-864-50 Box, State of Maine — HO (1958)	3.00	4.50	6.00
HO-864-100 Box, New Haven — HO (1958)	3.00	4.50	6.00
HO-864-125 Box, Rutland — HO (1958)	3.00	4.50	6.00
HO-864-150 Box, M&ST L — HO (1958)	3.00	4.50	6.00
HO-864-175 Box, Timken — HO (1958)	3.00	4.50	6.00
HO-864-200 Box, Monon — HO (1958)	3.00	4.50	6.00
HO-864-225 Box, Central of Georgia — HO (1958)	3.00	4.50	6.00
HO-864-250 Box, Wabash — HO (1958)	3.00	4.50	6.00
HO-864-275 Box, State of Maine — HO (1962)	3.00	4.50	6.00
HO-864-300 Box, Alaska — HO (1959)	3.00	4.50	6.00
HO-864-325 Box, D.S.S.A. — HO (1959)	3.00	4.50	6.00

	G	VG	E
HO-864-350 Box, State of Maine — HO (1959)	3.00	4.50	6.00
HO-864-400 Box, B&M — HO (1960)	3.00	4.50	6.00
HO-864-700 Box, Santa Fe — HO (1961)	3.00	4.50	6.00
HO-864-900 Box, NYC — HO (1959)	3.00	4.50	6.00
HO-864-925 Box, NYC — HO (1964)	3.00	4.50	6.00
HO-864-935 Box, NYC — HO (1963)	3.00	4.50	6.00
HO-865 Gondola with canisters — HO (1958)	5.00	7.00	10.00
HO-865-225 Gondola with scrap iron — HO (1960)	4.00	6.00	8.00
HO-865-250 Gondola with crates — HO (1960)	4.00	6.00	8.00
HO-865-300 Gondola with crates — HO (1963)	4.00	6.00	8.00
HO-865-350 Gondola, NYC — HO (1963)	3.00	4.50	6.00
HO-865-375 Gondola, NYC — HO (1963)	3.00	4.50	6.00
HO-865-400 Gondola, NYC with crates — HO (1963)	3.00	4.50	6.00
HO-865-435 Gondola — HO (1964)	3.00	4.50	6.00
HO-866-1 Cattle, M.K.T. — HO (1958)	3.00	4.50	6.00
HO-866-25 Cattle, Santa Fe — HO (1958)	3.00	4.50	6.00
HO-866-200 Circus car — HO (1959)	5.00	7.00	10.00
HO-870 Maintenance car with generator — HO (1959)	4.50	6.75	9.00
HO-872-1 Reefer, Fruit Growners — HO (1958)	3.00	4.50	6.00
HO-872-25 Reefer, Illinois Central — HO (1958)	3.00	4.50	6.00
HO-872-50 Reefer, El Capitan — HO (1958)	3.00	4.50	6.00
HO-872-200 Reefer, Railway Express — HO (1959)	3.00	4.50	6.00
HO-873 Rodeo car — HO (1962) ...	5.00	7.50	10.00
HO-874 Box, NYC — HO (1964) ...	3.00	4.50	6.00
HO-874-25 Box, NYC — HO (1965)	3.00	4.50	6.00
HO-874-60 Box, B&M — HO (1964)	3.00	4.50	6.00
HO-875 Flat car with missile — HO (1959)	5.00	7.50	10.00

	G	VG	E
876 Helios 21 Spaceship (1965)	6.00	9.00	12.00
HO-877 Miscellaneous car — HO (1958)	3.00	4.50	6.00
HO-879 Derrick — HO (1958)	4.00	6.00	8.00
HO-880 Maintenance car with light — HO (1959)	9.00	13.50	18.00
900 Express, trail car 2⅞″ (1904)	EXTREMELY RARE		
900 Box, ammunition — 0 (1917), part of armored train set	150.00	225.00	275.00
900 or B Catalog number for 230 and tender — 0 (1939), 0-6-0, similar to loco 227	350.00	550.00	700.00
HO-900 Operating platform — HO (1960)	5.00	7.50	10.00
901 Gondola — 0 (1919), gray or maroon	10.00	15.00	20.00
902 Gondola — 0 (1927), peacock ...	10.00	15.00	20.00
Same as above, apple green	7.50	11.25	15.00
HO-903 Track, straight 3″ — HO (1958)	.50	.75	1.00
HO-905 Track, straight 1½″ — HO (1958)	.25	.35	.50
HO-906 Track, straight 6″ — HO (1968)	.25	.35	.50
909 Smoke fluid (1957)	full bottle, two dollars		
HO-909 Track, straight 9″ — HO (1958)	.25	.35	.50
910 Grove of eleven trees (1932)	75.00	100.00	150.00
911 Country estate (1932), 191 villa, shrubbery and trees	150.00	200.00	250.00
912 Suburban home (1932), 189 villa, shrubbery and trees	150.00	200.00	250.00
913 Bungalow and garden (1932), bungalow, flowers and trees	150.00	200.00	250.00
914 Formal garden park (1932), two grass plots, centerpiece, flowering bushes, cream base	75.00	125.00	175.00
915 Curved tunnel mountain, large — 0 (1932)	100.00	150.00	225.00
916 Curved tunnel — 0 (1932)	75.00	135.00	175.00
917 Mountain, medium (1932)	100.00	150.00	225.00
918 Mountain, small (1932)	75.00	125.00	175.00

	G	VG	E
919 Park grass, 8 oz. (1932)	1.00	2.00	3.00
920 Scenic park, small (1932)	500.00	750.00	1000.00
920 Scenic display set (1957)	10.00	15.00	25.00
920-2 Tunnel portals (1958)	9.00	15.00	22.00
902-5 Rocks (1958)	one dollar		
920-8 Lichen (1958)	one dollar		
921 Scenic park, large (1932)	600.00	900.00	1400.00
921C Scenic park, center section (1932)	200.00	300.00	400.00
922 Lamp terrace (1932)	75.00	125.00	175.00
HO-922 Remote control switch, right — HO (1958)	.50	.75	1.00
923 Tunnel — Std. (1933)	100.00	150.00	200.00
HO-923 Remote control switch, left — HO (1958)	.50	.75	1.00
924 Curved tunnel — 072 (1935)	75.00	100.00	150.00
HO-925 Straight terminal track — HO (1958)	.25	.35	.50
HO-925-10 Insulating clip — HO (1960)	twenty-five cents		
926 Tube of lubrication (1955)	full tube, two dollars		
927 Flag plot (1937-42)	20.00	30.00	40.00
927 Lubrication and maintenance kit (1950-53)	2.00	4.00	6.00
927-3 Can of liquid track cleaner (1955)	three dollars		
928 Maintenance kit (1960-63)	2.00	4.00	6.00
HO-929 Uncoupling track 9″ — HO (1958)	1.00	1.50	2.00
HO-930 30° crossing — HO (1960) .	1.00	1.50	2.00
HO-939 Uncoupler — HO (1958) ...	.50	.75	1.00
HO-942 Manual switch, right — HO (1958)	.50	.75	1.00
943 Exploding ammo dump (1959) .	3.00	5.00	8.00
HO-943 Manual switch, left — HO (1958)	.50	.75	1.00
950 Railroad map (1958-66)	2.00	4.00	6.00
HO-950 Re-railer — HO (1958)	.50	.75	1.00
951 Farm set, plastic (1958), 13 pieces	2.00	4.00	6.00
952 Figure set, plastic (1958), 30 pieces	2.00	4.00	6.00

	G	VG	E
953 Figure set, plastic (1959), 32 pieces	2.00	4.00	6.00
954 Swimming pool and playground set, plastic (1959), 30 pieces	2.00	4.00	6.00
955 Highway set, plastic (1958), 22 pieces	2.00	4.00	6.00
956 Stockyard, plastic (1959), 18 pieces	2.00	4.00	6.00
957 Farm building and animal set, plastic (1958), 35 pieces	2.00	4.00	6.00
958 Vehicles, plastic (1958), 24 pieces	3.00	6.00	8.00
959 Barn set, plastic (1958), 23 pieces	2.00	4.00	6.00
960 Barn yard set, plastic (1959), 29 pieces	2.00	4.00	6.00
HO-960 Bumper track — HO (1960)	.25	.35	.50
961 School set, plastic (1959), 36 pieces	3.00	6.00	8.00
HO-961 Bumper track, illum. — HO (1961)	.30	.45	.60
962 Turnpike set, plastic (1958), 24 pieces	2.00	4.00	6.00
963 Frontier set, plastic (1959), 18 pieces	2.00	4.00	6.00
964 Factory, plastic (1959), 22 pieces	2.00	4.00	6.00
965 Farm set, plastic (1959), 36 pieces	3.00	6.00	8.00
966 Firehouse, plastic (1958), 45 pieces	3.00	6.00	8.00
967 Post office, plastic (1958), 25 pieces	2.00	4.00	6.00
968 TV transmitter, plastic (1958), 28 pieces	2.00	4.00	6.00
969 Construction set, plastic (1960), 23 pieces	2.00	4.00	6.00
970 Ticket booth (1958-60), cardboard	20.00	30.00	40.00
971 Box of lichen (1959)	three dollars		
972 Trees (1959)	three dollars		
973 Landscaping set (1959)	2.00	4.00	6.00
974 Scenery set (1962)	4.00	6.00	10.00
HO-975 Curved terminal track — HO (1958)	.25	.35	.50

	G	VG	E
980 Ranch set, plastic (1960), 14 pieces	2.00	4.00	6.00
981 Freight yard, set plastic (1960), 10 pieces	2.00	4.00	6.00
982 Suburban house, plastic (1960), 18 pieces	2.00	4.00	6.00
983 Farm set, plastic (1960), 7 pieces	2.00	4.00	6.00
HO-983 Curved track 18″ radius, 3″ — HO (1958)	.25	.35	.50
984 Rairoad set, plastic (1961), 22 pieces	2.00	4.00	6.00
HO-984 Curved track, 18″ radius, 4½″ — HO (1958)	.25	.35	.50
985 Freight area set, plastic (1961), 32 pieces	3.00	6.00	8.00
HO-985 Curved track, 15″ radius, 9″ — HO (1958)	.25	.35	.50
986 Farm set, plastic (1962), 20 pieces	2.00	4.00	6.00
HO-986 Curved track, 15″ radius, 4½″ — HO (1958)	.25	.35	.50
987 Town set, plastic (1962), 24 pieces	2.00	4.00	6.00
988 Railroad structure (1962), 16 pieces	2.00	4.00	6.00
HO-989 Curved track, 18″ radius, 9″ — HO (1958)	.25	.35	.50
HO-990 90° crossing — HO (1958) .	1.00	1.50	2.00
1000 Passenger car, motorized, 2⅞″ (1904)	EXTREMELY RARE		
1000 Trolley, trailer — Std. (1910) .	1200.00	1400.00	1600.00
1000 Trailer truck, 100 series — Std. (1910)	1200.00	1400.00	1600.00
1001 Loco, Scout steam — 027 (1948), 2-4-2, 1001T tender	8.00	12.00	17.00
1002 Winner set — (027) (Winner 1931)	10.00	15.00	20.00
1002 Gondola — 027 (1948)	2.00	3.00	4.00
1003 Winner set — 027 (Winner 1931)	10.00	15.00	20.00
1004 Winner set — 027 (Winner (1932)	10.00	15.00	20.00
1004 Box — 027 (1948)	5.00	7.50	10.00

	G	VG	E
1005 Winner set — 027 (Winner 1932)	10.00	15.00	20.00
1005 Tank — 027 (1948)	3.00	4.50	6.00
1006 Winner set — 027 (Winner 1932)	10.00	15.00	20.00
1007 Winner set — 027 (Winner 1932)	10.00	15.00	20.00
1007 Platform and background — 027 (1936)	15.00	20.00	30.00
1007 Caboose — 027 (1948)	1.75	2.62	3.50
1008 Uncoupling track — 027 (1957), per each	1.00	1.50	2.00
1008-50 Automatic uncoupling track — 027 (1961), each	1.00	1.50	2.00
1009 Manumatic uncoupling track set — 027 (1948)	2.00	3.00	4.00
1010 Interurban trolley, trailer — Std. (1910)	1200.00	1400.00	1800.00
1010 Winner loco, elec. — 027 (Winner 1931), 0-4-0	30.00	40.00	60.00
1010 Transformer, 35 watt (1961)	2.00	3.00	4.00
1011 Interurban trolley, motor car — Std. (1910)	1200.00	1400.00	1800.00
1011 Winner pullman — 027 (Winner 1931)	10.00	15.00	20.00
1011 Transformer, 15 watt (1961)	1.00	2.00	3.00
1012 Interurban trolley, trailer — Std. (1910)	1200.00	1400.00	1800.00
1012 Winner station transformer (Winner 1931)	15.00	20.00	25.00
1012 Ives station transformer (Ives 1931)	15.00	20.00	25.00
1012 Transformer, 35 watt (1950)	2.00	3.00	4.00
1013 Curved track — 027 (1934)	.25	.50	.75
1013 Ives curved track — 027 (Ives 1931)	.25	.50	.75
1013 Half section curved track — 027 (1968)	.25	.50	.75
1013-17 Track pins, steel — 027 (1938), per dozen	.50	.75	1.00
1014 Lockon — 027 (1931)	.25	.50	1.00
1014 Ives terminal clip — 027 (Ives 1931)	.25	.50	1.00

Lionel 415 Diesel Fueling Station
Courtesy H. A. Mueller, Continental Hobby House

	G	VG	E
1014 Transformer, 40 watt (1955) ..	2.00	3.00	4.00
1015 Winner loco, steam — 027 (Winner 1931), black, 0-4-0, 1016 tender	30.00	40.00	60.00
1015 Transformer, 45 watt (1956) ..	2.00	3.00	4.00
1016 Transformer, 35 watt (1959) ..	1.00	2.00	3.00
1017 Winner transformer station (Winner 1931)	15.00	20.00	25.00
1017 Lionel-Ives transformer station (1933).............................	15.00	20.00	25.00
1018 Straight track — 027 (1934) ..	.25	.50	.75
1018 Half section straight track 027 (1968)	.25	.50	.75
1019 Winner observation — 027 (Winner 1931)	8.00	12.00	15.00
1019 Remote control track set — 027 (1938)	1.00	1.50	2.00
1020 Winner baggage — 027 (Winner 1931)	8.00	12.00	15.00

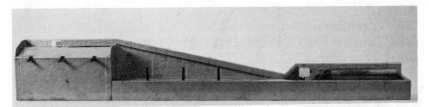

Lionel 364 Lumber Loader
Courtesy H. A. Mueller,
Continental Hobby House

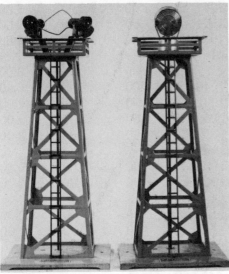

Lionel 395 Floodlight, 494
Rotary Beacon
Courtesy H. A. Mueller,
Continental Hobby House

	G	VG	E
1020 90° crossing — 027 (1955)	1.00	2.00	3.00
1021 90° crossing — 027 (1933)	1.00	2.00	3.00
1022 Curved tunnel — 0/027 (1935)	10.00	15.00	20.00
1022 Switch — 027 (1955), manual, pair	2.00	4.00	6.00
1023 Straight tunnel — 0/027 (1934)	10.00	15.00	18.00
1023 45° crossing — 027 (1955), each	.50	.75	1.00
1024 Manual switches — 027 (1935), per pair	2.00	3.00	4.00
1025 Bumper — 027 (1946)	2.00	3.00	4.00
1025 Transformer, 45 watt (1961) ..	2.00	3.00	4.00
1026 Transformer, 25 watt (1963) ..	1.00	2.00	3.00
1027 Transformer station (1934) ...	10.00	15.00	20.00
1028 Transformer, 25 watt (1935) ..	1.00	1.50	2.00
1029 Transformer, 25 watt (1936) ..	1.00	1.50	2.00
1030 Winner loco, elec. — 027 (Winner 1932), 0-4-0, orange with green roof	25.00	40.00	60.00

	G	VG	E
1030 Transformer, 40 watt (1936) ..	1.00	2.00	3.00
1032 Transformer, 90 watt (1948) ..	4.00	8.00	12.00
1033 Transformer, 90 watt (1948) ..	4.00	8.00	12.00
1034 Transformer, 75 watt (1948) ..	4.00	6.00	8.00
1035 Winner loco, steam — 027 (Winner 1932), 0-4-0, 1016 tender	25.00	40.00	60.00
1035 Transformer, 60 watt (1947) ..	1.00	2.00	3.00
1037 Transformer, 40 watt (1941) ..	1.00	1.50	2.00
1039 Transformer, 35 watt (1938) ..	1.00	1.50	2.00
1040 Transformer and whistle controller, 60 watt (1938)	1.00	2.00	3.00
1041 Transformer, 60 watt (1940) ..	1.00	2.00	3.00
1042 Transformer, 75 watt (1942) ..	1.00	2.00	3.00
1043 Transformer, 60 watt (1953) ..	1.00	2.00	3.00
1043 Transformer, 50 watt	1.00	2.00	3.00
1043-500fx) Girls train transformer, 60 watt (1957), ivory case	25.00	40.00	60.00
1044 Transformer, 90 watt (1957) ..	6.00	8.00	10.00
1045 Operating watchman (1938), nickle or brass sign	10.00	15.00	20.00
1045C Contractor (1938)	.50	.75	1.00
1046 Mechanical gateman and crossing (1936)	15.00	20.00	30.00
1047 Switchman with flat (1959-61)	20.00	30.00	45.00
1050 Passenger car, trailer 2⅞″ (1905)	EXTREMELY RARE		
1053 Transformer, 60 watt (1956) ..	2.00	3.00	4.00
1054 Set — 027 (1934)	300.00	450.00	600.00
1055 Loco, Alco A diesel, Texas Special — 0 (uncat 1960)	15.00	20.00	25.00
1060 Loco, Scout team — 027 (uncat 1960), 2-4-2, 1050T	5.00	8.00	12.00
1061 Loco, steam — 027 (1969), 2-4-2, 1061T tender	6.00	8.00	12.00
1062 Loco and tender — 027 (1963), 2-4-2, 1062T tender	6.00	8.00	12.00
1063 Transformer, 75 watt (1961) ..	2.00	4.00	6.00
1065 Loco, Alco A unit only, Diesel, Union Pacific — 0 (uncat)	15.00	20.00	25.00
1066 Loco, Alco A unit only, Diesel, Union Pacific — 0 (uncat)	15.00	20.00	25.00
1073 Transformer, 60 watt (1961) ..	1.00	2.00	3.00

	G	VG	E
1100 Summer trolley, trailer — Std. (1911)	1400.00	1600.00	2000.00
1100 Trailer trucks, 35 series — Std. (1924)	2.00	4.00	6.00
1100 Mickey Mouse handcar — Mech (1935), wind-up, orange base	350.00	500.00	700.00
Same as above, green base	300.00	400.00	600.00
Same as above, red base	250.00	300.00	500.00
1101 Trailer trucks with lights, 35 series — Std. (1924)	2.00	4.00	6.00
1101 Loco, 2-4-2	8.00	10.00	12.00
1103 Peter Rabbit Chick-Mobile-Mech (uncat 1935), wind-up, track operation	250.00	350.00	600.00
Same as 1103, floor operation	300.00	450.00	600.00
1105 Santa Claus Handcar - Mech (1935), wind-up, green base	500.00	700.00	900.00
Same as above, red base	400.00	600.00	800.00
1107 Donald Duck Rail Car - Mech (1936), wind-up, green roof	325.00	450.00	600.00
Same as above, red roof	300.00	400.00	500.00
1110 Loco, Scout steam — 027 (1949), 2-4-2	6.00	8.00	12.00
1119 Set — 027 (1950)	50.00	75.00	100.00
1120 Loco, Scout steam — 027 (1950). 2-4-2	6.00	8.00	12.00
1121 Switches, electric — 027 (1937), remote pair	10.00	15.00	20.00
1122 Switches, remote control — 027 (1952)	10.00	15.00	20.00
1122-100 Switch control — 027 (1957)	2.00	3.00	4.00
1122-234 Insulating pins — 027 (1957)	.50	.75	1.00
1122-520 027 to Super 0 adapter kit (1957)	1.00	2.00	3.00
1130 Loco, steam — 027 (1953), 2-4-2, 1130T tender	6.00	8.00	12.00
1144 Transformer, 75 watt (1968) ..	1.00	2.00	3.00
1200 Trailer truck 10 series — Std. (1923)	2.00	4.00	6.00
1201 Trailer truck 10 series w/lights — Std. (1923)	2.00	4.00	6.00

	G	VG	E
1229 Transformer, 220 volts (1938) .	10.00	15.00	18.00
1230 Transformer, 220 volts (1938) .	10.00	15.00	18.00
1239 Transformer, 220 volts (1941) .	10.00	15.00	18.00
1241 Transformer, 220 volts (1941) .	10.00	15.00	18.00
1300 Trailer truck, 200 series — Std. (1925)	2.00	4.00	6.00
1301 Trailer truck 200 series w/lights — Std. (1925)	2.00	4.00	6.00
1400 Trailer truck, 418 series — Std. (1925)	3.00	5.00	8.00
1401 Trailer truck, 418 w/lights — Std. (1925)	3.00	6.00	8.00
1463 Set — 027 (1950)	40.00	60.00	80.00
1465 Set — 027 (1952)	62.50	93.75	125.00
1471 Set — 027 (1950)	125.00	187.50	250.00
1473 Set — 027 (1950)	125.00	187.50	250.00
1481 Set — 027 (1951)	87.50	131.25	175.00
1483 Set — 027 (1952)	125.00	187.50	250.00
1484 Set — 027 (1952)	200.00	300.00	400.00
1501 Ives loco, steam - Mech (Ives 1931)	20.00	30.00	45.00
1503 Ives, loco, steam - Mech (Ives 1931)	20.00	30.00	45.00
1504 Ives pullman - Mech (Ives (1931)	10.00	15.00	20.00
1506 Ives, loco, steam - Mech (Ives 1931)	20.00	30.00	45.00
1506 L.I. loco, steam - Mech (1933) .	20.00	30.00	45.00
1506 Loco & Tender (1509T) Outfit - Mech (1935), set includes 1515 tank and 1517 caboose	60.00	90.00	125.00
1506L Loco & Tender (1502T) Outfit - Mech (1933)	40.00	60.00	80.00
1506-8 Bulb, 1½ volt - clear (1935) .	fifty cents		
1507 Set — 027 (1953)	125.00	187.50	250.00
1508 Loco & Tender (1509T) Outfit - Mech (1935), 0-4-0 Commodore Vanderbilt type, red with 1509 tender ...	150.00	175.00	225.00
1511 Loco & Tender (1516) Outfit - Mech (1936-37), 0-4-0 Commodore Vanderbilt type with 1516 tender, black	25.00	40.00	60.00
Same as above, red	35.00	60.00	80.00

94

	G	VG	E
1512 Winner gondola — 027 (Winner 1931)	8.00	12.00	15.00
1512 Ives gondola — 027 (Ives 1931)	8.00	12.00	15.00
1512 L.I. gondola — 027 (1933)	8.00	12.00	15.00
1512 Gondola — 027 (1936)	8.00	12.00	15.00
1513 Ives cattle — 027 (Ives 1932) .	8.00	12.00	15.00
1514 Ives box — 027 (Ives 1931) ...	8.00	12.00	15.00
1514 Winner box — 027 (Winner 1932)	8.00	12.00	15.00
1514 L.I. box — 027 (1933)	8.00	12.00	15.00
1514 Box — 027 (1934)	8.00	12.00	15.00
1515 Ives tank — 027 (Ives 1932) ..	8.00	12.00	15.00
1515 L.I. tank — 027 (1933)	8.00	12.00	15.00
1515 Tank — 027 (1934)	8.00	12.00	15.00
1516T Tender — 027 (1936)	8.00	12.00	15.00
1517 Winner caboose — 027 (Winner 1931)	8.00	12.00	15.00
1517 Ives caboose — 027 (Ives 1931)	8.00	12.00	15.00
1517 L.I. caboose — 027 (1933)	8.00	12.00	15.00
1517 Caboose — 027 (1931-37)	8.00	12.00	15.00
1519 Set — 027 (1954)	50.00	75.00	100.00
1520 Animal (1935)	50.00	75.00	100.00
1521 Loco & Tender (1516T) Outfit - Mech (1937)	160.00	240.00	320.00
1536 Mickey Mouse Circus Train Outfit consisting of cardboard figures, circus facade, tickets, Mickey as barker, train loco #1508, 1509 red, 1536 dinner, 1536 band, and 1536 animal car including original box ..	600.00	800.00	1000.00
1550 Ives switches - Mech (Ives 1931), remote, pair	10.00	15.00	20.00
1550 Switches - Mech (1933), pair, remote	10.00	15.00	20.00
1551 Set — 0 (1921)	75.00	112.50	150.00
1551 90° crossing - Mech (1936)	1.00	1.50	2.00
1551 Set - Mech (1936)	75.00	112.50	150.00
1555 Crossing, 90° - Mech (1933) .	1.00	1.50	2.00
1555W Set	62.50	93.75	125.00
1557W Set	75.00	112.50	150.00
1558 Ives bumper - Mech (Ives 1931)	2.00	3.00	4.00
1559 Ives crossing gate - Mech (Ives 1931)	4.00	6.00	8.00
1560 Ives station - Mech (Ives 1931)	10.00	15.00	20.00

	G	**VG**	**E**
1560 Station - Mech (1933)	10.00	15.00	20.00
1561 Ives tunnel - Mech (Ives 1931)	10.00	15.00	20.00
1562 Ives water tank - Mech (Ives 1931)	8.00	12.00	15.00
1563 Ives telegraph poles, 5 (Ives 1931)	12.00	18.00	25.00
1564 Ives bridge - Mech (Ives 1931)	3.00	6.00	9.00
1565 Ives single arm semaphore - Mech (Ives 1931)	4.00	6.00	8.00
1566 Ives double arm semaphore - Mech (Ives 1931)	5.00	8.00	12.00
1567 Ives danger signal - Mech (Ives 1931)	4.00	6.00	8.00
1568 Ives clock - Mech (Ives 1931) .	6.00	8.00	12.00
1569 Ives accessory set - Mech (Ives 1932)	10.00	15.00	22.00
1571 Ives telegraph posts - Mech (Ives 1932)	8.00	12.00	18.00
1572 L. Jr. telegraph posts - Mech (1934)	8.00	12.00	18.00
1573 Ives warning signal - Mech (Ives 1932)	4.00	6.00	8.00
1573W Set	100.00	150.00	200.00
1573 L. Jr. warning signal - Mech (1934)	4.00	6.00	8.00
1574 Ives clock - Mech (1932)	4.00	6.00	8.00
1574 L. Jr. clock - Mech (1934)	4.00	6.00	8.00
1575 Ives crossing gate - Mech (Ives 1932)	4.00	6.00	8.00
1585 Ives set - Mech (Ives 1931) ...	100.00	150.00	200.00
1588 Loco & Tender (1588T) Outfit - Mech (1936), 0-4-0 torpedo type, 1588 or 1516 tender	25.00	40.00	60.00
1590 Ives set - Mech (Ives 1932) ...	75.00	112.50	150.00
1615 Loco, steam — 027 (1955), 0-4-0 switcher, with 1615T tender	40.00	60.00	90.00
1625 Loco, steam — 027 (1958), 0-4-0 switcher, with 1625 tender	45.00	65.00	100.00
1630 Pullman — 027 (1938), blue sides, aluminum roof	15.00	20.00	25.00
Same as above, blue sides, gray roof	15.00	20.00	25.00
1631 Observation — 027 (1938), blue sides, aluminum roof	15.00	20.00	25.00

Lionel 93 Water Tower (tank) 0 ga, 1931-42, 46-49, silver with vermillion base, pea green tank with maroon base.
Photo by Steve Hintze

Lionel No. 30 Water Tower (tank), operating spout, 0/027 ga., 1947-50.
Photo by Steve Hintze

	G	VG	E
1640-100 Presidential kit (1960) ...	12.00	15.00	20.00
1649 Set — 027 (1961)	137.50	206.25	275.00
1651 Ives, loco, elec. — 027 (Ives 1931)	60.00	90.00	125.00
1651E L.I. loco, elec. — 027 (1933), 0-4-0, red cab, brown roof	60.00	90.00	125.00
1654 Loco, steam — 027 (1946), 2-4-2, 1654W tender	10.00	15.00	18.00
1655 Loco, steam — 027 (1945), 2-4-2, 6654W tender	10.00	15.00	18.00
1656 Loco, steam — 027 (1948), 0-4-0 switcher, 6403 tender	75.00	125.00	175.00
1661 Ives loco, steam — 027 (Ives 1932)	20.00	30.00	40.00
1661E L.I. loco, steam — 027 (1933), gloss black, 2-4-0, 1661 Tender	20.00	30.00	40.00
1662 Loco, steam — 072 (1940), 0-4-0 switcher, 2203 tender	100.00	150.00	225.00
1663 Loco, steam — 027 (1940), 0-4-0 switcher, 2201 tender	125.00	175.00	250.00
1664 or E Loco — Tender outfit — 027 (1938), 2-4-2, with 1689T, 1689W, 2666T, or 2666W tender, black or gunmetal gray	20.00	30.00	40.00

	G	VG	E
1665 Loco, steam — 027 (1946), 0-4-0 switcher with 2403B tender	75.00	125.00	225.00
1666 or E Loco and tender outfit — 027 (1938), 2-4-2 black with 2666T, 2666W, 2689T, 2689W or 1689W tender	20.00	30.00	40.00
Same as above, gunmetal gray	25.00	35.00	50.00
1668 or E Loco, steam — 027 (1937), 2-4-0, 1689T or 1689W tender, black .	20.00	30.00	40.00
Same as above, gunmetal gray	25.00	35.00	50.00
1673 Coach, streamliner - Mech (1936), red	10.00	15.00	18.00
1674 Pullman, streamliner - Mech (1936)	10.00	15.00	18.00
1675 Observation, streamliner - Mech (1936)	10.00	15.00	18.00
1677 Ives gondola — 027 (Ives 1931)	8.00	12.00	15.00
1677 L. I. gondola — 027 (1933)	8.00	12.00	15.00
1677 Gondola — 027 (1934)	8.00	12.00	15.00
1679 Ives box — 027 (Ives 1931) ...	8.00	12.00	15.00
1679 L.I. box — 027 (1933)	8.00	12.00	15.00
1679 Box — 027 (1934)	8.00	12.00	15.00
1680 Ives tank — 027 (Ives 1931) ..	8.00	12.00	15.00
1680 L.I. tank — 027 (1933)	8.00	12.00	15.00
1680 Tank — 027 (1934)	8.00	12.00	15.00
1681 or E L. Jr. loco, steam — 027 (1934), 2-4-0 black	20.00	30.00	40.00
Same as above, red	25.00	40.00	50.00
1682 Ives caboose — 027 (1931)	8.00	10.00	12.00
1682 L.I. caboose — 027 (1933)	8.00	10.00	12.00
1682 Caboose — 027 (1934)	8.00	10.00	12.00
1684 Loco, steam — 027 (1942), 2-4-2, 1689T, 1688T, 2689T, or 2689W tender, black	10.00	15.00	20.00
Same as above, gunmetal gray	15.00	20.00	25.00
1685 Pullman — 0 (uncat 1933), Ives transitional car, blue body, silver roof, 4 wheel trucks	75.00	125.00	200.00
Same as above, red body, maroon roof, 4 wheel trucks	60.00	90.00	150.00
Same as above, gray body, maroon roof, 6 wheel trucks	100.00	150.00	225.00
1686 Baggage — 0 (uncat 1933), Ives transitional car, blue body, silver			

	G	VG	E
roof, 4 wheel trucks	75.00	125.00	200.00
Same as above, red body, maroon roof, 4 wheel trucks	60.00	90.00	150.00
Same as above, gray body, maroon roof, 6 wheel trucks	100.00	150.00	225.00
1687 Observation — 0 (uncat 1933), Ives transitional car, blue body, silver roof, 4 wheel trucks	75.00	125.00	200.00
Same as above, red body, maroon roof, 4 wheel trucks	60.00	90.00	150.00
Same as above, gray body, maroon roof, 6 wheel trucks	100.00	150.00	225.00
1688 or E Loco, steam — 027 (1936), 2-4-2, 1689T tender, black	20.00	30.00	40.00
Same as above, gunmetal gray	25.00	35.00	45.00
1689E Loco, steam — 027 (1936), 2-4-2, 1689T tender, black	20.00	30.00	40.00
Same as above, gunmetal gray	25.00	35.00	45.00
1690 Ives pullman — 027 (Ives 1931), red with brown roof or red with red roof	9.00	15.00	18.00
1690 L.I. pullman — 027 (1933), red with red or brown roof	9.00	15.00	18.00
1690 Pullman — 027 (1934), red, with red or brown roof	9.00	15.00	18.00
1691 Ives observation — 027 (Ives 1931), red with red or brown roof ...	9.00	15.00	18.00
1691 L.I. observation — 027 (1933), red with red or brown roof	9.00	15.00	18.00
1691 Observation — 027 (1934), red with red or brown roof	9.00	15.00	18.00
1692 Pullman — 027 (uncat 1937), peacock body and roof	9.00	15.00	18.00
1693 Observation — 027 (uncat 1937), peacock body and roof	9.00	15.00	18.00
1694 Ives loco, elec. — 0 (Ives 1932)	40.00	60.00	80.00
1695 Ives pullman — 0 (Ives 1932) .	10.00	15.00	20.00
1696 Ives baggage — 0 (Ives 1932) .	10.00	15.00	20.00
1697 Ives observation — 0 (Ives 1932)	10.00	15.00	20.00
1697 Loco, tender and transformer outfit — 027 (1937)	40.00	60.00	80.00

	G	VG	E
1698E Loco, tender (1689) and transformer outfit — 027 (1936)	40.00	60.00	80.00
1699E Loco, tender (1688) and transformer outfit — 027 (1936)	40.00	60.00	80.00
1700 or E Power car, diesel, streamliner — 027 (1935), "Lionel Jr.", aluminum and red	20.00	30.00	40.00
1700 Special set — 027 (uncat 1935), 1700E, one 1701, one 1702, aluminum and red	60.00	75.00	90.00
1700 Special set — 027 (uncat 1936), 1700E, two 1701, one 1702, chrome and red	75.00	90.00	120.00
1701 Coach, streamliner — 027 (1935), aluminum and red or chrome	9.00	12.00	15.00
1702 Observation, streamliner — 027 (1935), aluminum and red or chrome	9.00	12.00	15.00
1703 Front coach with drawbar, streamliner — 027 (1935)	9.00	12.00	15.00
1707 Ives gondola — 0 (Ives 1932) .	8.00	12.00	15.00
1708 Ives cattle — 0 (Ives 1932)	8.00	12.00	15.00
1709 Ives box — 0 (Ives 1932)	8.00	12.00	15.00
1712 Ives caboose — 0 (Ives 1932) .	8.00	12.00	15.00
1717 Gondola — 0 (uncat 1933), orange and tan or yellow and green	12.00	15.00	18.00
1719 Box — 0 (uncat 1933), peacock with blue roof (orange doors), yellow and brown	12.00	15.00	18.00
1722 Caboose — 0 (uncat 1933), orange body or red body	12.00	15.00	18.00
1760 Ives loco, steam — Std. (Ives 1931)	200.00	300.00	400.00
1764 Ives loco, elec. — Std. (Ives 1932)	200.00	300.00	400.00
1766 Ives pullman — Std. (Ives 1932)	60.00	90.00	120.00
1766 Pullman — Std. (1934)	60.00	90.00	120.00
1767 Ives baggage — Std. (Ives 1932)	60.00	90.00	120.00
1767 Baggage — Std. (1934)	60.00	90.00	120.00
1768 Ives observation — Std. (Ives 1932)	60.00	90.00	120.00
1768 Observation — Std. (1934)	60.00	90.00	120.00

	G	VG	E
1770 Ives loco, steam — Std. (Ives 1932)	200.00	300.00	400.00
1771 Ives lumber — Std. (Ives 1931)	30.00	40.00	60.00
1772 Ives gondola — Std. (Ives 1931)	20.00	30.00	40.00
1773 Ives cattle — Std. (Ives 1931) .	30.00	40.00	60.00
1774 Ives box — Std. (Ives 1931) ...	30.00	40.00	60.00
1775 Ives tank — Std. (Ives 1931) ..	30.00	40.00	60.00
1776 Ives hopper — Std. (Ives 1931)	30.00	40.00	60.00
1777 Ives caboose — Std. (Ives 1931)	20.00	30.00	40.00
1778 Ives refrigerator — Std. (Ives 1931)	40.00	60.00	80.00
1779 Ives crane — Std. (Ives 1931) .	60.00	90.00	120.00
1810 Ives loco, elec. — 027 (Ives 1931)	40.00	60.00	80.00
1811 Ives pullman — 027 (Ives 1931)	8.00	12.00	15.00
1811 L.I. pullman — 027 (1933)	8.00	12.00	15.00
1811 Pullman — 027 (1934)	8.00	12.00	15.00
1812 Ives observation — 027 (Ives 1931)	8.00	12.00	15.00
1812 L.I. observation — 027 (1933) .	8.00	12.00	15.00
1812 Observation — 027 (1934)	8.00	12.00	15.00
1813 Ives baggage — 027 (Ives 1931)	8.00	12.00	15.00
1813 L.I. baggage — 027 (1933)	8.00	12.00	15.00
1813 Baggage — 027 (1934)	8.00	12.00	15.00
1815 Ives loco, steam — 027 (Ives 1931), black	30.00	40.00	60.00
1816 or W Power car, streamliner - Mech (1935), diesel wind-up, "Silver Streak"	25.00	40.00	60.00
1816 Streamliner set with 1816 — 027 (1935), 1816, 1817, 1818, chrome and orange	50.00	75.00	100.00
1817 Coach, streamliner - Mech (1935), chrome and orange	8.00	12.00	15.00
1818 Observation, streamliner - Mech (1935), chrome and orange ...	8.00	12.00	15.00
1835E Loco, steam — Std. (1934), 2-4-2, 1835T, 1835TW or 1835W tender	200.00	300.00	375.00
1851 Ives crossing, 90° — 0 (Ives 1931)	1.00	2.00	3.00

	G	VG	E
1853 Ives crossing, 45° — 0 (Ives 1931)	1.00	2.00	3.00
1854 Ives crossing, 45° — Std. (Ives 1931)	1.00	2.00	4.00
1855 Ives bumper — 0 (Ives (1931) .	2.00	3.00	4.00
1856 Ives bumper — Std. (Ives 1931)	2.00	4.00	6.00
1857 Ives bumper — 0 (Ives 1931) ..	2.00	3.00	4.00
1858 Ives bumper — Std. (Ives 1931)	2.00	4.00	6.00
1859 Ives tunnel — 0 (Ives 1931) ...	8.00	12.00	15.00
1860 Ives tunnel — 0 (Ives 1931) ...	8.00	12.00	15.00
1861 Ives tunnel — Std. (Ives 1931)	8.00	12.00	15.00
1862 Ives tunnel — Std. (Ives 1931)	8.00	12.00	15.00
1862 Loco, steam — 027 (1959), 4-4-0 civil war "General", 1862T tender ..	40.00	60.00	90.00
1863 Ives low bridge warning (Ives 1931)	3.00	5.00	7.00
1864 Ives block signal (Ives 1931) .	3.00	5.00	7.00
1865 Ives double arm block signal (Ives 1931)	4.00	6.00	8.00
1865 Coach — 027 (1959), Western & Atlantic	15.00	20.00	30.00
1866 Ives flagpole (Ives 1931)	10.00	15.00	20.00
1866 Baggage car — 027 (1959), Western & Atlantic	15.00	20.00	30.00
1867 Ives signal tower (Ives 1931) .	10.00	15.00	20.00
1868 Ives suburban house (Ives 1931)	15.00	20.00	30.00
1869 Ives Dutch colonial house (Ives 1931)	15.00	20.00	30..00
1870 Ives English cottage house (Ives 1931)	15.00	20.00	30.00
1871 Ives station (Ives 1931)	15.00	20.00	35.00
1872 Ives way station (Ives 1931) ..	15.00	20.00	35.00
1872 Loco, steam — super 0 (1959), 4-4-0, civil war "General", 1872W tender	75.00	125.00	175.00
1873 Ives station (Ives 1931)	15.00	20.00	35.00
1874 Ives station (Ives 1931)	15.00	20.00	35.00
1875 Ives freight station (Ives 1931)	15.00	20.00	35.00
1875 Coach Super 0 (1959), Western & Atlantic	50.00	75.00	100.00
1875W Coach w/whistle — Super 0 (1959), Western & Atlantic	40.00	60.00	80.00
1876 Ives power house (Ives 1931)	40.00	60.00	80.00

Lionel 155 Freight Shed, Std., 1940-42 (illum.).
Lionel 163 Freight Station Set, Std., 1930-42. Consisting of: 162 dump cart, 160 baggage cart, (2) 157 hand trucks.
Photo by Steve Hintze

Lionel 1045 Operating Watchman, 10 ga., 1938-42 46-50, nickel sign, also available with brass sign.
Photo by Steve Hintze

	G	VG	E
1876 Baggage — Super 0 (1959), Western & Atlantic	25.00	40.00	60.00
1877 Ives circuit breaker (Ives 1931)	1.00	2.00	3.00
1877 Flat with horses — 027 (1959), part of General set, six horses	15.00	25.00	40.00
1878 Ives crossing gate — 0 (Ives 1931)	2.00	4.00	6.00
1879 Ives crossing gate — Std. (Ives 1931)	2.00	4.00	6.00
1880 Ives flashing signal (Ives (1931)	2.00	4.00	6.00
1881 Ives traffic signal (Ives 1931) .	2.00	4.00	6.00
1882 Ives boulevard lamppost (Ives 1931)	15.00	20.00	30.00
1882 Loco, steam — Super 0 (uncat 1959), Sears Production, Civil War General, 4-4-0	125.00	175.00	250.00
1883 Ives crossing bell — Std. (Ives 1931)	6.00	9.00	12.00
1885 Ives target signal — Std. (Ives 1931)	4.00	6.00	8.00
1885 Coach — Super 0 (uncat 1959), Sears production, Western & Atlantic (Blue Shell)	75.00	125.00	175.00
1886 Ives target signal — 0 (Ives 1931)	2.00	4.00	6.00

	G	VG	E
1887 Ives transformer, 50 watt (Ives 1931)	1.00	2.00	3.00
1887 Flat w/horses — 027 (uncat 1959), Sears Production, six horses .	40.00	60.00	80.00
1888 Ives transformer, 75 watt (Ives 1931)	2.00	3.00	4.00
1889 Ives transformer, 100 watt (Ives 1931)	2.00	3.00	4.00
1890 Ives transformer, 150 watt (Ives 1931)	2.00	3.00	4.00
1891 Ives transformer, 50 watt (Ives 1931)	1.00	2.00	3.00
1893 Ives D. C. controller (Ives 1931)	1.00	1.50	2.00
1894 Ives rheostat (Ives 1931)	1.00	1.50	2.00
1895 Ives switch, manual — 0 (Ives 1931)	3.00	5.00	7.00
1896 Ives switch, manual — Std. (Ives 1931), single	5.00	7.00	9.00
1897 Ives switch, automatic — 0 (Ives 1931)	5.00	7.00	9.00
1898 Ives switch, automatic — Std. (Ives 1931)	7.00	9.00	12.00
1899 Ives crossing 90° — Std. (Ives 1931)	1.00	2.00	3.00
1901 Ives panel board (Ives 1932) ..	4.00	6.00	8.00
1902 Ives floodlight tower (Ives 1932)	6.00	9.00	12.00
1903 Ewing Merkle catalog (early Lionel) (1903)	20.00	40.00	60.00
1903 Lionel catalog (later) (1903) ..	20.00	40.00	60.00
1903 Ives semaphore — Std. (Ives 1932)	2.00	4.00	6.00
1904 Lionel catalog (1904)	20.00	40.00	60.00
1904 Ives semaphore — 0 (Ives 1932)	2.00	4.00	6.00
1905 Lionel catalog (1905)	20.00	40.00	60.00
1905 Ives lamp post (Ives 1932)	6.00	9.00	12.00
1906 Lionel catalog (1906)	20.00	40.00	60.00
1906 Ives freight station set (Ives 1932)	20.00	30.00	40.00
1907 Lionel catalog (1907)	20.00	40.00	60.00
1907 Ives automatic train control — 0 (Ives 1932)	6.00	8.00	12.00

	G	VG	E
1908 Lionel catalog (1908)	20.00	40.00	60.00
1908 Ives automatic train control — Std. (Ives 1932)	4.00	6.00	8.00
1909 Lionel catalog (1909)	20.00	40.00	60.00
1910 Lionel catalog (1910)	20.00	40.00	60.00
1910 Loco, elec. — Std. (1910), 0-6-0, dark olive green, "New York, New Haven and Hartford" in gold script on side of cab	600.00	800.00	1000.00
1910 Pullman — Std. (uncat 1910) dark olive green, maroon doors, "1910 Pullman 1910" gold lettering on sides	300.00	600.00	900.00
1911 Lionel catalog (1911)	20.00	40.00	60.00
1911 Loco, elec. — Std. (1910), 0-4-0, dark olive	400.00	500.00	600.00
Same as above, maroon	350.00	450.00	550.00
1911 Special loco, elec. — Std. (1911), 0-4-4-0, maroon, either "New York, New Haven and Hartford" or "New York Central Lines" gold rubber stamped on each variation	400.00	600.00	700.00
1912 Loco, elec. — Std. (1910), 0-4-4-0, dark olive green, same lettering variations as above	700.00	900.00	1100.00
Same as above "New York, New Haven and Hartford"	800.00	1000.00	1200.00
1912 Lionel catalog (1912)	20.00	40.00	60.00
1912 Special loco, elec. — Std. (1911), 0-4-4-0, all brass engine (polished) ..	1800.00	2400.00	2800.00
1913 Lionel catalog (1913)	20.00	40.00	60.00
1913 Lionel catalog, small (1913) ..	15.00	30.00	45.00
1914 Lionel catalog (1914)	20.00	40.00	60.00
1914 Lionel catalog, small (1914) ..	15.00	30.00	45.00
1915 Lionel catalog (1915)	20.00	40.00	60.00
1916 Lionel catalog (1916)	20.00	40.00	60.00
1917 Lionel catalog (1917)	20.00	40.00	60.00
1917 Lionel folder (1917)	10.00	15.00	20.00
1918 Lionel folder (1918)	10.00	15.00	20.00
1919 Lionel folder (1919)	10.00	15.00	20.00
1919 Lionel apology folder (1919) ..	20.00	30.00	40.00
1920 Lionel catalog (1920)	20.00	40.00	60.00
1920 Lionel folder (1920)	10.00	15.00	20.00

	G	VG	E
1921 Lionel folder (1921)	10.00	15.00	20.00
1922 Lionel catalog (1922)	20.00	40.00	60.00
1923 Lionel catalog (1923)	20.00	40.00	60.00
1924 Lionel catalog (1924)	20.00	40.00	60.00
1925 Lionel catalog (1925)	20.00	40.00	60.00
1926 Lionel catalog (1926)	20.00	40.00	60.00
1926-3 Ives bulb, 6 volt (Ives 1931)	fifty cents		
1926-3 Lionel-Ives bulb, 6 volt (1933)	fifty cents		
1927 Lionel catalog (1927)	20.00	40.00	60.00
1928 Lionel catalog (1928)	20.00	40.00	60.00
1928 Dealer Display - large cardboard background showing power station, roundhouses, etc.	175.00	262.50	350.00
1928 Ives bulb, 18 volt (Ives 1931) .	fifty cents		
1929 Lionel catalog (1929)	20.00	40.00	60.00
1930 Lionel catalog (1930)	20.00	40.00	60.00
1930 Winner folder (1930)	15.00	20.00	30.00
1931 Lionel catalog (1931)	20.00	40.00	60.00
1931 Winner folder (1931)	15.00	20.00	30.00
1932 Lionel catalog (1932)	20.00	40.00	60.00
1932 Winner folder (1932)	15.00	20.00	30.00
1933 Lionel catalog (1933)	20.00	35.00	50.00
1934 Lionel catalog (1934)	15.00	20.00	30.00
1935 Lionel catalog (1935)	15.00	20.00	30.00
1936 Lionel catalog (1936)	15.00	20.00	30.00
1937 Lionel catalog (1937)	15.00	20.00	30.00
1938 Lionel catalog (1938)	15.00	20.00	30.00
1939 Ives bulb, 12 volt (Ives 1931) .	fifty cents		
1939 Lionel catalog (1939)	15.00	20.00	30.00
1940 Ives bulb, 18 volt (Ives 1931) .	fifty cents		
1940 Lionel catalog (1940)	15.00	20.00	30.00
1941 Lionel catalog (1941)	15.00	20.00	30.00
1942 Lionel catalog (1942)	15.00	20.00	30.00
1945 Lionel folder (1945)	9.00	12.00	15.00
1946 Lionel catalog (1946)	10.00	15.00	20.00
1947 Lionel catalog (1947)	9.00	12.00	15.00
1948 Lionel catalog (1948)	9.00	12.00	15.00
1949 Lionel catalog (1949)	15.00	18.00	22.00
1950 Lionel catalog (1950)	10.00	15.00	25.00
1951 Lionel catalog (1951)	10.00	15.00	25.00
1952 Lionel catalog (1952)	9.00	12.00	15.00
1953 Lionel catalog (1953)	7.00	9.00	12.00
1954 Lionel catalog (1954)	7.00	9.00	12.00

	G	VG	E
1955 Lionel catalog (1955)	7.00	9.00	12.00
1956 Lionel catalog (1956)	5.00	7.00	9.00
1957 Lionel catalog (1957)	3.00	5.00	7.00
1958 Lionel catalog (1958)	3.00	4.00	6.00
1959 Lionel catalog (1959)	3.00	4.00	6.00
1960 Lionel catalog (1960)	3.00	4.00	5.00
1961 Lionel catalog (1961)	3.00	4.00	5.00
1962 Lionel catalog (1962)	2.00	4.00	5.00
1963 Lionel catalog (1963)	2.00	4.00	4.00
1964 Lionel catalog (1964)	2.00	3.00	4.00
1965 Lionel catalog (1965)	1.00	2.00	3.00
1966 & 67 Lionel catalog (1966) ...	1.00	2.00	3.00
1968 Lionel catalog (1968)	1.00	2.00	3.00
1969 Lionel catalog (1969)	1.00	2.00	3.00
2016 Loco, steam — 027 (1955), 2-6-4, 6026W tender	15.00	25.00	35.00
2018 Loco, steam — 027 (1956), 2-6-4, 6026W tender	15.00	25.00	40.00
2020 Loco, steam — 027 (1946), 6-8-6, 2020W, 2466WX or 6020W tender ...	35.00	50.00	75.00
2023 Loco, Diesel, Alco AA, U.P. — 027 (1950), yellow body, gray roof, or silver body with gray roof	40.00	60.00	80.00
2024 Loco, Diesel, Alco A, C&O — 027 (1969)	15.00	25.00	30.00
2025 Loco, steam — 027 (1947), 2-6-2, 6466WX or 6466W tender	20.00	30.00	45.00
2026 Loco, steam — 027 (1948), 2-6-2, 6466WX or 6466W tender	20.00	30.00	40.00
2026-58 Bulb, 18 volt - clear (1950)	fifty cents		
2028 Loco, Diesel, GP-7, PRR — 027 (1955), tuscan brown	40.00	60.00	75.00
2029 Loco, steam — 0 (1964), 2-6-4, 243W tender	15.00	20.00	25.00
2031 Loco, Diesel, Alco AA, R.I. — 027 (1952), black body, red middle stripe	30.00	45.00	75.00
2032 Loco, Diesel, Alco AA, Erie — 027 (1952), black body, yellow middle stripe	30.00	45.00	75.00
2033 Loco, Diesel, Alco AA, U.P. — 027 (1952), silver body	30.00	45.00	75.00
2034 Loco, steam — 027 (1952), 2-4-2	15.00	18.00	22.00

	G	VG	E
2035 Loco, steam — 027 (1950), 2-6-4, 2466W tender	20.00	30.00	40.00
2036 Loco, steam — 027 (1950), 2-6-4, 6466W tender	15.00	22.00	30.00
2037 Loco, steam — 027 (1953), 2-6-4, 6026W or 6026 tender	18.00	25.00	30.00
2037-500 Loco, steam - Girls train — 027 (1957), 2-6-4 Girls' Set, pink ..	400.00	500.00	600.00
2041 Loco, Diesel, Alco AA, R.I. — 027 (1969), black body, white stripe .	20.00	30.00	40.00
2046 Loco, steam — 027 (1950), 4-6-4, 2046W tender	35.00	50.00	75.00
2055 Loco, steam — 027 (1953), 4-6-4, 1025W or 2046W tender	30.00	45.00	60.00
2056 Loco, steam — 027 (1952), 4-6-4, 2046W tender	30.00	45.00	60.00
2065 Loco, steam — 027 (1954), 4-6-4, 2046W or 6026W tender	30.00	45.00	60.00
2167 Set — 0 (1950)	150.00	225.00	300.00
2173 Set — 0 (1950)	175.00	262.50	350.00
2175 Set — 0 (1951)	175.00	262.50	350.00
2191 Set — 0 (1952)	150.00	225.00	300.00
2200 Summer trolley, trailer — Std. (1910), non-powered, gold rubber-stamped, "2200 Rapid Transit 2200"	1200.00	1600.00	2000.00
2201 Set – 0 (1952)	125.00	187.50	250.00
2240 Loco, Diesel AB, F-3, Wabash — 027 (1956), grey and blue shell, single motor	125.00	175.00	225.00
2242 Loco, Diesel, AB, F-3, New Haven — 027 (1958), checkerboard scheme, silver and black, single motor	150.00	225.00	300.00
2243 Loco, Diesel AB, F-3, Santa Fe — 027 (1955), silver shell, red nose, single motor	75.00	100.00	145.00
2245 Loco, Diesel AB, F-3, Texas Special — 027 (1954), red shell, single motor	125.00	175.00	225.00
2255W Set	112.50	168.75	225.00
2257 Caboose, (non-illuminated) ...	1.00	1.50	2.00
2321 Loco, Diesel, FM, Lackawanna — 0 (1954), double motor, grey	125.00	175.00	225.00
Same as above, grey with maroon roof.................................	150.00	200.00	250.00

	G	VG	E
2322 Loco, Diesel, FM, Virginian — 0 (1965), double motor, yellow, blue roof	150.00	200.00	250.00
Same as above, yellow, black roof	200.00	350.00	500.00
2328 Loco, Diesel, GP-7, Burlington — 027 (1955), silver shell	40.00	60.00	80.00
2329 Loco, elec, rectifier, Virginian — 0 (1958), blue shell, yellow striping	125.00	200.00	250.00
2330 Loco, elec, GG-I-0 (1950), New Brunswick Green, five gold stripes, double motor	200.00	300.00	400.00
2331 Loco, Diesel, FM, Virginian — 0 (1955), double motor, yellow shell, black stripe, gold lettering	200.00	350.00	500.00
Same as above, yellow shell, blue stripe, yellow lettering	150.00	200.00	250.00
2332 Loco, elec, GG-I (1947), single motor, New Brunswick Green, five gold stripes	125.00	175.00	225.00
Same as above, five silver stripes	200.00	275.00	325.00
Same as above, satin black, five gold stripes or silver stripes	300.00	500.00	800.00
2333 Loco, Diesel, AA, F-3, A. Santa Fe or NYC — 0 (1948), Santa Fe, silver, red nose	90.00	150.00	225.00
B. Same as above, NYC, gray	90.00	150.00	225.00
C. NYC RR in large bold letters	125.00	175.00	275.00
2337 Loco, Diesel, GP-7, Wabash — 027 (1958), blue and gray body, white striping	50.00	75.00	100.00
2338 Loco, Diesel, GP-7, Milwaukee Rd — 027 (1955), black and orange	60.00	85.00	110.00
2339 Loco, Diesel, GP-7, Wabash — 0 (1957), blue and gray with white striping	50.00	75.00	100.00
2340-1 Loco, elec, GG-1, Maroon — 0, (1955), double motor, tuscan brown, five stripes	200.00	300.00	400.00

	G	VG	E
2340-25 Loco, elec, GG-1, Green — 0 (1955), double motor, New Brunswick green, five stripes	200.00	325.00	425.00
2341 Loco, Diesel, FM, Jersey Central — 0 (1956), double motor, orange body, blue stripe	300.00	500.00	700.00
2343 Loco, Diesel, AA, F-3, Santa Fe — 0 (1950), double motor, silver with red nose	90.00	135.00	185.00
2343C Loco, Diesel, B, Santa Fe — 0 (1950)	30.00	40.00	60.00
2344 Loco, Diesel, AA, F-3, NYC — 0 (1950), double motor, gray	100.00	150.00	200.00
2344C Loco, Diesel, B, F-3, NYC — 0 (1950)	30.00	40.00	60.00
2345 Loco, Diesel, AA, F-3, Western Pacific — 0 (1952), double motor, silver and orange			
A. Screen roof	175.00	225.00	325.00
B. Louvered roof	150.00	200.00	250.00
2346 Loco, Diesel, GP-7, Boston and Maine — 027 (1965), blue shell, black cab, white trim	60.00	90.00	125.00
2347 Loco, Diesel, GP-7, C&O — 027 (uncat 1962), Sears, blue shell, yellow lettering	500.00	700.00	900.00
2348 Loco, Diesel, GP-9, M.St.L. — 027 (1958), red shell, blue roof	75.00	125.00	185.00
2349 Loco, Diesel, GP-0, Northern Pacific — 0 (1959), black shell, red striping, gold lettering	95.00	125.00	160.00
2350 Loco, elec, New Haven — 0 (1956), black shell, orange and white striping	90.00	145.00	185.00
2351 Loco, elec, Milwaukee Rd — 0 (1957), yellow shell, black roof, red stripe	90.00	145.00	185.00
2352 Loco, Diesel, PRR — 0 (1958), tuscan brown	90.00	145.00	185.00
2353 Loco, Diesel, AA, F-3, Santa Fe — 0 (1953), double motor, silver, red nose	90.00	145.00	185.00
2353C Loco, Diesel, F-3, Santa Fe — 0 (1954)	30.00	40.00	60.00

	G	VG	E
2354 Loco, Diesel, AA, F-3, NYC — 0 (1953), double motor, gray	125.00	165.00	225.00
2354C Loco, Diesel, B, F-3, NYC — 0 (1954)	30.00	40.00	60.00
2355 Loco, Diesel, AA, F-3, Western Pacific — 0 (1953), double motor, silver and orange	160.00	225.00	300.00
2356 Loco, Diesel, AA, F-3, Southern Ry — 0 (1954), double motor, green .	160.00	225.00	300.00
2356C Loco, Diesel, B, F-3, Southern Ry — 0 (1954)	30.00	40.00	60.00
2357 Caboose — 0 (1948)	3.00	6.00	9.00
2358 Loco, elec. Great Northern — 0 (1959), orange and green shell, yellow stripes	125.00	175.00	250.00
2359 Loco, Diesel, GP-9, B&M — 027 (1961), blue shell, black cab, white trim	60.00	90.00	135.00
2360-1 Loco, elec, GG-1, single stripe, (1961), double motor, tuscan brown, decal letters and numbers rubber-stamped stripe	225.00	325.00	425.00
Same as above, heavy heat stamped letters and numbers	250.00	375.00	475.00
Same as 2360-1, light pressed letters and numbers, rubber-stamped stripe	200.00	300.00	375.00
2360-10 Loco, elec, GG-1, 5 stripes — 0 (1956), tuscan brown, double motor, heat-stamped letter and number, five rubber-stamped stripes	250.00	350.00	450.00
2360-25 Loco, elec, GG-1, green — 0 (1956), New Brunswick green, heat stamped letters and numbers, double motor, five rubber stamped stripes	225.00	325.00	425.00
2363 Loco, Diesel, AB, F-3, Illinois Central — 0 (1955), double motor, brown shell, orange stripe, yellow trim	175.00	250.00	350.00
2365 Loco, Diesel, GP-7, C&O — 027 (1962), blue shell	50.00	75.00	100.00
2367 Loco, Diesel, AB, F-3, Wabash — 0 (1955), double motor, gray and blue shell, white stripe and trim	150.00	260.00	325.00

	G	VG	E
2368 Loco, Diesel, AB, F-3, B&O — 0 (1956), blue shell with black, white and yellow trim, double motor	200.00	300.00	400.00
2373 Loco, Diesel, AA, F-3, Canadian Pacific — Super - 0 (1957), double motor, gray and maroon, yellow trim	250.00	350.00	450.00
2378 Loco, Diesel, AB, F-3, Milwaukee Rd — 0 (1956), double motor, gray with orange stripe	225.00	325.00	425.00
2379 Loco, Diesel, AB, F-3, Rio Grande — Super 0 (1957), double motor, yellow body, silver roof and stripe	200.00	275.00	325.00
2383 Loco, Diesel, AA, F-3, Santa Fe — Super 0 (1958), silver, red nose, double motor	90.00	125.00	185.00
2400 Pullman — 027 (1948), Maplewood, green shell, gray roof, yellow trim	15.00	25.00	40.00
2401 Observation — 027 (1948), Hillside	15.00	25.00	40.00
2402 Pullman — 027 (1948), Chatham	15.00	25.00	40.00
2404 Vista Dome — 027 (1964), Santa Fe, aluminum, blue lettering .	10.00	15.00	25.00
2405 Pullman — 027 (1964), Santa Fe, aluminum, blue lettering	10.00	15.00	25.00
2406 Observation (1964), Santa Fe, aluminum, blue lettering	10.00	15.00	25.00
2408 Vista Dome — 027 (1964), Santa Fe, aluminum, blue lettering .	10.00	15.00	25.00
2409 Pullman — 027 (1964), Santa Fe, aluminum, blue lettering	10.00	15.00	25.00
2410 Observation (1964), Santa Fe, aluminum, blue lettering	10.00	15.00	25.00
2411 Flat w/load of pipes — 027 (1946), gray metal frame	5.00	8.00	12.00
2412 Vista Dome — 027 (1959), silver, blue stripe through windows, illuminated	15.00	20.00	35.00
2414 Pullman — 027 (1959), silver, blue stripe through windows, illuminated	15.00	20.00	25.00

	G	VG	E
2416 Observation — 027 (1959), silver, blue stripe through windows, illuminated	15.00	20.00	25.00
2419 Wrecker caboose — 027 (1946), D.L. & W., gray metal frame, gray cab	15.00	22.00	30.00
2420 Wrecker caboose with light — 0 (1946), gray metal frame, D.L.&W., gray cab	20.00	30.00	40.00
2420-20 Bulb, 14 volt - clear (1946)	fifty cents		
2421 Pullman — 027 (1950), aluminum, gray roof, black stripe	15.00	25.00	35.00
Same as above, silver roof, no stripe	10.00	20.00	25.00
2422 Pullman — 027 (1950), aluminum, gray roof, black stripe	15.00	25.00	35.00
Same as above, silver roof, no stripe	10.00	20.00	25.00
2423 Observation — 027 (1950), aluminum, gray roof, black stripe ..	15.00	25.00	35.00
Same as above, silver roof, no stripe	10.00	20.00	25.00
2426 Tender — 0 (1946), aluminum, gray roof, black stripe	15.00	25.00	35.00
Same as above, silver roof, no stripe	10.00	20.00	25.00
2429 Pullman — 027 (1952), aluminum, gray roof, black stripe	15.00	25.00	35.00
Same as above, silver roof, no stripe	10.00	20.00	25.00
2430 Pullman — 027 (1946), blue, silver roof (sheet metal)	10.00	15.00	20.00
2431 Observation — 027 (1946), blue, silver roof (sheet metal)	10.00	15.00	20.00
2432 Vista Dome — 027 (1954), "Clifton", silver, red lettering	15.00	20.00	25.00
2434 Pullman — 027 (1954), "Newark", silver, red lettering	15.00	20.00	25.00
2435 Pullman — 027 (1954), "Elizabeth", silver, red lettering	15.00	20.00	25.00
2436 Observation — 027 (1954), "Summit", silver, red lettering	15.00	20.00	25.00
Same as above, "Mooseheart"	20.00	30.00	40.00
2440 Pullman — 027 (1946), blue, silver roof	15.00	20.00	25.00
Same as above, green, dark green roof	15.00	20.00	25.00
2441 Observation — 027 (1946), blue, silver roof	15.00	20.00	25.00
Same as above, green, dark green roof	15.00	20.00	25.00

	G	VG	E
2442 Pullman — 027 (1946), brown sheet metal	15.00	20.00	25.00
2242 Vista Dome — 027 (1956), "Clifton", aluminum, red window stripe	15.00	20.00	25.00
2443 Observation — 0 (1956), brown sheet metal	15.00	20.00	25.00
2444 Pullman — 0 (1956), aluminum, red window stripe	15.00	20.00	25.00
2452 Gondola — 027 (1945), "Pennsylvania"	2.00	4.00	6.00
2452X Gondola — 027 (1946), "Pennsylvania"	2.00	4.00	6.00
2454 Box — 027 (1946), "Baby Ruth"	3.00	5.00	8.00
Same as above, "Pennsylvania"	15.00	30.00	45.00
2456 Hopper — 0 (1948), Lehigh Valley	2.00	4.00	6.00
2457 Caboose — 0 (1945), "Pennsylvania" N5 type	4.00	8.00	12.00
2458 Box, automatic — 0 (1945), "Pennsylvania", double door	6.00	8.00	12.00
2460 Operating crane — 0 (1946), Bucyrus Erie	10.00	15.00	20.00
2461 Transformer car — 027 (1947), gray metal frame	8.00	12.00	18.00
2465 Tank - double dome — 027 (1946), Sunoco	2.00	4.00	6.00
2472 Caboose — 027 (1946), "Pennsylvania", N5 type	2.00	4.00	6.00
2481 Pullman — 027 (1950), illuminated, yellow, red stripes, gray roof Anniversary Set	45.00	75.00	100.00
2482 Pullman — 027 (1950), illuminated, yellow, red stripes, gray roof, Anniversary Set	45.00	75.00	100.00
2483 Observation — 027 (1950), illuminated yellow, red stripes, gray roof, Anniversary Set	45.00	75.00	100.00
2521 Observation — Super 0 (1962), "Pres. McKinley", illuminated, extruded aluminum shell, gold stripe with President's name	50.00	75.00	100.00
2522 Vista Dome — Super 0 (1962), "Pres. Harrison", extruded aluminum			

114

	G	VG	E
shell, illuminated, gold stripe with President's name	50.00	75.00	100.00
2523 Pullman — Super 0 (1962), "Pres. Garfield", illuminated, extruded aluminum shell, gold stripe with President's name	50.00	75.00	100.00
2530 Baggage — 0 (1956), Railway Express Agency, extruded aluminum shell, large door	60.00	80.00	120.00
Same as above, small doors	40.00	60.00	80.00
2531 Observation — 0 (1952), illuminated, "Silver Dawn", extruded aluminum shell	20.00	30.00	40.00
2532 Vista Dome — 0 (1952), "Silver Range"	25.00	37.50	50.00
2533 Pullman — 0 (1952), "Silver Cloud"	30.00	45.00	60.00
2534 Pullman — 0 (1952), "Silver Bluff"	28.00	42.00	56.00
2541 Observation — 0 (1955), "Alexander Hamilton", Penn., extruded aluminum, brown stripes, illuminated	50.00	75.00	100.00
2542 Vista Dome — 0 (1955), "Betsy Ross", Penn.	50.00	75.00	100.00
2543 Pullman — 0 (1955), "William Penn" Penn	50.00	75.00	100.00
2544 Pullman — 0 (1955), "Molly Pitcher", Penn	50.00	75.00	100.00
2550 Budd R.D.C. Mail-Baggage Trailer — 0 (1957), Baltimore and Ohio dummy to match motorized Budd 404, silver shell, blue lettering	90.00	150.00	200.00
2551 Observation — Super 0 (1957), "Banff Park", extruded aluminum shell, two brown stripes, top Canadian Pacific, bottom, name of car, illuminated	60.00	90.00	125.00
2552 Vista Dome — Super 0 (1957), "Skyline 500"	60.00	90.00	125.00
2553 Pullman — Super 0 (1957), "Blair Manor"	75.00	120.00	160.00
2554 Pullman — Super 0 (1957), "Graig Manor"	75.00	120.00	160.00

	G	VG	E
2555 Tank-one-dome — 0 (1945)	9.00	13.50	18.00
2555 Set — Super 0 (1946), Sunoco .	10.00	15.00	20.00
2559 Budd car coach - trailer — 0 (1957), Baltimore & Ohio, silver shell, blue lettering, dummy to match motorized 400 Budd	75.00	125.00	185.00
2560 Crane — 027 (1946), "Lionel Lines"	10.00	15.00	20.00
2561 Observation — 0 (1959), "Santa Fe Set" "Vista Valley", extruded aluminum shell	30.00	50.00	75.00
2562 Vista Dome — 0 (1959), "Royal Pass"	30.00	50.00	75.00
2563 Pullman — 0 (1959), "Indian Falls"	30.00	50.00	75.00
2570 Set — Super 0 (1961)	125.00	187.50	250.00
2600 Pullman — 0 (1938), red body and roof	30.00	45.00	70.00
2601 Observation — 0 (1938), red body and roof	30.00	45.00	70.00
2602 Baggage — 0 (1938), red body and roof	30.00	45.00	70.00
2613 Pullman — 0 (1938), 0 Gauge Blue Comet, two-tone blue	75.00	140.00	180.00
Same as above, state green	40.00	75.00	110.00
2614 Observation — 0 (1938), 0 Gauge, Blue Comet, two-tone blue ..	75.00	140.00	180.00
Same as above, state green	40.00	75.00	110.00
2615 Baggage — 0 (1938), 0 Gauge Blue Comet, two-tone blue	75.00	140.00	180.00
Same as above, state green	40.00	75.00	110.00
2620 Floodlight — 0 (1938), red frame on searchlight	10.00	15.00	20.00
2623 Pullman, Irvington — 0 (1941), Tuscan brown bakelite	60.00	90.00	120.00
2623 Pullman, Manhattan — 0 (uncat 1941), Tuscan brown bakelite ...	50.00	75.00	100.00
2624 Pullman, Manhattan — 0 (uncat 1941), Tuscan brown bakelite ...	125.00	175.00	250.00
2625 Pullman, Irvington — 0 (1946), Tuscan brown bakelite	50.00	75.00	100.00
Same as above, Manhattan	60.00	90.00	120.00
Same as above, Madison	60.00	90.00	120.00

	G	VG	E
2627 Pullman, Madison — 0 (1946), Tuscan brown bakelite	50.00	75.00	100.00
2628 Pullman, Manhattan — 0 (1946), Tuscan brown bakelite	50.00	75.00	100.00
2630 Pullman — 0 (1938), light blue and silver or gray roof	10.00	15.00	25.00
2631 Observation — 0 (1938), light blue and silver or gray roof	10.00	15.00	25.00
2640 Pullman — 0 (1938), light blue and silver roof	15.00	20.00	30.00
Same as above, state green and dark green roof	10.00	15.00	25.00
2641 Observation — 0 (1938), light blue and silver roof	15.00	20.00	30.00
Same as 2641, state green and dark green roof	10.00	15.00	25.00
2642 Pullman — 0 (1941), light blue and silver or gray roof	15.00	20.00	30.00
2643 Observation — 0 (1941), light blue and silver or gray roof	15.00	20.00	30.00
2651 Flat — 0 (1938), bright green with lumber load	10.00	15.00	20.00
2652 Gondola — 0 (1938), yellow ...	10.00	15.00	20.00
Same as above, brown	10.00	15.00	20.00
2653 Hopper — 0 (1938), light green	10.00	18.00	25.00
Same as above, black	15.00	25.00	45.00
2654 Tank — 0 (1938), aluminum, "Sunoco"	10.00	18.00	25.00
Same as above, orange "Shell"	10.00	18.00	25.00
Same as above, light gray, "Sunoco"	10.00	18.00	25.00
2655 Box — 0 (1938), cream body, maroon roof	10.00	15.00	20.00
Same as above, cream body, tuscan brown roof	15.00	20.00	30.00
2656 Cattle — 0 (1938), light gray body, red roof	10.00	18.00	25.00
2657 Caboose — 0 (1938), red body and red roof	10.00	15.00	20.00
Same as above, red body and brown roof	10.00	15.00	20.00
2659 Dump — 0 (1938), green, black frame	10.00	15.00	20.00
2660 Crane — 0 (1938), red roof, green boom	10.00	18.00	25.00

	G	VG	E
2672 Caboose — 027 (1942), Pennsylvania N5 type, tuscan brown	8.00	12.00	15.00
2677 Gondola — 027 (1940), red with black frame	5.00	10.00	15.00
2679 Box — 027 (1938), yellow, blue roof............................	5.00	10.00	15.00
Same as above, yellow, maroon roof	5.00	10.00	15.00
2680 Tank — 027 (1938), aluminum "Sunoco"	5.00	10.00	15.00
Same as above, orange, "Shell"	5.00	10.00	15.00
Same as above, gray, "Sunoco"	5.00	10.00	15.00
2682 Caboose — 027 (1938), red with red roof	5.00	10.00	15.00
Same as above, brown with brown roof..............................	5.00	10.00	15.00
2717 Gondola — 0 (uncat 1938), orange and tan	10.00	18.00	25.00
2719 Box — 0 (uncat 1938), peacock and blue roof	10.00	18.00	25.00
2722 Caboose — 0 (uncat 1938), red with maroon roof	10.00	18.00	25.00
2755 Tank — 0 (1941), gray "Sunoco"	30.00	45.00	60.00
2757 Caboose — 0 (1941), PRR-N5 type, tuscan brown	10.00	18.00	25.00
2758 Box - automobile — 0 (1941), "Pennsylvania", tuscan body	15.00	20.00	30.00
2810 Crane — 0 (1938), yellow cab and red roof	40.00	60.00	90.00
2811 Flat — 0 (1938), aluminum with eight logs	20.00	30.00	45.00
2812 Gondola — 0 (1938), bright green	15.00	20.00	25.00
Same as above, dark green	15.00	20.00	25.00
2813 Cattle — 0 (1938), cream body, maroon roof	30.00	45.00	60.00
2814 Box — 0 (1938), light yellow body, maroon roof	30.00	45.00	60.00
Same as above, orange body, brown roof..............................	125.00	225.00	325.00
2814R Refrigerator — 0 (1938), white body, brown roof.............	250.00	350.00	450.00
2815 Tank — 0 (1938), silver, Sunoco	30.00	45.00	60.00
Same as above, orange, Shell	40.00	60.00	80.00

	G	VG	E
2816 Hopper — 0 (1938), red	30.00	45.00	60.00
Same as above, black, white rubber-stamped lettering	75.00	125.00	175.00
2817 Caboose — 0 (1938), light red body and roof	25.00	40.00	60.00
Same as above, red, tuscan roof, white rubber-stamped lettering	60.00	90.00	120.00
2820 Floodlight — 0 (1938), two searchlights, green base, plate-stamped lights	25.00	40.00	60.00
Same as 2820, green base, cast lights	45.00	60.00	90.00
2855 Tank - one-dome — 0 (1946), black S.U.N.X.	25.00	40.00	60.00
Same as above, gray	30.00	45.00	70.00
2954 Box — 047 (1940), scale, tuscan brown, "Pennsylvania"	75.00	140.00	180.00
2955 Tank — 072 (1940), scale, black, "S.U.N.X."	90.00	160.00	200.00
2956 Hopper — 072 (1940), scale, black, B&O	90.00	160.00	200.00
2957 Caboose — 072 (1940), "NYC", scale, tuscan brown	75.00	140.00	180.00
3300 Summer trolley, trailer — Std. (1910), gold rubber-stamped, "3300 Electric Rapid Transit 3300", non-powered	1200.00	1800.00	2400.00
3330 Flat with submarine — 0 (1960)	15.00	20.00	25.00
3330-100 Operating submarine kit (1960)	7.00	9.00	12.00
3349 Turbo missile firing car — 0 (1960)	10.00	15.00	20.00
3356 Operating horse car with horses and corral — 0 (1956)	20.00	25.00	45.00
3356-2 Operating horse car — 0 (1956), green, car alone	10.00	15.00	20.00
3356-100 Set of nine horses — 0 (1956), black horses	2.00	4.00	6.00
3356-150 Horse corral — 0 (1956), white fencing (corral only)	10.00	14.00	18.00
3357 Operating cop and hobo car — 0 (1962), blue box car with hydraulic lift and figures	20.00	30.00	40.00

	G	VG	E
3359 Operating dump car — 0 (1955), two gray dump bins	15.00	20.00	25.00
3360 Operating Burro crane — 0 (1956), yellow cab and boom, motorized, inc. track trips	75.00	125.00	175.00
3361 Operating lumber — 0 (1955) .	8.00	12.00	15.00
3362 Operating helium tank car (1961), green frame	8.00	12.00	15.00
3364 Operating log dump car — 0 (1966), green frame	8.00	12.00	15.00
3366 Operating circus car — 0 (1959), white stock car, nine horses (white) and corral	75.00	125.00	160.00
3366-100 Set of nine white horses — 0 (1959)	6.00	9.00	12.00
3370 Operating sheriff and outlaw car — 0 (1961), green stock car	15.00	20.00	25.00
3376 Operating giraffe car — 0 (1960), blue stock car, including track trips, with teletails and poles	20.00	25.00	30.00
Same as above, green stock car	25.00	35.00	45.00
3410 Operating helicopter launching car — 0 (1961), blue flat with helicopter	10.00	15.00	20.00
3413-150 Mercury capsule launching car — 0 (1961), red flat, gray platform	20.00	40.00	60.00
3419 Operating helicopter launching car — 0 (1959), blue flat with helicopter	15.00	20.00	25.00
3424 Operating brakeman car set — 0 (1956), blue box car, set of track trips and teletails with poles	20.00	30.00	45.00
3424-100 Two low bridge warning poles — 0 (1956), with track clips ...	8.00	12.00	15.00
3428 Operating mail car — 0 (1959), red white and blue box car, man dumps mail bag	20.00	30.00	45.00
3429 U.S.M.C. helicopter car — 0 (1960), olive frame	15.00	20.00	25.00
3434 Chicken sweeper car — 0 (1959), brown stock car, man at door sweeps back and forth	30.00	45.00	60.00

	G	VG	E
3435 Operating aquarium car — 0 (1959),			
A. Green box with four clear windows, fish move around on two spindles ..	50.00	70.00	100.00
B. Green box gold letters marked "Tank 1" and "Tank 2"	60.00	90.00	120.00
3444 Animated hobo gondola — 0 (1957), "Erie", red gondola, cop chases hobo around freight load	20.00	30.00	45.00
3451 Operating lumber — 0 (1946), black diecast base, black platform with log stakes	10.00	15.00	20.00
3454 Operating merchandise — 0 (1946), silver box car, discharges five brown cubes	20.00	30.00	45.00
3456 Operating hopper car — 0 (1950), black "N&W", drops ore	15.00	20.00	25.00
3459 Operating dump — 0 (1946), die cast frame, black	9.00	13.00	15.00
Same as above, silver	20.00	30.00	45.00
Same as above, green	15.00	20.00	30.00
3460 Piggy-back flat — 0 (1955), red flat with two trailer containers	9.00	12.00	15.00
3461 Operating lumber — 0 (1949) black die-cast frame	10.00	15.00	20.00
Same as above, green frame	15.00	20.00	30.00
3462 Milk car set — 0 (1947), white box car, platform (green base), five cans, man discharges cans onto platform	10.00	15.00	20.00
3462-70 Set of five milk cans (1952)	1.00	2.00	3.00
3462P Milk car platform — 0 (1952)	3.00	5.00	7.00
3464 Operating box, Santa Fe — 0 (1949), orange shell, black doors, plunger mechanism opens door with man	9.00	12.00	15.00
3464 Operating box-NYC — 0 (1952), brown shell, black doors, plunger mechanism opens door with man ...	10.00	15.00	18.00
3469 Operating dump — 0 (1949), black die cast frame	9.00	12.00	15.00
3470 Aerial target launching car — 0 (1962), blue flatcar, white top shell,			

	G	VG	E
blue balloon carriage, batter operation inflates balloons	15.00	25.00	40.00
3472 Operating milk car set — 027 (1949), white box car, five cans, man discharges cans onto platform, green base	10.00	15.00	20.00
3474 Operating box, W.P. — 027 (1952), silver box, yellow feather, plunger mechanism	15.00	20.00	25.00
3482 Operating milk car set — 0 (1954), white box car, man discharges cans onto platform (green base), five cans	10.00	15.00	20.00
3484 Operating box, Pennsy — 0 (1953), tuscan brown, plunger mechanism	15.00	20.00	25.00
3484-25 Operating box, Santa Fe — 0 (1954), orange shell, orange doors, plunger mechanism	15.00	25.00	35.00
3494 Operating box, NYC Pacemaker — 0 (1955), red and gray, red doors, plunger mechanism	20.00	30.00	45.00
3494-150 Operating box, MP — 0 (1956), blue and gray, plunger mechanism	20.00	30.00	45.00
3494-275 Operating box, B.A.R. — 0 (1956), State of Maine, red, white and blue, plunger mechanism	20.00	30.00	40.00
3494-550 Operating box, Monon — 0 (1957), maroon shell with white stripe, plunger mechanism	75.00	100.00	150.00
3494-615 Operating box, Soo Line — 0 (1957), tuscan brown, plunger mechanism	90.00	120.00	175.00
3509 Operating satellite car — 0 (1959), green flat, black and silver satellite, yellow radar scope, manually operated	9.00	12.00	15.00
3510 Same as above, red flat	10.00	15.00	20.00
3512 Fireman and ladder car — 0 (1959), red frame and structure, black ladders	20.00	30.00	40.00
Same as above, silver ladders	30.00	45.00	60.00

	G	VG	E
3519 Automatic satellite car — 0 (1961), remote track operated	10.00	15.00	20.00
3520 Searchlight — 0 (1952), gray diecast frame, orange generator	10.00	15.00	22.00
3530 G.M. generator car — 0 (1956), blue box car with white markings, transformer pole, remote searchlight	20.00	30.00	45.00
3535 AEC Security car — 0 (1960), red shell, white lettering, gray gun and gray rotating searchlight, one man	20.00	30.00	45.00
3540 Operating radar scanning car — 0 (1959), red flat, gray structure, yellow radar scope and silver radar antenna, revolving	35.00	50.00	75.00
3545 Operating TV monitor car — 0 (1961), black base, blue structure, yellow camera and screen, two men	35.00	50.00	75.00
3559 Operating ore dump — 0 (1946), black die-cast frame	9.00	12.00	15.00
3562 Operating barrel car, black — 0 (1954), six wood barrels	30.00	45.00	60.00
3562-25 Operating barrel car, gray — 0 (1954), blue lettering	10.00	15.00	20.00
Same as above, red lettering	30.00	45.00	60.00
3562-50 Operating barrel car, yellow — 0 (1955)	10.00	15.00	20.00
3562-75 Operating barrel car, orange — 0 (1958)	10.00	15.00	20.00
3619 Reconnaisance helicopter car — 0 (1962), yellow shell, black double door, with helicopter	20.00	30.00	40.00
3620 Searchlight — 0 (1954), gray diecast frame, orange generator	12.00	18.00	25.00
3650 Searchlight extension car — 0 (1956), gray diecast frame, gray generator, remote searchlight with wire	15.00	22.00	30.00
3651 Operating lumber — 0 (1939), black frame, nickel stakes, with logs and bin	15.00	20.00	25.00
3652 Operating gondola — 0 (1939), yellow	15.00	22.00	30.00

	G	VG	E
3656 Operating cattle car — 0 (1950), "Armour", orange stock car, set includes car, cattle and corral, white lettering	20.00	30.00	40.00
Same as 3656, black lettering	30.00	40.00	60.00
3656-34 Set of nine cattle — 0 (1952), black	3.00	5.00	7.00
3656-150 Cattle car platform — 0 (1952), green base, ivory fencing	9.00	12.00	15.00
3657 Dump Car, silver with brown bin (1939)	75.00	125.00	175.00
3659 Operating dump — 0 (1939), black frame, red hopper	15.00	20.00	25.00
3662 Operating milk — 0 (1955), white shell, brown roof, includes five cans and platform	15.00	20.00	25.00
3662-79 Set of five milk cans — 0 (1955)	2.00	3.00	4.00
3665 Operating Minuteman missile car — 0 (1961), white shell, blue double door roof, with missile	20.00	30.00	40.00
3666 Operating Marine missile car — 0 (1960), Sears, white shell, blue double door roof, with missile	25.00	35.00	50.00
3672 Operating Bosco box — 0 (1959), yellow shell and brown roof, set includes seven Bosco cans and brown and yellow platform	50.00	75.00	110.00
3672-79 Set of seven Bosco cans — 0 (1959), brown and yellow	10.00	15.00	20.00
3811 Operating flat — 0 (1939), black frame with lumber	20.00	30.00	45.00
3814 Operating merchandise — 0 (1939), tuscan body and roof, discharges five cubes	75.00	100.00	125.00
3820 Operating submarine car — 0 (1960), olive, "U.S.M.C.", gray	15.00	22.00	30.00
3830 Operating submarine car — 0 (1960), blue "Lionel", gray submarine	12.00	18.00	22.00
3854 Operating merchandise — 0 (1946), tuscan brown, doors open, and eject five merchandise cubes	150.00	200.00	250.00
3859 Operating dump — 0 (1938), black	20.00	30.00	45.00

	G	VG	E
3927 Track cleaner car — 0 (1956), orange shell, motor-operated cleaning disk, includes two gray washol containers	20.00	40.00	60.00
3927-50 Package of 25 track cleaner pads — 0 (1956)	three dollars		
3927-75 Can of liquid track cleaner (full), — (1956)	two dollars		
4357 Caboose, electronic — 0 (1948), green and white, "Electronic Control" decal, red metal Pennsylvania N5 type	30.00	40.00	60.00
4400 Summer trolley, trailer — Std. (1910)	1400.00	1800.00	2400.00
4452 Gondola, electronic — 0 (1946), black, Pennsylvania	30.00	45.00	60.00
4454 Box, electronic — 0 (1946), Baby Ruth, P.R.R., orange with brown doors	25.00	35.00	45.00
4457 Caboose, electronic — 0 (1946)	30.00	40.00	60.00
4671 Loco, steam, electronic — 0 (1946), 6-8-0, 4671W tender	75.00	100.00	125.00
5100 Straight roadway — 0 (1963) .	.50	.75	1.00
5101 Straight roadway — 0 (1963) .	.50	.75	1.00
5102 Railroad and roadway crossing — 0 (1963)	.50	.75	1.00
5103 Straight roadway with power connection — 0 (1963)	.50	.75	1.00
5104 Lane change over — 0 (1963) .	.50	.75	1.00
5105 Roadway intersection — 0 (1963)	.50	.75	1.00
5106 Inner curved roadway — 0 (1963)	.50	.75	1.00
5107 Inner curved roadway — 0 (1963)	.50	.75	1.00
5108 Outer curved roadway — 0 (1963)	.50	.75	1.00
5109 Outer curved roadway — 0 (1963)	.50	.75	1.00
5150 Banking set (1963)	2.00	4.00	6.00
5151 Trestle set — 0 (1963)	2.00	4.00	6.00
5152 Guard rail and flag set — 0 (1963)	2.00	4.00	6.00
5154 Electric lap counter — 0 (1963)	2.00	4.00	6.00

	G	VG	E
5155 Pacesetter timer — 0 (1963) ...	2.00	4.00	6.00
5156-24 Rail clips — 0 (1963)	1.00	2.00	3.00
5157-34 Roadway clips — 0 (1963) .	1.00	2.00	3.00
5158 Barrels (1963)	1.00	2.00	3.00
5159 Lubrication kit (1963)	2.00	3.00	4.00
5159-50 Lubrication kit (1968)	2.00	3.00	4.00
5160 Official viewing stand (1963) .	4.00	6.00	8.00
5163 Maintenance kit (1965)	2.00	3.00	4.00
5200 Ferrari racing car — 0 (1963) .	2.00	3.00	4.00
5201 "D" Jaguar racing car — 0 (1963)	2.00	3.00	4.00
5202 Corvette racing car — 0 (1963)	2.00	3.00	4.00
5210 Cooper racing car — 0 (1963) .	2.00	3.00	4.00
5211 B.R.M. racing car — 0 (1963) .	2.00	3.00	4.00
5222 Cooper racing car — 0 (1964) .	2.00	3.00	4.00
5223 Corvette racing car — 0 (1964)	2.00	3.00	4.00
5230 Ferrari racing car — 0 (1964) .	2.00	3.00	4.00
5231 B.R.M. racing car — 0 (1964) .	2.00	3.00	4.00
5232 "D" Jaguar racing car — 0 (1964)	2.00	3.00	4.00
5233 Ford racing car — 0 (1964) ...	2.00	3.00	4.00
5234 Buick racing car — 0 (1964) ..	2.00	3.00	4.00
5235 Jaguar XKE racing car — 0 (1964)	2.00	3.00	4.00
5236 Buick Riviera racing car — 0 (1964)	2.00	3.00	4.00
5237 Buick Riviera racing car — 0 (1964)	2.00	3.00	4.00
5238 Ford racing car — 0 (1964) ...	2.00	3.00	4.00
5239 Ford convertible racing car — 0 (1964)	1.00	3.00	5.00
5240 Ford police racing car — 0 (1964)	1.00	3.00	5.00
5242 Conversion kit (1966)	2.00	4.00	6.00
5300 Racemaster power pack (1963)	1.00	3.00	5.00
5302 Racemaster power pack (1965)	1.00	3.00	5.00
5304 HO control transformer (1965)	2.00	4.00	6.00
5310 Touch-A-Matic speed control (1963)	1.00	2.00	3.00
5320 Touch-A-Matic speed control (1963)	1.00	2.00	3.00
5321 Touch-A-Matic speed control (1965)	1.00	2.00	3.00

	G	VG	E
5322 Touch-A-Matic speed control (1965)	1.00	2.00	3.00
5400 Straight roadway — HO (1963)	.50	.75	1.00
5401 Straight roadway with power connector — HO (1963)	.50	.75	1.00
5402 Railroad and roadway crossing — HO (1963)	1.00	1.50	2.00
5403 Roadway intersection — HO (1963)	1.00	1.50	2.00
5404 Lane change over — HO (1963)	1.00	1.50	2.00
5405 Curved roadway — HO (1963)	.50	.75	1.00
5406 Curved roadway, 45° — HO (1963)	.50	.75	1.00
5407 Inner curved roadway, 90° — HO (1963)	.50	.75	1.00
5408 Outer curved roadway, 45° — HO (1963)	.50	.75	1.00
5409 Inner curved roadway, 45° — HO (1963)	.50	.75	1.00
5410 Straight roadway — HO (1963)	.50	.75	1.00
5411 Straight roadway — HO (1963)	.50	.75	1.00
5412 Straight roadway — HO (1963)	.50	.75	1.00
5415 Straight roadway with power connection — HO (1963)	.50	.75	1.00
5421 Touch-A-Matic speed controller — HO (1965)	1.00	2.00	3.00
5422 Touch-A-Matic speed controller — HO (1965)	1.00	2.00	3.00
5425 Loop-the-loop kit — HO (1960)	4.00	8.00	12.00
5430 Universal roadway kit — HO (1966)	4.00	6.00	8.00
5431 Mystery route selector — HO (1966)	2.00	4.00	6.00
5433 Car lane controller — HO (1965)	2.00	3.00	4.00
5434 Car lane controller — HO (1965)	2.00	3.00	4.00
5450 Trestle set — HO (1963)	1.00	2.00	3.00
5455 Car lane controller — HO (1966)	2.00	3.00	4.00
5457 Relay kit — HO (1966)	2.00	4.00	6.00
5459 Operating dump, electronic — 0 (1948), black "Lionel Lines"	20.00	30.00	40.00

	G	VG	E
5478 Guard rail and flag set — HO (1966)	2.00	4.00	6.00
5431 Buick Riviera racing car — HO (1965)	1.00	3.00	5.00
5532 Buick patrol racing car — HO (1965)	1.00	3.00	5.00
5533 Ford hardtop racing car — HO (1965)	1.00	3.00	5.00
5534 Ford convertible racing car — HO (1965)	1.00	3.00	5.00
5535 Ford police racing car — HO (1965)	1.00	3.00	5.00
5537 Rolls Royce racing car — HO (1965)	1.00	3.00	5.00
5538 Bentley racing car — HO (1965)	1.00	3.00	5.00
5539 Jaguar XKE racing car — HO (1965)	1.00	3.00	5.00
5540 Car lane control car, Thunderbird — HO (1965)	2.00	4.00	6.00
5541 Car lane control car - Jaguar XKE — HO (1965)	2.00	4.00	6.00
5542 Car lane control car, Thunderbird — HO (1965)	2.00	4.00	6.00
5767-15 Valise carrying pack — HO (1961)	4.00	6.00	8.00
6002 Gondola — 027 (1949), NYC ..	3.00	6.00	9.00
6004 Box — 027 (1950), Baby Ruth P.R.R.	2.00	3.00	4.00
6007 Caboose — 027 (1950), Lionel Lines, SP type	1.00	1.50	2.00
6009 Remote control track — 027 (1953)	3.00	4.50	6.00
6012 Gondola — 027 (1955), black, Lionel	1.00	2.00	3.00
6014 Box — 027 (1951), Air Ex	4.00	6.00	8.00
6014 Box, Baby Ruth — 027 (1955), P.R.R.	2.00	3.00	4.00
6014 Box, Frisco — 027 (1957)	2.00	4.00	6.00
6014 Box, Bosco — 027 (1958), P.R.R.	4.00	6.00	8.00
6014-85 Box, Frisco — 027 (1969) ..	2.00	4.00	6.00
6014-325 Box, Frisco — 027 (1964)	2.00	4.00	6.00

	G	VG	E
6014-325 Frisco Savings Bank car — 027 (1963)	2.00	4.00	6.00
6014-335 Box, Frisco — 027 (1965)	2.00	4.00	6.00
6014-410 Box, Frisco — 027 (1969)	2.00	4.00	6.00
6014 WIX creme white	30.00	45.00	60.00
6015 Tank — 027 (1954), silver, one dome, Sunoco	2.00	3.00	4.00
6017 Caboose, Lionel — 027 (1951), brown	1.00	2.00	3.00
6017-50 Caboose, Marine — 027 (1958), dark blue	10.00	15.00	20.00
6017-100 Caboose, B&M (1959), blue	6.00	9.00	12.00
6017-185 Caboose, ATSF — 027 (1959), gray	4.00	6.00	8.00
6017-200 Caboose, Navy — 027 (1960), dark blue	15.00	20.00	25.00
6017-225 Caboose ATSF — 027 (1961)	4.00	6.00	8.00
6019 Remote control track (1948) ..	1.00	2.00	3.00
6024 Box, Nabisco — 027 (1957) ...	8.00	12.00	18.00
6024 Box, RCA-Whirlpool — 027 (uncat 1957), red	15.00	20.00	25.00
6025 Tank — 027 (1956), "Gulf", orange	3.00	6.00	9.00
Same as above, gray	4.00	8.00	12.00
Same as 6025, black	4.00	8.00	12.00
6027 Caboose, Alaska — 027 (1959), blue	15.00	20.00	25.00
6029 Uncoupling track set — 027 (1955)	1.00	2.00	3.00
6032 Gondola — 027 (1952), black "Lionel"	1.00	2.00	3.00
6034 Box — 027 (1953), Baby Ruth, P.R.R.	2.00	4.00	6.00
6035 Tank — 027 (1950), gray, single dome	2.00	3.00	4.00
6037 Caboose — 027 (1952), brown, "Lionel Lines"	1.00	2.00	3.00
6042 Gondola (uncatalogued) "Lionel"	6.00	9.00	12.00
6044 Box, Airex — 027 (uncat)	4.00	6.00	8.00
6045 Tank car, green, Cities Service	6.00	9.00	12.00
6047 Caboose — 027 (1962), "Lionel Lines"	1.00	2.00	3.00

	G	VG	E
6050 Savings bank car — 027 (1961), white and green	10.00	15.00	20.00
6050 Savings bank car, Libby Tomato Juice — 027 (uncat 1961), Libby promotional car	10.00	15.00	20.00
6050-100 Savings bank car, Swift's — 027 (1963), red	4.00	6.00	8.00
6050-110 Savings bank car, Swift's — 027 (1962), red	4.00	6.00	8.00
6057 Caboose, Lionel Lines — 027 (1959), red	1.00	2.00	3.00
6057-50 Caboose, H.H. — 027 (1962), orange	4.00	6.00	8.00
6058 Caboose, C&O — 027 (1961), yellow	5.00	10.00	15.00
6059-50 Caboose, M&St.L — 027 (1961), maroon	2.00	4.00	6.00
6059-60 Caboose, M&St.L — 027 (1969), shiny or flat red	2.00	4.00	6.00
— **6062** Gondola — 027 (1959), glossy black	8.00	12.00	18.00
6076 Hopper, A.T.S.F. — 027 (1959), gray	2.00	4.00	6.00
6076-75 Hopper, LV — 027 (1963), gray or black or red	2.00	4.00	6.00
6076-100 Hopper, Lionel — 027 (1963)	2.00	4.00	6.00
6110 Loco, steam — 027 (1951), 2-4-2	4.00	8.00	12.00
6111 Flat — 027 (1955), with logs or pipes	1.00	2.00	3.00
6112 Gondola with canisters — 027 (1956), "Lionel", blue	2.00	3.00	4.00
Same as above, white	8.00	12.00	18.00
6112-25 Set of four canisters — 027 (1956), white or red	two dollars		
6119 Work caboose — 027 (1955) ...	6.00	9.00	12.00
6119-25 Work caboose, D.L.&W — 027 (1957)	6.00	9.00	12.00
6119-100 Work caboose — D.L.&W. — 027 (1963)	4.00	6.00	8.00
6119-110 Work caboose, D.L.&W. — 027 (1964)	4.00	6.00	8.00
6121 Flat with pipes — 027 (1956) .	1.00	2.00	3.00

	G	VG	E
6130 Work caboose, Santa Fe — 027 (1965)	6.00	9.00	12.00
6139 Remote control uncoupling track — 027 (1963)	1.00	2.00	3.00
6142 Gondola with canisters — 027 (1963)	1.00	2.00	3.00
6142-75 Gondola with canisters — 027 (1963)	1.00	2.00	3.00
6142-100 Gondola with canisters — 027 (1964)	1.00	2.00	3.00
6142-125 Gondola — 027 (1964) ...	1.00	2.00	3.00
6142-150 Gondola — 027 (1964) ...	1.00	2.00	3.00
6149 Remote control uncoupling track — 027 (1964)	1.00	2.00	3.00
6157 Caboose — 027 (uncat), brown	1.00	2.00	3.00
6162 Gondola with canisters, NYC — 027 (1963), red	2.00	4.00	6.00
6162-25 Gondola with canisters — 027 (1959), blue	2.00	4.00	6.00
6162-50 Gondola with canisters - Alaska — 027 (1959), yellow	20.00	30.00	40.00
6162-100 Gondola with canisters, NYC — 027 (1964)	2.00	4.00	6.00
6162-110 Gondola with canisters, NYC — 027 (1965)	2.00	4.00	6.00
6167 Caboose, Lionel — 027 (1963) .	1.00	1.50	2.00
6167-50 Caboose, D.R.W. — 027 (1963)	1.00	1.50	2.00
6167-85 Caboose, U.P. — 027 (1969)	1.00	1.50	2.00
6167-100 Caboose, Lionel — 027 (1964)	1.00	1.50	2.00
6167-125 Caboose, unlettered — 027 (1964)	1.00	1.50	2.00
6175 Rocket car — 027 (1958), red and white rocket, red or black frame	10.00	15.00	22.00
6176 Hopper — 027 (1964), yellow ..	2.00	4.00	6.00
6176-50 Hopper, L.V. — 027 (1964), yellow	2.00	4.00	6.00
6176-75 Hopper, L.V. — 027 (1964), gray	2.00	4.00	6.00
6219 Work caboose - C&O — 027 (1960), blue cab	8.00	15.00	20.00

	G	VG	E
6220 Loco, SW2 Diesel, NYC or Santa Fe — 027 (1949), black, similar to #622, with bell	60.00	90.00	140.00
6250 Loco, SW2 Diesel Seaboard — 027 (1954), blue and orange	40.00	70.00	100.00
6257 Caboose — 027 (1948)	4.00	6.00	8.00
6257-25 Caboose — 027 (uncat) ...	1.00	1.50	2.00
6257-50 Caboose — 027 (uncat) ...	1.00	1.50	2.00
6257-100 Caboose — 027 (1964) ...	1.00	1.50	2.00
6262 Wheel car — 0 (1956), black or red frame with eight set of wheels ..	8.00	12.00	18.00
6264 Forklift Accessory Flatcar, red frame, brown lumber rack	8.00	12.00	18.00
6311 Flat — 0 (1955), brown, no load	1.00	2.00	3.00
6315 Tank car, "Gulf" — 0 (1956), orange, (3 dome)	10.00	15.00	22.00
6315-60 Chemical car — 0 (1963), orange, single dome tank, "Lionel Lines"	9.00	12.00	18.00
6342 Culvert car — 0 (1957), red gondola, with inclined rake for culvert pipes	6.00	9.00	12.00
6343 Barrel ramp car — 0 (1961), red, gray ramp	5.00	8.00	10.00
6346 Covered hopper, Alcoa — 0 (1956), silver	10.00	15.00	22.00
6352 Refrigerator car for ice depot — 0 (1955), Pacific Fruit Express, orange shell, door on roof for deposit of ice blocks, side door discharges ..	20.00	30.00	45.00
6356 Stock, NYC — 0 (1954), yellow	10.00	15.00	22.00
6357 Caboose — 027 (1948), maroon, red, tuscan brown	4.00	6.00	8.00
6361 Timber flat — 0 (1960), green frame with three lumber branches ..	10.00	15.00	22.00
6362 Rail truck car — 0 (1955), orange frame with three sets of trucks	5.00	10.00	15.00
6376 Circus car — 0 (1956), white stock car	15.00	22.00	30.00
6401 Flat — 0 (1965), with two vans	9.00	12.00	15.00
6402-50 Flat with cable reels — 0 (1964), gray frame with orange reels	6.00	9.00	12.00

	G	VG	E
6405 Flat with piggyback van — 0 (1961), brown frame with two trailer vans	9.00	12.00	15.00
6407 Flat with rocket — 0 (1963), red frame, gray supports with red and white rocket, blue nose (actually a pencil sharpener)	20.00	30.00	45.00
6408 Flat with pipes — 0 (1963)	2.00	4.00	6.00
6409-25 Flat with pipes — 0 (1963)	2.00	4.00	6.00
6411 Flat with logs — 027 (1948), gray diecast frame, five logs	6.00	9.00	12.00
6413 Mercury capsule car — 0 (1962), blue frame with two gray Mercury capsules	10.00	15.00	25.00
6414 Evans loader car — 0 (1955), red frame, black metal car rack with four cars	12.00	18.00	25.00
6414-25 Set of four autos — 0 (1955)	6.00	9.00	12.00
6415 Tank, Sunoco — 0 (1953), silver, three-dome	9.00	12.00	18.00
6415-60 Tank, Sunoco — 0 (1969) .	9.00	12.00	18.00
6416 Four-boat loader — 0 (1961), red frame, black metal boat rack ...	25.00	35.00	50.00
6417 Caboose, P.R.R. — 0 (1953), #536417, N5C type, tuscan brown ..	10.00	15.00	20.00
Same as above, Lehigh Valley gray	20.00	30.00	45.00
Same as above, Tuscan	300.00	500.00	700.00
6418 Depressed center girder flat — 0 (1955), gray die-cast frame with two orange girder sections, four sets of trucks	20.00	30.00	45.00
6419 Wrecker caboose — 027 (1948), L&W, gray cab	10.00	15.00	20.00
6419-100 Wrecker caboose, N&W — 027 (1954), light gray cab, #576419 .	20.00	30.00	45.00
6420 Wrecker caboose — 0 (1949), DL&W, dark gray, die-cast frame with searchlight	30.00	45.00	60.00
6424 Twin auto car — 0 (1956), black frame, two autos	6.00	9.00	12.00
6425 Tank, Gulf — 0 (1956), silver, three-dome........................	10.00	15.00	22.00
6427 Caboose — 0 (1954), # 64273, tuscan brown, N5C type	9.00	12.00	15.00

133

	G	VG	E
6427-60 Caboose, Virginian — 0 (1958), #6427, blue shell, yellow lettering, N5C type	40.00	60.00	80.00
6427-500 Caboose, Girls' train — 0 (1957), #57-6427, blue shell, white lettering	60.00	90.00	125.00
6428 Box, U.S. Mail — 0 (1960), red, white and blue	9.00	12.00	15.00
6429 Wrecker caboose — 0 (1963), gray diecast frame, gray cab	9.00	12.00	15.00
6430 Flat with piggyback van — 0 (1956), red frame with two trailer vans	9.00	12.00	15.00
6434 Poultry car — 0 (1958), red stock car, gray doors, illuminated ..	12.00	18.00	22.00
6436 Hopper, N&W — 0 (1955), red	9.00	12.00	18.00
6436-1 Hopper, L.V. — 0 (1956), black	9.00	12.00	18.00
6436-25 Hopper, L.V. — 0 (1956), maroon	9.00	12.00	18.00
6436-57 Hopper, L.V. — 0 (1957), lilac, maroon lettering, girls' set	60.00	90.00	120.00
6436-100 Hopper, LV — 0 (1957) ..	9.00	12.00	18.00
6437 Caboose — 0 (1961), Pennsylvania, N5C, tuscan brown	9.00	12.00	15.00
6440 Pullman — 027 (1948), green sheetmetal body, dark green roof ...	10.00	15.00	22.00
6441 Observation — 027 (1948), green sheetmetal body, dark green roof.................................	10.00	15.00	22.00
6442 Pullman — 027 (1949), brown sheetmetal body and roof	15.00	20.00	25.00
6443 Observation — 027 (1949), brown sheetmetal body and roof ...	15.00	20.00	25.00
6445 Fort Knox Gold car — 0 (1961), silver with four clear windows, showing gold bullion	30.00	45.00	75.00
6446-25 Covered hopper — 0 (1956), N&W gray	12.00	15.00	18.00
6446-54 Covered cement, N&W — 0 (1954), black	15.99	22.00	30.00
Same as above, gray	12.00	15.00	18.00
6447 Caboose — 0 (1963), tuscan brown, N5C type..................	10.00	15.00	20.00
6448 Exploding target range car — 0 (1961), red shell, white lettering	3.00	5.00	8.00

	G	VG	E
6454 Box, P.R.R. — 027 (1948), tuscan brown	6.00	9.00	15.00
6454 Box, NYC — 027 (1949), brown	6.00	9.00	15.00
6454 Box, Erie — 027 (1950), brown	6.00	9.00	15.00
Same as above, SP	6.00	9.00	15.00
6456 Hopper — 0 (1948), maroon, black, gray	4.00	6.00	8.00
Same as above, shiny red, yellow letters	15.00	20.00	25.00
Same as above, white letters	20.00	30.00	40.00
6457 Caboose — 0 (1949), brown or maroon, SP type	6.00	8.00	10.00
6460 Crane — 0 (1952) black cab	10.00	15.00	20.00
Same as above, gray cab	15.00	20.00	25.00
6461 Transformer car — 027 (1949), gray diecast frame, black transformer	5.00	9.00	12.00
6462-25 Gondola, NYC — 0 (1954), black, bright red, green	4.00	6.00	8.00
6462-500 Gondola, Girls' train — 0 (1957), "NYC", pink	60.00	90.00	120.00
6463 Rocket fuel tank car — 0 (1962), white shell, two dome, red lettering	5.00	7.50	10.00
6464-1 Box, W.P. — 0 (1953), silver	15.00	20.00	25.00
6464-25 Box, G.N. — 0 (1953), orange	10.00	15.00	20.00
6464-50 Box, M&St.L — 0 (1953), maroon	10.00	15.00	20.00
6464-75 Box, R.I. — 0 (1953), green	15.00	20.00	35.00
6464-100 Box, W.P. — (1954), silver with yellow feather	20.00	30.00	50.00
Same as above, orange with blue feather	125.00	200.00	300.00
6464-125 Box, "Pacemaker" — 0 (1954), red and gray	20.00	30.00	40.00
6464-150 Box, M.P. — 0 (1954), blue and gray	20.00	30.00	40.00
6464-175 Box, R.I. — 0 (1954), silver	25.00	40.00	60.00
6464-200 Box, P.R.R. — 0 (1954), tuscan brown	20.00	25.00	30.00
6464-226 Box, S.P. — 0 (1954), black	15.00	20.00	35.00
6464-250 Box, W.P. — 0 (1966), orange with blue feather	25.00	35.00	45.00
6464-275 Box "State of Maine" — 0 (1955), red, white and blue	15.00	20.00	25.00

	G	VG	E
6464-300 Box, Rutland — 0 (1955), green and yellow..................	20.00	30.00	40.00
6464-325 Box, B&O "Sentinel" — 0 (1956), silver and aqua	75.00	100.00	125.00
6464-350 Box, M.K.T. — 0 (1956), maroon..........................	40.00	60.00	80.00
6464-375 Box, C.G. — 0 (1956), maroon and silver	20.00	30.00	40.00
6464-400 Box, B&O "timesaver" — 0 (1956), blue and orange	15.00	20.00	30.00
6464-425 Box, N.H. — 0 (1956), black	10.00	15.00	20.00
6464-450 Box, G.N. — 0 (1956), olive and orange	15.00	25.00	40.00
6464-475 Box, B&M — 0 (1957), blue	10.00	15.00	20.00
6464-500 Box, Timken — 0 (1957), yellow and white..................	20.00	30.00	40.00
6464-510 Box, Girls train, NYC — 0 (1957), lilac	100.00	150.00	225.00
6464-515 Box, Girls train, M,K,T, — 0 (1957), yellow	100.00	150.00	225.00
6464-525 Box, M&St.L. — 0 (1957), red	15.00	20.00	25.00
6464-650 Box, D.R.G.W. — 0 (1957), yellow and silver..................	20.00	30.00	40.00
6464-700 Box, Santa Fe — 0 (1961), red	20.00	30.00	40.00
6464-725 Box, New Haven — 0 (1962), black	10.00	15.00	20.00
6464-825 Box, Alaska — 0 (1959), blue and yellow	50.00	75.00	100.00
6464-900 Box, NYC — 0 (1960), light green	20.00	30.00	40.00
6465 Tank — 027 (1948), silver "Sunoco", two-dome...............	2.00	3.00	4.00
6465 Tank — 027 (1958) Gulf, black, two-dome	6.00	8.00	12.00
Same as 6465, black, Lionel Lines, two-dome	4.00	6.00	8.00
Same as above, orange, Lionel Lines, two-dome	4.00	6.00	8.00
6465 Tank — 027 (1960), green Cities Service, two-dome	6.00	8.00	12.00

	G	VG	E
6466T, W, or WX Tender — 027 (1948)	14.00	21.00	28.00
6467 0 — Bulkhead Car (1956), red frame, two black bulkheads	9.00	12.00	15.00
6468 Automobile, B&O — 0 (1953), blue (double door)	10.00	15.00	20.00
6468-25 Automobile, N.H. — 0 (1956), orange (double door)	15.00	20.00	25.00
6469 Liquefied gas tank car — 0 (1963), red frame, white cylinder	15.00	20.00	25.00
6470 Exploding box — 0 (1959), red with white lettering, spring mechanism	4.00	6.00	8.00
6472 Refrigerator — 0 (1950), white box car	4.00	6.00	8.00
6473 Horse Transport Car (1963), yellow, two horse heads bob in and out	10.00	15.00	20.00
6475 Pickle car — 0 (1960), Heinz 57	50.00	75.00	100.00
6475 Pineapple car — 0 (uncat 1960), Libby	20.00	30.00	45.00
6475 Pickles Car	15.00	20.00	25.00
6476 Hopper — 0 (1957), red, white letters	2.00	4.00	6.00
6476-25 Hopper, L.V. — 0 (1963), gray, black letters	2.00	4.00	6.00
6476-75 Hopper, L.V. — 0 (1963), red. white letters	2.00	4.00	6.00
6477 Pipe car — 0 (1957), same as 6467, except has sidestakes	9.00	12.00	15.00
6500 Beechcraft Bonanza Transport Car — 0 (1962), black frame with red and white plane	15.00	20.00	25.00
6501 Flat with motor boat — 0 (1962), red frame with white and brown boat	15.00	20.00	25.00
6502 Flat with girder — 0 (1962), blue flat with orange bridge	2.00	4.00	6.00
6511 Pipe car — 0 (1953), brown or red flat with three aluminum colored pipes	6.00	8.00	10.00
6512 Cherry picker car — 0 (1962), black or blue frame, gray ladder support, black ladder with man	12.00	18.00	24.00

	G	VG	E
6517 Caboose, bay window — 0 (1955), red, "Lionel Lines"	20.00	30.00	40.00
6517 Caboose, bay window, Erie — 0 (uncat), red, Erie	125.00	175.00	225.00
6518 Transformer car — 0 (1956), gray diecast frame, four sets of trucks, black transformer	20.00	30.00	45.00
6519 Allis Chalmers car — 0 (1958), orange car, gray reactor	15.00	20.00	25.00
6520 Operating searchlight — 0 (1949), gray diecast base, green	30.00	45.00	75.00
Same as above, orange or maroon gen	10.00	20.00	30.00
Same as above, tan gen	75.00	120.00	160.00
6530 Fire prevention car — 0 (1960), red shell, white lettering	10.00	15.00	20.00
6536 Hopper, M&St.L. — 0 (1958), red with white lettering	9.00	12.00	18.00
6544 Missile firing car — 0 (1960), blue frame, gray launch platform, red firing control with four white rockets	10.00	18.00	25.00
6555 Tank — 0 (1949), silver "Sunoco" single dome (metal tank)	10.00	15.00	22.00
6556 Stock, M.K.T. — 0 (1958), Katy, red shell, white lettering and doors	40.00	60.00	90.00
6557 Smoking caboose — 0 (1958), "Lionel", SP-type, tuscan brown with smoke unit (liquid type)	40.00	60.00	90.00
6560 Crane — 0 (1955), "Bucyrus Erie" black frame, gray cab	12.00	18.00	25.00
Same as above, red cab	10.00	15.00	20.00
6560-25 Crane — 0 (1961), "Bucyrus Erie", black frame, red cab #6560-25	12.00	18.00	25.00
6561 Cable car — 0 (1953), gray diecast frame with two orange or gray spools wrapped with aluminum wire	9.00	12.00	15.00
6562 Gondola, NYC — 0 (1956), gray	4.00	6.00	8.00
Same as above, red	3.00	5.00	7.00
Same as above, black	2.00	4.00	6.00
6572 Railway Express Reefer — 0 (1958), green	20.00	25.00	30.00
Same as above, light green	15.00	20.00	25.00
6630 IRBM missile launcher car — 0 (1960), black frame, blue ramp, with			

	G	VG	E
red and white missile	15.00	22.00	30.00
6636 Hopper, Alaska — 0 (1959), black with orange lettering	15.00	20.00	25.00
6640 U.S.M.C. Missile Launcher (1960), olive frame, black ramp, with white missile	15.00	22.00	30.00
6646 Stock — 0 (1957), "Lionel Lines", orange shell, black lettering	2.00	4.00	6.00
6650 IRBM Missile car — 0 (1959), red frame, blue support, black ramp with red and white missile	15.00	20.00	25.00
6650-80 Missile for 6650 — 0 (1959), five white missiles	4.00	6.00	8.00
6651 Marine cannon car — 0 (uncat 1960), olive frame and cannon with four cannon loads	18.00	25.00	35.00
6656 Stock — 0 (1950), yellow shell, black lettering	2.00	4.00	6.00
6657 Caboose, D.R.G.W. — 0 (1957), SP type, yellow cab with silver lower stripe, black lettering	40.00	60.00	90.00
6660 Flat car with boom — 0 (1958), red flat, yellow crane, turn control ..	10.00	15.00	22.00
6670 Flat car with derrick — 0 (1959), red flat, yellow crane, no turn control	10.00	15.00	20.00
6672 Refrigerator — 0 (1954), "Santa Fe" reefer, white shell, brown roof, black lettering	15.00	20.00	25.00
Same as above, blue lettering	10.00	15.00	20.00
6736 Hopper, Detroit & Mackinac — 0 (1960), red shell, white lettering ...	10.00	15.00	22.00
6800 Flat with airplane — 0 (1957), red frame with black and yellow plane	10.00	15.00	22.00
6801 Flat with white boat — 0 (1957), red flat	8.00	12.00	16.00
6801-50 Flat with yellow boat — 0 (1957), red flat	8.00	12.00	16.00
6801-75 Flat with blue boat — 0 (1957), red flat	8.00	12.00	16.00
6802 Flat with bridge — 0 (1958), red flat with black bridge	2.00	4.00	6.00

	G	VG	E
6803 Flat with tank and sound truck — 0 (1958), red frame, two gray vehicles	15.00	25.00	35.00
6804 Flat with sound truck — 0 (1958), red frame, two gray trucks ..	15.00	25.00	35.00
6805 Atomic energy car — 0 (1958), red frame, two gray radioactivity containers, lights under containers .	15.00	20.00	30.00
6806 Flat with radar and medical truck - 0 (1958), red frame, two gray vehicles	15.00	25.00	35.00
6807 Flat with duck — 0 (1958), amphibian boat, red frame, one gray boat	15.00	25.00	35.00
6808 Flat with tank and searchlight — 0 (1958), red flat with two gray vehicles	15.00	25.00	35.00
6809 Flat with medical trucks — 0 (1958), red frame, two gray vehicles	15.00	25.00	35.00
6810 Flat with piggyback van — 0 (1958), red frame, one trailer container, "Cooper Jarretting"	6.00	9.00	12.00
6812 Track maintenance car — 0 (1959), red frame, gray, blue or yellow platform, with two blue men	10.00	15.00	22.00
6814 First aid caboose — 0 (1959), "Rescue Unit", white frame, cab and tool boxes, two stretchers, oxygen tank and man	20.00	35.00	50.00
6816 Flat with bulldozer — 0 (1959), "Allis-Chalmers" orange bulldozer, red flat	10.00	15.00	22.00
6816-100 Bulldozer — 0 (1959)	6.00	9.00	12.00
6817 Flat with scraper — 0 (1959), same as 6816, except bulldozer replaced by scraper	10.00	15.00	22.00
6817-100 Scraper — 0 (1959)	6.00	9.00	12.00
6818 Flat with transformer — 0 (1958), red frame, black transformer	6.00	9.00	12.00
6819 Flat with helicopter — 0 (1959), red frame with gray helicopter	8.00	12.00	15.00
6820 Aerial missile car — 0 (1960), blue frame, navy helicopter	10.00	15.00	22.00
6821 Flat with crates — 0 (1959), red frame, tan crates	4.00	8.00	12.00

	G	VG	E
6822 Searchlight car — 0 (1961), red frame, gray searchlight, black housing with blue man	10.00	15.00	20.00
6823 IRBM Missile car — 0 (1959), red frame, gray supports, two white missiles	10.00	15.00	22.00
6824 First Aid caboose — 0 (1960), "Rescue Unit", olive frame, cab, tool boxes, with two stretchers, oxygen tank and man	30.00	40.00	60.00
6825 Flat with arch bridge — 0 (1959), red frame, black bridge, or gray bridge	6.00	9.00	12.00
6826 Flat with trees — 0 (1959), red frame with bundles of life-like Xmas trees	10.00	15.00	22.00
6827 Flat with power shovel — 0 (1960), black frame, yellow and black steam shovel	20.00	30.00	45.00
6828 Flat with construction crane— 0 (1960), black frame, yellow and black crane	25.00	35.00	50.00
6828-100 Construction crane — 0 (1960)	12.00	18.00	25.00
6830 Submarine car — 0 (1960), blue frame, gray sub, "U.S. Navy"	10.00	15.00	22.00
47618 Caboose - paper train (uncat 1943)	15.00	20.00	25.00
61100 Box - paper train (uncat 1943)	15.00	20.00	25.00
(A) Transformer, 40 watt (1916)	1.00	1.50	2.00
(A) Transformer, 90 watt (1947)	2.00	4.00	6.00
(B) Transformer, 50 watt (1917)	1.00	1.50	2.00
(B) Transformer, 75 watt (1923)	1.00	1.50	2.00
(C) Curved track — Std. (1906)	.50	1.00	1.50
(C) Transformer, 75 watt (1922)	2.00	3.00	4.00
(C) Ives transformer, 75 watt (Ives 1931)	2.00	3.00	4.00
(C) Ives curved track — Std. (Ives 1931)	.50	1.00	1.50
(½C) Half section curved track — Std. (1906)	.50	.75	1.00
(O-C) Curved tract — 0 (1915)	.50	.75	1.00
(O-C) Ives curved track — 0 (Ives 1931)	.50	.75	1.00

	G	VG	E
(O-C-18) Steel pins, dozen — 0/Std. (1937)	1.00	1.50	2.00
(CC) Curved track with battery connections — Std. (1915)	.50	.75	1.50
(0-CC) Curved track with battery connections — 0 (1915)	.50	.75	1.50
(CO-1) Ives track clip — 0 (Ives 1931)	.50	.75	1.00
(CO-1) Track clip — 0 (1937)	.50	.75	1.00
(CS-1) Ives track clip — Std. (Ives 1931)	.50	.75	1.00
(CS-1) Track clip — Std. (1937)	.50	.75	1.00
(0-CS) Curved track with insulated rails — 0 (1926)	.50	.75	1.00
(CTC) Lockon — 0/027 (1947)	.50	.75	1.00
(EUC-1) Electronic control unit (1946)	10.00	18.00	25.00
(EUC-50) Electronic control instruction booklet (1946)	2.00	4.00	6.00
(F) Transformer, 60 watt (1930)	1.00	1.50	2.00
(H) Transformer, 75 watt (1938)	1.00	1.50	2.00
(I) Racing car curved track, 30" diameter — Std. (1912)	20.00	30.00	40.00
(K) Transformer, 150 watt (1914) ...	2.00	4.00	6.00
(KW) Transformer, 190 watt (1950) .	20.00	25.00	30.00
(K-1) Ives mechanical key - Mech (Ives 1931)	2.00	4.00	6.00
(K-2) Square mechanical key - Mech (1934)	2.00	4.00	6.00
(L) Transformer, 75 watt (1914)	1.00	1.50	2.00
(L) Racing car curved track, 36" diameter — Std. (1915)	25.00	30.00	45.00
(LTC) Lockon with light — 0/027 (1950)	2.00	4.00	6.00
(LW) Transformer, 125 watt (1956) .	8.00	12.00	15.00
(MC) Ives curved track — Mech (Ives 1931)	.50	.75	1.00
(MC) Curved track — Mech (1933) ..	.50	.75	1.00
(MWC) Ives curved track — Mech (Ives 1931)	.50	.75	1.00
(MWC) Curved track — Mech (1933)	.50	.75	1.00
(MS) Ives straight track — Mech (Ives 1931)	.50	.75	1.00
(MS) Straight track — Mech (1933) .	.50	.75	1.00
(N) Transformer, 50 watt (1942)	1.00	1.50	2.00

	G	VG	E
(O) Racing car curved track, 36" diameter — Std. (1912)	20.00	30.00	45.00
(Q) Transformer, 50 watt (1915)	1.00	1.50	2.00
(Q) Transformer, 75 watt (1939)	1.00	2.00	3.00
(Q-90) Transformer, 75 watt (1939) ..	1.00	2.00	3.00
(Q-90) Bulb, 8 volt - clear (1939)	fifty cents		
(R) Transformer, 100 watt (1939) ...	2.00	3.00	4.00
(RCS) Remote control track — 0 (1938)	1.00	2.00	3.00
(RW) Transformer, 110 watt (1948) .	2.00	4.00	6.00
(S) Straight track — Std. (1906)	.50	.75	1.00
(S) Transformer, 50 watt (1915)	1.00	1.50	2.00
(½S) Half section straight track — Std. (1906)	.50	.75	1.00
(O-S) Straight track — 0 (1915)	.50	.75	1.00
(O-S) Ives straight track — 0 (Ives 1931)	.50	.75	1.00
(SC) Straight track with battery connections — Std. (1915)	.50	.75	1.00
(O-SC) Straight track with battery connections — 0 (1915)	.50	.75	1.00
(SCS) Insulated curved track — Mech (1935)	.50	.75	1.00
(SMC) Curved track — Mech (1935) .	.50	.75	1.00
(SS) Straight track with insulated rails — Std. (1926)	.50	.75	1.00
(SS) Ives straight track with insulated rails — Std. (Ives 1931)	.50	.75	1.00
(O-SS) Straight track with insulated rails — 0 (1926)	.50	.75	1.00
(O-SS) Ives straight track with insulated rails — 0 (Ives 1931)	.50	.75	1.00
(STC) Lockon — Std. (1921)	.50	.75	1.00
(STC) Ives lockon — Std. (Ives 1931)	.50	.75	1.00
(SW) Transformer, 130 watt (1961) ..	2.00	4.00	6.00
(T) Transformer, 75 watt (1915)	1.00	1.50	2.00
(O-TC) Lockon — 0 (1921)	.50	.75	1.00
(TOC) Curved track — 0 (1962)	.50	.75	1.00
(TOC-½) Half section curved track — 0 (1966)	.50	.75	1.00
(TOC-51) Steel pins, dozen — 0 (1962)	fifty cents		
(TOS) Straight track — 0 (1962)	.50	.75	1.00
(TOS-½) Half section straight track — 0 (1966)	.50	.75	1.00

	G	VG	E
(T-011-43) Fiber pins, dozen — 0 (1962)	fifty cents		
(T-020) 90° crossing — 0 (1962)	2.00	3.00	4.00
(T-022) Remote control switches — 0 (1962)	15.00	22.00	30.00
(TW) Transformer, 115 watt (1953) .	2.00	4.00	6.00
(U) Transformer, 50 watt (1933)	1.00	1.50	2.00
(UCS) Remote control uncoupling track set — 0 (1949)	2.00	3.00	4.00
(UTC) Lockon, universal (1937)	.50	.75	1.00
(V) Transformer, 150 watt (1939) ...	2.00	4.00	6.00
(VW) Transformer, 150 watt (1948) .	9.00	12.00	15.00
(W) Ives transformer, 75 watt (Ives (1932)	1.00	1.50	2.00
(W) Transformer, 75 watt (1933)	1.00	1.50	2.00
(Z) Transformer, 250 watt (1939)....	20.00	25.00	30.00
(ZW) Transformer, 250 watt (1948)..	30.00	45.00	65.00
(ZW) Transformer, 275 watt (1953)..	35.00	45.00	65.00

MARX TRAIN HISTORY
R. L. MacNary

Louis Marx started working at age 16 (in 1912) with Ferdinand Strauss but left in 1917 over a dispute in his philosophy of volume sales. He reportedly was a millionaire by the time he reached age 26. The first trains he sold, The Joy Line, were actually produced by the Girard Model Works under a commission sales agreement. These appeared in 1927 or 1928 and were sold through the mid-1930's when Marx had completely acquired Girard and started to produce his own now widely recognized line of 6″ tin trains. The tin clockwork trolley seems to have been produced during the late 1920's, also.

The early, fragile #350 engine and matching Joy Line cars were produced for a very short time. By 1930, Girard had started using a heavier stamped steel frame for these cars and also cast iron engines (both clockwork and electric). The third major Joy Line engine type appeared in 1932. It was of stamped steel. These were produced at least into 1935 after the complete take-over of Girard by Marx. These stamped-steel engines came in various red and black color combinations and both clockwork and electric.

Richard MacNary was raised during WW II along the Monon RR in Hammond, Indiana (Chicago area) on a steady, if not expensive, diet of paper, cardboard, and wood "Victory" toys as well as a few left over Barclay and Manoil lead soldiers. Setting up a pre-war MARX Commodore Vanderbilt train set which was shared with an older sister was one of the thrills of those war-time Christmas seasons. In 1948, a #999 freight set was purchased, the first "new" train for many years.

While the first Lionel came along in 1951 (a used 2026), it was only after the Army and a couple of college degrees that collecting really took hold. A fairly complete post-war (1946-1969) Lionel collection was amassed along with original catalogs back as far as 1922. Several original MARX pre-war catalogs are now in his collection, too, along with a color ad for the introduction of the M10,005 streamliner.

Richard is the Atlanta District Manager for the Ohio Brass Company, a manufacturer of high voltage electrical equipment. He, wife Marilyn, two children, two dogs, a dumb cat, and various snakes, hamsters, etc., have now lived in Atlanta long enough to possess a fine grits tree orchard in the North Georgia mountains.

He is still looking for six or seven tin-litho MARX pieces including the **red 994** Nickel Plate loco and tender and the **rabbit** for the Bunny Express Train. "There is no such thing as a complete MARX (train) collection. Just when you think you have it all, something else shows up."

The first trains to have been produced after the 1935 acquisition and believed to be wholly Marx inspired were the Commodore Vanderbilt and the 6″ cars that in various colors and markings would be produced into the 1970's. The first cars, all 4 wheel, have somewhat unusual colors and numbers and are mounted on black frames lithographed in silver to appear as 8 wheel cars. These had so-called left over Joy Line couplers. The Commodore Vanderbilt engine with a swinging coupler peg extending down through its cab floor is quite difficult to find but it is the proper engine for these first cars. The cars were also sold for a short period later, I believe, as they also accept the standard Marx hook coupler; their general availability seems much too high to have been limited only to the swinging peg Commodores.

From the late 1930's up to WW II would have to be a golden age of Marx Tin Trains if there was one. These trains were produced in a wide variety of colors, in 4 wheel as well as 8 wheel, with simple hook couplers and complex automatic couplers, in articulated (cheap and also fancy) passenger trains and in the well recognized 6″ passenger cars. And this period also saw the introduction of the most popular Marx trains, The Army Train in all its functional beauty.

Just prior to WW II, Marx produced a line of 3/16″ scale freight cars. Contrary to another review of Marx trains, the die-cast #999 made its appearance prior to the stopping of all non-war essential production in May of 1942. While there may not have been many produced, you may wish to refer to Spiegel's *Holiday Greetings 1942* catalog for an excellent view of this pre-war set. The 3/16″ line may have been produced to give American Flyer a good run as it follows closely behind the Gilbert (American Flyer) introduction of 3/16″ scale trains in 1939. The Marx 3/16″ trains were continued after the war well into the 1950's.

By the early 1950's a corresponding set of 3/16″ passenger cars had been manufactured in NYC two tone gray with a nicely proportioned, die-cast Pacific #333 engine and tender heading up this consist. These cars went through several color and marking changes over the next several years finally ending up in Western Pacific markings pulled by a plastic E3 three unit diesel which was longer than the normal three car set. Continuing a practice started in the late 1930's, Marx sometimes included both freight cars and passenger cars in a single set to enhance the "play value" of the train set while at the same time quietly capitalizing on the suspected higher profit margin for cars without the expenses of more track, transformer, engine, packaging, and sales overheads.

By late 1949 or early 1950, Marx was producing a line of 7″ tin trains which included the Mickey Mouse Meteor set, a collectors jewel for both Disney and Marx collectors. These trains may have been a successful attempt to run *Unique* trains out of business, if not the whole Unique operation. The majority of Unique Manufacturing Company toys seem to have been made with left over or leased Marx dies with new lithography. One can speculate that as long as Marx was through with the dies, it was a good situation; as soon as Unique introduced a brand new line of their own toy trains in 1949, that all changed. Not long after Unique disappeared in 1952, the Marx line of 7″ cars started its conversion to plastic. The basic 7″ tin cars lasted to 1962 with the Wm. Crooks (General type) old time passenger cars.

The period from the early 1950's until the demise of train production in 1979 saw a wide assortment of plastic trains, some of which are quite nice. The die-cast #666 engine, as sold with the deluxe 8 wheel plastic Army trains is a dependable, excellent smoking unit (Marx trains of this period could out-smoke any Lionel or American Flyer — what did they know that the "giants" didn't?)

Louis sold his company (owned entirely by him and his brother Dave) to Quaker Oats in 1972 for $51.3 million. Quaker Oats tried to run it the same way as one of their other rather successful divisions but it just didn't work out. After losing a noticeable amount of money in 1975, they sold to the English combine of Dunbee-Combex-Marx. In February of 1980, Chapter XI bankruptcy was filed, thus ending one of the best known lines of toys and trains which had spanned over a half century of production. Louis Marx had out-lived and his train line out-lasted his competitors' by basically selling trains that "ran better than they should for the price."

I would like to issue special thanks to Larry Jensen and Tom Croyts for their help in updating the listing for the 2nd edition.

Additional information on Louis Marx and his trains can be found in these references:

1. Greenberg's *Guide to Marx Trains* by Eric Matzke, Greenberg Publishing Company, 1978.
2. *Fortune*, January 1946 (Reprinted in *Antique Toy World*, February and March 1972)
3. *Railroad Model Craftsman*, December 1957 Carstens Publications, 1957 - article by Roger Arcara, now slightly out of date.
4. Any Sear, Wards, Spiegels, Butler Bros., etc., Christmas catalogs from 1928 to at least 1970.

MARX

General Notes:
1. Numbers listed, i.e. 552, appear on the engine or car.
2. Numbers in parenthesis, i.e. (551), are generally accepted catalog numbers even though they don't appear on the engine or car.
3. Major variations are shown by small letters (a), (b) etc.
4. No divisions have been attempted by truck style, frame type, or coupler variation as these permutations are too numerous for this volume.
5. All transformers and track sections are so common they aren't listed separately. At the most, working Marx transformers are worth $1.00 each and track worth .10 to .25 each.
6. Prices for complete sets may be obtained by adding together each car and engine; sets with original boxes, add 20%.
7. Remember, there are very few *mint* Marx trains even though hundreds and hundreds of thousands have been made.

	G	VG	M
(0211) Signal Set, plastic, 3 pieces ..	.50	1.00	1.50
(061) Telephone Pole, 7″, plastic	.05	.10	.15
(062) Lamp Post, 6″, plastic, dummy	.05	.10	.15
(063) Semaphore, 6⅛″, plastic, mech.	.05	.10	.15
(064) Crossing Gate, 8¼″, plastic ...	.05	.10	.15
(065) Water Tower, 8¼″, plastic	.10	.15	.20
(067) Twin Crossing Light, 6″, plastic, dummy	.05	.10	.15

41 Loco, 4-4-0, Flashlight

	G	VG	M
(073/3) Lamp Post Set, lighted, Boulevard	1.00	2.00	3.00
1 (a) Loco, 4-4-0, plastic, black, marked "Wm. Crooks" and "#1", electric drive, with smoke	20.00	30.00	40.00
(b) Same as above, 0-4-0, clockwork, no smoke	10.00	15.00	20.00
(c) Similar, 0-4-0, shorter stack, no smoke, electric	8.00	10.00	12.00
1 Baggage car, 7" tin, both 4 wheel and 8 wheel, yellow body, black frame, black & yellow lettering "St. Paul and Pacific"	8.00	10.00	15.00
3 Passenger Car, 7" tin, 4 wheel and 8 wheel, yellow body and black frame with yellow lettering "St. Paul and Pacific"	5.00	8.00	10.00
(9) "The Cannon Ball Express", pedal-operated ride-on train, engine, metal, red & yellow	20.00	30.00	50.00
20 (a) Loco, 0-4-0, plastic HO, black with orange lettering "NH"	1.00	2.00	3.00
(b) Same as above, white "AT&SF"	1.00	2.00	3.00
(c) Same as above, white "Rock Island"	1.00	2.00	3.00
(d) Same as above, white "NYC" ...	1.00	2.00	3.00
21 (a) Loco, diesel "A" unit, large tin litho, red and silver with black lettering "Santa Fe", powered "A" unit ..	5.00	9.00	12.00
(b) Same as above, non-powered "A" unit	4.00	6.00	8.00
21 Loco, diesel GP7/9, plastic HO, red and gray with black lettering "Monon" (*worst looking engine ever produced*)	1.00	2.00	3.00
24 Drop Center Searchlight, plastic, deluxe 8 wheel, black with gray searchlight, yellow generator	4.00	6.00	8.00
41 Loco, 4-4-0, plastic floor toy, flashlight, green, gold, red, old-time design	10.00	15.00	20.00
44 (a) Loco, streamlined steam, tin, litho, engine and tender one piece, gray-red-white with "Super Chief", clockwork	10.00	15.00	20.0

	G	VG	M
(b) Same as 44(a), friction, (lighter gray)	10.00	15.00	20.00
45 Caboose, plastic, 8 wheel, brown with white "45"	1.00	1.50	2.00
47 Hopper, plastic HO, red with white lettering "Huron Portland Cement"	1.00	1.50	2.00
49 Loco, riding floor toy, plastic, black 2-4-0, marked "PIONEER" on cab and "49" on tender	5.00	7.50	10.00
(51) Loco, diesel, plastic, 8 wheel powered "A" unit, orange with black lettering "ALLSTATE"	20.00	25.00	30.00
(52) Same as above, dummy "A" unit	20.00	25.00	30.00
(53) Same as above, dummy "A" unit	20.00	25.00	30.00
(U1) Loco, diesel, plastic, 8 wheel powered "A" unit, orange with black lettering "Union Pacific"	9.00	12.00	15.00
(U2) Same as above, dummy "A" unit	9.00	12.00	15.00
(U3) Same as above, dummy "B" unit	9.00	12.00	15.00
(I) Loco, diesel switcher, plastic, 4 wheel, orange with black lettering "Illinois Central"	5.00	8.00	10.00
(M) Loco, diesel switcher, plastic, 4 wheel, blue and white lettering "Missouri Pacific"	6.00	9.00	12.00
54 (a) Loco, diesel, small tin litho, red-yellow-black with yellow and white lettering	10.00	12.00	15.00
"Kansas City Southern" *powered* "A" unit			
(b) Same as above, dummy "A" unit	10.00	12.00	15.00
((55) (a) Similar to 54, 4 wheel dummy "B" unit	8.00	10.00	12.00
(b) Same as above, 8 wheel dummy "B" unit	8.00	10.00	12.00
56 Flat Car, plastic, 8 wheel, maroon with yellow side rails, white letter "56"	2.00	4.00	6.00
59 (a) Cattle Car, 6″ tin, 4 wheel and 8 wheel brown with red lettering "Union Pacific"	2.00	3.00	4.00
(b) Same as above, with punched out slotted sides	3.00	6.00	8.00

	G	VG	M
62 (a) Loco, diesel, medium tin litho, silver and blue with black and white lettering "Baltimore & Ohio", *powered* "A" unit	5.00	8.00	10.00
(b) Same as above, dummy "A" unit	5.00	8.00	10.00
81F (a) Loco, diesel, small tin litho, red and gray with yellow and white lettering "Monon" *powered* "A" unit	10.00	12.00	15.00
(b) Same as above, *dummy* "A" unit	10.00	12.00	15.00
(c) Same as above, clockwork (wind-up) motor	12.00	16.00	20.00
(82) (a) Similar 81F, *4 wheel*, dummy "B" unit	8.00	10.00	12.00
(b) Same as above, *8 wheel* dummy "B" unit	8.00	10.00	12.00
93 Loco, streamlined steam, tin litho, engine and tender one piece, black and blue with yellow lettering "LU-MAR LINES", clockwork	10.00	15.00	20.00
99 (a) Loco, diesel, plastic, black with white lettering "Rock Island", powered "A" unit	5.00	13.00	15.00
(b) Similar to 99, dummy "A" unit ..	4.00	12.00	14.00
99 (c) Loco, riding floor train, plastic, red 2-4-2T, marked "THE CHIEF" under cab window, "MARX RR" embossed on tender, and "99" on headlite..........................	10.00	15.00	20.00
109 (a) Hopper, plastic, *HO blue* with white lettering "Lehigh Portland Cement"	.50	1.00	1.50
(b) Same as above, *gray* with black lettering	.50	1.00	1.50
112 Loco, diesel switcher, plastic, red with white lettering "Lehigh Valley"	3.00	5.00	7.00
161 Drop Center Searchlite, plastic, HO, black with white lettering "GEX"	1.00	2.00	3.00
198 Loco, 0-4-0, plastic, clockwork, red or black with "Marline" cast on side	3.00	5.00	7.00
200 Trolley, tin litho, green and red with white "RAPID TRANSIT"	100.00	150.00	200.00
201 Observation, 6″ tin, 4 wheel, red with black lettering, black and silver or all black frame	5.00	8.00	10.00

Marx Army Train, plastic, early 1960's
Top left to right: 400 olive drab loco, black tender
Middle left to right: 572M(b) flat with truck 572M(b) flat with truck, 572M(e) flat with
    search light
Bottom left to right: 572M(c) flat with duck, 572M(d) flat with armored car, 558(a)
    observation
Courtesy Richard MacNary

Marx Cape Carnaveral Sets, late 1950's
Top left to right: 1798 switcher, X-246 4 wheel tank car, 467 4 wheel caboose
Middle left to right: 1799 4 wheel gondola, 1796 8 wheel missile launcher, 1799 8 wheel
    gondola
Bottom left to right: 1798 switcher, 246 8 wheel tank car, 8 wheel searchlight
Courtesy Richard MacNary

152

	G	VG	M
(232) Loco - see (597) "Commodore Vanderbilt"			
(233) Loco - see (635) "Mercury"			
234 (a) Passenger Car, 3/16" scale, tin litho, 8 wheel two tone gray with white lettering "New York Central"	5.00	7.00	10.00
(b) Same as above, Vista Dome	5.00	7.00	10.00
234 Caboose, plastic 8 wheel, ARMY olive drab with white lettering "USA"	3.00	5.00	7.00
(235) Loco - see 396, 397 "Canadian Pacific			
(236) Passenger Car, 3/16" scale, tin litho, 8 wheel observation, two tone gray with white lettering "New York Central" and "Meteor"	5.00	7.00	10.00
242 Loco, floor toy, plastic 4-4-2 lettered "SPARKLING FRICTION RR"	5.00	7.50	10.00
245 Coach, 6" tin, 4 wheel, red with black lettering "Bogota" black and silver or all black frame	5.00	8.00	10.00
246 Coach, 6" tin, 4 wheel, red with black lettering "Montclair" black and silver or all black frame	5.00	8.00	10.00
246 Tank car, plastic, 8 wheel, white (cream) with red lettering "Chemical Rocket Fuel" and "Danger"	1.00	3.00	5.00
X-246 Tank Car, plastic, 4 wheel, white (cream) with red lettering "Chemical Rocket Fuel"	1.00	2.00	3.00
246 Passenger Car, 6" tin, 4 wheel and 8 wheel, CANADIAN PACIFIC, maroon with gold lettering "Montreal"	25.00	35.00	45.00
247 Same as above, "Toronto"	25.00	35.00	45.00
248 Same as above, "Quebec"	25.00	35.00	45.00
249 Same as above, "Ottawa"	25.00	35.00	45.00
250 Same as above, "Winnipeg"	25.00	35.00	45.00
(309B) Tunnel, tin litho	2.00	3.00	4.00
(321) Railroad Signal Set, steel	3.00	5.00	7.00
251 Same as 246, "Vancouver"	25.00	35.00	45.00
252 Same as above, "Calgary"	25.00	35.00	45.00
253 Same as above, "Hamilton"	25.00	35.00	45.00

(896) Hiawatha loco and passenger car

2 different early Marx "Honeymoon Specials"

	G	VG	M
256 Tank Car, 3/16″ scale, tin litho, 8 wheel silver with red lettering "N.I.A.X." and "Niagara Falls, NY"	2.00	3.00	4.00
284 Tank Car, plastic, deluxe, 8 wheel, gray with red lettering "UTLX"	1.00	3.00	5.00
333 Loco, 4-6-2, die-cast, black, marked "333"	20.00	25.00	30.00
Tender, die-cast, for 333 engine only, black, marked "New York Central" .	7.00	10.00	12.00
333 Loco, floor toy, plastic 4-4-4 with whistle & bell	5.00	7.50	10.00
C-350 Caboose, plastic, 8 wheel, red with white lettering "MONON"	1.00	3.00	5.00
350 Loco, tin, clockwork, "Joy Line" 0-4-0 red & gold body, blue frame ...	50.00	90.00	150.00
- Loco, cast iron, clockwork, 0-4-0, black, no markings	30.00	60.00	90.00
- Loco, cast iron, electric, 0-4-0, black, no markings	40.00	80.00	110.00
- Loco, stamped steel, clockwork, 0-4-0, red frame, black top or black frame, red top	15.00	25.00	40.00

	G	VG	M
- Loco, stamped steel, electric 0-4-0, red frame, black top	15.00	25.00	40.00
- Loco, stamped steel, clockwork, 0-4-0, all black	15.00	25.00	40.00
351 (a) Tender, tin, "Joy Line" yellow, blue frame, marked "Koal Kar"	20.00	40.00	60.00
(351b) Tender, tin, unmarked, black top, black frame	10.00	15.00	20.00
(351c) Tender, tin, unmarked, longer than 351a, all black or red	12.00	18.00	25.00
352 (a) Gondola, tin "Joy Line" marked "Venice Gondola" blue body, blue frame	20.00	40.00	60.00
352 (b) Gondola, tin, Joy Line, marked "Venice gondola" blue body, black frame	20.00	30.00	40.00
352 (c) Gondola, tin, Joy Line, marked "Bunny Express", either baby chicks or ducklings with red or blue backgrounds	25.00	35.00	50.00
352 (d) Gondola, tin, Marx, Same style as 352 but with wood litho stakes, red or orange backgrounds	25.00	35.00	45.00
353 (a) Tank Car, tin, Joy Line, marked "Everful Tank Car", gold body, blue frame	20.00	40.00	60.00
(b) Tank Car, tin, Joy Line, marked "Everful Tank Car", gold body, black frame	20.00	30.00	40.00
354 (a) Side Dump, tin, Joy Line, marked "Contractor Dump Car", yellow body, blue frame	20.00	40.00	60.00
(b) Side Dump, tin, Joy Line, marked "Contractor Dump Car" yellow body, black frame	20.00	30.00	40.00
355 (a) Boxcar, tin, Joy Line, marked "Hobo Rest", red body, blue frame .	20.00	40.00	60.00
(b) Boxcar, tin Joy Line, marked "Hobo Rest", red body, black frame	20.00	30.00	40.00
356 (a) Caboose, tin Joy Line, marked "Eagle Eye Caboose", red body, blue frame	20.00	40.00	60.00
(b) Caboose, tin, Joy Line, marked "Eagle Eye Caboose" red body, black frame	20.00	30.00	40.00

Deluxe Army Train, 1960's
Top left to right: 666 loco, tender
Middle left to right: 586(c) flat with auto, 586(c) flat with tank, 2236 gondola
Bottom left to right: 2824 missile launcher, 234 caboose
Courtesy Richard MacNary

Pre-War Tin Army Trains
Top left to right: 572AA A.A. gun, 563A flat with lumber, 558(a) observation
Middle left to right: 557(b) radio car without antenna, 557(a) radio car with antenna, 558(a)
    observation (illuminated)
Bottom left to right: 561(c) searchlight, 572A flat with airplane, 572MG flat with machine
    gun.
Courtesy Richard MacNary

	G	VG	M
357 (a) Coach, tin, marked "The Joy Line Coach" green body, yellow round roof, blue frame	35.00	50.00	75.00
(b) Coach, tin, marked "The Joy Line Coach", orange or red roof, green body, black frame	20.00	30.00	40.00
358 (a) Observation, tin, Joy Line, marked "Observation", orange or red roof, green body, black frame (only)	20.00	30.00	40.00
(b) Observation, tin, Joy Line, marked "Observation", orange or red roof, green body, black frame, with light .	35.00	50.00	75.00
(391) Loco, 0-4-0 and 2-4-2, Canadian Pacific various boiler colors and side boards	18.00	22.00	25.00
(396) Loco, 0-4-0 and 2-4-2, Canadian Pacific style various boiler colors and side boards	18.00	22.00	25.00
397 Loco, 2-4-2, Canadian Pacific style, various boiler colors and side boards	18.00	22.00	25.00
400 (a) Loco, 0-4-0, plastic, black, clockwork and electric	2.00	3.00	4.00
(b) Same as above, with rubber bulb and powder smoke	6.00	7.00	9.00
(c) Same as above, ARMY olive drab	5.00	7.00	10.00
(d) Same as above, dark gray	3.00	4.00	5.00
(401) Loco, 0-4-0, plastic, clockwork, black "Mar" cast on side	1.00	2.00	3.00
(404) Block Signal, stamped steel, 6⅝" high	3.00	5.00	7.00
(408) Twin Light Lamp Post, stamped steel 7¼" high	3.00	4.00	5.00
(409) Twin Light Blinking Caution Signal, stamped steel, 7¼" high	3.00	5.00	7.00
(412) RR Derrick Loader, boom on top, straddles track, winch	4.00	6.00	8.00
(413) Switchman tower with light, stamped steel, 9¼"	3.00	5.00	7.00
(414) RR Crossing Warning Bell	3.00	5.00	7.00
(416) Floodlight, black, plastic, 4 bulbs	.75	1.25	1.50
X415 Tank Car, plastic, HO, white			

	G	VG	M
and blue (or black) with red lettering "Hydrocarbon Rocket Fuel"	.25	.50	.75
(416-A) Floodlight Tower, stamped steel, two bulbs, red, black or silver .	3.00	5.00	7.00
(418) Automatic Bell Ringing Signal, stamped steel, 7½″ tall	3.00	4.00	5.00
(419) Lamp Post, stamped steel, single bulb........................	2.50	3.50	4.50
(423) Automatic Twin Light Highway Crossing Signal, flashing, two bulbs, 7½″ high	3.00	5.00	7.00
(424) Radio Control Tower, stamped steel and tin, operated by "voice", 9½″ × 2¾″ × 2¾″	5.00	7.00	9.00
(429) Lamp Post, stamped steel, twin bulbs	4.00	6.00	8.00
(434) Block Signal, stamped steel, 7″	2.00	3.00	4.00
(436) Searchlight Tower, large plastic	1.00	2.00	3.00
(438) Automatic Crossing Gate, stamped steel, 9″ gate arm	3.00	5.00	7.00
(439) Semaphore with light, stamped steel, 9″	4.00	6.00	8.00
458 (a) Observation, tin, Joy Line, marked "Observation", orange or red roof, green body, black frame	20.00	30.00	40.00
458 (b) Same as above, with light ..	35.00	50.00	75.00
X467 Caboose, plastic, 4 wheel and 8 wheel, red with white lettering "Rocket Computing Center	5.00	7.00	9.00
490 (a) Loco, 0-4-0, plastic, black	2.50	3.00	4.00
(b) Same as above, with white stripe	3.00	5.00	7.00
500 Loco, both 0-4-0 and 2-4-2, Canadian Pacific style, ARMY olive drab	25.00	35.00	50.00
500 Tender, 6″ tin, 4 wheel and 8 wheel, ARMY olive drab with white lettering "Army Supply Train"	6.00	9.00	12.00
504 Caboose, plastic, 4 wheel, blue with yellow lettering "B & O"	2.00	5.00	7.00
C-504 Caboose, 7″ tin, 4 wheels, blue and black with yellow and white C-518 lettering "B&O"	3.00	5.00	7.00
547 (a) Baggage car, 6″ tin, 4 wheel, red with black lettering "Express			

	G	VG	M
Baggage", black and silver or all black frame	9.00	12.00	15.00
(b) Same as above, red with silver lettering	8.00	10.00	12.00
(c) Same as above, red with yellow lettering (4 wheel and 8 wheel)	8.00	10.00	12.00
548 Gondola, 6" tin, 4 wheel and 8 wheel, light blue with blue and white lettering "Guernsey Milk" and "CRI&P"	9.00	12.00	15.00
(550) (a) Wrecker/Crane, tin, 6", 4 wheel orange cab, red boom, black lettering "Wrecker", black and silver or all black frame, with rail clips . . .	8.00	12.00	16.00
(b) Same as above, 4 wheel and 8 wheel, no clips	7.00	10.00	13.00
553 Tank Car, 6" tin, 4 wheel, silver with red lettering "UTLX"	4.00	6.00	8.00
(551) (a) Tender, 6" tin, 4 wheel, black with silver lettering "New York Central", black and silver frame	2.00	3.00	4.00
(b) Same as above, 4 wheel and 8 wheel, black, red or nickel frame . . .	2.00	3.00	4.00
(c) Same as above, red, 4 wheel	4.00	6.00	8.00
(d) Same as above, blue with gray band	5.00	7.50	10.00
(e) Same as above, copper (or brass)	4.00	6.00	8.00
(f) Same as above, black with gray bank	2.00	3.00	4.00
(g) Same as above, black, marked with "Union Pacific" (late)	2.00	3.00	4.00
(h) Same as above, black marked with "1st DIV." St.P & P.R.R. (late)	3.00	4.00	5.00
552 (a) Gondola, 6" tin, 4 wheel, red with black lettering "CRI&P", black and silver or all black frame	9.00	12.00	15.00
(b) Same as above, 4 wheel and 8 wheel, green with red and white lettering	2.00	3.00	4.00
(c) Same as 552(b), light blue with blue and white lettering	2.00	4.00	6.00
(d) Same as above, yellow and brown with brown and white lettering "Groceries and Sundries" (Car marked 552G)	9.00	12.00	15.00

H&P Japanese Copy 3/16" Train
Top left to right: 2-6-2 Diecast loco, H&P tender
Middle left to right: 174520 H&P box car, 1530000 H&P gondola
Bottom left to right: Japanese transformer, 752 H&P tank car, 201507 H&P caboose
Courtesy Richard MacNary

	G	VG	M
(e) Same as above, ARMY olive drab with black and white lettering "Ordinance Department" (with original shells, add $20.00)	8.00	10.00	12.00
(f) Same as above, dark blue, 8 wheel	4.00	6.00	8.00
553 (a) Tank Car, 6" tin, 4 wheel, yellow with black lettering "Middle States Oil" and "Santa Fe", black and silver or all black frame	9.00	12.00	15.00
(b) Same as above, 4 wheel and 8 wheel, silver with red and black lettering "Santa Fe" and "Middle States Oil"	1.00	2.00	3.00
554 High side gondola, 6" tin, 4 wheel red with yellow lettering "General Coal Co." and N.P." herald	2.00	4.00	6.00
554 (a) Hopper, 6" tin, 4 wheel and 8 wheel red with yellow lettering "General Coal Co." and "N.P." herald ...	2.00	4.00	6.00
(b) Same as above, blue with white lettering	2.00	4.00	6.00

160

Three types of #999's (tenders and cabooses)
Top: Late version with disc drivers and plastic coal pile on tender
Middle: Very common version produced after WW II for many years.
Bottom: Early style, probably Pre-WW II with spoked pilot and 3 piece slider pick-up.
Courtesy Richard MacNary

	G	VG	M
555 (a) Refrigerator car, 6″ tin, both 4 wheel and 8 wheel, cream with red roof and red lettering marked "C&S", sliding doors	4.00	8.00	12.00
(b) Same as above, cream with blue roof, and blue lettering, sliding doors	4.00	6.00	8.00
(c) Same as above, 4 wheel only, cream with red roof and red lettering, solid litho doors	12.00	16.00	20.00
(d) Same as above, 4 wheel and 8 wheel, cream with blue roof and blue lettering, solid litho doors	4.00	8.00	12.00
556 (a) Caboose, 6″ tin, 4 wheel and 8 wheel, red with white lettering "NYC"	.50	1.00	1.50
(b) Same as above, with light	6.00	9.00	12.00
(556) Cable Car, 6″ tin, 4 wheel and perhaps 8 wheel, large wooden cable reel mounted through base with string "cable"	6.00	9.00	12.00
(---) Wheel car, 6″ tin, 4 wheel with second car riveted on top with extra wheels, top frame is red	10.00	12.00	14.00

161

	G	VG	M
(---) Rail Car, 6″ + 6″ tin, 4 + 4 wheels, two flat cars permanently coupled together, carries 10-12 individual rails	12.00	15.00	18.00
(557) (a) Passenger Car, 6″ tin, 4 wheel and 8 wheel ARMY olive drab with lettering "Radio Car" and "Army Supply Tain", with roof top antenna	9.00	12.00	15.00
(b) Same as above, without roof top antenna (no holes)	15.00	20.00	25.00
(c) Same as above, red with black and white lettering "Bogota" or "Montclair"	3.00	6.00	9.00
(d) Same as above, green with yellow lettering "Bogota" or "Montclair" 4 wheel only	6.00	9.00	12.00
(e) Same as above, blue with ivory lettering "Bogota" or "Montclair" 4 wheel only	6.00	9.00	12.00
(558) (a) Observation Car, 6″ tin, 4 wheel ARMY olive drab with white lettering, with and without light ...	9.00	12.00	15.00
(b) Same as above, red with black and white lettering "Observation", 4 wheel or 8 wheel	3.00	6.00	9.00
(c) Same as above, green with yellow lettering "Observation", 4 wheel only	6.00	9.00	12.00
(d) Same as above, blue with ivory lettering "Observation", 4 wheel only	6.00	9.00	12.00
(559) (a) Floodlight, 6″ tin, 4 wheel, two lights	6.00	9.00	12.00
(b) Same as above, ARMY olive drab	20.00	25.00	30.00
(561) (a) Searchlight Car, 6″ tin, 4 wheel, one light	6.00	9.00	12.00
(b) Same as above, 8 wheel	50.00	60.00	75.00
(c) Same as above, ARMY olive drab, (4 wheel)	20.00	25.00	30.00
(562D) Flat Car, 6″ tin, 4 wheel and 8 wheel, with different colored stamped steel dump trucks	12.00	15.00	18.00
(563A) Lumber Car, 6″ tin, 4 wheel and 8 wheel, with four pieces of lumber & clamp	6.00	9.00	12.00
564 Caboose, plastic, 8 wheel, brown with white lettering "All State"	.50	1.00	1.50

Nickel plate Set with 7" cars
Top left to right: 994(a) loco, tender
Middle left to right: 37956 PRR box car, 80982 Wabash gondola
Bottom: 956 NKP caboose
Courtesy Richard MacNary

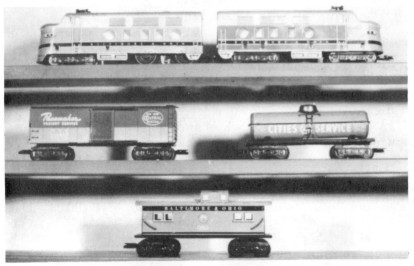

B&O set with 7" cars
Top left to right: 62(a) loco (powered A), 62(b) loco (dummy A)
Middle left to right: 174580 NYC box car, 3532 CITGO tank car
Bottom: C513 B&O caboose
Courtesy Richard MacNary

	G	VG	M
567 Dump Car, 6″ tin, 4 wheel and 8 wheel, yellow with red lettering "Side Dumping Car" and "New York Central" both copper and brass bases ..	4.00	6.00	8.00
(572A) Flat Car, 6″ tin, 4 wheel, ARMY olive drab with olive drab airplane	40.00	50.00	60.00
(572M) (a) Flat Car, 6″ tin, 4 wheel ARMY olive drab with stamped steel olive drab dump truck	30.00	40.00	50.00
(b) Same as above, with gray plastic 2½ ton truck, 1950's	9.00	12.00	15.00
(c) Same as above, with gray plastic "Duck"	9.00	12.00	15.00
(d) Same as above, with gray plastic armored car	9.00	12.00	15.00
(e) Same as above, with gray search-lite truck	9.00	12.00	15.00
(f) Same as above, with gray plastic tank	9.00	12.00	15.00
(g) Same as above, with gray plastic staff car	9.00	12.00	15.00
(572ST) (a) Flat Car, 6″ tin, 4 wheel ARMY olive drab with #5 tin litho tank	40.00	50.00	60.00
(b) Same as above, with midget sparkling tank (also 8 wheel)	30.00	40.00	50.00
(572FG) Flat car, 6″ tin, 4 wheel and 8 wheel, ARMY olive drab with attached field gun	20.00	25.00	30.00
(572AA) Flat Car, 6″ tin, 4 wheel and 8 wheel, ARMY olive drab with attached AA gun	20.00	25.00	30.00
(572G) Flat Car, 6″ tin, 4 wheel and 8 wheel, ARMY olive drab with attached large bore siege gun	20.00	25.00	30.00
(572MG) Flat Car, 6″ tin, 4 wheel and 8 wheel, ARMY olive drab with attached machine gun	20.00	25.00	30.00
(2572) Ramp Car, 6″ tin, 3/16″ 8 wheel trucks, ARMY olive drab with end un-loading ramp and OD truck	25.00	35.00	45.00
(574) Barrel Car, 6″ tin, 4 wheel and 8 wheel with 7 wooden barrels	9.00	12.00	15.00

164

"Green Giant Valley Express" HO train set

999(e) Plastimarx loco, 0-4-0, Mexico and special cars

Plastimarx set

Valley Express

Plastimarx set

3/16" Trains
Top left to right: 999 loco, 951A tender, 71499 NKP gondola
Middle left to right: 17899 T&P gondola, 347000 PRR gondola, 254000 B&O gondola
Bottom left to right: 256 NICET tank car, 2532 Cities Service tank car, 652 Shell tank car
Courtesy Richard MacNary

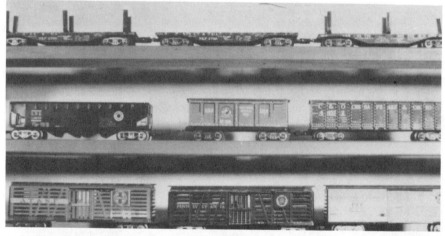

3/16" Trains
Top left to right: NKP 2700 flat with stakes, NKP 2700 flat without stakes, B&M 33773 flat
　　with stakes
Middle left to right: 13079 LNE Hopper, 554 N.P. green transition car, 44572 C&O high side
　　gondola
Bottom left to right: 13549 ATSF stock car, 53941 PRR stock car, 35461 PFE reefer
Courtesy Richard MacNary

166

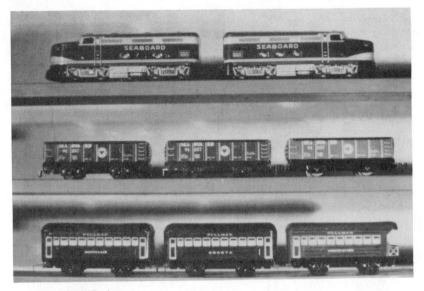

Seaboard RR Trains
Top left to right: 4000 loco (powered), 4000 loco (dummy)
Middle left to right: 91257 blue gondola, 91257 red gondola, 91257 brown gondola
Bottom left to right: 557(d) Montclair, 556(d) Bogota, 558(c) observation
Courtesy Richard MacNary

3/16" Trains
Top left to right: 70311 PRR box car, 1950 GATX box car, 1950 GATX box car
Middle left to right: 3200 NY,NH,M box car, 9100 UP box car, 174580 NYC box car
Bottom left to right: 20102 NYC caboose, 92812 Reading caboose
Courtesy Richard MacNary

167

	G	VG	M
(586) (a) Flat Car, plastic, 8 wheel, red with white lettering "Rock Island" .	1.00	2.00	3.00
(b) Same as above, maroon with yellow lettering "Erie"	1.00	2.00	3.00
(c) Same as above, ARMY olive drab with white lettering "USA" and silver plastic tank (truck, etc.)	7.00	9.00	12.00
586 Caboose, plastic, 8 wheel, brown with white lettering "Rock Island", wrecker type	1.00	2.00	3.00
588 (a) Loco, diesel switcher, 4 wheel, black with white lettering "New York Central"	2.00	4.00	8.00
(b) Same as above, maroon with yellow lettering	2.00	4.00	8.00
(c) Same as above, gray with black lettering	2.00	4.00	8.00
(591) Loco, 0-4-0 tin, black (no markings)...............................	1.00	3.00	5.00
(592) Loco, 0-4-0 tin, black (no markings)...............................	1.00	3.00	5.00
(593) Loco, 0-4-0, tin, black (no markings)...............................	1.00	3.00	5.00
(595) Loco, 0-4-0, tin, black (no marking), electric	1.00	3.00	5.00
(597) (a) Loco, 0-4-0, stamped steel, "Commodore Vanderbilt" style, early with Joy Line swinging peg coupler, green or black, clockwork only	20.00	30.00	40.00
(b) Same as above, electric or clockwork, regular hook coupler, red or gray	15.00	20.00	25.00
(c) Same as above, ARMY olive drab	40.00	50.00	60.00
(d) Same as above, black	10.00	12.00	15.00
C 630 Caboose, plastic, HO, red with white lettering "NH"	.50	1.00	1.50
C 635 Caboose, plastic, 8 wheel, red with white lettering "New Haven" .	.50	1.00	1.50
(635) Loco, 0-4-0, tin, black, (no marking)...............................	1.00	3.00	5.00
(635) (a) Loco, 0-4-0, stamped steel, "Mercury" style, articulated, gray, red, or black, electric or clockwork ..	15.00	18.00	20.00
(b) Same as above, blue, regular hook coupler, clockwork only	20.00	25.00	30.00

Articulated & Plastic Trains
Top: Erie
Middle: Roy Rogers
Bottom left to right: clockwork, plastic
Courtesy Richard MacNary

	G	VG	M
643 (a) Caboose, plastic, 4 wheel, green with yellow (or gold) lettering "Western Pacific"	2.00	4.00	6.00
(b) Same as above, 8 wheel Bay Window	4.00	6.00	8.00
645 Caboose, plastic HO, work type, red with white lettering "NH"	.50	1.00	1.50
645 Caboose, plastic HO, bay window green with yellow lettering "Western Pacific"	.50	1.00	1.50
652 Tank Car, 3/16" scale, tin litho, 8 wheel, orange with red lettering "SCCX" & "SHELL"	5.00	7.00	9.00
(657) (a) Passenger Car, tin litho, streamline, 4 wheel trailing truck for M10,000 train, tan and cream with red lettering "Union Pacific" and "Coach"	6.00	8.00	10.00
(b) Same as above, maroon and silver, black lettering	8.00	10.00	12.00
(c) Same as above, green and cream, red lettering	4.00	6.00	8.00

	G	VG	M
(657) (d) Passenger Car, tin litho, streamline, 2 wheel for M10,005 train, green & cream (white) with red lettering "REA/RPO" and "Union "Pacific"	4.00	6.00	8.00
(e) Same as 657(d), marked "Los Angeles"	4.00	6.00	8.00
(f) Same as above, marked "Omaha"	4.00	6.00	8.00
(g) Same as above, marked "Denver"	4.00	6.00	8.00
(657) (h) Passenger Car, tin litho, streamline, 2 wheel for M10,005 train, red and silver with blue lettering "REA/RPO" and "Union Pacific" ..	6.00	8.00	10.00
(i) Same as above, marked "Los Angeles"	6.00	8.00	10.00
(j) Same as above, marked "Omaha"	6.00	8.00	10.00
(k) Same as above, marked "Denver"	6.00	8.00	10.00
(657) (l) Passenger Car, tin litho, streamline, 2 wheel for M10,005 train, yellow and brown, with orange lettering "REA/RPO" and "Union Pacific"	7.00	9.00	11.00
(m) Same as above, marked "Los Angeles	7.00	9.00	11.00
(n) Same as above, marked "Omaha"	7.00	9.00	11.00
(o) Same as above, marked "Denver"	7.00	9.00	11.00
(657) (p) Passenger Car, tin litho, streamline, 2 wheel for NYC Mercury train, gray with white lettering "US Mail-Baggage"	8.00	10.00	12.00
(q) Same as above, marked "Chicago"	8.00	10.00	12.00
(r) Same as above, marked "Toledo"	8.00	10.00	12.00
(s) Same as above, marked "Cleveland"	8.00	10.00	12.00
(657) (t) Passenger Car, tin litho, streamline, 2 wheel for NYC Mercury train, copper (brass) with black lettering "US Mail-Baggage"	10.00	12.00	14.00
(u) Same as above, marked "Chicago"	10.00	12.00	14.00
(v) Same as above, marked "Toledo"	10.00	12.00	14.00
(w) Same as above, marked "Cleveland"	10.00	12.00	14.00
(657) (x) Passenger Car, tin litho, streamline, 2 wheel, for NYC Mercury			

	G	VG	M
train, red with white lettering "Chicago"	8.00	10.00	12.00
(y) Same as above, marked "Toledo"	8.00	10.00	12.00
(z) Same as above, marked "Cleveland"	8.00	10.00	12.00
(658) (a) Passenger Car, Observation, tin litho, streamline, 4 wheel trailing truck for M10,000 train, tan and cream with red lettering "Union Pacific" and "Coach Buffet"	6.00	8.00	10.00
(b) Same as above, maroon and silver with black lettering	8.00	10.00	12.00
(c) Same as above, green and cream with red lettering	4.00	6.00	8.00
(658) (d) Passenger Car, Observation, tin litho, streamline, 2 wheel for M10,005 train, green and cream (white) with red lettering "Squaw Bonnet"	4.00	6.00	8.00
(e) Same as above, red and silver with blue lettering "Squaw Bonnet"	6.00	8.00	10.00
(f) Same as above, yellow and brown with orange lettering "Squaw Bonnet"	7.00	9.00	11.00
(658) (g) Passenger Car, Observation, tin litho, streamline, 2 wheel for NYC Mercury train, gray with white lettering "Detroit"	8.00	10.00	12.00
(h) Same as 658(g), copper (brass), black lettering "Detroit"	10.00	12.00	14.00
(i) Same as above, red, white lettering, "Detroit"	8.00	10.00	12.00
(663) Pole Car, 6″ tin, 4 wheel and 8 wheel with 13 poles and clamp, black	6.00	9.00	12.00
666 (a) Loco, 2-4-2, die cast, black, with and without white stripe, with and without smoke	7.00	10.00	12.00
(b) Same as above, ARMY olive drab, with smoke	15.00	20.00	25.00
694 Caboose, 6″ tin, 4 wheel, red with black letters, "New York Central", black and silver or all black frame .	4.00	8.00	12.00
702 Loco, diesel switcher, plastic, 4 wheel, green with yellow (or gold) lettering "Western Pacific"	2.00	4.00	8.00

Pennsylvania Coal Train
Top left to right: 897(a) loco, tender, 556 caboose
Middle left to right: 567 dump car, 567 dump car, 567 dump car
Bottom left to right: dump tray, 1614 dumping station
Courtesy Richard MacNary

Joy Line
Top left to right: 350 loco, 351(a) tender, 356(a) caboose
Middle left to right: 350 loco, 352(d) gondola, 352(d) gondola
Bottom left to right: 350 loco, 351(a) tender, 357(a) coach
Courtesy Richard MacNary

Joy Line
Top left to right: (late) loco, 351(c) tender, 357(b) coach, 458 observation
Bottom left to right: (middle) loco, 351(b) tender, 357(b) coach, 357(b) coach
Courtesy Richard MacNary

	G	VG	M
720 Loco, streamline steam, tin litho, one piece engine and tender, red-white-blue marked "Coronation Express" (made in Great Britain), friction powered	15.00	20.00	25.00
(734) Loco - see 994/995 "Mickey Mouse" type			
(735) Loco - see 994/995 "Nickel Plate" style			
799 Loco, diesel switcher, plastic, 4 wheel, black with white lettering "Rock Island"	2.00	4.00	8.00
817 Box Car/Refrigerator, 6" tin, 4 wheel, yellow with black letters "Colorado & Southern", black and silver or all black frame	9.00	12.00	15.00
(834) Loco - see 400 Loco			
(896) Loco, Hiawatha type, tin litho, red and white, 4½" long with passenger car 3¾" long	10.00	15.00	20.00
897 (a) Loco, 0-4-0, tin black, litho with gray and white details	15.00	20.00	25.00
(b) Same as above, ARMY olive drab	25.00	35.00	40.00
(898) Loco, 0-4-0, tin, black enamel, electric	2.00	5.00	7.00
901 (a) Loco, diesel, plastic, 8 wheel, green with yellow lettering "Western Pacific", powered "A" unit	6.00	9.00	12.00
(b) Same as 901(a), gray with black lettering	9.00	12.00	15.00

173

	G	VG	M
(c) Same as 901(a), green dummy "A" unit	6.00	9.00	12.00
(d) Same as above, gray dummy "A" unit	9.00	12.00	15.00
(902) (a) Similar 901 (a) dummy "B" unit, green	6.00	9.00	12.00
(b) similar 902 (c) dummy "B" unit, gray	9.00	12.00	15.00
949 Gondola, 7″ tin, 4 wheel, white with blue lettering "Marlines" and brown cow	20.00	25.00	30.00
(951A) Tender, 6″ tin, 4 wheel & 8 wheel, "wedge" style, black with white lettering "New York Central"	3.00	5.00	7.00
952 Tender 6″ tin, 4 wheel, "wedge" style, ARMY olive drab, marked "Army Supply Train"	10.00	15.00	20.00
956 Caboose, 7″ tin, 4 wheel, red and gray with black/white lettering "Nickel Plate Road"	2.00	4.00	6.00
956 Caboose, 6″ tin, 4 wheel, green and yellow with black lettering "Seaboard Air Lines"	6.00	8.00	10.00
(961A) Similar to 951A but with light on top	7.00	9.00	12.00
969 Caboose, plastic, 4 wheel and 8 wheel, red with white lettering "Kansas City Southern"	1.00	2.00	3.00
972 Caboose, 7″ tin, 8 wheel, red-yellow-black with black & yellow lettering "Kansas City Southern" ..	5.00	7.00	9.00
973 Same as above (different number)	5.00	7.00	9.00
974 Same as above, (different number)	5.00	7.00	9.00
980 Same as above (different number)	5.00	7.00	9.00
994 (a) Loco, 0-4-0, tin litho, black Nickel Plate style, white "994", electric or clockwork	6.00	8.00	10.00
(b) Same as above, red	12.00	15.00	20.00
(c) Same as above, Mickey Mouse Meteor, clockwork only	45.00	60.00	75.00
999 (a) Loco, 2-4-2, die cast, black, early with spoked pilot, 3 piece slider pick-up	5.00	10.00	15.00

	G	VG	M
(b) Same as 999(a)...............	1.00	2.00	3.00
(c) Same as above, last style, disc drivers...........................	2.00	5.00	8.00
999 (d) Loco, tin litho, red and black, clockwork, floor type	50.00	75.00	100.00
999 (e) Loco, 0-4-0, plastic, black Plastimarx (made in Mexico) (set) ..	25.00	35.00	45.00
1007 Passenger Car, Observation, 3/16" scale, tin litho, 8 wheel, silver with red lettering "Western Pacific"	8.00	10.00	12.00
1015 Caboose, work, plastic, 8 wheel, black and orange with white lettering "Illinois Central Gulf"	2.00	4.00	6.00
1020 Wrecker, plastic, 8 wheel, black with white lettering "IC"	3.00	4.00	5.00
(1020) Railroad Trestle Bridge, steel	4.00	6.00	8.00
1024 Flat Car, plastic, 8 wheel, black with white lettering "IC"	3.00	4.00	5.00
1095 (a) Loco, diesel, plastic, 8 wheel, red and gray (or silver) with black lettering "Santa Fe", powered "A" unit	6.00	8.00	10.00
(b) Same as above, dummy "A" unit	6.00	8.00	10.00
(1096) Similar to 1095, dummy "B" unit	6.00	8.00	10.00
1182 Rite-O-Way Signs, plastic	1.00	2.00	3.00
1217 (a) Passenger Car, full length Vista Dome, 3/16" scale, tin litho, 8 wheels, silver with red lettering "Western Pacific"	8.00	10.00	12.00
(b) Same as above, Coach, (no Vista Dome)	15.00	18.00	20.00
1231 (a) Caboose, plastic, 4 wheel, blue with white lettering "Missouri Pacific"..........................	.50	1.00	2.00
(b) Same as above, white with black lettering	.50	1.00	2.00
1235 Caboose, 7" tin, 4 wheel, red and silver with white lettering "Southern Pacific"...........................	2.00	4.00	6.00
1281 Rite-O-Way Signs, plastic	1.00	2.00	3.00
(1305) Railroad Girder Bridge, stamped steel, various RR names ...	2.00	3.00	4.00

Flat cars with trucks
Top left to right: 562D stake bed, 562D dump, 562D dump
Middle left to right: 562D tank, 562D auto, 562D bus
Bottom left to right: 562D wrecker, 562D stake bed, 562D dump
Courtesy Richard MacNary

6" Tin cars, miscellaneous
Top left to right: 561(a) searchlight (late plastic), 563A lumber, 550 wrecker
Middle left to right: wheel car, 563A lumber, 550 wrecker
Bottom left to right: 574 barrel car, 572 airplane car, 556 cable car
Courtesy Richard MacNary

	G	VG	M
(1404) Block Signal, stamped steel, 5 lights	4.00	6.00	8.00
(1430) Station, tin litho, "Union Station" 12″ × 6¾″ × 3½″	5.00	7.00	9.00
(1440) Grade Crossing Signal Man, tin and plastic, automatic	3.00	5.00	10.00
1476 Box Car, 7″ tin, 4 wheel, yellow with blue frame, Mickey Mouse figures (Dumbo, etc.)	30.00	35.00	40.00
(---) Gondola, 7″ tin, 4 wheel, blue with blue frame, Mickey Mouse figures (Pluto etc.)	30.00	35.00	40.00
1500 Caboose, plastic, 8 wheel, orange with black lettering "Rio Grande" ..	.50	1.00	2.00
(1614) Automatic Dumping Unit, tin litho, arms swing out to dump car #567, 3¾″ × 2¾″ square	10.00	15.00	20.00
1621 Loco, 2-4-2, plastic, HO, "New Haven"	2.00	4.00	6.00
1654 Caboose, plastic HO, orange and red, marked "UNION PACIFIC" ...	1.00	1.50	2.00
1666 (a) Loco, 2-4-2, plastic, gray, smoke	12.00	15.00	18.00
(b) Same as above, black	10.00	12.00	15.00
1678 Hopper, 6″ tin, 4 wheel, olive with black lettering "General Coal Co." black and silver frame or all black frame	9.00	12.00	15.00
1796 (a) Flat Car with missile launcher, plastic, 4 wheel, white with blue lettering	3.00	5.00	7.00
(b) Same as above, deluxe 8 wheel, white with blue lettering	4.00	6.00	8.00
1798 Loco, diesel switcher, plastic, 4 wheel, red-white-blue with white lettering "Cape Canaveral Express" ..	15.00	20.00	25.00
1799 (a) Gondola, plastic, 4 wheel, blue with white lettering "USAX Danger"	3.00	4.00	5.00
(b) Same as above, 8 wheel, red with white lettering "USAX Danger"	4.00	6.00	8.00
1829 Loco, 4-6-4, plastic, black	12.00	15.00	18.00
1935 (a) U.S. Mail Car, 6″ tin, 4 wheel			

Copper Trains
Top left to right: 397 C.P. loco, 551(e) tender
Middle left to right: 561(a) searchlight, 559(a) floodlight, 556(b) caboose with light
Bottom left to right: 597(b) C.V. loco, 551(e) tender
Courtesy Richard MacNary

	G	VG	M
green with yellow letters "NYC" & "U.S. Mail Car 1935", black and silver frame	10.00	15.00	20.00
(b) Same as above, red with yellow lettering, 4 wheel and 8 wheel	3.00	6.00	9.00
1963 Work Caboose, plastic, 8 wheel, blue frame, red shed, white tank, white lettering "USAX Missile Express" and red lettering on tank "Rocket Fuel"	10.00	15.00	20.00
1950 (a) Box Car, 3/16" scale, tin litho, 8 wheel, green with yellow lettering "GAEX-DF" on yellow diagonal stripe	6.00	8.00	10.00
(b) Same as above, just "DF" on yellow stripe	6.00	8.00	10.00
1951 Caboose, 7" tin, 8 wheel, red with black lettering "AT&SF"	2.00	4.00	6.00
1958 AT&SF work caboose, plastic, HO	1.00	1.50	2.00
1961 Caboose, plastic, HO, red and black with white lettering "Rock Island"	.50	1.00	1.50

178

Various locomotives
Top left to right: Marline C.P. loco, 961A tender, 556(b) caboose with light
Middle left to right: C.P. loco, 551(c) tender
Bottom left to right: C.V. loco, 551(c) tender
Courtesy Richard MacNary

	G	VG	M
1977 (a) Caboose, plastic, 8 wheel and 4 wheel, red with white lettering "Santa Fe"	1.00	2.00	3.00
(b) Same as above, red-yellow-gray, 8 wheel only	6.00	8.00	10.00
1988 Caboose, plastic, 4 wheel, orange with black lettering "Bessemer & Lake Erie"	2.00	5.00	8.00
1998 (a) Loco, diesel switcher, plastic, 8 wheel, maroon with yellow lettering "AT&SF"	10.00	15.00	20.00
(b) Same as above, black with white lettering "AT&SF"	10.00	15.00	20.00
(c) Same as above, blue with white lettering "All State"	10.00	15.00	20.00
(d) Same as above, yellow & gray with red lettering "Union Pacific"	10.00	15.00	20.00
(e) Same as above, gray & red with black or white lettering "Rock Island"	10.00	15.00	20.00
2002 (a) Loco, diesel, plastic, 8 wheel, powered "A" unit, black-red-white lettering "New Haven"	12.00	15.00	18.00

	G	VG	M
(b) Same as 2002(a)	12.00	15.00	18.00
(2003) Similar to 2002, dummy "B" unit	12.00	15.00	18.00
(2002) Hand Car, plastic, two men, red or brown base	5.00	15.00	25.00
2028 "Flintstones" Bedrock Handcar, Set	25.00	50.00	75.00
2071 Passenger Car, 6″ tin, 4 wheel, silver with blue lettering "New York Central"	6.00	9.00	12.00
2072 Same as above, Observation ..	6.00	9.00	12.00
2124 Rail Diesel Car, plastic, 8 wheel, passenger, gray (silver) with black lettering "Boston & Maine	35.00	50.00	75.00
2130 Caboose/Work, plastic, 8 wheel, olive drab with white lettering "U.S.A." and star	10.00	15.00	20.00
2225 (a) Caboose, bay window, plastic, 8 wheel, dark red with white lettering "Santa Fe"	3.00	5.00	7.00
(b) Same as above, orange with black lettering "All State"	5.00	7.00	10.00
(c) Same as above, blue with white lettering "All State"	5.00	7.00	10.00
2226 Caboose, plastic, bay window, HO, red with white lettering "Santa Fe"	.25	.50	.75
2236 Gondola, plastic, 8 wheel, ARMY olive drab with white lettering "U.S.A."	5.00	7.00	9.00
(2246) Flat Car, plastic, deluxe, 8 wheel, ARMY olive drab with plastic jeep, truck, etc.	7.00	10.00	12.00
2260 "Guide-A-Train" Set, plastic ..	12.50	19.00	25.00
2366 Caboose, plastic, 8 wheel, dark red with white lettering "Canadian Pacific"	5.00	7.00	10.00
2532 (a) Tank Car, 3/16″ scale, tin litho, 8 wheel, green with white lettering "Cities Service"	5.00	7.00	9.00
2532 (b) Tank Car, plastic, 4 wheel and 8 wheel, green with white lettering "Cities Service"	1.00	1.50	2.00

180

Floor Trains
Top left to right: loco, tender, coach
Middle left to right: gondola, gondola
Bottom left to right: loco/tender, gondola
Courtesy Richard MacNary

Western Pacific Set
Top left to right: 901(a) loco (powered A), 902 loco (dummy B)
Middle left to right: 5543(c) flat with two tanks, 21429 hopper
Bottom left to right: 5553(b) tank car, 4528(b) flat with tractors, 643 caboose
Courtesy Richard MacNary

	G	VG	M
2552 Loco, 2-8-2 Kit, plastic snap-together 5/16″ = 1′ scale (very nice) .	10.00	15.00	20.00
(2572) Ramp Car, 6″ tin, 3/16″, 8 wheel trucks, ARMY olive drab with end unloading ramp and OD truck .	25.00	35.00	45.00
2700 (a) Flat Car, 3/16″ scale, tin litho, 8 wheel, black with white lettering "NKP" with 3 sets of stakes	5.00	7.00	9.00
(b) Same as above, no stakes (no holes)	5.00	7.00	9.00
2731 Tender, plastic, deluxe 8 wheel, block with white lettering "SANTA FE" and "2731"	5.00	7.00	9.00
2824 (a) Gondola, plastic, 8 wheel, missile launcher, yellow with red lettering "USAF"	9.00	12.00	15.00
(b) Same as above, olive drab	9.00	12.00	15.00
2824 (c) Flat Car, plastic, deluxe 8 wheel, Army olive drab, white lettering, missile launcher	7.00	9.00	12.00
2858 Box Car, plastic, deluxe 8 wheel, ARMY olive drab with white lettering "Bureau of Ordinance"	9.00	12.00	15.00
(2889) Station, whistling, tin litho, battery operated, 9″ × 5½″ × 2⅝″	3.00	5.00	8.00
2900 Station, "Glendale Freight Depot", tin litho, lamp post, mechanical gate 13⅝″ × 10″ × 5″	20.00	25.00	30.00
(2940) Station, illuminated, tin litho, "Grand Central Station", 17″ × 11″ × 4¾″	20.00	25.00	30.00
(2959/2970) Station, whistling, tin litho, "Girard" 9″ × 5½″ × 5″	5.00	7.00	10.00
(2980) Station, diesel horn, tin litho, "Oak Park", same as (2970) 9″ × 5½″ × 5″	8.00	12.00	15.00
3000 Loco, 0-4-0 and 2-4-2, Canadian Pacific style, various boiler colors and side boards	10.00	15.00	20.00
3000 Loco, Riding Floor Toy, stamped steel, red or gray front wheels steer thru handle in boiler top	20.00	30.00	40.00
3152 (a) Passenger Car, 3/16″ scale,			

	G	VG	M
tin litho, 8 wheel, silver with red lettering "Santa Fe"	8.00	10.00	12.00
(b) Same as above, solid window ...	8.00	10.00	12.00
(c) Same as above, vista dome	8.00	10.00	12.00
(d) Same as above, vista dome with solid windows	8.00	10.00	12.00
3197 (a) Passenger Car, 3/16″ scale, tin litho, 8 wheel, observation, silver with red lettering "Santa Fe"	8.00	10.00	12.00
(b) Same as 3197(a), solid windows .	8.00	10.00	12.00
3200 Box Car, 3/16″ scale, tin litho, 8 wheels, brown with white lettering "NY, NH, & H"	6.00	8.00	10.00
3280 (a) Box Car, plastic, 8 wheel, orange with black lettering "Santa Fe"	.50	1.00	1.50
(b) Same as above, 4 wheel, white with black or red lettering	.25	.50	.75
3281 (a) Box Car, plastic HO, green with white lettering "SFRD" and "SANTA FE"	1.00	1.50	2.00
3281 (b) Same as above except orange with black lettering	1.00	1.50	2.00
(3550) Wrecker, 3/16″ scale with ugly plastic top on tin litho base, 8 wheel, gray and black	10.00	15.00	20.00
3557 (a) Passenger Car, 3/16″ scale, tin litho, 8 wheel, all silver with blue lettering "New York Central"	10.00	12.00	15.00
(b) Same as above, solid windows ..	10.00	12.00	15.00
(c) Same as above, vista dome	10.00	12.00	15.00
(d) Same as above, vista dome, solid windows	10.00	12.00	15.00
3558 (a) Passenger car, 3/16″ scale, tin litho, 8 wheel, observation, silver with blue lettering "NYC"	10.00	12.00	15.00
(b) Same as above, solid windows ..	10.00	12.00	15.00
(3561) Flat Car, 3/16″ scale with ugly plastic searchlight on tin litho base, 8 wheel, red and black	10.00	15.00	20.00
(3563) Lumber Car, 3/16″ scale with lumber load on tin litho base, 8 wheel, black	5.00	7.50	10.00

Illinois Central Work Train, Set #27152
Top left to right: (I) loco, 1020 wrecker
Middle left to right: 24 searchlight, 1024 flat with racks
Bottom: 1015 work caboose
Courtesy Richard MacNary

Small plastic diesels
Top left to right: 799 RI loco, 588(c) NYC loco
Middle left to right: 702 WP loco (gold), 588(a) NYC loco
Bottom left to right: 702 WP loco (yellow), 588(b) NYC loco
Courtesy Richard MacNary

Missouri Pacific Set #7360
Top left to right: (m) loco, flat with auto
Bottom left to right: 9553(c) tank car, 1231 caboose
Courtesy Richard MacNary

Lehigh Valley Set
Top left to right: 112 loco, 3280(b) box car
Bottom left to right: 715100 gondola, 95050 caboose
Courtesy Richard MacNary

Marline Set
Top left to right: 198 loco, tender
Bottom left to right: box car, caboose
Courtesy Richard MacNary

Gray 1666 Set with sound
Top left to right: 1666 loco, tender with sound
Bottom left to right: 34178 box car, 1977 caboose
Courtesy Richard MacNary

	G	VG	M
3824 (a) Caboose, 6″ tin, 4 wheel, yellow, orange and brown, orange lettering "Union Pacific", black frame	1.00	2.00	3.00
(b) Same as above, brown frame	2.00	4.00	6.00
3824 (c) Caboose, bay window, plastic, 8 wheel, dark red with white lettering "Union Pacific"	2.00	3.00	4.00
(d) Same as above, work caboose	3.00	5.00	7.00
3827 Tank Car, plastic, HO, green with white lettering "Sinclair"	.25	.50	.75
3855 Caboose, 7″ tin, 4 wheel, red-gray-white with white lettering "MONON"	3.00	5.00	8.00
3880 Railroad Station, plastic, 11¾″ × 6¼″ × 4⅝″	.50	1.00	1.50
3900 (a) Caboose, plastic, 8 wheel, orange (or yellow) with black lettering "Union Pacific"	.50	1.00	1.50
(b) Same as above, brown with white lettering	.50	1.00	1.50
(c) Same as above, 4 wheel, yellow with black lettering	.50	1.00	1.50
3903 Caboose, plastic HO, bay window, red with white lettering "Union Pacific"	.50	.75	1.00
4000 (a) Loco, diesel, plastic, 8 wheel, powered "A" unit, black with white lettering "New York Central"	10.00	12.00	15.00
(b) Same as above, dummy "A" unit	10.00	12.00	15.00

186

	G	VG	M
(c) Same as 4000(a), dummy "B" unit	10.00	12.00	15.00
(d) Same as above, green, powered "A" unit	12.00	15.00	18.00
(e) Same as above, dummy "A" unit	12.00	15.00	18.00
4000 (f) Loco, diesel, small tin litho, 4 wheel, powered "A", green with yellow lettering "Seaboard"	10.00	12.00	15.00
(g) Same as above, dummy "A"	10.00	12.00	15.0
4000 (h) Loco, diesel HO plastic "A" unit black, marked NYC	2.00	3.00	4.00
4015 Reefer, plastic HO, white marked "NYC"	1.00	2.00	3.00
(4414, 16, 18) Station, tin litho, "Glendale" 20⅝" × 10" × 6"	15.00	22.50	30.00
4427 Caboose, plastic, 8 wheel, red with white or black lettering "Santa Fe"	1.00	1.50	2.00
4484 Box Car, 7" tin, 4 wheel, blue-white-red, white and blue lettering "BAR" and "State of Maine"	2.00	5.00	8.00
4485/4500 Box Car, 6" tin, 4 wheel, blue to white-red, white and blue lettering "BAR" and "State of Maine"	3.00	5.00	8.00
4528 (a) Flat Car, plastic, deluxe, 8 wheel, maroon with yellow lettering "Erie" searchlight	1.00	3.00	5.00
(b) Same as above, flat with farm tractors	3.00	4.00	5.00
(4556) (a) Caboose, plastic, 4 wheel and 8 wheel, red white lettering "Southern Pacific"	.50	1.00	1.50
(b) Same as above, green, 4 wheel only	.50	1.00	1.50
4564 Caboose, plastic, 8 wheel, red with white or black lettering "New York Central"	.50	1.00	1.50
4566 Flat Car, plastic, deluxe, 8 wheel, drop center with 2 cable reels, blue with white lettering "C.W.E.X."	1.00	3.00	5.00
4571 (a) Flat Car, plastic deluxe, 8 wheel, searchlight, red with white lettering "W.E.C.X."	1.00	3.00	5.00
(b) Same as above, white "U.S.A.F."	5.00	7.00	9.00

	G	VG	M
(c) Same as 4571(a), maroon with white "A.T. & S.F."	2.00	3.00	4.00
4581 Flat Car, plastic, deluxe, 8 wheel, red with white lettering "B.K.X.", searchlight	2.00	4.00	6.00
4583 Flat Car, plastic, deluxe, 8 wheel, black with white lettering "G.E.X.", searchlight	2.00	3.00	4.00
4586 Caboose, plastic, work type, 8 wheels, red with white lettering "Union Pacific" with light	2.00	4.00	6.00
(4587) Same as above, "AT & SF"	2.00	4.00	6.00
(4588) Same as above, "All State"	2.00	4.00	6.00
(4589) Same as above, "New York Central", no light, with tank	5.00	7.00	10.00
4590 Same as above, "AT & SF"	3.00	5.00	7.00
5011/5026 Baggage Car, 6" tin, 4 wheel, blue and gray body with white lettering "New York Central" and "U.S. Mail"	3.00	5.00	7.00
(5424) RR Freight Terminal, tin litho, 28" × 11" × 8" (some come with plastic trucks & accessories)	10.00	15.00	20.00
5532 Gondola, plastic, 4 wheel and 8 wheel, blue with white lettering "All State"	.50	1.00	2.00
(5543) (a) Tank Car, plastic, deluxe, 8 wheel, two tanks maroon and white lettering "All State"	2.00	4.00	6.00
(b) Same as above, blue and orange with black lettering "Gulf"	2.00	4.00	6.00
(c) Same as above, maroon and green with white "Cities Service"	2.00	4.00	6.00
5545 (a) Flat Car, plastic, deluxe, 8 wheel, maroon with white lettering "C.B.&Q", orange "All State"trailers	5.00	7.00	9.00
(b) Same as above, silver or red "Burlington" trailers	6.00	9.00	12.00
(c) Same as above, "Erie" girders	2.00	4.00	6.00
(5553) (a) Tank Car, plastic, deluxe, 8 wheel, three domes blue and white with red lettering "EXXON"	2.00	4.00	6.00
(b) Same as above, black and blue with white "All State"	1.00	2.00	3.00

Marx-Tronic Electric Train Set #2893, page 217

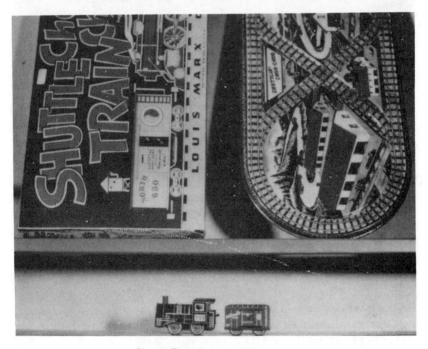

Shuttle Train Set, page 217
Courtesy Richard MacNary

Small tin trains
Top left to right: #44 "Super Chief" loco/tender (clockwork)
#44 "Super Chief" loco/tender (friction)
Bottom left to right: #93 "Lumar Lines" loco/tender, #720 "Coronation Express loco/tender
Courtesy Richard MacNary

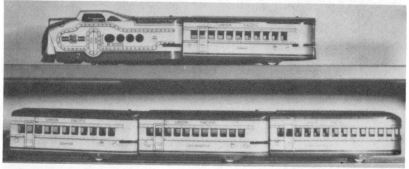

M10,005 Silver & Red
Top left to right: M10,005(a) loco, 657(j) Omaha coach
Bottom left to right: 657(k) Denver coach, 657(i) Los Angeles coach, 658(e) Squaw Bonnet
observation
Courtesy Richard MacNary

	G	VG	M
5563 Caboose, 6″ tin, 4 wheel, black, yellow and red body, red and yellow lettering "Kansas City Southern" ..	6.00	8.00	10.00
5586 Caboose, plastic, work type, 8 wheels, red brown with yellow lettering "Western Pacific"	3.00	5.00	7.00
5594 Flat Car, operating, plastic, 8 wheel, maroon with yellow lettering, "Erie"	3.00	5.00	7.00
5595 Box Car, plastic, operating, deluxe 8 wheel, cream with red lettering "Farm Master Brand	4.00	6.00	8.00
(5772) NYC diesel loco, HO	2.00	4.00	6.00
6000 (a) Loco, diesel, medium tin litho,			

	G	VG	M
8 wheel powered "A" unit, orange with black lettering "Southern Pacific"	9.00	12.00	15.00
(b) Same as above, dummy "A" unit	9.00	12.00	15.00
6028 Erie flat car with side racks, HO	.50	.75	1.25
6096 Loco, 4-6-4, plastic HO, black with white lettering & stripe, with NYC tender	7.00	10.00	15.00
(6150) Wrecker, plastic HO, black with white "NYC" emblem	2.00	3.00	4.00
(6420) Trestle bridge, HO	.25	.50	.75
6938 Loco, GP-7, plastic, HO, black and gold with gold lettering "Northern Pacific"	4.00	6.00	8.00
7210 Box Car, plastic "HO", green with white and yellow lettering Railway Express Agency	3.00	6.00	9.00
9100 Box Car, 3/16″ scale, tin litho, 8 wheels, red and black with white lettering "Union Pacific"	6.00	8.00	10.00
(9553) (a) Tank Car, plastic, 8 wheel, blue with white lettering "All State"	2.00	3.00	4.00
Same as above, white with red "All State Rocket Fuel	2.00	4.00	6.00
(c) Same as above, orange with black "Gulf" 4 wheel and 8 wheel	1.00	2.00	3.00
M10,000 (a) Loco, streamliner, tin litho, 4 drivers, 4 trailing wheels, electric, tan and cream with red lettering "Union Pacific"	20.00	25.00	30.00
(b) Same as above, maroon and silver, black lettering	25.00	30.00	35.00
(c) Same as above, green and cream, red lettering	18.00	22.00	25.00
(NOTE: for matching articulated cars, see numbers (657) and (658)			
M10,003 Loco, streamliner, tin litho, clockwork, one unit, tan and cream with black lettering "Union Pacific"	30.00	40.00	50.00
M10,005 (a) Loco, streamliner, tin litho, 4 drivers, electric and clockwork, silver and red with blue lettering "Union Pacific"	12.00	16.00	18.00

191

Marx Handcars
Top: Moon Mullins & Kayo — deluxe, page 217
Middle left to right: 2002 late (brown), 2002 late (red)
Bottom left to right: Flintstones (set 2028) Barney & Fred handcar with plastic base,
    Mickey Mouse & Donald Duck plastic handcar with tin base, page 217
Courtesy Richard MacNary

Three miscellaneous engines
Top: #999 clockwork — floor train
Middle left to right: 898 loco, 951 "nickel plate road" short tender
Bottom left to right: 391 loco, C.P. tender
Courtesy Richard MacNary

Marx "Blue Comet"
Top left to right: 635(b) loco, 551(d) tender
Bottom left to right: 557(e) Bogota, 557(e) Montclair, 558(d) observation
Courtesy Richard MacNary

	G	VG	M
(b) Same as M10,0005(a), yellow and brown with orange lettering	15.00	18.00	20.00
(c) Same as above, white (or cream) and green with orange lettering	12.00	16.00	18.00
(NOTE: For matching articulated cars, see number (657) and (658)			
10049 Flat Car with lumber load, plastic HO, black with white lettering "LV"	1.00	1.50	2.00
10961/10976 Refrigerator Car, 6″ tin, 4 wheel, yellow with gray roof and black letters, marked "Fruit Growers Express"	3.00	5.00	8.00
11874 Box Car, plastic, HO, green or red with white lettering "Great Northern"	1.00	2.00	3.00
13079 Hopper, 3/16″ scale, tin litho, 8 wheel black with white lettering "LNE"	7.00	10.00	12.00
13549 Stock Car, 3/16″ scale, tin litho, 4 and 8 wheels, orange and yellow with brown lettering "AT & SF"	6.00	8.00	10.00
13795 (a) Stock Car, plastic, 8 wheel, yellow with black lettering "AT & SF"	.50	1.00	2.00
(b) Same as above, brown with white lettering (4 wheel also)	.50	1.00	2.00
(c) Same as above, maroon (red) with white lettering	.50	1.00	2.00

Handcar Set
Mickey Mouse & Donald Duck plastic handcar with tin base, page 217
Courtesy Richard MacNary

	G	VG	M
17858 (a) Caboose, plastic, bay window, 8 wheel, red with white lettering "Rock Island"	1.00	3.00	5.00
(b) Same as above, 4 wheel and 8 wheel (regular caboose)	.50	1.00	2.00
17899 Gondola, 3/16" scale, tin litho, 8 wheels, gray with white lettering "T&P"	5.00	7.00	9.00
18326 (a) Caboose, plastic, 4 wheel and 8 wheel, red with white lettering "New York Central" some with "Pacemaker"	.50	1.00	1.50
(b) Same as above, brown, white lettering	.50	1.00	1.50
(c) Same as above, yellow, black lettering	.50	1.00	1.50
(d) Same as above, white (cream) black	.50	1.00	1.50
(e) Same as above, white-black-green, red lettering (8 wheel only)	.50	1.00	1.50
(18326) (f) Same as above, orange, black lettering (no number)	.50	1.00	1.50
(g) Same as above, green, white lettering	.50	1.00	1.50

194

	G	VG	M
(h) Same as 18326(g), white, black lettering	.50	1.00	1.50
(i) Same as above, green, white lettering	.50	1.00	1.50
(j) Same as above, yellow, black lettering (4 wheel only)	.50	1.00	1.50
18918 Box Car, plastic, deluxe 8 wheel, brown with white lettering "Great Northern"	4.00	6.00	8.00
19847 (a) Tank Car, 6″, tin, 4 wheel, black with white lettering "Sinclair"	3.00	5.00	7.00
(b) Same as above, green with white lettering "Sinclair"	3.00	5.00	7.00
20053 Box Car, plastic, deluxe, 8 wheel, dark red (or brown) with white lettering "Seaboard"	4.00	6.00	8.00
20102 (a) Caboose, 6″ tin, 4 wheel, red and gray body with white lettering "NYC"	2.00	3.00	4.00
(b) Same as above, with light	6.00	8.00	12.00
20102 (c) Caboose, 3/16″ scale, tin litho, 8 wheel red and gray, white lettering "NYC"	1.00	2.00	3.00
20110/20124 Caboose, 7″ tin, 4 wheel and 8 wheel, red and gray with white "NYC" & "Pacemaker"	2.00	5.00	8.00
20295 Caboose, plastic HO, black and red with white lettering "NYC"	.50	.75	1.00
20298 Caboose, plastic HO, bay window, red with white lettering "NYC"	.50	1.00	1.50
21429 Hopper, plastic, deluxe, 8 wheel, black with yellow (orange) lettering "Lehigh Valley"	2.00	3.00	4.00
21913 (a) Hopper, plastic, 4 wheel and 8 wheel, black with yellow lettering "Lehigh Valley"	.50	1.00	1.50
(b) Same as above, blue with white lettering	.50	1.00	1.50
(c) Same as above, orange with black lettering	.50	1.00	1.50
(d) Same as 21913(a), red and white lettering	.50	1.00	1.50

Disneyland express, page 217
Tin articulated with tin base
Courtesy Richard MacNary

Scenic Express Set, page 221
Tin and plastic articulated "Erie" with tin base.
Courtesy Richard MacNary

196

Deluxe plastic freight cars
Top left to right: 54099 stock car, 54099 stock car
Middle left to right: 5595 refrigerator, 249319 box car
Bottom left to right: 4587 work caboose, 20053 box car
Courtesy Richard MacNary

Canadian Pacific cars
Top left to right: 246 Montreal, 248 Quebec, 247 Toronto
Middle left to right: 249 Ottawa, 250 Winnipeg
Bottom left to right: 251 Vancouver, 252 Calgary, 253 Hamilton
Courtesy Richard MacNary

	G	VG	M
(e) Same as 21913(a), green with white lettering (4 wheel only)	.50	1.00	1.50
25000 Hopper, plastic HO, black with orange lettering "LV" (Lionel's Number)	.50	.75	1.00
28236 (a) Hopper, plastic, deluxe 8 wheel, brown with white lettering "Virginian"	5.00	7.00	9.00
(b) Same as above, maroon	5.00	7.00	9.00
(c) Same as above, red	5.00	7.00	9.00
28500 High Side Gondola, 6" tin, 4 wheel green with silver lettering "Lehigh Valley"	2.00	4.00	6.00
30982 Gondola, 7" tin, 4 wheel, yellow with black lettering "Wabash"	6.00	8.00	10.00
31055 Caboose, 6" tin, 4 wheel, red and gray body, white lettering "Monon"	4.00	6.00	8.00
33618 Caboose, plastic HO, red and white, bay window "ERIE"	.50	.75	1.00
33621 Caboose, plastic HO, yellow with black lettering "C&O"	.50	.75	1.00
33773 Flat Car, 3/16" scale, tin litho, 8 wheel black with white lettering "B&M"	6.00	9.00	12.00
34178 Box Car, plastic, 8 wheel, green with white lettering, "Great Northern"	1.00	2.00	3.00
35461 Refrigerator, 3/16" scale, tin litho, 8 wheel brown roof, yellow sides with black lettering "PFE"	6.00	8.00	10.00
36000 Gondola, 7" tin, 4 wheel, brown with white lettering "C&O"	1.00	2.00	3.00
36000 Gondola, plastic HO, blue with white lettering "C&O"	.50	.75	1.00
37950/37959 Box car, 7" tin, 4 wheel, red and gray with gray roof, black lettering "Pennsylvania" and "Merchandise Service"	2.00	5.00	8.00
37960/37975 Box Car, 6" tin, 4 wheel, red and gray with gray roof, black lettering, marked "Merchandise Service" & "Pennsylvania" (also one with no number)	2.00	5.00	8.00

Mexican, Set #5063, page 221
Plaxtimarx train set with accessories
Courtesy Richard MacNary

Speedway Set #2065
Mechanical speedway with one tin train, one plastic train and plastic track
Courtesy Richard MacNary

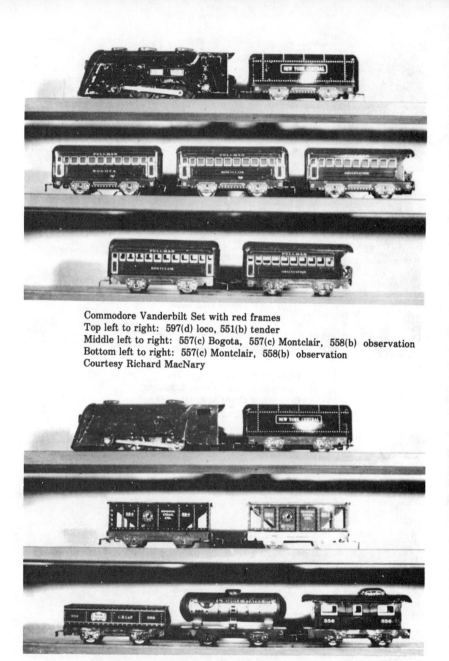

Commodore Vanderbilt Set with red frames
Top left to right: 597(d) loco, 551(b) tender
Middle left to right: 557(c) Bogota, 557(c) Montclair, 558(b) observation
Bottom left to right: 557(c) Montclair, 558(b) observation
Courtesy Richard MacNary

Commodore Vanderbilt Set with nickel frames
Top left to right: 597B loco, 551(b) tender
Middle left to right: 554(b) hopper, 554(a) hopper
Bottom left to right: 552(b) gondola, 553(b) tank car, 556 caboose
Courtesy Richard MacNary

Commodore Vanderbilt Set with red frames
Top left to right: 597(d) loco, 951A tender
Middle left to right: 555(b) refrigerator, 553(b) tank car, 555(c) refrigerator
Bottom left to right: 552(b) gondola, 554(b) hopper, 556 caboose
Courtesy Richard MacNary

Canadian Pacific Set with red 8 wheel frames & automatic couplers
Top left to right: 391 loco, tender
Middle left to right: 557(c) Bogota, 557(c) Montclair, 556 caboose
Bottom left to right: 555(b) refrigerator car, 562D flat with truck, 554(b) hopper
Courtesy Richard MacNary

201

Allstate Train
Top left to right: loco, 284 tank car
Middle left to right: 28236 hopper, 28236 hopper
Bottom left to right: 21429 hopper, 2225(c) caboose
Courtesy Richard MacNary

Allstate Train
Top left to right: 52 loco, 53 loco
Middle left to right: 51 loco, 4571 searchlight
Bottom left to right: 4528 flat with lumber, 5594 log car, 2225(b) caboose
Courtesy Richard MacNary

Deluxe plastic freight cars
Top left to right: 5545 flat with trailers, 51100 flat with autos
Middle left to right: 5590 wrecker, 51170 gondola
Bottom left to right: 339234 gondola, 259199 box car, 2366 caboose
Courtesy Richard MacNary

Deluxe box cars
Top left to right: 18918 box car, 147815 box car
Middle left to right: 43461 box car, 186028 box car
Bottom left to right: 176893 box car, 77003 box car
Courtesy Richard MacNary

Late Clockwork Set
Top left to right: loco, 551(b) tender
Middle left to right: 2071 pullman, 2071 pullman, 2072 observation
Bottom: custom painted #5344 "Commodore Vanderbilt"
Courtesy Richard MacNary

Canadian Pacific Passenger Set
Top left to right: 3000 loco, tender, 246 "Montreal"
Middle left to right: 247 "Toronto", 248 "Quebec", 249 "Ottawa", 250 "Winnipeg"
Bottom left to right: 251 "Vancouver", 252 "Calgary", 253 "Hamilton"
Courtesy Richard MacNary

Kansas City Southern & 6" cars
Top left to right: 54(a) loco (powered A), 55(b) loco (dummy B - 8 wheels)
Middle left to right: 55(a) loco (dummy B - 4 wheels), 54(b) loco (dummy A)
Bottom left to right: 567 NYC dump car, 561(a) searchlight, 5563 caboose
Courtesy Richard MacNary

MONON & 6" cars
Top left to right: 81F(a) loco (powered A), 84(b) loco (dummy B- 8 wheels)
Middle left to right: 82(a) loco (dummy B - 4 wheels), 81F(b) loco (dummy A)
Bottom left to right: PRR box car (no number), 562D flat with truck, 31055 caboose
Courtesy Richard MacNary

205

Various locomotives
Top: C.P. with light blue letter boards
Middle: C.P. with flat black (crackle) tender
Bottom: C.P. gray and maroon
Courtesy Richard MacNary

	G	VG	M
39520 (a) Flat Car, plastic, deluxe 8 wheel, tool box generator, winch, maroon with yellow "S.P."	1.00	3.00	5.00
(b) Same as above, black with white lettering "S.P."	1.00	3.00	5.00
40397 Box Car, plastic HO, black with white and red "NEW HAVEN"	2.00	3.00	4.00
43461 Box Car, plastic, deluxe 8 wheel, white (or cream) with red lettering "Pacific Fruit Express"	4.00	6.00	8.00
44534 Flat Car, plastic, deluxe 8 wheel, gray with blue lettering "S.A.L.", black or gray pipe	2.00	4.00	6.00
44572 High Side Gondola, 3/16" scale, tin litho, 8 wheels, black with white lettering "C&O"	5.00	7.00	9.00
46010 (a) Box Car, 6" tin, 4 wheel and 8 wheel, sliding door, brown with yellow lettering "SSW Cotton Belt Route"	4.00	6.00	8.00
(b) Same as above, red with yellow lettering	4.00	6.00	8.00

Late Clockwork Set
Top left to right: loco, 551(b) tender, 241708 B&O gondola
Middle left to right: 19847 SINCLAIR tank car, 552(c) CRI&P gondola, 556 NYC caboose
Bottom left to right: developmental loco, developmental loco (from Marx archives)
Courtesy Richard MacNary

	G	VG	M
(c) Same as 46101(a), red with silver lettering	4.00	6.00	8.00
(d) Same as above, blue with white lettering	4.00	6.00	8.00
(e) Same as above, yellow with white lettering	4.00	6.00	8.00
(f) Same as above, orange with white lettering	4.00	6.00	8.00
51100 (a) Flat Car, double auto carrier, plastic, deluxe 8 wheel, maroon with yellow lettering "Southern", 4 autos	2.00	4.00	6.00
(b) Same as above, blue with white lettering	3.00	5.00	7.00
51170 (a) Gondola, plastic, 8 wheel, black with white lettering "Erie"	1.00	2.00	3.00
(b) Same as above, orange with black lettering	3.00	4.00	5.00
(c) Same as above, blue with white lettering	1.00	2.00	3.00

MONON Freight Set
Top left to right: 81F(a) loco (powered "A"), 82(a) loco (dummy "B")
Middle left to right: 19847 SINCLAIR tank car, 28500 high side gondola,
     31005 Monon caboose
Bottom left to right: 81F(c), loco, C-350 Caboose
Courtesy Richard MacNary

Tin ATSF & 7" cars, set #45225
Top: 21 Santa Fe loco
Middle left to right: 44572 C&O high side gondola, 1950 GAEX box car
Bottom left to right: 652 SHELL tank car, 1951 ATSF caboose
Courtesy Richard MacNary

208

	G	VG	M
51998 (a) Box Car, 6″ tin, 4 wheel and 8 wheel, sliding door, blue with white lettering "Chicago and North Western" "400 Stream Liners"	4.00	6.00	8.00
(b) Same as above, brown with orange lettering	4.00	6.00	8.00
(c) Same as above, red with silver lettering	4.00	6.00	8.00
(d) Same as above, red with silver lettering, 4 wheel only	4.00	6.00	8.00
(e) Same as above, orange with white lettering	4.00	6.00	8.00
(f) Same as above, yellow with white lettering	4.00	6.00	8.00
53941 Stock Car, 3/16″ scale, tin litho, 8 wheel brown with white lettering "Pennsylvania"	30.00	40.00	50.00
54099 (a) Stock Car, plastic, deluxe 8 wheel, red with white lettering "Missouri Pacific" & "I-GN"	4.00	6.00	8.00
(b) Same as above, yellow with black lettering	6.00	8.00	10.00
(c) Same as above, green with white lettering	4.00	6.00	8.00
54201 Gondola, plastic HO red with white "WESTERN MARYLAND" ..	2.00	3.00	4.00
70018 Hopper, plastic, HO, red with white lettering "Western Maryland"	.50	1.00	1.50
70311 Box Car, 3/16″ scale, tin litho, 8 wheels, brown with white lettering "Pennsylvania"	6.00	8.00	10.00
71499 Gondola, 3/16″ scale, tin litho, 8 wheel, black with white lettering "NKP" & "NYC & STL"	5.00	7.00	9.00
74005 Box Car, plastic HO blue with white "B&M"	2.00	3.00	4.00
74563 Flat Car, plastic, deluxe with lumber, red with white (or black) lettering "A.C.L."	2.00	4.00	6.00
77003 Box Car, plastic, deluxe 8 wheel, blue with white lettering "B&M"	4.00	6.00	8.00
78450 Tank Car, plastic HO, gray with black "GATX" and "HOOFER"	1.00	2.00	3.00

Guid-A-Train, Set #2260
Tin articulated train, battery operated with curved pieces for corners.
Courtesy Richard MacNary

Mechanical Trains
Top: Honeymoon Express, (early) with original box, page 221
Bottom: Musical Choo-Choo, Linemar (in girls' train colors), page 221
Courtesy Richard MacNary

	G	VG	M
80410 Flat Car, 3/16″ scale, tin litho, 8 wheel black with white lettering "C&O"	5.00	7.00	9.00
80982 Gondola, 7″ tin litho 4 wheels, yellow with black markings "WABASH"	2.00	3.00	4.00
86000 (a) High Side Gondola, 6″ tin, 4 wheel bright blue with red lettering "Lackawanna"	6.00	9.00	12.00
(b) Hopper, 6″ tin, 4 wheel, bright blue with red lettering "Lackawanna"	2.00	3.00	4.00
90171 (a) Box Car, 6″ tin, 4 wheel and 8 wheel, yellow, with white lettering "B&LE" & "Bessemer"	4.00	6.00	8.00
(b) Same as above, orange with black lettering	4.00	6.00	8.00
(c) Same as 90171(b), brown and white lettering	4.00	6.00	8.00
(d) Same as above, blue with white lettering	4.00	6.00	8.00
(e) Same as above, red with silver lettering (4 wheel only)	4.00	6.00	8.00
90798 Caboose, plastic HO, red marked "CRI&D"	1.00	2.00	3.00
91257 (a) Gondola, 6″ tin, 4 wheel, light brown with white lettering "Seaboard"	10.00	15.00	20.00
(b) Same as above, blue with white lettering	5.00	7.50	10.00
(c) Same as above, red with white lettering	2.00	3.00	4.00
91453 Refrigerator car, 6″ tin, 4 wheel, yellow with black letters, marked "Colorado & Southern RR", black and silver or all black frame	6.00	9.00	12.00
92812 Caboose, 3/16″ scale, tin litho, 8 wheels, red with white lettering "Reading"	1.00	2.00	3.00
95050 Caboose, plastic, 4 wheel, red with white lettering "Lehigh Valley"	.50	1.00	1.50
(---) Caboose, plastic, 4 wheel, red with white (or silver) lettering "Marlines"	5.00	7.00	9.00

Three NYC Engines
Top left to right: loco, 551(b) tender, 20102 caboose
Middle left to right: 597(b) loco, 551(c) tender, 556 caboose
Bottom left to right: 635(a) loco, 551(f) tender, 556 caboose
Courtesy Richard MacNary

Mickey Mouse Meteor Set
Top left to right: 994(c) loco, tender
Middle left to right: 1476 box car, gondola
Bottom: 691521 caboose
Courtesy Richard MacNary

666 Set with 7" cars
Top left to right: 666 loco, 951 tender
Middle left to right: 4484 box car, 36000 C&O gondola
Bottom: 20118 NYC caboose
Courtesy Richard MacNary

B&O and Southern Pacific Locos, medium size tin
Top left to right: 62(a) B&O loco (powered A), 62(b) B&O loco (dummy A)
Middle left to right: C507 B&O caboose, 1235 Southern Pacific caboose
Bottom left to right: 6000 Southern Pacific loco (powered A), 6000 Southern Pacific loco
     (dummy A)
Courtesy Richard MacNary

666 Set with 3/16" cars
Top left to right: 666 loco, 951 NYC tender
Middle left to right: 3557(a) NYC pullman, 3558(a) NYC observation
Bottom left to right: 174580 NYC box car, 652 SHELL tank car, 20102 NYC caboose
Courtesy Richard MacNary

	G	VG	M
104436 Box Car, plastic HO, red with white lettering "Union Pacific"	1.00	1.50	2.00
131000 (a) Gondola, plastic, 4 wheel, yellow with black lettering "SCL" ..	1.00	2.00	3.00
(b) Same as above, blue with white lettering	3.00	4.00	5.00
147815 (a) Box Car, plastic, deluxe 8 wheel, red with white lettering "Rock Island"	4.00	6.00	8.00
(b) Same as above, orange with black lettering	8.00	10.00	12.00
160149 Gondola, plastic HO, gray with black lettering "Southern Pacific"	1.00	2.00	3.00
161755 Box Car, plastic, 4 wheel, yellow with black lettering "NYC" .	1.00	2.00	3.00
174479 Box Car, plastic, 4 wheel, green with white lettering "NYC" ..	.50	1.00	1.50
174580/174595 Box Car, 6" tin, 4 wheel, red and gray, black roof, white lettering "NYC Pacemaker"	4.00	6.00	8.00
174580 Box Car, 3/16" scale, tin litho, 8 wheel, red and gray, black roof, white lettering "NYC"	6.00	8.00	10.00

214

Set #15300MB
Ward's Famous Switch Train Set, with equipment shown plus two electric switches, track, 90° cross over and transformer
Courtesy Richard MacNary

	G	VG	M
174853 Box Car, plastic HO, red with white lettering "NYC"	1.00	1.50	2.00
176893 Box Car, plastic, deluxe 8 wheel, green with white lettering "New York Central"	4.00	6.00	8.00
186028 Box Car, plastic, deluxe 8 wheel, red with white lettering "Union Pacific"	4.00	6.00	8.00
200309 (a) Gondola, plastic, 8 wheel, brown with white lettering "L&N', with sewer tiles	4.00	6.00	8.00

	G	VG	M
(b) Same as 200309(a), yellow with black lettering	4.00	6.00	8.00
241708 Gondola, 6″ tin, 4 wheel, yellow with black lettering "B&O" .	1.00	1.50	2.00
249319 (a) Box Car, plastic, deluxe 8 wheel, operating, red with white lettering "Marlines	4.00	6.00	8.00
(b) Same as 249319(a), white, with red lettering	4.00	6.00	8.00
254000 Gondola, 3/16″ scale, tin litho, 8 wheel, gray with white lettering "B&O" & "Baltimore and Ohio"	5.00	7.00	9.00
259199 Box Car, plastic, deluxe 8 wheel, gray with white lettering "CANADIAN PACIFIC"	10.00	12.50	15.00
339234 (a) Gondola, plastic, 8 wheel, brown with white lettering "Canadian Pacific"	4.00	6.00	8.00
(b) Same as above, black	4.00	6.00	8.00
(c) Same as above, red	4.00	6.00	8.00
347000 (a) Gondola, plastic, 4 wheel and 8 wheel gray with red lettering "Pennsylvania"	.25	.50	.75
(b) Same as above, red or blue, white lettering	.50	1.00	1.50
(c) Same as above, orange, black lettering	1.00	2.00	3.00
(d) Same as above, yellow, black lettering	1.00	2.00	3.00
347000 Gondola, 3/16″ scale, tin litho, 8 wheels, black with white lettering "Pennsylvania"	5.00	7.00	9.00
347100 Gondola, plastic, 8 wheels, gray with red lettering "Pennsylvania"	.50	1.00	2.00
384299 (a) Box Car, 6″ tin, 4 wheel and 8 wheel, sliding door, blue with white lettering "B&O" & "Baltimore and Ohio"	4.00	6.00	8.00
(b) Same as above, orange with white lettering	4.00	6.00	8.00
(c) Same as above, yellow with white lettering	4.00	6.00	8.00

	G	VG	M
(d) Same as above, red with silver lettering	4.00	6.00	8.00
(e) Same as above, brown with white lettering	4.00	6.00	8.00
(f) Same as above, blue with white lettering, solid door, 4 wheel only ...	6.00	8.00	10.00
467110 (a) Box Car, plastic, 4 wheel and 8 wheel red with white lettering "B&O"	.50	1.00	1.50
(b) Same as 467110(a), blue with white lettering	.50	1.00	1.50
(c) Same as above, orange with black lettering	.50	1.00	1.50
(d) Same as above, yellow with black lettering (4 wheel only)	.50	1.00	1.50
499898 Work Caboose, plastic HO, red with "NYC" markings	.50	.75	1.00
691521 Caboose, 7" tin, 4 wheel, orange Mickey Mouse figures (Pinocchio, etc.)	40.00	60.00	80.00
715100 (a) Gondola, plastic, 4 wheel and 8 wheel, blue with white lettering "NYC"	.50	1.00	1.50
(b) Same as above, green with black lettering	.50	1.00	1.50
(c) Same as above, red with black (or white) lettering	.50	1.00	1.50
738701 High side gondola, 6" tin, 4 wheel red with silver lettering "Pennsylvania"	1.00	2.00	3.00
738701 Hopper, 6" tin, 4 wheel, tuscan (red-brown) with white lettering "Pennsylvania"	2.00	4.00	6.00
--- "Moon Mullins & Kayo" Hand car, deluxe	150.00	200.00	300.00
--- Same as above, simple spring wound	125.00	175.00	250.00
--- "Disneyland Express" with tin board	40.00	60.00	80.00
--- "Mickey Mouse & Donald Duck" Hand Car set	75.00	100.00	150.00
--- "Shuttle Choo-Choo" (with MARX logo—	20.00	30.00	40.00
--- MARX-TRONIC set #2893	10.00	15.00	20.00

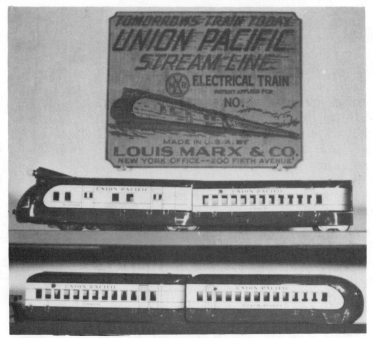

M10,000 Red & Silver
Top left to right: M10,000 loco, 657(b) coach
Bottom left to right: 657(b) coach, 658(b) coach-buffet
Courtesy Richard MacNary

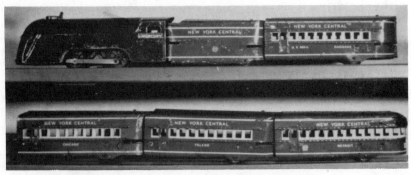

Gray Mercury Set
Top left to right: 635(a) loco, tender, 657(p) mail-baggage
Bottom left to right: 657(g) "Chicago", 657(r) "Toledo", 658(g) "Detroit"
Courtesy Richard MacNary

Lionel No. 126 Station, circa 1935.
Courtesy T. W. Sefton Collection.

Lionel No. 840 Power Station, circa 1928-37.
Courtesy T. W. Sefton Collection.

Lionel No. 9V Locomotive. Scarce hand-reverse model, circa 1928-29.
Courtesy T. W. Sefton Collection.

Lionel No. 408E
Locomotive, Twin
Motors, circa 1927-31.

*Courtesy
T. W. Sefton Collection.*

Lionel No. 9E
Locomotive in two-tone
green, circa 1933.

*Courtesy
T. W. Sefton Collection.*

Ives No. 40 Windup Loco & Tender, circa 1917.
Courtesy T. W. Sefton Collection.

Ives 3240, Electric Locomotive, No. 1 gauge, circa 1914-20.
Courtesy T. W. Sefton Collection.

Ives 3243, Locomotive, standard gauge, circa 1923.
Courtesy T. W. Sefton Collection.

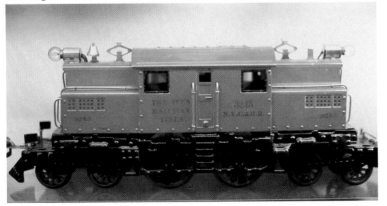

Lionel No. 490 Observation Car with Ives decals, circa 1931. When Ives went bankrupt in 1930, Lionel took over and kept the name for a few years.

Courtesy T. W. Sefton Collection.

Lionel No. 18 Parlor Car in scarce orange color, circa 1920.

Courtesy T. W. Sefton Collection.

Lionel No. 381E Locomotive, circa 1928-33.

Courtesy T. W. Sefton Collection.

American Flyer Circus Train
Courtesy Richard MacNary

Marx Wm. Crooks Set

Top L: 1(a) Loco, **Top R:** Tender—8 wheel **Middle L:** #1 Baggage—8 wheel. **Middle R:** #3 Coach—8 wheels **Bottom L to R:** 551(h) Tender—4 Wheel, #1 Baggage—4 wheel, #3 Coach—4 wheel

Courtesy Richard MacNary

Marx 7" Cabooses

Top L: C513, B&O Caboose. **Top R:** C507 B&O Caboose **Middle L to R:** 1235 So. Pac. Caboose, 956 NKP Caboose, 691521 Mickey Mouse Caboose **Bottom L;** 1951 ATSF Caboose, **Bottom R:** 20118 NYC Caboose

Courtesy Richard MacNary

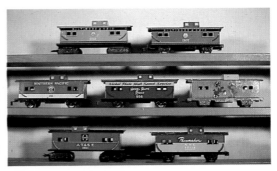

Marx Santa Fe ³⁄₁₆" Passenger Set (solid windows)

Top L: 21, Loco "A", **Top R:** Loco-dummy "A" **Middle:** 3152(b) Pullmans **Bottom:** 3197(b) Observation

Courtesy Richard MacNary

Marx Pre-War Army Locomotives

Top L: 500, 2-4-2 Canadian Pacific. **Top R:** 500 Tender **Middle L:** 897, 0-4-0 Canadian Pacific Litho, C/W. **Middle R:** 952 Tender **Bottom L:** 597(c), 0-4-0 C.V., painted olive drab. **Bottom R:** 952 Tender

Courtesy Richard MacNary

Marx Pre-War Tin Army Trains

Top L: 2572, Flat with truck and unloading ramp. **Top R:** 552(e) Gondola **Middle L to R:** 572ST(a) Flat with #5 Tank, 572ST(b) Flat with plain olive drab midget tank, 572ST(c) Flat with litho midget tank **Bottom L to R:** 572G Flat with siege gun, 552(e) Gondola, 572FG Flat with field gun

Courtesy Richard MacNary

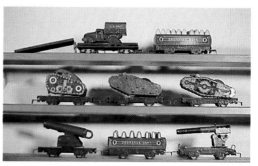

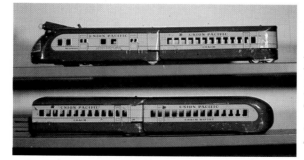

Marx 10,000 (Green & Cream)

Top L: M10,000 Loco. **Top R:** 657(c) Coach **Bottom L:** 657(c) Coach. **Bottom R:** 658(c) Coach-Buffet

Courtesy Richard MacNary

Marx Red Mercury Set

Top L: Mercury Loco. **Top R:** Tender **Bottom L to R:** 657(x) "Chicago", 657(r) "Toledo", 658(i) "Detroit"

Courtesy Richard MacNary

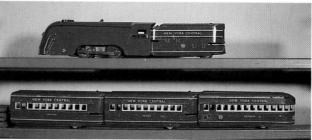

Lionel Small Units #1

Top L: 41 Loco "US Army". **Top R:** 42 Loco "Picatinny Arsenal" **Bottom L:** 51 Loco "Navy Yard". **Bottom R:** 53 Loco-Snowplow "Rio Grande"

Courtesy Richard MacNary

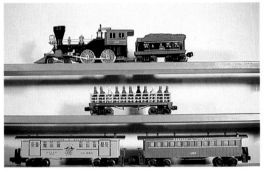

Lionel Sears "General" Set (uncataloged "Pumpkin" Set)

Top L: 1882 Loco. **Top R:** 1882T Tender **Middle:** 1887 Horse Car **Bottom L:** 1866 Baggage. **Bottom R:** 1885 Coach

Courtesy Richard MacNary

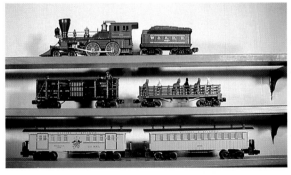

Lional 0-27 "General" Set

Top L: 1862 Loco. **Top R:** 1862T Tender **Middle L:** 3370 Wells Fargo Car "Sheriff & Outlaw". **Middle R:** 1877 Horse Car **Bottom L:** 1866 Baggage. **Bottom R:** 1865 Coach

Courtesy Richard MacNary

Lionel North Pacific Attack Set

Top: 2349 Loco **Middle L:** 6463 Tank Car. **Middle R:** 3540 Radar Tracking Car **Bottom L:** 6805 Radioactive Waste Car. **Bottom R:** 3535 Security Car

Courtesy Richard MacNary

Lionel USMC Set #2

Top L: 6809 Flat with two trucks. **Top R:** 6808 Flat with AA & truck **Middle:** 6807 Flat with Duwk **Bottom L to R:** 1625 Loco, 1615 Tender, 6017 Caboose

Courtesy Richard MacNary

Lionel (uncataloged) Army & USMC

Top L: 6651 Gun. **Top R:** 617 Caboose **Middle L:** Hopper. **Middle R:** 6112 Gondola **Bottom L:** 221 Loco. **Bottom R:** 221 Loco

Courtesy Richard MacNary

Lionel US Navy Set

Top L: 224 Loco. **Top R:** 224 Loco **Middle L:** 6820 Flat with Helicopter. **Middle R:** 6544 Missile Car **Bottom L:** 6830 Flat with Submarine, **Bottom R:** 6017 Caboose

Courtesy Richard MacNary

Lionel Small Units #4

Top L: 55 Tie-Jector. **Top R:** 54 Ballast Tamper **Middle L:** 6530 Box Car. **Middle R:** 52 Fire Car **Bottom L:** Maintenance Car. **Bottom R:** 3512 Ladder Car

Courtesy Richard MacNary

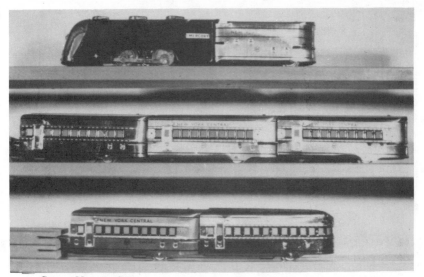

Copper Mercury Set
Top left to right: 635(a) loco, tender
Middle left to right: 657(t) mail-baggage, 657(v) "Toledo", 657(w) "Cleveland"
Bottom left to right: 657(u) "Chicago", 658(h) "Detroit"
Courtesy Richard MacNary

Santa Fe 3/16" Passenger Set (punched out windows)
Top left to right: 1829 loco, 2731 tender
Middle left to right: 3152(c) pullman - vista dome, 3152(a) pullman
Bottom: 3197(a) observation
Courtesy Richard MacNary

219

Marx "HO"
Top left to right: 20(c) loco, tender, 109(b) hopper, 1961 caboose
Middle left to right: 370 loco, 370 loco, C-630 caboose
Bottom left to right: 6096 loco, tender, 20298 caboose
Courtesy Richard MacNary

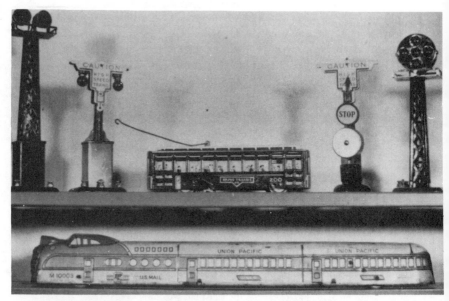

Tin Trolley & M 10,003
Top left to right: 416A floodlight tower, 409 crossing with two lights, #200 trolley,
    414 crossing with bell, 1404 block signal
Bottom: M10,003 Streamliner (one piece - clockwork)
Courtesy Richard MacNary

	G	VG	M
---Floor Train loco, two gondolas....	10.00	15.00	20.00
--- Floor Train, Standard gauge	25.00	35.00	50.00
--- Floor Train, Tin Litho #999, clockwork	50.00	75.00	10.00
--- "Honeymoon Express", early	75.00	125.00	150.00
--- Same as above, late	35.00	45.00	55.00
--- "Musical Choo Choo", Linemar ..	10.00	15.00	20.00
--- "Plastimarx" Mexican Marx Set #5063	15.00	20.00	30.00
--- "Scenic Express" with tin board .	5.00	10.00	15.00
--- "Green Giant Valley Express", HO set, promotional	25.00	35.00	50.00

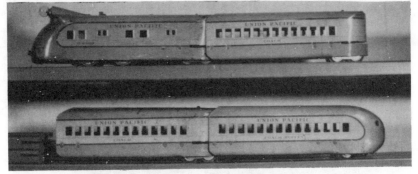

M10,000 Tan & Cream (yellow)
Top left to right: M10,000 loco, 657(a) coach
Bottom left to right: 657(a) coach, 658(a) coach-buffet
Courtesy Richard MacNary

Marx "HO"
Top left to right: 20(b) loco, tender, 160149 gondola, 2226 caboose
Middle left to right: 21 loco 6938 loco
Bottom left to right: loco, loco, 2226 caboose
Courtesy Richard MacNary

Western Pacific 3/16" Passenger Set
Top left to right: 902(b) loco (dummy B), 901(d) loco (dummy A)
Middle left to right: 1217(a) vista dome, 901(b) loco (powered A)
Bottom left to right: 1007 observation, 1217(a) vista dome
Courtesy Richard MacNary

NYC 3/16" Passenger Set
Top left to right: 333 loco, tender
Middle left to right: 234(b) pullman - vista dome, 234(a) pullman
Bottom left to right: 234(a) pullman, 236 observation "Meteor"
Courtesy Richard MacNary

Tin Articulated Trains
Top: Denver & Rio Grande
Middle: Lumar Line
Bottom: Marville Local
Courtesy Richard MacNary

Tin Disney Articulated Trains
Top: Casey Jr. Disneyland Special
Middle: Disneyland
Bottom: Disneyland Express
Courtesy Richard MacNary

Tin Stations
Top left to right: 1430 Union Station, 1430 Union Station
Bottom: 2940 Grand Central Station
Courtesy Richard MacNary

Tin Stations
Top left to right: 2980 "Oak Park", 2970 "Girard"
Bottom: 2900 "Glendale"
Courtesy Richard MacNary

224

BUDDY "L"

Buddy "L" toys were first manufactured by the Moline Pressed Steel Company, Moline, Illinois, in 1921, and were named after the son of the owner, Fred Lundahl. Lundahl had started the company about eight years earlier, manufacturing auto and truck parts (fenders, etc.). The toys were originally made as special items for his son, but as Buddy Lundahl's playmates began to clamor for similar toys of their own and their fathers began asking Lundahl senior to make duplicate toys for their sons, Lundahl went into the toy business. Buddy "L" toys were large, typically 21 to 24 or more inches long for trucks and fire engines. Construction was of very heavy steel, strong enough to support a man's weight. These were made until the early 1930's, when the line was modified and lighter-weight materials were employed. Before this time, Fred Lundahl had died, having already lost control of the company. The company has changed names several times, being known as the Buddy "L" Corp., Buddy "L" Toy Co., etc., in recent years dropping the quotes around the L. Continuing to make toys till the present day, the company even put out a few wooden toys during World War II, when its main plant made nothing but war-related items. The Buddy "L" trains were first manufactured in 1921 and ended production in 1931.

BUDDY "L" — List compiled by Thomas W. Sefton

	G	VG	E
BUDDY L Industrial Train, 1929-31 2″ Gauge			
50 A-G Various complete sets	150.00	225.00	300.00
51 Locomotive (decals BL 12, BL 14, or BL 16), dark green	45.00	67.50	90.00
52 Stake Car (flatcar), red	20.00	30.00	40.00
53 Rock Car, red	20.00	30.00	40.00
54 Gondola, red	20.00	30.00	40.00
55 Ballast Car (side dump), red	20.00	30.00	40.00
56 Rocker Dump Car, red	20.00	30.00	40.00
? Handcar, rare, orange	250.00	375.00	500.00
70 Straight Track, 24″, dark green, per section	5.00	7.50	10.00
71 Curved Track, dark green, per section	1.50	2.25	3.00
72 R Switch, dark green	10.00	15.00	20.00
73 L Switch, dark green	10.00	15.00	20.00
74 Turn-Out Curve, dark green	2.00	3.00	4.00

Buddy L 1002 Box Car, Buddy L 1003 Tank Car.
Photo Courtesy PB Eighty-Four New York

Buddy L 1004 Stock Car, Buddy L. 1001 Caboose.
Photo Courtesy PB Eighty-Four New York

Buddy L 1002 box car, Buddy L 1006 flat car.
Photo Courtesy PB Eighty-Four New York

No. 50 — Buddy "L" Industrial Train. Consists of Locomotive, Rack Car, Rocker Dump Car, Coal Car, Stake Car and Ballast Car. The Locomotive is 10¼ inches long, 4 inches wide and 6½ inches high. The cars are 8 inches long. This train operates on 2 inch gauge steel tracks, 12 sections of 24 inch curved track included with each set. Packed one set in a box

Buddy L 1002 box car, 1003 tank car
Photo Courtesy PB 84

Buddy L 1002 box car, 1006 flat car
Photo Courtesy PB 84

Buddy L 1004 Stock Car; Buddy L 1001 Caboose
Photo Courtesy PB Eighty Four New York

Buddy L 1002 Box Car
T. W. Sefton Collection

227

Buddy L 1020 Locomotive Wrecking Crane
T. W. Sefton Collection

	G	VG	M
75 90° Crossing, dark green	10.00	15.00	20.00
76 60° Crossing, dark green	14.00	21.00	28.00
77 Loose Latch Plate, dark green ..	.75	1.00	1.25
78 ¼ straight 6", dark green	.75	1.00	1.25
79 ½ straight 12", dark green	1.00	2.00	3.00
80 3 stall roundhouse and turntable, dark green	166.00	249.00	332.00
81 1 stall roundhouse and turntable, dark green	100.00	150.00	200.00

BUDDY L Outdoor Railroad, 3¼" gauge

	G	VG	M
1000 Locomotive & Tender (decal 963), black, 1921-31	300.00	450.00	600.00
1001 Caboose (decal 3017), red, 1921-31	400.00	600.00	800.00
1002 Boxcar, red, 1921-31	125.00	187.50	250.00
1003 Tankcar, dark red, yellow, silver, 1921-31	150.00	225.00	300.00
1004 Stockcar, red, 1921-31	125.00	187.50	250.00
1005 Coal Car (gondola), black, 1921-31	75.00	112.50	150.00
1006 Flatcar, black, 1926-31	75.00	112.50	150.00
1007 Hopper (bottom dump), black, 1928-31	175.00	262.50	350.00

	G	VG	M
1008 Ballast Car (side dump) 23" long), black, 1928-31	225.00	337.50	450.00
1009 Construction Car (single truck - 11" long), dark green, 1930-31	530.00	795.00	1060.00
1020 Locomotive Wrecking Crane, black/red, 1927-30	425.00	637.50	850.00
1021 Locomotive Dredge, black/red, 1927-30	500.00	750.00	1000.00
1022 Locomotive Pile Driver, black/red, 1927-30	750.00	1125.00	1500.00
1023 Locomotive Shovel, black/red, 1928-30	500.00	750.00	1000.00
1200 Straight Track 4'	12.50	18.75	25.00
1201 Curved Track 4' (26' diameter)	10.00	15.00	20.00
1202 Right-hand switch 7'	50.00	75.00	100.00
1203 Left-hand switch 7'	50.00	75.00	100.00
Trestle Sections, black	50.00	75.00	100.00
Supporting Piers, black	25.00	37.50	50.00

AMERICAN FLYER
by Catherine Hintze

First known as "Chicago Flyer" under the ownership of W.O. Coleman Sr. and later Coleman Jr., the company's train line hardly gave any serous competition to either Lionel or Ives, the two leading competitive giants in the American toy train market at the time. This was basically due to the firm's lack of creativity, poor quality control, and diversification into other fields. In 1937, as financial problems were gaining the upper hand over Coleman, Alfred Carlton (A.C.) Gilbert (already well-established with his successful marketing of his "Mystic Magic" chemistry set and "Erector" set lines), had the opportunity to purchase the Flyer company for a low-percent royalty basis spread out over the next ten years. Thus was born American Flyer, as best remembered today. During the next several years, Gilbert marketed a successful 3/16 scale-like line. Through considerable expense, along with excellent marketing practices and a heightened quality standard, American Flyer had placed itself as a competitor Lionel would have to take seriously (Lionel having already purchased Ives in 1928). As wartime production put a halt to most toy manufacturing, both American Flyer and Lionel feverishly prepared new lines and innovations for the post-war operation. After the War, Lionel showed first, as it took almost a year for American Flyer to convert back to peacetime production (Lionel, being well-established and financially sound, was able to make the conversion more quickly). In 1946, the decision to go two-rail (for realism) in S-gauge was standardized. Gilbert felt this type of track had the edge over Lionel's traditional three-rail system, but it created many technical problems which would have to be overcome at considerable expense. To his dismay, the public's acceptance was not all he had hoped, but nevertheless, the two-rail system was marketed to the end. Through the fifties, with several expansions made on their New Haven, Connecticut, facilities, American Flyer produced many high-quality trains and accessories which ranked them second only to Lionel. The production of such steam locos as the Atlantic, PRR K-5, Hudson, Northern and an 0-8-0 switcher, along with beautifully scale-like passenger and freight (both operating and non-operating) cars, have made American Flyer both a collector's and an operator's dream. The competitive knife was sharp, with Lionel winning out on several important patent right battles. One major legal bout was over the knuckle-type coupler. First introduced by Lionel in 1945, it took American Flyer seven years before they could produce their version, free from any infringements. In 1949, Lionel also won out on a whistle unit patent. American Flyer came out with a "choo choo" chugger to counter Lionel's whistle as an alternative. They produced a whistling billboard which just didn't have the same effect as Lionel's whistle coming directly from the engine itself. Again the public showed preference for Lionel's inboard whistle unit which children could control by a remote button, usually found on the transformer. As public demand for trains in general was slackening through the later 1950s and early 60s, both American Flyer and Lionel were forced to diversify and cheapen their line. Competition from Marx for a low-budget line was strong, as were "fad toys" (market a new toy or game every 90 days) from such toy manufacturers as Ideal and Mattel. The space-age boom of the sixties also took control of a considerable part of the toy market. American Flyer was spending less on their train line and channeling more capital into other toy angles, hoping to show a profit overall. In 1961, A.C. Gilbert Sr. died, and within a year Jack Wrather (owner of the tv programs "Lassie" and "The Lone Ranger") purchased 52% of the business for four million dollars. The following four years were very turbulent. The firing and hiring of new management and drastic cutbacks presaged what was to come. A. C. Gilbert Jr. died in 1964, leaving behind a company whose future was very much in question, a far cry from the proud and positive era of the fifties. Sales were up by 30% in 1965, but this hardly offset production costs and borrowed capital. American Flyer finally succumbed, and in 1966 Lionel purchased the remnants of what was once a very serious adversary, and put a complete halt to the production of all American Flyer trains.

AMERICAN FLYER

	G	VG	M
(1) 25 watt transformer	.90	1.50	5.00
(1) 35 watt transformer	1.08	1.80	6.00
(1½) 45 watt transformer	1.26	2.10	7.00
(1½) 50 watt transformer	1.44	2.40	8.00
(1½B) 50 watt transformer	1.44	2.40	8.00
(2) 75 watt transformer	1.80	3.00	10.00
(8B) Transformer	2.70	4.50	15.00
(8B) Transformer with uncoupler, track, manual & buttons	3.60	6.00	20.00
(8B) 100 watt transformer with bulb covers	3.60	6.00	20.00

American Flyer No. 484 caboose, "0" scale

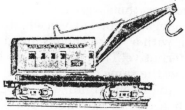

American Flyer No. 3025 wrecker, "0" scale

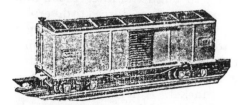

American Flyer No. 478 box car, "0" scale

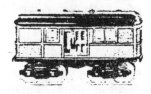

American Flyer No. 1205 double truck U.S. mail car with sliding doors, "0" scale

	G	VG	M
(8B) 100 watt transformer without bulb covers	2.70	4.50	15.00
(10) Loco, electric (1925)	36.00	60.00	200.00
(10) Cast iron 0-4-0 wind-up loco	27.00	45.00	150.00
(12) Cast iron loco-0 ga	27.00	45.00	150.00
(12) Smoke Cartridges	.63	1.05	3.50
(13) 0-4-0 wind-up loco and tender, black, orange and green	31.25	52.50	175.00
(16) Loco, 0-4-0, electric, 0 ga	10.80	18.00	60.00
(18B) Transformer	13.50	22.50	75.00
(19B) 300 watt transformer with volt and amp	13.50	22.50	75.00
(119) Hiawatha Loco, Tin-Plate Wind-Up with tender, 0	36.00	60.00	200.00
(119) Hiawatha Loco, Tinplate Electric, 0	54.00	90.00	300.00
(119) Hiawatha loco with tender, 0	90.00	150.00	500.00
(120) Tender-0 ga	9.00	15.00	50.00
(121) Tender, 0. Ga., Black, White, "No. 121"	10.80	18.00	60.00
(234) Engine, diesel, HO, Chesapeake & Ohio	27.00	45.00	150.00
(401) Loco 2-4-2, 0 ga.	27.00	45.00	150.00
(401) Penn. loco 2-4-4	22.50	37.50	125.00
(404) Pullman, 0 Ga.	13.50	22.50	75.00
(405) Observation, 0 Ga.	13.50	22.50	75.00
(420) A.F. Lines loco, 0 Ga	31.25	52.50	175.00

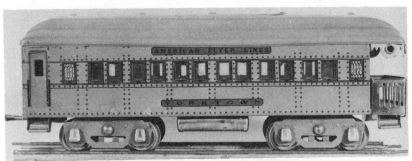

A. F. "Yorktown" Obser., Std. orange, green litho, brass trim.
Courtesy H. A. Mueller, Continental Hobby House

A. F. "Eagle" Pullman, Std., red litho, brass trim.
Courtesy H. A. Mueller, Continental Hobby House

A. F. "Eagle" Observatory, Std., red litho, brass trim.
Courtesy H. A. Mueller, Continental Hobby House

A. F. Coach, 0, two-tone green, yellow
Courtesy H. A. Mueller, Continental Hobby House

A. F. Gondola, 0, green, brass trim.
Courtesy H. A. Mueller, Continental Hobby House

A. F. Caboose, 0, red, black, brass trim.
Courtesy H. A. Mueller,
Continental Hobby House

A. F. Coach, 0, red, yellow
Courtesy H. A. Mueller,
Continental Hobby House

A. F. Hiawatha Obs., 0, yellow, maroon,
gray, brass trim
Courtesy H. A. Mueller,
Continental Hobby House

A. F. "Illini" Obser., 0, two-tone green, black litho
Courtesy H. A. Mueller, Continental Hobby House

234

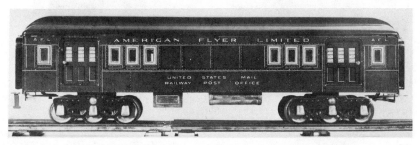

A. F. Hiawatha 4-4-4 Engine and tender, 0, orange, gray, black, nickel trim
Courtesy H. A. Mueller, Continental Hobby House

A. F. Limited U.S. Mail car, Std., blue, yellow litho, brass trim
Courtesy H. A. Mueller, Continental Hobby House

	G	VG	M
(420) Die-cast loco and tender, 0 Ga. . . .	27.00	45.00	150.00
(421) Tender, 0 Ga.	9.00	15.00	50.00
(423) Loco-0 ga	27.00	45.00	150.00
(429) Loco, 0-6-0, 0 Ga.	27.00	45.00	150.00
(446) Loco 4-6-4, HO	18.00	30.00	100.00
(476) Gondola, 0	1.80	3.00	10.00
(478) Box car-0 ga.	3.60	6.00	20.00
(480) Tank car, Shell, yellow, 0	3.60	6.00	20.00
(482) Lumber Car, 0 ga.	2.70	4.50	15.00
(484) Caboose - 0 ga.	2.70	4.50	15.00
(486) Hopper, 0 Ga.	2.70	4.50	15.00
(488) Floodlight Car	2.70	4.50	15.00
(490) Whistle car, red-0 ga.	9.00	15.00	50.00
(494) Baggage car-0 ga.	9.00	15.00	50.00
(495) Coach car, red (2 pcs.) 0 ga. . . .	9.00	15.00	50.00
(500) Pullman, 0 Ga., litho	7.20	12.00	40.00
(500) Tank Car-HO	3.60	6.00	20.00
(501) Hopper-HO	3.60	6.00	20.00
(506) Caboose-HO	3.60	6.00	20.00
(513) Observation, 0 Ga.	23.50	39.00	130.00

A. F. "Illini" coach, 0, two-tone green, black litho
Courtesy H. A. Mueller, Continental Hobby House

	G	VG	M
(515) Coach car, tinplate litho, yellow/red/black/orange (early)--0 ga.	9.00	15.00	50.00
(553) Loco, steam	9.00	15.00	50.00
(555) Tender, black	1.80	3.00	10.00
(556) Loco, royal blue	18.00	30.00	100.00
(561) Loco, steam	12.60	21.00	70.00
(564) Tender	2.70	4.50	15.00
(565) Loco	12.60	21.00	70.00
(597) Passenger and freight station	8.40	14.40	48.00
(736) Missouri Pacific closed slate cattle car w/cattle corral and 2 cattle, has button	9.00	15.00	50.00
(1025) Railway Express mail car-0 ga.	7.20	12.00	40.00
(1026) Passenger car, 0 Ga.	13.50	22.50	75.00
(1045) 25 watt transformer	.90	1.50	5.00
(1096) 0-4-0 box cab loco with square headlight, rubber stamped-0 ga.	45.00	75.00	250.00
(1097) Engine, 0-4-0, 0 Ga., Orange, Green, Red litho, Nickel trim	45.00	75.00	250.00
(1102) Coach, 0 Ga.	20.00	36.00	120.00
(1103) Passenger car	9.00	15.00	50.00
(1105) American Express baggage car	14.40	24.00	80.00
(1105) "Canadian National Railways Dominion Flyer", 0 ga., Red, Black litho, nickel trim	9.00	15.00	50.00

A. F. Obser., 0, red, yellow
Courtesy H. A. Mueller,
Continental Hobby House

A. F. Lumber Car, 0, yellow
Courtesy H. A. Mueller,
Continental Hobby House

A. F. Lumber Car, 0, black, nickel trim
Courtesy H. A. Mueller, Continental Hobby House

	G	VG	M
(1106) Coach, "Dominion Flyer", 0 ga., brown, black litho	9.00	15.00	50.00
(1106) Parlor car, yellow/black/green litho.-0 ga.	9.00	15.00	50.00
(1106) Parlor car, green litho./black roof, 4 wheels	9.00	15.00	50.00
(1106) Lumber Car (1930), Black	4.50	7.50	25.00
(1107) Coach car, litho.-0 ga.	9.00	15.00	50.00
(1108) Baggage car, litho.-0 ga.	9.00	15.00	50.00
(1109) Sand Car, red litho, 0 Ga.	9.00	15.00	50.00
(1112) Boxcar (1925) Red Litho	9.00	15.00	50.00
(1112) Boxcar (1930) Yellow Litho ..	9.00	15.00	50.00
(1113) Gondola (1925) Green Litho ..	4.50	7.50	25.00
(1114) Caboose, 0, Red, Green, White litho, with brass trim	5.40	9.00	30.00
(1118) Tank car, litho. gray/white/ black-0 ga.	8.10	13.50	45.00

237

	G	VG	M
(1120) Caboose, 0 Ga.	7.20	12.00	40.00
(1120) Passenger car, 0 Ga.	9.00	15.00	50.00
(1122) Bluestreak passenger car, 0 Ga.	7.20	12.00	40.00
(1123) Passenger car, 0 Ga.	7.20	12.00	40.00
(1123) Tuscan passenger car, 0 Ga. .	7.20	12.00	40.00
(1127) Caboose, 0 Ga.	4.50	7.50	25.00
(1200) Baggage car, litho., 4 wheel-0 ga.	13.25	22.50	75.00
(1200) Baggage car, litho., 8 wheel-0 ga.	13.25	22.50	75.00
(1201) Passenger car, red litho./black roof.................................	13.25	22.50	75.00
(1202) Electric service baggage car-0 ga.	13.25	22.50	75.00
(1202) Express baggage car	12.60	21.00	70.00
(1203) Passenger car, blue litho./ black roof.........................	13.25	22.50	75.00
(1203) Coach car, litho., 8 wheel (early)-0 ga.	13.25	22.50	75.00
(1205) Baggage car-0 ga.	13.25	22.50	75.00
(1205) Mail car-0 Ga.	16.20	27.00	90.00
(1206) Coach car-0 ga.	13.25	22.50	75.00
(1206) Passenger car	13.25	22.50	75.00
(1206) Pullman-0 ga.	13.25	22.50	75.00
(1207) Observation Car (1926)	13.25	22.50	75.00
(1217) Electric loco 0-4-0, 0 ga.	45.00	75.00	250.00
(1218) Electric loco 0-4-0, black/red/ yellow-0 ga.	45.00	75.00	250.00
(1218) Engine, 0-4-0, black, lettering on side, nickel and brass trim	45.00	75.00	250.00
(1218) Loco, red/black/yellow-0 ga. .	45.00	75.00	250.00
(1223) Coach car-0 ga.	5.40	9.00	30.00
(1270) Loco, 0 Ga.	14.40	24.00	80.00
(1290) Transformer	1.80	3.00	10.00
(1306) Passenger car	9.00	15.00	50.00
(1316) Set-0 Ga. (1931) 3110-3013-3012-3014	36.00	60.00	200.00
(1350) Set-0 Ga. (1932) 3316-3171-3171-3172	45.00	75.00	250.00
(1366RT) Set-0 Ga. (1934) 3193-1214-1213-1217	40.50	67.50	225.00
(1433) Set (1925) "The All American", 4019-4040-4041-4042, Maroon	144.00	240.00	800.00

	G	VG	M
(1448) Set (1935) "The Warrior", 4681-4695-4671-4331-4331-4331-4332	360.00	600.00	2000.00
(1453) Set (1926) "The President's Special", 4039-4080-4081-4081	900.00	1500.00	5000.00
(1466) Set (1927) Second "The President's Special", 4687-4080-4081-4082	900.00	1500.00	5000.00
(1473) Set (1928) "The Statesman", 4654-4151-4151-4152, Orange with Orange car roofs	270.00	450.00	1500.00
(1473) Set (1930) "The Statesman", 4654-4151-4151-4152, Orange with Green car roofs	270.00	450.00	1500.00
(1474) Set (1933) "The Brigadier", Red 4644R/C loco-4331-4332	162.00	270.00	900.00
(1489) Set (1929) "The President's Special" 4689-4390-4391-4393-4392, two-tone Blue	990.00	1650.00	5500.00
(1491) Set (1931) "The Iron Monarch", 4694-4692-4693-4340-4341-4342	360.00	600.00	2000.00
(1493) Set (1932) "The New Minuteman", 4696-4695-4693-4390-4391-4392	396.00	660.00	2200.00
(1688) Loco 2-4-2	18.00	30.00	100.00
(1730RW) U.P. Streamliner 51" long (1935)	72.00	120.00	400.00
(1835TW) Tender	36.00	60.00	200.00
(1925) Catalog	40.00	60.00	80.00
(1926) Catalog	35.00	52.50	70.00
(1927) Catalog	35.00	52.50	70.00
(1928) Catalog	35.00	52.50	70.00
(1929) Catalog	35.00	52.50	70.00

A. F. "Pleasant View" obs., Std., red, black litho, brass trim
Courtesy H. A. Mueller, Continental Hobby House

239

A. F. Obs., 0, two-tone green, yellow
Courtesy H. A. Mueller, Continental Hobby House

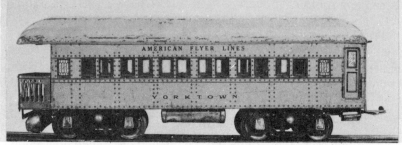

A. F. "Yorktown" Obs., Std., orange, maroon, black litho, brass trim
Courtesy H. A. Mueller, Continental Hobby House

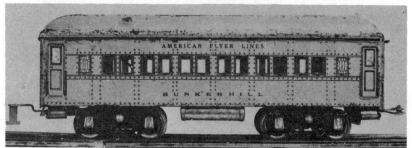

A. F. "Bunker Hill" car, Std., orange, maroon, black litho, brass trim
Courtesy H. A. Mueller, Continental Hobby House

A. F. 4393 "President's Special - Academy", Std., peacock, blue, brass trim
Courtesy H. A. Mueller, Continental Hobby House

	G	VG	M
(1930) Catalog	35.00	52.50	70.00
(1931) Catalog	30.00	45.00	60.00
(1932) Catalog	30.00	45.00	60.00
(1933) Catalog	30.00	45.00	60.00
(1934) Catalog	25.00	37.50	50.00
(1935) Catalog	25.00	37.50	50.00
(1936) Catalog	25.00	37.50	50.00
(1937) Catalog	25.00	37.50	50.00
(1938) Catalog	25.00	37.50	50.00
(1939) Catalog	20.00	30.00	40.00
(1940) Catalog	20.00	30.00	40.00
(1941) Catalog	15.00	22.50	30.00
(1944) Catalog	No	Price	Found
(1945) Catalog	No	Price	Found
(1946) Catalog (D1451) 32 pages	23.00	33.00	50.00
(1947 Catalog (D1473), 32 pages	20.00	30.00	45.00
(1948) Catalog (D1507), 32 pages ...	20.00	30.00	45.00
(1949) Catalog (D1536), 40 pages ...	10.00	15.00	20.00
(1950) Catalog (D1604), 56 pages ...	10.00	15.00	20.00
(1951) Catalog (D1640), 48 pages ...	7.00	11.00	15.00
(1952) Catalog (D1677), 48 pages ...	7.00	11.00	15.00
(1953) Catalog (D1715), 52 pages ...	7.00	11.00	15.00
(1954) Catalog (D1760), 48 pages ...	7.00	11.00	15.00
(1955) Catalog (D1801), 44 pages ...	7.00	11.00	15.00
(1956) Catalog (D1866), 52 pages ...	6.00	9.00	12.00
(1957) Catalog (D2006), 48 pages ...	7.00	11.00	15.00
(1958) Catalog (D2047), 48 pages ...	12.00	18.00	25.00
(1959) Catalog (D2115), 24 pages ...	6.00	9.00	12.00
(1960) Catalog (D2230), 20 pages ...	6.00	9.00	12.00
(1961) Catalog (D2239), 36 pages ...	6.00	9.00	12.00
(1962) Catalog (D2278), 36 pages ...	3.00	5.00	7.00
(1963) Catalog (X-863-3), 32 pages ..	3.00	5.00	7.00
(1964) Catalog (X-264-6), 40 pages ..	2.00	3.50	5.00
(1965) Catalog (X165-12RV), 20 pages	5.00	7.00	10.00
(1966) Catalog (X466-1), 24 pages ...	3.00	4.50	6.00
(2010) Double arc lamp post, 12½″ high	5.40	9.00	30.00
(2020) Electric Loco, 4-4-4, 0 Ga.	108.00	180.00	600.00
(2029) remote control whistle unit ..	8.10	13.50	45.00
(3000) Baggage, 0, Two-tone Green, Black litho	10.80	18.00	60.00
(3001) Illini Pullman, 0 Ga.	10.80	18.00	60.00
(3006) Flat car	2.70	4.50	15.00

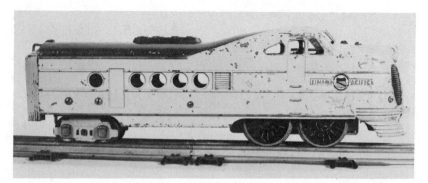

A. F. "Union Pacific" Engine-Passenger Car unit, 0, brown, yellow
Courtesy H. A. Mueller, Continental Hobby House

A. F. Tank Car, 0, yellow, black, nickel trim
Courtesy H. A. Mueller, Continental Hobby House

A. F. Valley Forge Obser. Std., brown, black litho, brass trim.
Courtesy H. A. Mueller, Continental Hobby House

242

A. F. "Streamline" 0-4-4-0, 0, orange, silver
Courtesy H. A. Mueller, Continental Hobby House

A. F. 2-6-4 Loco, 0, black, white, copper and brass trim, with tender.
Courtesy H. A. Mueller, Continental Hobby House

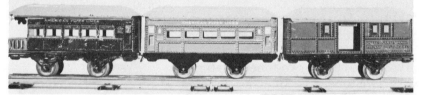

A. F. Coaches, Observation, Passenger, "United States Mail Railway Post Office", 0, maroon, brown, blue, orange roofs, brass trim.
Courtesy H. A. Mueller, Continental Hobby House

	G	VG	M
(3008) Box Car, 0 ga., Yellow, Black litho	9.00	15.00	50.00
(3009) Dump car, decaled set-0 ga. ...	5.40	9.00	30.00
(3010) Tank Car, 0 ga., Gray, Black Nickel trim	9.00	15.00	50.00
(3011) Loco	27.00	45.00	150.00
(3012) Box car, rubber stamped, decaled set-0 ga.....................	9.00	15.00	50.00
(3012) Electric loco 0-4-0, litho. headlight in cab-0 ga.	27.00	45.00	150.00
(3013) Gondola, decaled set-0 ga. ...	5.40	9.00	30.00
(3014) Caboose, decaled set-0 ga. ...	5.40	9.00	30.00
(3015) Loco	36.00	60.00	200.00
(3017) Caboose, 8 wheels-0 ga.	5.75	9.60	32.00
(3018) Tank car, 8 wheels-0 ga.	5.75	9.60	32.00
(3018) Tank car, yellow/black/copper trim-0 ga.	6.30	10.50	35.00

243

	G	VG	M
(3019) Electric loco, dark green/black frame/maroon windows, rubber stamped, headlight-0 ga.	126.00	210.00	350.00
(3019) Dump car, 8 wheels-0 ga.	5.75	9.60	32.00
(3019) Dump car-0 ga.	5.40	9.00	30.00
(3020) 4-4-4 Engine, 0 ga., Black, Yellow, Nickel trim	72.00	120.00	400.00
(3020) 4-4-4 Engine, 0 ga., Maroon, Black, Nickel trim	81.00	135.00	450.00
(3025) Crane car-0 ga.	9.00	15.00	50.00
(3046) Lumber car, 8 wheels-0 ga. ...	7.20	12.00	40.00
(3100) Loco 0-4-0 red/black/gold/ brass trim and plates-0 ga.	40.50	67.50	225.00
(3102) Loco (1926) Litho	35.10	58.50	195.00
(3105) Loco, blue	31.50	52.50	175.00
(3107) 0-4-0 Engine, 0 ga.	36.00	60.00	200.00
(3109) 0-4-0 Engine, 0 ga, Green, Brown, Brass trim	36.00	60.00	200.00
(3110) Loco 0-4-0, headlight in cab-0 ga.	35.10	58.50	195.00
(3112) 0-4-0 Engine and "United States Mail Railway Post Office" baggage car	10.80	18.00	60.00
(3113) Loco 0-4-0, two tone blue-0 ga. with two-tone blue Coaches lettered "Nationwide Lines" (made for J.C. Penney Co. - extremely rare), Set Complete in Original boxes	1800.00	3000.00	10,000.00
(3113) Same set as above, AF Bluebird, American Flyer Lines lettering	324.00	540.00	1800.00
(3115) 0-4-0 Engine, 0 ga., Peacock, Blue, Brass trim	36.00	60.00	200.00
(3116) 0-4-0 Engine, 0 ga., Turq., Black, Brass trim	36.00	60.00	200.00
(3117) 0-4-0 Engine, 0 ga., Red, Brass trim	36.00	60.00	200.00
(3141) Coach car, red/black/gold/ brass trim-0 ga.	14.40	24.00	80.00
(3141) Pullman, 0 ga., Red, Black, Brass trim	10.80	18.00	60.00
(3142) Observation car, red/black/ gold/brass trim-0 ga.	14.40	24.00	80.00
(3150) Baggage car	14.40	24.00	80.00
(3151) Passenger car	12.60	21.00	70.00

	G	VG	M
(3152) Observation car, 0 ga., Two-tone Orange, brass trim	10.80	18.00	60.00
(3152) Passenger car	12.60	21.00	70.00
(3161) Passenger car	12.60	21.00	70.00
(3162) Observation, 0 Ga., Turq., Blue, Gray, Brass trim	10.80	18.00	60.00
(3171) Pullman, 0 ga., Beige, Green, Brass trim	10.80	18.00	60.00
(3172) Obser., 0 ga., Beige, Green, Brass trim	10.80	18.00	60.00
(3180) Club, "Potomac", 0 ga., Beige, Green, Brass trim	14.40	24.00	80.00
(3180) Club, 0 ga., Two-tone Red, Green, Brass trim	14.40	24.00	80.00
(3181) Pullman, "Potomac", 0 ga., Beige, Green, Brass trim	14.40	24.00	80.00
(3182) Obser., "Potomac", 0 ga., Beige, Green, Brass trim	14.40	24.00	80.00
(3185) Loco, turquoise/teal blue	72.00	120.00	400.00
(3189) Tender, tin (1933)	7.20	12.00	40.00
(3192) Loco (1937)	45.00	75.00	250.00
(3195) Cast iron loco	45.00	75.00	250.00
(3198) Cast iron loco-0 ga.	40.50	67.50	225.00
(3206) Flatcar with lumber, orange .	7.20	12.00	40.00
(3207) Gondola-0 ga.	5.40	9.00	30.00
(3208) Car, Orange/Blue (1938)	9.00	15.00	50.00
(3210) Tank Car, Silver/Green (1938)	9.00	15.00	50.00
(3211) Caboose-0 ga.	5.40	9.00	30.00
(3212) Milk Car (1938)	9.00	15.00	50.00
(3216) Log Car (1937)	9.00	15.00	50.00
(3219) Dump Car (1938)	9.00	15.00	50.00
(3280) Club car, turquoise/teal blue	18.00	30.00	100.00
(3281) "Jeffersonian" Pullman, 0 ga., Two-tone Red, Green	32.40	54.00	180.00
(3281) Pullman, turquoise/teal blue .	18.00	30.00	100.00
(3282) Observation car, turquoise/teal blue	18.00	30.00	100.00
(3282) Observation car, turquoise/teal blue	18.00	30.00	100.00
(3307) Loco, bell in cab-0 ga.	36.00	60.00	200.00
(3380) Baggage car, red/dark red roof/brass window inserts and decals, 8 wheel, lighted-0 ga.	18.00	30.00	100.00

A. F. Loco and tender, 0-4-0, 0, gray, yellow, copper trim.
Courtesy H. A. Mueller, Continental Hobby House

A. F. 2-4-2 Loco and Tender, 0, black, brass trim
Courtesy H. A. Mueller, Continental Hobby House

A. F. Limited "Washington", Std., brown, black litho, brass, nickel trim.
Courtesy H. A. Mueller, Continental Hobby House

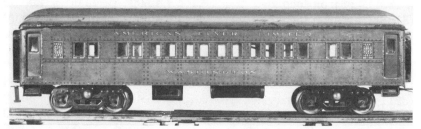

A. F. West Point Coach, Std., blue, yellow litho, brass trim.
Courtesy H. A. Mueller, Continental Hobby House

A. F. Box Car, 0, beige-blue, brass trim
Courtesy H. A. Mueller,
Continental Hobby House

A. F. "America" Obs. Std., green, orange,
black litho, brass trim.
Courtesy H. A. Mueller,
Continental Hobby House

A. F. 13 0-4-0 Wind-up Loco and tender, 0, black, orange, green
Courtesy H. A. Mueller, Continental Hobby House

	G	VG	M
(3381) Coach car red/dark red roof/ brass window insert and decal, 8 wheel, lighted-0 ga.	18.00	100.00	100.00
(3382) Observation car, red/dark red roof/brass window insert and decal, 8 wheel, lighted-0 ga.	18.00	30.00	100.00
(4000) Loco—Std. ga.	63.00	105.00	350.00
(4000) Loco, maroon-Std. ga.	72.00	120.00	400.00
(4002) Loco and Tender, 2-6-4, 0 ga., Black, White, Copper trim	36.00	60.00	200.00
(4006) Hopper car, Std. ga.	63.00	105.00	350.00
(4010) Tank car, yellow-Std. ga......	46.80	78.00	260.00
(4011) Caboose-Std. ga.	32.40	54.00	180.00
(4012) Lumber, Std., Blue, Black, Brass trim	18.00	30.00	100.00
(4017) Gondola-Std. ga., Green	18.00	30.00	100.00
(4018) Box car, beige/blue-Std. ga. ..	49.50	82.50	275.00
(4019) Engine, 0-4-0,, Std., Maroon, Black, Brass trim	63.00	105.00	350.00

247

	G	VG	M
(4020) Cattle car, green/blue-Std. ga.	54.00	90.00	300.00
(4020) Cattle car, two tone blue-Std. ga.	54.00	90.00	300.00
(4021) Caboose-Std. ga., Two-tone Red, Brass trim	36.00	60.00	200.00
(4022) Lumber car-Std. ga., Orange, Turq., Brass trim	36.00	60.00	200.00
(4023) Lumber car with load-Std. ga.	36.00	60.00	200.00
(4039) Loco-Std. ga. 0-4-0, Brown, Black, Brass trim	135.00	225.00	750.00
(4040) Mail car, litho. red-Std. ga.	38.50	64.50	215.00
(4040) "United States Mail Railway Post Office", Std. Ga., Green, Orange, Black litho	36.00	60.00	200.00
(4040) Baggage car, maroon-Std. Ga.	38.50	64.50	215.00
(4041) Pullman, maroon-Std. ga.	38.50	64.50	215.00
(4042) Observation car, maroon-Std. ga.	38.50	64.50	215.00
(4080) Baggage car-Std. ga.	54.00	90.00	300.00
(4081) Washington car-Std. ga.	54.00	90.00	300.00
(4082) Valley Forge car-Std. ga.	54.00	90.00	300.00
(4122) Mail car two-tone blue	40.50	67.50	225.00
(4250) "Lone Scout" Club, Std., Turq., Red litho, Brass trim	40.50	67.50	225.00
(4251) "Lone Scout" Pullman, St. Ga., Turq., Red litho, Brass	40.50	67.50	225.00
(4252) "Lone Scout" Obser., Std. Ga., Turq., Red, Brass trim	40.50	67.50	225.00
(4321) 0-6-0 Loco, with tender, 0 Ga., black, white, nickel trim	18.00	60.00	200.00
(4331) Pullman car, red-Std. ga.	40.50	67.50	225.00
(4331) Observation Car, red with brass doors-Std. ga.	40.50	67.50	225.00
(4331) Pullman, two tone red/brass inserts and brass windows-Std. ga.	40.50	67.50	225.00
(4332) Passenger car, red-Std. ga.	36.00	60.00	200.00
(4332) Observation Car, red with brass doors-Std. ga.	40.50	67.50	225.00
(4332) Observation car, two tone red/brass inserts and brass windows-Std. ga.	40.50	67.50	225.00
(4340) "Pocohontas" Club car, beige/green/green trucks/brass plates/brass windows-Std. ga.	40.50	67.50	225.00

	G	VG	M
(4340) Club car, "Hamiltonian", Std. Ga., Two-tone Red, Brass trim	40.50	67.50	225.00
(4341) Pullman, beige/green/green trucks/brass plates/brass windows-Std. ga.	40.50	67.50	225.00
(4341) "Hamiltonian" Pullman, Std. ga., Two-tone Red, brass trim	40.50	67.50	225.00
(4341) "Pocahontas" Pullman, Std. Ga., Beige, Green, Brass trim	45.00	75.00	250.00
(4342) "Pocahontas", Observation car,/beige/green/green trucks/brass plates/brass windows-Std. ga.	40.50	67.50	225.00
(4342) Observation car, "Hamiltonian", Std. Ga., Two-tone Red, Brass trim	40.50	67.50	225.00
(4343) "Pocahontas", Std. Ga., Observation, Beige, Green, Brass trim	45.00	75.00	250.00
(4350) Club Car, blue green with red roof-Std. ga.......................	40.50	67.50	225.00
(4351) Club Car, blue green with red roof-Std. ga.......................	40.50	67.50	225.00
(4352) Club Car, blue green with red roof-Std. ga.......................	40.50	67.50	225.00
(4380) "Flying Colonel-Madison", Std. Ga., Blue, Brass trim	54.00	90.00	300.00
(4380) "Hancock" Baggage, Std. Ga., Beige, Green, Brass trim	54.00	90.00	300.00
(4381) "Flying Colonel-Adams", Std. Ga., Blue, Brass trim	54.00	90.00	300.00
(4381) "Hancock" Pullman, Std., Ga., Green, Beige, Brass trim	54.00	90.00	300.00
(4382) "Flying Colonel-Hancock" Obs., Std., Ga., Blue, Brass trim	54.00	90.00	300.00
(4382) "Hancock" Obs. Std. Ga., Beige, Green, Brass trim	54.00	90.00	300.00
(4390) "West Point" club car, two-tone blue-Std. ga.	90.00	150.00	500.00
(4391) "Annapolis" pullman car, two-tone blue-Std. ga.	90.00	150.00	500.00
(4392) "Army-Navy" observation car, two-tone blue-Std. ga.	90.00	150.00	500.00
(4393) "President's Special" Academy diner car, two-tone blue-Std. ga.	126.00	210.00	700.00
(4615) Loco 2-4-2, 0 ga.	99.00	165.00	550.00

	G	VG	M
(4633) Loco	63.00	105.00	350.00
(4635) Shasta Loco, re/brass trim-Std. ga...............................	90.00	150.00	500.00
(4637) Eng. 0-4-0, Auto Bell, Std. Ga., Green, Beige, Brass trim	81.00	135.00	450.00
(4637) Shasta Loco, green-Std. ga. ...	108.00	180.00	600.00
(4642) Box car, red/black-Std. ga. ...	54.00	90.00	300.00
(4643) 0-4-0 Engine, Std. Ga., Green-Black, brass trim	72.00	120.00	400.00
(4644) Engine 0-4-0, Std. ga., Red, Gray, Brass trim	63.00	105.00	350.00
(4644) Eagle Pullman, litho.-Std. ga.	36.00	60.00	200.00
(4644) Eagle observation, litho.-Std. ga...............................	36.00	60.00	200.00
(4644) Shasta loco, red/gray-Std. ga. ...	99.00	165.00	550.00
(4653) Engine, 0-4-0, Std. Ga., Orange, Black, Brass trim	54.00	90.00	300.00
(4654) Loco-Std. ga.	63.00	105.00	350.00
(4660) Loco	75.00	125.00	375.00
(4667) Engine, 0-4-0, Std. Ga., Red, Black, Brass trim	64.80	108.00	360.00
(4670) Loco, 2-4-2, and tender, Std. Ga., Black, Green stripe, Brass trim	72.00	120.00	400.00
(4670) Loco, 4-4-2, with tender, Std. Ga., Black, Green stripe, Brass, Nickel trim	126.00	210.00	700.00
(4671) Cast iron loco	104.00	180.00	600.00
(4672) Consist Loco 4670, Tender 4671	126.00	210.00	700.00
(4677) Loco	90.00	150.00	500.00
(4677) Loco-0 ga.	63.00	105.00	350.00
(4678) Engine, 0-4-0,, Std., Red, Gray, Brass trim	67.50	112.50	375.00
(4680) Loco 2-4-4, Std. ga.	104.00	180.00	600.00
(4680) "Golden State" Loco-Std. ga. .	126.00	210.00	700.00
(4680) Loco-Std. ga.	108.00	180.00	600.00
(4682) Consist (1933) Loco 4680, 4671 Coal Tender	126.00	210.00	700.00
(4683) Loco	90.00	150.00	500.00
(4684) Loco	90.00	150.00	500.00
(4686) "The Ace" Engine, 4-4-4, Std. Ga., Two-tone Blue, Black, Red, Brass trim	90.00	150.00	500.00
(4687) "President Special" loco-Std. ga. (blue litho.)	360.00	600.00	2000.00

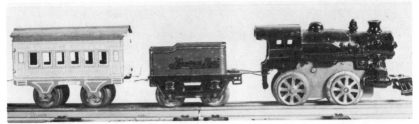

A. F. 0-4-0 Loco, Wind-up, tender, "Empire Express" coach, black, red, yellow, blue litho on coach.
Courtesy H. A. Mueller, Continental Hobby House

A. F. No 10 0-4-0 Wind-up Loco, tender, 515 Coach, 0, black, orange, yellow.
Courtesy H. A. Mueller, Continental Hobby House

A. F. 2-4-2 Loco with "No. 121" Tender, 0, black, white, copper trim.
Courtesy H. A. Mueller, Continental Hobby House

A. F. 0-4-0 Wind-up Loco, "328" Tender, "Chicago" coach, green, black, yellow.
Courtesy H. A. Mueller, Continental Hobby House

251

A. F. Limited, Annapolis Obs. Std., blue, yellow litho, brass trim.
Courtesy H. A. Mueller, Continental Hobby House

A. F. 0-4-0 Loco and tender, 1107 Coach, 0, black loco and tender, litho coach.
Courtesy H. A. Mueller, Continental Hobby House

A. F. 1218 0-4-0 Engine, 1105 "Canadian National Railways-Dominion Flyer", 0, red, black, litho on car, nickel trim.
Courtesy H. A. Mueller, Continental Hobby House

A. F. 3107 0-4-0 Engine, 3150 Baggage, 0, peacock, blue, gray, brass trim
Courtesy H. A. Mueller, Continental Hobby House

252

A. F. 1114 Caboose, 0, red, green, white litho, brass trim.
Courtesy H. A. Mueller,
Continental Hobby House

A. F. 1106 Coach "Dominion Flyer", 0, brown, black litho.
Courtesy H. A. Mueller,
Continental Hobby House

A. F. 1097 Engine, 0-4-0, 0, orange, green, red litho, nickel trim, 500 Pullman.
Courtesy H. A. Mueller, Continental Hobby House

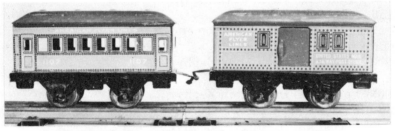

A. F. 1108 Baggage, 1107 Pullman, 0, red, green, orange litho.
Courtesy H. A. Mueller, Continental Hobby House

A. F. 1218 0-4-0 Engine, black, 3150 Baggage, two-tone orange, 0, nickel and brass trim.
Courtesy H. A. Mueller, Continental Hobby House

	G	VG	M
(4687) 4-4-4 Engine, Std. Ga., Blue, Black, Brass trim	360.00	600.00	2000.00
(4689) "The Commander" Engine, 4-4-4 Std. Ga., Peacock, Blue-Black, Brass, Nickel trim	504.00	840.00	2800.00
(4692) Flyer/Ives loco-Std. ga.	270.00	450.00	1500.00
(4692) Ives loco-Std. ga.	144.00	240.99	800.00
(4693) Tender	36.00	60.00	200.00
(4693) Loco, 4-4-2, Std. Ga., with Tender, Black, Green stripe, Brass Nickel trim	108.00	180.00	600.00
(4693) Loco, 4-4-2, Std. Ga., Blue, Brass and Copper Trim	126.00	210.00	700.00
(4693) Ives "Golden State" tender-Std. ga.	63.00	105.00	350.00
(4694) Flyer/Ives loco-Std. ga.	104.00	180.00	600.00
(4694) Loco-Std. ga.	162.00	270.00	900.00
(4694) Loco, beige/green/green trucks/brass plates/brass windows-Std. ga.	162.00	270.00	900.00
(4695) Loco-Std. ga.	162.00	270.00	900.00
(5160) Union Pacific caboose	1.80	3.00	10.00
(5640) Hudson, 4-6-4, 0 Ga., with Tender	36.00	60.00	200.00
(9217) Street lamp, green metal, approx. 6″ high	3.00	4.00	10.00
(9900) Loco-0 ga., Burlington Zephyr, tinplate wind-up	45.00	75.00	250.00
(9900) Loco-0 ga. Burlington Zephyr, tinplate electric	63.00	105.00	350.00
(9900) Loco-0 ga. Burlington Zephyr, Aluminum Cast Electric	81.00	135.00	450.00
(19220) Auto Rama T intersections for HO	.90	1.50	5.00
(22006) 25 watt transformer	1.80	3.00	10.00
(25671) Track trip	.54	.90	3.00
(26672) Track trip	.54	.90	3.00
(26782) Trestle set	3.25	5.40	18.00
(31004) Switcher loco 0-6-0, HO	17.50	28.50	95.00
"America" Observation car, Std. Ga., Green, Orange, black litho, Brass trim	27.00	45.00	150.00
"Annapolis" Observation car, Std. Ga., Blue, Yellow litho, Brass trim ..	27.00	45.00	150.00

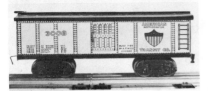

A. F. 3008 Box Car, 0, yellow, black litho.
Courtesy H. A. Mueller,
Continental Hobby House

A. F. 3000 Baggage, 0, two-tone green, black litho.
Courtesy H. A. Mueller,
Continental Hobby House

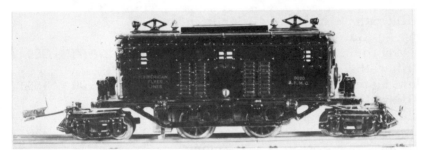

A. F. 3020 4-4-4 Engine, 0, black, yellow, nickel trim.
Courtesy H. A. Mueller, Continental Hobby House

	G	VG	M
Box Car, 0 Ga., Beige, Blue, Brass trim	14.40	24.00	80.00
Bubbling watertower	3.25	5.40	18.00
"Bunker Hill" passenger, Std., Ga., Orange, Maroon, Black litho, Brass trim	31.50	52.50	175.00
Caboose, 0 Ga., Red, Black, Brass trim, 8 wheel	10.80	18.00	60.00
Cattle for cattle corral, 4 black, 4 brown	2.70	4.50	15.00
Central station, large, plastic, with sound	35.10	58.50	195.00
"Chicago" Coach, Green, Yellow, 0 Ga.	10.80	18.00	60.00
Circus train set, complete	216.00	360.00	1200.00
Coach, 0 Ga., Blue, Orange roof	14.40	24.00	80.00
Coach, 0 Ga., Red, Yellow	14.40	24.00	80.00
Coach, 0 Ga., Two-tone Green, Yellow	14.40	24.00	80.00
Crossover, 90°, 0 ga.	1.14	1.80	6.00

	G	VG	M
Crossover, 45°, 0 ga.	1.45	2.40	8.00
"Eagle" Observatory, Std. Ga, Red litho, Brass trim	31.50	52.50	175.00
"Eagle" Pullman, Std. Ga, Red litho, Brass trim	31.50	52.50	175.00
"Empire Express" Coach, Yellow, Blue litho, 0 Ga.	14.40	24.00	80.00
Franklin loco, with 2 cars	31.10	58.50	195.00
Franklin loco, with 3 cars	49.50	82.50	275.00
Gondola, 0 Ga., Green, Brass trim, 3000 series	8.10	13.50	45.00
"Hiawatha" Engine, 4-4-4, and tender, 0 Ga., Orange, Gray, Black, nickel trim	162.00	270.00	900.00
"Hiawatha" Observation, 0 Ga., Yellow, Maroon, Gray, Brass trim	27.00	45.00	150.00
"Hiawatha" passenger coaches, maroon/yellow/gray 0 ga., set of three	81.00	135.00	450.00
"Hiawatha" Set, 0 Ga., Engine, tender, 3 cars	243.00	405.00	1350.00
"Hiawatha" Set, 0 Ga., Tinplate litho electric, Engine, tender, 3 cars	108.00	180.00	600.00
"Hiawatha" Set, 0 Ga., Tinplate litho Windup, Engine, tender, 3 cars	126.00	210.00	700.00
"Illini" Coach, 0 Ga., Two-tone Green, Black litho	14.40	24.00	80.00
"Illini" Observation, 0 Ga., Two-tone Green, Black litho	14.40	24.00	80.00
"Limited" U.S. Mail Car, Std. Ga., Blue, Yellow litho, Brass trim	27.00	45.00	150.00
Loco, 0-4-0, and tender, Black, 0 Ga.	27.00	45.00	150.00
Loco, 0-4-0, and Tender, 0 ga., Gray, Yellow, Copper trim	27.00	45.00	150.00
Loco, 0-4-0, Wind-up, 0 ga., with Tender, Black loco, Red tender	22.50	37.50	125.00
Loco, 0-4-0, 0 Ga., with "328" tender, Black	28.80	48.00	160.00
Loco, 2-4-2, and Tender, 0 G., Black, Brass trim	28.80	48.00	160.00
Loco, 2-4-2, 0 Ga., with "No. 121" Tender, Black, White, Copper trim ..	31.50	52.50	175.00
Loco, 2-6-4, 0 Ga., Black, white, Copper and Brass trim, with Tender	40.50	67.50	225.00

	G	VG	M
Lumber Car, 0, Black, Nickel trim ..	6.30	10.50	35.00
Lumber Car, 0 Ga., Yellow	6.30	10.50	35.00
Observation Car, 0 Ga., Red, Yellow, large 8-wheel car	14.40	24.00	80.00
Observation Car, 0 Ga., Two-tone Green, Yellow, large 8-wheel car	14.40	24.00	80.00
"Nationwide Lines" Railway post office car, red/blue/yellow/dark red roof litho.-0 ga., made for J. C. Penney	36.00	60.00	200.00
Wells Fargo & Co. Overland Flyer box car body	31.50	52.50	175.00
Pleasant Valley ovservation car-Std. ga.	36.00	60.00	200.00
"Pleasant View" observation car, red/dark red roofs, Std. ga.	36.00	60.00	200.00
"Pleasant View" passenger car-Std. ga.	36.00	60.00	200.00
Race car track (44 pcs.) 3 lane controllers, 1 connecting track	5.40	9.00	30.00
Station, mystic talking with button	27.00	45.00	150.00
"Streamline" Engine and attached car, 0-4-4-0, 0 Ga., Orange, Silver ...	22.50	37.50	125.00
Switches, electric autom	6.30	10.50	35.00
Switches, manual	2.70	4.50	15.00
Tank Car, 0 Ga., Yellow, Black, Nickel trim	7.20	12.00	40.00
Track, HO curved or straight	.20	.30	.50
Union Pacific "City of Denver" loco, yellow/brown 0 ga.	36.00	60.00	200.00
Union Pacific center coaches-0 ga. .	18.00	30.00	100.00
Union Pacific observation car-0 ga.	18.00	30.00	100.00
"Valley Forge" Observation Car, Std. Ga., Brown, Black litho	54.00	90.00	300.00
"Washington" Limited, Std. Ga., Brown, Black litho, Brass, Nickel trim	54.00	90.00	300.00
"West Point" Coach, Std. Ga., Blue, Yellow litho, Brass trim	54.00	90.00	300.00
"Yorktown" Observation, Std. Ga., Orange, Green litho, Brass trim	54.00	90.00	300.00
"Yorktown" Observation, Std. Ga., Orange, Maroon, Black litho, Brass trim	54.00	90.00	300.00

AMERICAN FLYER "S" GAUGE AND FUNDIMENSIONS
By Frank L. Ferrara

Some "S" Gauge Definitions and Notes

Gauge of Track ⅞" or 0.875" (space between rails)
Scale 1/64. Scale to the Foot 3/16"

G - Good. All complete and original, well-used, with scratches and perhaps small dents, perhaps dirty, but not broken.
VG - Very Good. Relatively clean, few scratches, no dents or rust, complete and original.
E - Excellent. Extremely clean, minute scratches, no discoloration, no dents or rust. All complete and original.
Mint - Appears as it did when it was manufactured. Original carton, inserts and instructions must come with it. Add 20-25% over excellent value for mint.
2-4-2, 0-6-0, refers to the number of wheels under each section of the unit.

L/C - Link coupler.
K/C - Knuckle coupler.
P/M - Pike Master.
Reefer - Refrigerator Box Car
Coach - Pullman or Passenger Car
Combine - Baggage/Club Car

FRANK L. FERRARA

An enthusiastic American Flyer "S" Gauge collector, Frank L. Ferrara is a police officer living in Bergen County, New Jersey. As far back as he can remember, his father and two older brothers set up a train layout for the Christman holidays. When he was five, his parents gave him his first American Flyer train set as a Christmas present, a gift he still owns today. As his brothers grew older, the tradition of setting up a layout for the holidays was discontinued. In 1979, a few months before Christmas, his oldest brother suggested that they set up a train layout for the holidays in his home. Looking to expand the existing layout they had when younger, Frank looked into purchasing track and rolling stock at train shows. It was at this time that he got the "itch" for train collecting. His collection over the years has grown extensively, and setting up layouts has again become a tradition in the Ferrara home. Recently married, Frank hopes to share his knowledge and joy of train collecting with his anticipated children.

AMERICAN FLYER S GAUGE
List compiled by Frank L. Ferrara

	G	VG	E
1B Transformer, 50 watt, 1956	1.00	2.00	3.00
2/2B Transformer, 75 watt, 1947-52	1.00	3.00	5.00
4B Transformer, 75/100/110 watt, 1949-56	3.00	6.00	9.00
5/5A/5B Transformer, 50 watt, 1946	1.00	3.00	5.00
6/6A Transformer, 75 watt, 1946 ...	3.00	5.00	7.00
7B Transformer, 75 watt, 1946	3.00	5.00	7.00
8B Transformer, 100 watt, 1946-52 ..	12.00	18.00	25.00
9B Transformer, 150 watt, 1946	12.00	18.00	25.00
12B Transformer, 250 watt, 1946-52	15.00	22.00	30.00
15B Transformer, 110 watt, 1953-56	10.00	15.00	20.00
16B Transformer, 190 watt, 1953 ...	12.00	18.00	25.00

A. F. 3109 0-4-0 Engine, 0, green, beige, brass trim.
Courtesy H. A. Mueller,
Continental Hobby House

A. F. 3910 Tank Car, 0, gray, black, nickel trim
Courtesy H. A. Mueller,
Continental Hobby House

A. F. 3110 0-4-0 Engine, 0, red, nickel and brass trim.
Courtesy H. A. Mueller, Continental Hobby House

	G	VG	E
16B Transformer, 175 watt, 1954-56	12.00	18.00	25.00
17B Transformer, 190 watt	12.00	18.00	25.00
18B Transformer, 190 watt, 1953 (dual controls)	15.00	22.00	30.00
19B Transformer, 300 watt, 1952-55 (dual controls)	23.00	33.00	45.00
20 (247((20))) Coach, Fy & PRR, Yellow, 1959-60, K/C	15.00	22.00	30.00
21/21A Imitation Grass, ½ lb., 1949-56, full bag	three dollars		
22 Scenery Gravel, 22 oz., 1949-56, full bag	three dollars		
23 Artificial Coal, ½ lb., 1949-56, full bag	three dollars		
24 Multicolor Wire, 25′ roll, 1949-56 .	five dollars		
25 Smoke Fluid Cartridges, 12 in box, 1947-56, full box	five dollars		
26 Service Kit, 1952-56	3.00	4.50	6.00
27 Track Cleaning Fluid, 8 oz., 1952-56	three dollars		
28/28A Track Ballast, 8 oz., 1950-53	three dollars		
29/29A Imitation Snow, 4 oz., 1950-53	three dollars		
30 (247((30))) Baggage, FY & PRR, yellow, 1959-60, K/C	15.00	22.00	30.00
30/30A Highway sign set (3 yellow, 5 white), 1949-52 (in excellent condition, requires box)	6.00	8.00	12.00
30B Transformer, 300 watt, 1953-55 (dual control)	25.00	38.00	50.00
31/31A Railroad Signs, 8 white signs (Excellent requires box)	7.00	11.00	15.00
32 City Street Set, 8 pieces, 1949-50 (Excellent requires box)	7.00	11.00	15.00
32A Park Set, 12 pieces, 1951 (Excellent requires box)	10.00	15.00	20.00
33 Passenger and Train Figure Set, 8 figures (Excellent requires box), 1951-52	12.00	18.00	25.00
34 Railway Figure Set, 25 pieces, 1953 (Excellent requires box)	20.00	30.00	40.00
35 Brakeman with Lantern, three brakemen (Excellent requires box) ..	10.00	15.00	20.00
40 (247((40))) Combine, FY&PRR, yellow, 1959-60 K/C	15.00	22.00	30.00

A. F. 3112 0-4-0 Engine and "United States Mail Railway Post Office" car, 0, orange litho, brass trim.
Courtesy H. A. Mueller, Continental Hobby House

A. F. 3115 0-4-0 Engine, 0, peacock, blue, brass trim.
Courtesy H. A. Mueller, Continental Hobby House

A. F. 3110 0-4-0 Engine, 0, black, nickel and brass trim
Courtesy H. A. Mueller, Continental Hobby House

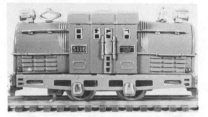

A. F. 3116, 0-4-0, 0, turq., black, brass trim.
Courtesy H. A. Mueller,
Continental Hobby House

A. F. 3141 Pullman, 0, red, black, brass trim.
Courtesy H. A. Mueller,
Continental Hobby House

A. F. 3151 Passenger and 3152 Observation, 0, two-tone orange, brass trim.
Courtesy H. A. Mueller, Continental Hobby House

A. F. 3117 0-4-0 Engine, 0, red, brass trim.
Courtesy H. A. Mueller, Continental Hobby House

A. F. 3171 Pullman, 0, beige, green, brass trim
Courtesy H. A. Mueller, Continental Hobby House

	G	VG	E
40 Smoke Set, 1953-55	1.00	2.00	3.00
50 (247((50))), Combine, FY&PRR, 1960-61, K/C	25.00	38.00	50.00
50 District School (Illuminated), 1953-54	25.00	38.00	50.00
55 Box Car, G.Fox & Co., Brown, 1947, L/C (rare)	400.00	800.00	1200.00
55 (240((55))) Box Car, Gold Belt Line, 1960-61, K/C, P/M	20.00	30.00	40.00
65 (245((65))), Flat Car, F.Y.& P.R.R., cannon load, 1960-61, K/C	60.00	90.00	120.00
88 (210)88 Steam Loco, FY88&P, Franklin 4-4-0, 1959, K/C	38.00	56.00	75.00
160 Station Platform, non-illuminated, 1953	30.00	45.00	60.00
161 Bungalow (Illuminated), 1953 ..	30.00	45.00	60.00
162 Factory, "Mysto-Magic Company"	38.00	56.00	75.00
163 Flyerville Station, 1953	30.00	45.00	60.00
164 Barn, illuminated, 1953	38.00	56.00	75.00
165 Grain Elevator, illuminated, 1953	38.00	56.00	75.00
166 Church, illuminated, 1953	38.00	56.00	75.00
167 Town Hall, illuminated, 1953 ...	38.00	56.00	75.00
168 Hotel, illuminated, 1953	38.00	56.00	75.00
234 (21((234))) GP-7, Chesapeake & Ohio, 1961-62, K/C	82.00	123.00	165.00

263

A. F. 3172 Observation, 0, beige, green, brass trim.
Courtesy H. A. Mueller, Continental Hobby House

	G	VG	E
247 Tunnel, 11″, 1946-48	6.00	9.00	12.00
248 Tunnel, 14″, 1946-48	7.00	11.00	15.00
249 Tunnel, 11½″, 1947-56	6.00	9.00	12.00
263 Steam Loco, P.R.R., switcher, 0-6-0, 1957, K/C	245.00	410.00	590.00
270 News & Frank Stand, 1952-53 ..	30.00	45.00	60.00
271 "Whistle Stop Set" - Newsstand, Franks stand, Waiting stand, 1952-53	38.00	56.00	75.00
272 Glendale Station, illuminated ..	30.00	45.00	60.00
273 Suburban Station, illuminated, 1952-53	30.00	45.00	60.00
274 Harbor Junction Freight Station, illuminated, 1952-53	30.00	45.00	60.00
275 Eureka Diner, Illuminated, 1952-53	30.00	45.00	60.00
282 Steam Loco, C&NW, Pacific, 4-6-2, 1952-53, L/C, K/C	19.00	28.00	38.00
283 Steam Loco, C&NW, Pacific, 4-6-2, 1954-57, K/C	20.00	30.00	40.00
285 Steam Loco, C&NW, Pacific, 4-6-2, 1952, L/C	39.00	58.00	78.00
287 Steam Loco, C&NW, Pacific	20.00	30.00	40.00
289 Steam Loco, C&NW, Pacific 4-6-2, 1956, K/C	80.00	120.00	160.00
290 Steam Loco, Reading, Pacific 4-6-2, 1949-51, L/C	25.00	37.00	49.00

	G	VG	E
293 Steam Loco, NYNH & Hartford, Pacific 4-6-2, 1953-58, K/C	35.00	52.00	69.00
295 Steam Loco, A.F., Pacific 4-6-2, 1951, L/C	49.00	73.00	97.00
296 Steam Loco, New Haven, Pacific 4-6-2, 1955 K/C	87.00	131.00	175.00
299 Steam Loco, Reading AFL, Atlantic 4-4-2, 1954 L/C	68.00	100.00	135.00
300 Steam Loco, Reading, Atlantic 4-4-2, 1946-47, L/C	22.00	32.00	42.00
300AC Steam Loco, Reading, Atlantic 4-4-2, 1949-51, LC	18.00	27.00	36.00
301 Steam Loco, Reading, Atlantic 4-4-2, 1946-53, L/C	13.00	19.00	27.00
302 Steam Loco, Reading, Atlantic 4-4-2, 1948-1952-53, L/C	13.00	19.00	27.00
302 AC Steam Loco, Reading, Atlantic, 4-4-2, 1950-51, L/C	13.00	19.00	27.00
303 Steam Loco, Reading, Atlantic 4-4-2, 1954-57, K/C	13.00	19.00	27.00
307 Steam Loco, Reading, Atlantic 4-4-2, 1954-55, K/C	10.00	15.00	20.00
308 Steam Loco, Reading, Atlantic 4-4-2, 1956, K/C	13.00	19.00	27.00
310 Steam Loco, P.R.R., K-5, 4-6-2, 1946 L/C "Pennsylvania" tender ...	49.00	73.00	98.00
310 Steam Loco, A.F.L. PRR K-5, 4-6-2, 1947, L/C	35.00	52.00	70.00
312 Steam Loco, P.R.R., K-5, 4-6-2, 1946-48, 1952, L/C	30.00	45.00	60.00
312 AC Steam Loco, PRR, K-5, 4-6-2, 1949-51, L/C	33.00	49.00	65.00
313 Steam Loco, PRR, K-5, 4-6-2, 1955-57, K/C	49.00	73.00	98.00
314AW, Steam Loco, PRR, K-5, 4-6-2, 1949-50, L/C	63.00	94.00	125.00
315 Steam Loco, PRR, K-5, 4-6-2, 1952, L/C	35.00	52.00	69.00
316 Steam Loco, PRR, K-5, 4-6-2, 1953-54, K/C	50.00	75.00	100.00
320 Steam Loco, New York Central, Hudson 4-6-4, 1946-47, L/C	50.00	75.00	100.00
321 Steam Loco, New York Central, Hudson 4-6-4, 1946-7 L/C Tender with "New York Central System" in oval	65.00	97.00	130.00

	G	VG	E
321 Steam Loco, New York Central, Hudson 4-6-4, 1946-47 L/C Tender "New York Central"	87.00	131.00	175.00
322 Steam Loco, New York Central, Hudson 4-6-4, 1947-48, L/C Tender with "New York Central System" in oval	58.00	86.00	115.00
322 Steam Loco, New York Central, Hudson 4-6-4, 1946, L/C, "New York Central" on tender	87.00	131.00	175.00
322 AC Steam Loco, New York Central, Hudson 4-6-4, 1949-51, L/C	40.00	60.00	80.00
324 AC Steam Loco, New York Central, Hudson 4-6-4, 1950, L/C	48.00	71.00	95.00
325AC Steam Loco, New York Central, Hudson 4-6-4, 1951 L/C	40.00	60.00	80.00
K325 Steam Loco, New York Central, Hudson 4-6-4, 1952, K/C	40.00	60.00	80.00
326 Steam Loco, New York Central, Hudson 4-6-4, 1953-57, K/C	40.00	60.00	80.00
332 Steam Loco, Union Pacific, Northern 4-8-4, 1946-49, L/C, Tender lettered "Union Pacific", rare	600.00	900.00	1200.00
332 Steam Loco, Union Pacific, Northern 4-8-4, 1946-49, L/C. "Union Pacific" on shield on tender	82.00	123.00	165.00
332 AC, Steam Loco, Union Pacific, Northern 4-8-4, 1950-51, L/C	82.00	123.00	165.00
334 DC Steam Loco, Union Pacific, Northern 4-8-4, 1950 L/C	97.00	147.00	195.00
K335 Steam Loco, Union Pacific, Northern, 1952, K/C	82.00	123.00	165.00
336 Steam Loco, Union Pacific, Northern 4-8-4, 1953-57, K/C	82.00	123.00	165.00
342 Steam Loco,nickelplate, Switcher 0-8-0, 1946, L/C, Tender lettered "Nickel Plate Road"	405.00	607.00	810.00
342 Steam Loco, nickelplate, Switcher 0-8-0, 1947-48, 1952, L/C, Tender reads "A.F.L.& Nickel Plate Road" .	49.00	73.00	98.00
342 AC Steam Loco, nickel plate, Switcher, 0-8-0, 1949-51, L/C	45.00	67.00	90.00

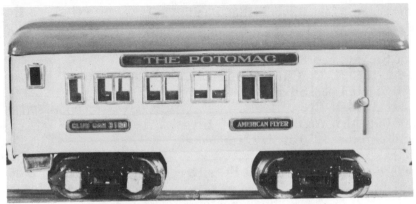

A. F. 3180 Club, "Potomac", 0, beige, green, brass trim.
Courtesy H. A. Mueller, Continental Hobby House

A. F. 3181 Pullman, "Potomac", 0, beige, green, brass trim.
Courtesy H. A. Mueller, Continental Hobby House

	G	VG	E
342 DC Steam Loco, nickelplate, Switcher 0-8-0, 1948-50, L/C	45.00	67.00	90.00
343 Steam Loco, nickelplate, Switcher 0-8-0, 1953-58, K/C	58.00	86.00	115.00
346 Steam Loco, nickelplate, Switcher, 0-8-0, 1955, K/C	90.00	135.00	180.00
350 Steam Loco, B&O, Royal Blue, Pacific 4-6-2, 1948-50, L/C	49.00	73.00	98.00
353 Steam Loco, A.F. Circus, Pacific 4-6-2, 1950-51, L/C	58.00	86.00	115.00

	G	VG	E
354 Steam Loco, Silver Bullet, Pacific 4-6-2, 1954, K/C	40.00	60.00	80.00
355 Switcher, C&NW, 1957, K/C ...	35.00	52.00	69.00
356 Steam Loco, Silver Bullet, Pacific 4-6-2, 1953, L/C., Chrome	68.00	100.00	135.00
356 Steam Loco, Silver Bullet, Pacific 4-6-2, 1953, L/C	35.00	52.00	70.00
360-361 Alco A&B, Santa Fe, silver and chrome, 1950-52, L/C (priced as set)	97.00	147.00	195.00
360-364 Alco A&B, Santa Fe, silver finish, 1951-52, L/C (priced as set) ..	97.00	147.00	195.00
370 GP-7, G.M.A.F. Road Switcher, 1950-53, coupler bar	40.00	60.00	80.00
371 GP-7, G.M.A.F. Road Switcher, 1954, K/C	40.00	60.00	80.00
372 GP-7, Union Pacific, Road Switcher 1955-57 K/C, "Built by Gilbert" on side	58.00	86.00	115.00
372 GP-7, Union Pacific, Road Switcher, 1955-57, K/C without "Built by Gilbert" on side	63.00	94.00	125.00
374-375 GP-7, Texas & Pacific, Road Switcher, 1955, K/C, priced as set ..	85.00	127.00	170.00
375 GP-7, GM, A.F., Road Switcher, 1953 K/C, rare	197.00	296.00	395.00
377-78 GP-7, Texas & Pacific, Road Switcher, 1956-57, K/C, priced as set	63.00	94.00	125.00
405 Alco A, Silver Streak, 1952, L/C	48.00	71.00	95.00
460 A.F. Bulb Assortment (54), boxed set	30.00	45.00	60.00
466 Alco A, Silver Comet, 1953-55, K/C	33.00	49.00	65.00
470-471-473 Alco A-B-A, Santa Fe, 1953-57, K/C, priced as set	110.00	210.00	220.00
472 Alco A, Santa Fe, 1956, K/C ...	73.00	109.00	145.00
474-475 Alco A-A, Silver Rocket, 1953-55, K/C	75.00	112.00	150.00
477-478 Alco A-B, Silver Flash, 1953-54, K/C	87.00	131.00	175.00
479 Alco A, Silver Flash, 1955, K/C	49.00	73.00	98.00
480 Alco B, Silver Flash, 1955, K/C	162.00	244.00	325.00
481 Alco A, Silver Flash, 1956, K/C	58.00	86.00	115.00
484-485-486 Alco A-B-A, Santa Fe, 1956-57, K/C, priced as set	125.00	187.00	250.00

	G	VG	E
490-491-493 Alco A-B-A, Northern Pacific, 1956-57, K/C, priced as set, rare	195.00	292.00	390.00
497 Alco A, New Haven, 1957, K/C .	53.00	79.00	105.00
499 GE Electric, New Haven, with Pantographs, 1956, K/C	97.00	147.00	195.00
500 Combine, AFL, chrome finish, 1952, L/C	63.00	94.00	125.00
500 Combine, AFL, silver finish, 1952, L/C	63.00	94.00	125.00
501 Coach, AFL, chrome finish, 1952, L/C	48.00	71.00	95.00
501 Coach, AFL, silver finish, 1952, L/C	48.00	71.00	95.00
502 Vista Dome, AFL, chrome finish, 1952, L/C	48.00	71.00	95.00
502 Vista Dome, AFL, silver finish, 1952, L/C	48.00	71.00	95.00
503 Observation, AFL, silver finish, 1952, L/C	48.00	71.00	95.00
503 Observation, AFL, chrome finish, 1952, L/C	48.00	71.00	95.00
520 Knuckle Coupler Kit, 1954-56 ...	1.00	2.00	3.00
561 Diesel Billboard, Santa Fe Alco Picture on billboard, 1955-56	7.00	11.00	15.00
561 Billboard Horn, Santa Fe Alco ABA Picture on billboard, 1956	10.00	15.00	20.00
566 Whistling Billboard, Santa Fe Alco or Steam Engine picture on billboard	7.00	11.00	15.00
568 Whistling Billboard, 1956	10.00	15.00	20.00
571 Truss Girder Bridge, 1955-56 ...	1.00	2.00	3.00
577 Whistling Billboard, "Ringling Bros. and Barnum & Bailey", 1946-50	10.00	15.00	20.00
577NL Whistling Billboard (same as 577), 1950	11.00	16.00	22.00
578 Station Figure Set (Excellent requires box)	20.00	30.00	40.00
579 Single Street Lamp, 1946-49	3.00	6.00	9.00
580 Double Street Lamp, 1946-49 ...	5.00	7.50	10.00
581 Girder Bridge lettered "Lackawanna" or "American Flyer", 1946-56	3.00	6.00	9.00
582 Automatic Blinker Signal, 1946-48	20.00	30.00	40.00

A. F. 3180 Club, 0, two-tone red, green, brass trim.
Courtesy H. A. Mueller,
Continental Hobby House

A. F. 3211 Caboose, 0, red, brass trim.
Courtesy H. A. Mueller
Continental Hobby House

A. F. 3281 "Jeffersonian" Pullman, 0, two-tone red, green
Courtesy H. A. Mueller
Continental Hobby House

A. F. 3282 "Golden State" Observation, 0, two-tone red, green, brass trim.
Courtesy H. A. Mueller
Continental Hobby House

A. F. 3182 "The Potomac" Observation, 0, beige, green, brass trim.
Courtesy H. A. Mueller, Continental Hobby House

	G	VG	E
583 Electro Magnetic Crane (single button control), 1946-49	30.00	45.00	60.00
583A Electro Magnetic Crane (double button control), 1950-53	33.00	49.00	65.00

	G	VG	E
584 Bell Danger Signal, 1946-47	17.00	26.00	35.00
585 Tool Shed, 1946-52	7.00	11.00	15.00
586F Wayside Station, 1946-56	20.00	30.00	40.00
587 Block Signal, 1946-47	10.00	15.00	20.00
588 Semaphore Signal, 1946-48	20.00	30.00	40.00
589 Passenger & Freight Station, illuminated, 1946-56	10.00	15.00	20.00
590 Control Tower, illuminated, manufactured by Bachman for A.C. Gilbert, 1955-56	20.00	30.00	40.00
591 Crossing Gate, single arm, 1946-48	12.00	18.00	25.00
592 Crossing Gate, double arm	12.00	18.00	25.00
592A Crossing Gate, double arm, 1951-53	12.00	18.00	25.00
593 Signal Tower, illuminated, 1946-54	20.00	30.00	40.00
594 Animated Track Gang Set, 1946-47, rare	500.00	900.00	1500.00
596 Water Tank, 1946-56	17.00	26.00	35.00
598 Talking Station Record (Replacement), 1946-56	6.00	9.00	12.00
599 Talking Station Record (Replacement), 1956	6.00	9.00	12.00
600 Crossing Gate with Bell, 1954-56	17.00	26.00	35.00
605 Flat Car, AFL, Log Load, 1953, L/C	9.00	13.50	18.00
606 Crane Car, AFL, 1953, L/C	12.00	18.00	25.00
607 Work Caboose, AFL, 1953, L/C .	6.00	9.50	13.00
609 Flat Car, AFL, Girder Load, 1953, L/C	9.00	14.00	19.00
612 Freight and Passenger Station with Crane, illuminated, 1946-54 ...	30.00	45.00	60.00
613 Box Car, Great Northern, brown, 1953, L/C,K/C	10.00	15.00	21.00
620 Gondola, Southern, black, 1953, L/C	5.00	7.50	10.00
622 Box Car, GAEX, 1953, L/C	10.00	15.00	21.00
623 Reefer, Illinois Central, orange, 1953, L/C	10.00	15.00	21.00
625G Tank Car, Gulf, Silver, 1952-53, L/C	7.00	11.00	15.00
627 Flat Car, AFL, girder load, 1950, L/C	10.00	15.00	20.00

271

	G	VG	E
627 Flat Car, C&NW, girder load, 1947-50, L/C	11.00	16.00	22.00
629 Stock Car, Missouri Pacific, red, 1943-53, L/C	10.00	15.00	21.00
630 Caboose, AFL, red, 1946-53, L/C, K/C	6.00	9.00	12.00
630 Caboose, Reading, red, 1946-53, L/C, K/C	3.00	4.50	6.00
631 Gondola, Texas & Pacific, 1946-53, L/C	3.00	4.50	6.00
632 Hopper, Lehigh-New England, grey, 1946-53, L/C	7.00	11.00	15.00
633 Reefer, B&O, 2 color variations, red or brown, 1948-53, L/C	10.00	15.00	21.00
633 Box Car, B&O, 3 color variations on sides, white, red, brown, 1948-53, L/C	10.00	15.00	21.00
634 Floodlight, C&NW, AFL, 1946-49, 1953, L/C, K/C	12.00	18.00	25.00
635 Crane Car, C&NWRY, 1946-49, L/C	12.00	18.00	25.00
636 Flat Car, Erie, depressed center, with spool load, 1948-53, L/C	11.00	16.00	22.00
637 Box Car, MKT, yellow, 1949-53, L/C	7.00	10.50	14.00
638 Caboose, AFL, red, 1949-53, L/C, K/C	3.00	4.50	6.00
639 Box Car, A.F., brown or yellow, 1949-52, L/C	7.00	10.50	14.00
639 Reefer, A.F., yellow, 1951-52, L/C	7.00	10.50	14.00
640 Hopper, A.F., grey, 1949-53, L/C	6.00	9.00	12.00
640 Hopper, Wabash, black, 1953, L/C	7.00	11.00	15.00
641 Gondola, Frisco, brown, 1953, L/C	13.00	19.00	26.00
641 Gondola, A.F., red or green, 1949-51, L/C	4.00	6.00	8.00
642 Box Car, Seaboard, lt. brown, 1953, L/C	10.00	15.00	21.00
642 Box Car, A.F., brown or red, 1950-52, L/C	10.00	15.00	21.00
642 Reefer, A.F., brown or red, 1952, L/C	10.00	15.00	21.00

	G	VG	E
643 Flat Car, A.F. Circus, with circus load, 1950-53, L/C	35.00	52.00	70.00
644 Crane Car, Industrial Brownhoist A.F., 1950-53, L/C	15.00	20.00	30.00
645 Work Caboose, A.F. 1950-51, L/C	9.00	13.50	18.00
645A Work Caboose, AFL, 1951-53, L/C	8.00	12.00	16.00
647 Reefer, Northern Pacific, orange side, 1952-53, L/C	10.00	15.00	21.00
648 Track Cleaning Car, A.F., depressed center, 1952-54, L/C, K/C ..	10.00	15.00	20.00
649 Coach (Circus), yellow, 1950-52, L/C	28.00	41.00	55.00
650 Coach, New Haven, green or red, 1946-53, L/C	12.00	18.00	24.00
651 Baggage, New Haven, green or red, 1946-52, L/C	12.00	18.00	24.00
651 Baggage, AFL, green or red, 1953, L/C	12.00	18.00	24.00
652 Pullman, green or red, 1946-53, L/C	25.00	38.00	50.00
653 Combine, green or red, 1946-53, L/C	25.00	38.00	50.00
654 Observation, green or red, 1946-52, L/C	25.00	38.00	50.00
655 Coach, AFL, green or red, 1953, L/C	14.00	21.00	28.00
655 Coach, Silver Bullet, silver or chrome, 1953, L/C	14.00	21.00	28.00
660 Combine, AFL, aluminum or chrome, 1950-52, L/C	17.00	26.00	35.00
661 Coach, AFL, aluminum or chrome, 1950-52, L/C	17.00	26.00	35.00
662 Vista-Dome AFL, aluminum or chrome, 1950-52, L/C	17.00	26.00	35.00
663 Observation, AFL, aluminum or chrome, 1950-52, L/C	17.00	26.00	35.00
668 Manual Switch, Left, non-illuminated	3.00	5.00	7.00
669 Manual Switch, right, non-illuminated	3.00	5.00	7.00
690 Track Terminal, 1946-56	.30	.60	.90
691 Track Pins, 1946-48, 12 per pack	.25	.50	.75
692 Fiber Track Pin, 1946-48, four per pack	.25	.50	.75

	G	VG	E
693 Track Lock, 26 per pack	.75	1.00	1.25
694 Automatic Coupler Truck Unit, 1946-53, link coupler	1.00	1.50	2.00
700 Straight Track	.20	.30	.40
701 Straight Track	.10	.20	.30
702 Straight Track	.20	.30	.40
703 Curve Track, ½ section	.10	.20	.30
704 Manual Uncoupler	.50	.75	1.00
705 Remote Uncoupler, 1946-47	1.00	1.50	2.00
706 Remote Uncoupler, 1948-56	1.00	1.50	2.00
707 Track Terminal	.25	.50	.75
708 Diesel Whistle Control	2.00	3.00	4.00
709 Lockout Eliminator, 1950-56	2.00	3.00	4.00
710 Steam Whistle Control	2.00	3.00	4.00
711 Mail Pick-up, used with 718-719 mail cars	2.00	3.00	4.00
713 Mail Hook, includes track terminal, 1953-55	3.00	5.00	7.00
714 Log unloading car, A.F. log load, 1951-54, L/C	10.00	15.00	20.00
715 Auto Unloading Car, AFL, car load, 1946-54, L/C, K/C	12.00	18.00	25.00

A. F. 3161 Coach, 3162 Observation, 0, turq., blue gray, brass trim.
Courtesy H. A. Mueller, Continental Hobby House

A. F. 4002 Loco and Tender, 2-6-4, 0, black, white, copper trim.
Courtesy H. A. Mueller, Continental Hobby House

A. F. 4010 Tank, Std., yellow, blue brass trim.
Courtesy H. A. Mueller, Continental Hobby House

A. F. 4012 Lumber, Std., blue, black, brass trim.
Courtesy H. A. Mueller, Continental Hobby House

A. F. 4018 Box, Std., brown, turq., brass trim.
Courtesy H. A. Mueller, Continental Hobby House

	G	VG	E
716 Operating Hopper, AFL, 1946-51, L/C	9.00	13.50	18.00
717 Log Unloading Car, AFL, log load, 1946-52, L/C	11.00	16.00	22.00

	G	VG	E
178 Mail Pickup, AFL/New Haven, red or green, 1946-54, L/C	14.00	21.00	28.00
719 Coal Dump Car, CB&Q, maroon, 1950-54, L/C	15.00	22.00	30.00
720/720A, Remote Control Switches (pair left and right, with controls) ..	10.00	15.00	20.00
722/722A Manual Control Switches (pair left and right)	3.00	6.00	9.00
726 Rubber Road Bed, black or gray, straight	.50	.75	1.00
727 Rubber Road Bed, black or gray, curve	.30	.60	.90
728 Rerailer, 1956	3.00	4.50	6.00
730 Bumper, 1946, green	2.00	3.00	4.00
730 Bumper, 1946, red	20.00	30.00	40.00
731 Pike Planning Kit (1952-56)	5.00	7.00	10.00
732 Operating Baggage Car, AFL, green or red, 1950-54, L/C, K/C	20.00	30.00	40.00
734 Operating Box Car, AF, brown/ red, 1950-54, L/C	11.00	16.00	22.00
735 Animated Coach, AFL-New Haven, red, 1952-54, L/C, K/C	24.00	36.00	48.00
748 Overhead Footbridge, gray and silver, 1951-52	10.00	15.00	20.00
749 Street Lamp Set, three plastic lamps, 1950-52	6.00	9.00	12.00
750 Trestle Bridge, black, silver, metallic blue	15.00	20.00	30.00
751/751A Log Loader, 1946-50	30.00	60.00	90.00
752 Seaboard Coaler, 1946-50	60.00	90.00	120.00
752A Seaboard Coaler, 1951-52	50.00	75.00	100.00
753 Trestle Bridge with Beacon, 1952	15.00	22.00	30.00
754 Double Trestle Bridge, 1950-52 ..	17.00	26.00	35.00
755 Talking Station, illuminated, similar to 589 station, except 755 has record and player, 1948-58, green roof	20.00	30.00	40.00
755 Same as above, brown roof	30.00	45.00	60.00
758 Sam the Semaphore Man, 1949-50	10.00	15.00	20.00
758A Same the Semaphore Man, 1950-56	28.00	41.00	55.00
759 Bell Danger Signal, 1953-56	10.00	15.00	20.00
760 Automatic Highway Flasher, 1949-56	3.00	6.00	9.00
761 Semaphore (2 track trips), 1949-56	11.00	16.00	22.00

A. F. 4022 Lumber, Std., orange, turq., brass trim.
Courtesy H. A. Mueller, Continental Hobby House

	G	VG	E
762 Billboard (2 in 1 whistle) 1949-50, two-button control	12.00	18.00	24.00
763 Mountain Set, three pieces, 1949-50	12.00	18.00	25.00
764 Express Office, illuminated, 1950-51	33.00	49.00	65.00
766 Animated Station, four plastic passengers, 1952-54, with 735 Pullman	30.00	45.00	60.00
766 Same as above, with 935 Pullman	38.00	56.00	75.00
767 Roadside Diner, Branford Diner, illuminated, 1950-54	20.00	30.00	40.00
768 Oil Supply Depot, 1950-53, Gulf .	17.00	26.00	35.00
768 Same as above, Shell	15.00	22.00	30.00
769/769A, Revolving Aircraft Beacon, 1951-56	10.00	15.00	20.00
770 Baggage Loading Platform, 1950-52	23.00	33.00	45.00
771 Operating Stockyard Set, 1950-54, includes 8 black and white rubber cattle with brush bases, 736 Cattle Car	20.00	30.00	40.00
771K, same as 771, except has 976 cattle car with knuckle couplers	23.00	33.00	45.00
772 Water Tower, 1950-56, plain tank	12.00	18.00	25.00
772 Same as above, checkerboard design on tank	15.00	22.00	30.00
773 Oil Derrick, glass bubble road and light, 1950-52, grey tower, red base (Colber)	7.00	11.00	15.00
773 Same as above, grey tower, grey base	11.00	16.00	22.00

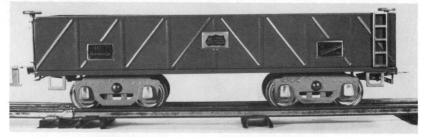

A. F. 4017 Gondola, Std., green, brass trim.
Courtesy H. A. Mueller, Continental Hobby House

	G	VG	E
773 Same as above, red tower, red base	11.00	16.00	22.00
774 Floodlight Tower, illuminated, 1951-56	10.00	15.00	20.00
775/775K, Baggage Loading Platform, 1953-56	23.00	33.00	45.00
778 Street Lamp Set, 1953-56, similar to 749	3.00	6.00	9.00
779 Oil Drum Loader, 1955-56, eight oil barrels	45.00	67.00	90.00
780 Railroad Trestle Set, 24 plastic pieces, 1953-56	4.00	6.50	9.00
781 Railroad Abutment Set, 1953	17.00	26.00	35.00
782 Railroad Abutment Set, 1953	12.00	18.00	25.00
783 Hi-Trestle Sections, 1954-56	3.00	6.00	9.00
784 Railroad Hump Set, 1955	20.00	30.00	40.00
785 Operating Coal Loader, 1955-56	60.00	90.00	120.00
787 Log Loader, 1955-56	38.00	56.00	75.00
788 Suburban Station, illuminated, 1956	10.00	15.00	20.00
789 Station and Baggage-Smasher, illuminated, 1956	33.00	49.00	65.00
792 Railroad Terminal, 1954-56	33.00	49.00	65.00
793 Union Station, illuminated, 1955-56	23.00	33.00	45.00
794 Union Station, illuminated, includes firebox, mailbox, lampposts	30.00	45.00	60.00
795 Union Station Terminal, 1954	55.00	82.00	110.00
799 Automatic Talking Station, 1954-56	30.00	45.00	60.00
801 Hopper, B&O, Black, 1956-57, K/C	9.00	13.50	18.00

	G	VG	E
802 Reefer, Illinois Central, orange, 1956-57, K/C	10.00	15.00	21.00
803 Box Car, Santa Fe, 1956, K/C ..	10.00	15.00	21.00
804 Gondola, Norfolk & Western, black, 1956-57, K/C	4.00	6.00	8.00
805 Gondola, Pennsylvania, 1956-57, K/C	4.00	6.00	8.00
806 Caboose, AFL, red, 1956, K/C, P/M	3.00	5.00	7.00
807 Box Car, Rio Grande, white, 1957, K/C	13.00	19.00	27.00
900 Combine, Northern Pacific, green, 1956, L/C, K/C	50.00	75.00	100.00
901 Coach, Northern Pacific, green, 1956, L/C, K/C	50.00	75.00	100.00
902 Vista Dome, Northern Pacific, green, 1956, L/C, K/C	50.00	75.00	100.00
903 Observation, Northern Pacific, green, 1956, L/C, K/C	50.00	75.00	100.00
904 Caboose, AFL, red, 1956, K/C ..	3.00	5.00	7.00
905 Flat Car, AFL, log load, 1954, K/C	7.00	11.00	15.00
906 Crane Car, AFL, 1954, K/C	10.00	15.00	20.00
907 Work Caboose, AFL, 1954, K/C .	8.00	12.00	16.00
909 Flat Car, AFL, Girder Load, 1954, K/C	7.00	11.00	15.00
910 Tank Car, Gilbert Chemical, green, 1954, K/C	38.00	56.00	75.00
911 Gondola, C&O, black, 1955-57, K/C, Pipe Load	7.00	10.50	14.00
912 Tank Car, Koppers, black, 1955-56, K/C	24.00	36.00	48.00
913 Box Car, Great Northern, 1953-58, K/C	13.00	19.00	27.00
914 Log Unloading Car, AFL, Log load, 1953-57, K/C	10.00	15.00	20.00
915 Auto Unloading Car, AFL, car load, 1953-57, K/C	12.00	18.00	25.00
916 Gondola, D&H, 1955-57, K/C, Cannister load	6.00	9.50	13.00
918 Mail Pick-Up, AFL/New Haven, red, 1953-56, K/C	10.00	15.00	20.00
919 Coal Dump Car, CB&Q, 1953-57, K/C	20.00	30.00	40.00
920 Gondola, Southern, black, 1953-57, K/C	6.00	9.50	13.00

	G	VG	E
921 Hopper, CB&Q, Coal load, 1953-57, K/C	9.00	13.50	18.00
922 Box Car, GAEX, green, 1953-56, K/C	13.00	19.00	27.00
923 Reefer, Illinois Central, orange, 1954-55, K/C	10.00	15.00	21.00
924 Hopper, Jersey Central, coal load, grey, 1953-57, K/C	7.00	11.00	15.00
925 Tank Car, Gulf, silver, 1953-56, K/C	7.00	11.00	15.00
926 Tank Car, Gulf, silver, 1955-56, K/C	13.00	19.00	26.00
928 Flat Car, New Haven, lumber load, 1956-57, K/C	9.00	13.00	18.00
928 Flat Car, New Haven, log load, 1954, K/C	9.00	13.00	18.00
929 Stock Car, Missouri Pacific, red, 1952-56, K/C	10.00	15.00	21.00
930 Caboose, AF, red, 1952, L/C	9.00	14.00	19.00
930 Caboose, AFL, red/brown, 1953-57, K/C	3.00	4.50	6.00
931 Gondola, Texas & Pacific, green, 1952-55, K/C	6.00	9.50	13.00
933 Box Car, Baltimore & Ohio, white sides, 1953-54, K/C	10.00	15.00	21.00
934 Floodlight, Southern Pacific, 1954-55, K/C	11.00	16.00	22.00
934 Floodlight, C&NW, 1953-54, K/C	11.00	16.00	22.00
934 Caboose, AFL, red, 1955, K/C	17.00	26.00	35.00

A. F. 3380 Baggage, 0, two-tone red, brass trim.
Courtesy H. A. Mueller, Continental Hobby House

280

	G	VG	E
935 Caboose, bay window, brown, 1957, K/C	8.00	12.00	16.00
936 Flat Car, Erie, depressed center, spool load, 1953-54, K/C	10.00	15.00	20.00
936, Flat Car, Pennsylvania, depressed center, spool load, 1953-54, K/C	20.00	30.00	40.00
937 Box Car, MKT, yellow, 1953-55, K/C	10.00	15.00	21.00
938 Caboose, AFL, red, 1954-55, K/C	3.00	4.50	6.00
940 Hopper, Wabash, black, 1953-57, K/C	7.00	11.00	15.00
941 Gondola, Frisco, 1953-57, K/C ..	5.00	8.00	11.00
942 Box Car, Seaboard, 1954, K/C ..	10.00	15.00	21.00
944 Crane Car, Industrial Brownhoist, AF, 1952-57, K/C	12.00	18.00	25.00
945 Work Caboose, AFL, 1953-57, K/C	8.00	12.00	16.00
946 Floodlight, Erie, depressed center, 1953-54, K/C	12.00	18.00	25.00
947 Reefer, Northern Pacific, orange, 1953-58, K/C	13.00	19.00	27.00
951 Baggage, AFL/Railway Express Agency, green or red, 1953-56, K/C .	11.00	16.00	22.00
952 Pullman, Pikes Peak, green or red, K/C, 1953-56	25.00	38.00	50.00
953 Combine, Niagara Falls, green or red, 1953-56, K/C	25.00	38.00	50.00
954 Observation, Grand Canyon, green or red, 1953-56, K/C	25.00	38.00	50.00
955 Coach, AFL, green or red, 1954, K/C	14.00	21.00	28.00
955 Coach, Silver Bullet, 1954, K/C .	14.00	21.00	28.00
956 Flat Car, Monon, Piggyback Van load, 1956-57, K/C	12.00	18.00	25.00
957 Operating Box Car, Erie, 1957 K/C with aluminum barrels	29.00	43.00	58.00
958 Tank Car, Mobilgas, red, 1957, K/C	7.00	11.00	15.00
960 Combine, AFL, "Columbus", chrome or silver, 1953-57, K/C, without color stripe	15.00	22.00	30.00
960 As above, New Haven, orange stripe	17.00	26.00	35.00
960 As above, Santa Fe, red stripe ..	20.00	30.00	40.00

A. F. 4021 Caboose, Std., two-tone red, brass trim.
Courtesy H. A. Mueller
Continental Hobby House

A. F. 4019 0-4-0 Engine, Std., maroon, black, brass trim.
Courtesy H. A. Mueller
Continental Hobby House

A. F. 4250 "Lone Scout" Club, Std., turq., red litho, brass trim.
Courtesy H. A. Mueller
Continental Hobby House

A. F. 4040 "United States Mail Railway Post Office", Std., green, orange, black litho.
Courtesy H. A. Mueller
Continental Hobby House

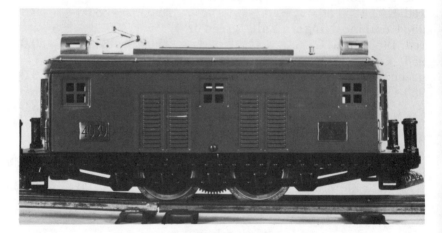

A. F. 4039 Engine 0-4-0, Std., brown, black, brass trim.
Courtesy H. A. Mueller, Continental Hobby House

A. F. 4252 "Lone Scout" Observation, Std., turq., red, brass trim.
Courtesy H. A. Mueller, Continental Hobby House

A. F. 4251 "Lone Scout" Pullman, Std., turq., red litho, brass trim.
Courtesy H. A. Mueller, Continental Hobby House

	G	VG	E
960 As above, Silver Comet, blue stripe	12.00	18.00	25.00
960 As above, Silver Flash, brown stripe	25.00	38.00	50.00
960 As above, Silver Rocket, green stripe	15.00	22.00	30.00
961 Coach, AFL "Jefferson", chrome or silver, 1953-57, K/C, without color stripe	15.00	22.00	30.00
961 As above, orange stripe	17.00	26.00	35.00
961 As above, red stripe	20.00	30.00	40.00
961 As above, blue stripe	NOT MANUFACTURED		
961 As above, brown stripe	25.00	38.00	50.00
961 As above, green stripe	15.00	22.00	30.00
962 Vista-Dome "Hamilton", chrome or silver, 1953-57, K/C, without color stripe	15.00	22.00	30.00

A. F. 4332 Observation, Std., red, brass trim.
Courtesy H. A. Mueller
Continental Hobby House

A. F. 4331 Pullman, Std., red, brass trim.
Courtesy H. A. Mueller
Continental Hobby House

A. F. 4340 "Hamiltonian" Club Car, Std.,
two-tone red, brass trim.
Courtesy H. A. Mueller
Continental Hobby House

A. F. 4343 Pocohontas, Std., Observation,
beige, green, brass trim.
Courtesy H. A. Mueller
Continental Hobby House

A. F. 4343 Pocahontas Observation, Std.,
beige, green, brass trim.
Courtesy H. A. Mueller
Continental Hobby House

A. F. 4341 Pocahontas Pullman, Std., beige,
green, brass trim.
Courtesy H. A. Mueller
Continental Hobby House

A. F. 4637 Engine, 0-4-0, Auto Bell, Std.,
green, beige, brass trim.
Courtesy H. A. Mueller
Continental Hobby House

A. F. 4391 "President's Special-Annapolis"
Std., peacock blue, brass trim.
Courtesy H. A. Mueller
Continental Hobby House

A. F. 4321 0-60 Loco, with tender, 0, black, white, nickel trim.
Courtesy H. A. Mueller, Continental Hobby House

A. F. 4380 Hancock Baggage Std., beige, green, brass trim.
Courtesy H. A. Mueller, Continental Hobby House

A. F. 4381 Hancock Pullman, Std., beige, green, brass trim.
Courtesy H. A. Mueller, Continental Hobby House

A. F. 4382 Hancock Observation, Std., beige, green, brass trim.
Courtesy H. A. Mueller, Continental Hobby House

A. F. 4694 4-4-2 loco, Std., and tender, black, red, brass trim, Ives "Golden State".
Courtesy H. A. Mueller, Continental Hobby House

A. F. 4670 4-4-2 Loco with Tender, Std., black, green stripe, brass, nickel trim (rear truck missing in photo).
Courtesy H. A. Mueller, Continental Hobby House

A. F. 4693 4-4-2 Loco, Std., blue, brass and copper trim.
Courtesy H. A. Mueller, Continental Hobby House

A. F. 4693 4-4-2 Loco, Std., tender, black, green stripe, brass, nickel trim.
Courtesy H. A. Mueller, Continental Hobby House

286

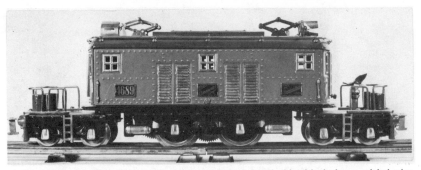

A. F. 4689 4-4-4 "The Commander" Engine, Std., peacock, blue-black, brass, nickel trim.
Courtesy H. A. Mueller, Continental Hobby House

	G	VG	E
962 As above, orange stripe	17.00	26.00	35.00
962 As above, red stripe	20.00	30.00	40.00
962 As above, blue stripe	12.00	18.00	25.00
962 As above, brown stripe	25.00	38.00	50.00
962 As above, green stripe	15.00	22.00	30.00
963 Observation, "Washington", chrome or silver, 1953-57, K/C, without color stripe	15.00	22.00	30.00
963 As above, orange stripe	17.00	26.00	35.00
963 As above, red stripe	20.00	30.00	40.00
963 As above, blue stripe	12.00	18.00	25.00
963 As above, brown stripe	25.00	38.00	50.00
963 As above, green stripe	15.00	22.00	30.00
969 Rocket Launcher, 1957-58, K/C .	12.00	18.00	25.00
970 Walking Brakeman Car, Seaboard, 1956-57, K/C	15.00	22.00	30.00
971 Lumber Unloading Car, Southern Pacific, Lumber load, 1956-57, K/C .	15.00	22.00	30.00
973 Operating Milk Car, Gilbert, white, 1956, K/C, with plastic cans .	20.00	30.00	40.00
974 Operating Box Car, Erie, 1955, K/C	29.00	43.00	58.00
974 Operating Box Car, AFL, 1953-54, K/C	28.00	41.00	55.00
975 Animated Coach, red, 1955, K/C	12.00	18.00	25.00
977 Caboose, AFL, brown, 1955-58, K/C, "Moving Brakeman"	10.00	15.00	20.00
978 Observation Action Car, Grand Canyon, 1956-58, K/C	53.00	79.00	105.00
979 Caboose, bay window, brown, 1957, K/C, "Moving Brakeman"	12.00	18.00	25.00

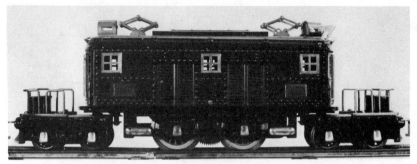

A. F. 4687 4-4-4 Engine, Std., blue, black, brass trim.
Courtesy H. A. Mueller, Continental Hobby House

	G	VG	E
980 Box Car, B&O, blue, 1956-57, K/C	24.00	36.00	48.00
981 Box Car, Central of Georgia, black, 1956, K/C	24.00	36.00	48.00
982 Box Car, State of Maine, red, white and blue, 1956-57, K/C	24.00	35.00	47.00
983 Box Car, Missouri Pacific, blue/gray, 1956, K/C	18.00	27.00	36.00
984 Box Car, New Haven, orange, 1956-57, K/C	18.00	27.00	36.00
985 Box Car, Boston & Maine, blue, 1957, K/C	18.00	27.00	36.00
988 Reefer, ART, orange, 1956-57, K/C	17.00	25.00	34.00
989 Reefer, C&NW, 1956-58, K/C	30.00	45.00	60.00
994 Stock Car, Union Pacific, yellow, 1957 K/C	24.00	36.00	48.00
C1001 Box Car, White's Stores, 1962, K/C	325.00	487.00	650.00
C2001 Box Car, Post, white, with or without Hayjector, 1962, K/C, P/M	24.00	36.00	48.00
L2001 Steam Loco, Casey Jones, 4-4-0, 1963	20.00	30.00	40.00
L2002 Steam Loco, Erie, 4-4-0, 1963	90.00	135.00	180.00
L2002 Steam Loco, Burlington Route, 4-4-0, 1963	107.00	161.00	215.00
L2004 F-9, Rio Grande, 1962, K/C	49.00	73.00	97.00
C2009 Gondola, Texas & Pacific, light green, 1962-64, P/M	7.00	10.50	14.00

A. F. 4686 "The Ace" Engine, 4-4-4, Std., two-tone blue, black, red, brass trim.
Courtesy H. A. Mueller, Continental Hobby House

A. F. 4670 Loco, 2-4-2 and Tender, Std., black, green stripe, brass trim.
Courtesy H. A. Mueller, Continental Hobby House

A. F. 4667 0-4-0 Engine, Std., red, black, brass trim.
Courtesy H. A. Mueller, Continental Hobby House

FUNDIMENSIONS
By Frank L. Ferrara

In the late 1960s Lionel purchased American Flyer, and with the sale came the original American Flyer dies. The revival of American Flyer "S" gauge trains came in 1979 when Fundimensions (manufactuer of Lionel) produced three "S" gauge cars, a Santa Fe box car, a Gulf tank car, and a B&O hopper. This first production evolved into the much-desired train sets, rolling stock, and accessories available today. Hopefully Fundimensions will continue to produce American Flyer for years to come and keep the "S" gauge tradition going strong.

2300 Operating Oil Drum Loader, 1983, FUNDIMENSIONS, mint price is 60.00

8153-8154-8155, Alco A-B-A, B&O, 1981, K/C, FUNDIMENSIONS, mint price is 260.00

8251-8252-8253, Alco A-B-A, Southern Pacific, 1981-82, K/C, FUNDIMENSIONS, mint price is 260.00

8251-8252-8253, Alco A-B-A, Erie, 1982, K/C, FUNDIMENSIONS, mint price is 260.00

8350 GP-7, Boston & Maine, 1983, K/C, FUNDIMENSIONS, mint price is 120.00

9000 Flat Car, B&O, Van Load, 1981, K/C, FUNDIMENSIONS mint price is 20.00

9002 Flat Car, Boston & Maine, log load, 1983, K/C, FUNDIMENSIONS, mint price is 15.00

9100 Tank Car, Gulf, white, 1979, K/C, FUNDIMENSIONS, mint price is 25.00

Tank Car, Union, blue, 1980, K/C, FUNDIMENSIONS, mint price is 20.00

9102 Tank Car, B&O, 1981, K/C, FUNDIMENSIONS, mint price is 20.00

9104 Tank Car, Boston & Main, 1983, K/C, FUNDIMENSIONS, mint price is 15.00

9200 Hopper, B&O, black, 1979, K/C, FUNDIMENSIONS, mint price is 25.00

9201 Hopper, B&O, 1981, K/C, FUNDIMENSIONS, mint price is 20.00

9203 Hopper, Boston & Maine, silver, 1983, K/C, FUNDIMENSIONS, mint price is 15.00

9300 Gondola, Burlington, green, 1980, K/C, FUNDIMENSIONS, mint price is 20.00

9301 Gondola, B&O, with containers, 1981, K/C, FUNDIMENSIONS, mint price is 20.00

9400 Caboose, bay window, Chessie System, yellow, 1980, K/C, FUNDIMENSIONS, mint price is 20.00

9401 Caboose, B&O, red/black, 1981, K/C, FUNDIMENSIONS, mint price is 20.00

9402 Caboose, bay window, Boston & Maine, 1983, K/C, FUNDIMENSIONS, mint price is 15.00

9500 Combine, Southern Pacific, 1981, K/C, FUNDIMENSIONS, mint price is 35.00

9501 Coach, Southern Pacific, 1981, K/C, FUNDIMENSIONS, mint price is 35.00

9502 Vista Dome, Southern Pacific, 1981, K/C, FUNDIMENSIONS, mint price is 35.00

9503 Observation, Southern Pacific, 1981, K/C, FUNDIMENSIONS, mint price is 35.00

9504 Combine, Erie, 1982, K/C, FUNDIMENSIONS, mint price is 35.00

9505 Coach, Erie, 1982, K/C, FUNDIMENSIONS, mint price is 35.00

9506 Vista Dome, Erie, 1982, K/C, FUNDIMENSIONS, mint price is 35.00

A. F. 4678 0-4-0 Engine, Std., red, gray, brass trim.
Courtesy H. A. Mueller, Continental Hobby House

	G	VG	E
9507 Observation, Erie, 1982, K/C, FUNDIMENSIONS, mint price is 35.00			
9700 Box Car, Santa Fe, red, 1979, K/C, FUNDIMENSIONS, mint price is 25.00			
9701 Box Car, The Rock, blue, 1980, K/C, FUNDIMENSIONS, price in mint is 20.00			
9702 Box Car, B&O, Sentinel, 1981, K/C, FUNDIMENSIONS, mint price is 20.00			
9703 Box Car, Boston & Maine, blue, 1983, K/C, FUNDIMENSIONS, mint price is 15.00			
21004 Steam Loco, P.R.R., Switcher 0-6-0, 1957, K/C	78.00	116.00	155.00
21005 Steam Loco, P.R.R., Switcher, 0-6-0, 1958, K/C	97.00	147.00	195.00
21084 Steam Loco, C&NW, Pacific, 4-6-2, 1957, K/C	40.00	60.00	80.00
21085 Steam Loco, C&NW or CMSP&P Pacific 4-6-2, 1962-3, 1965, K/C, P/M .	24.00	36.00	48.00
21095 Steam Loco, New Haven, Pacific 4-6-2, 1958 K/C, rare	325.00	275.00	650.00
21099 Steam Loco, New Haven, Pacific 4-6-2, 1958, K/C	90.00	135.00	180.00
21100 Steam Loco, Reading, Atlantic, 4-4-2, 1957, K/C	12.00	18.00	24.00

A. F. 4643 0-4-0 Engine, Std., green-black, brass trim.
Courtesy H. A. Mueller, Continental Hobby House

	G	VG	E
21105 Steam Loco, Reading, Atlantic, 4-4-2, 1957-60, K/C	13.00	19.00	27.00
21106 Steam Loco, Reading, Atlantic 4-4-2, 1959, K/C	24.00	35.00	47.00
21107 Steam Loco, Burlington, Atlantic, 4-4-2, 1965, K/C	23.00	34.00	46.00
21107 Steam Loco, PRR, Atlantic 4-4-2, 1964-66, K/C	17.00	26.00	35.00
21115 Steam Loco, PRR, K-5, 4-6-2, 1958, K/C	125.00	187.00	250.00
21129 Steam Loco, New York Central, Hudson, 4-6-4, 1958, K/C	115.00	173.00	230.00
21130 Steam Loco, New York Central, Hudson, 1959-60, 1962-63, K/C	80.00	120.00	160.00
21139 Steam Loco, Union Pacific, Northern, 4-8-4, 1958, K/C	107.00	161.00	215.00
21140 Steam Loco, Union Pacific, Northern, 4-8-4, 1959-60, K/C	137.00	201.00	265.00
21145 Steam Loco, Nickel Plate Road, Switcher, 0-8-0, 1958, K/C	107.00	161.00	215.00
21155 Steam Loco, Docksider Switcher, 0-6-0, 1958, K/C	80.00	120.00	160.00
21156 Steam Loco, Docksider Switcher, 0-6-0, 1959, K/C	90.00	135.00	180.00
21158 Steam Loco, Docksider Switcher, 0-6-0, 1960, K/C	45.00	67.00	90.00
21160 Steam Loco, Reading Atlantic 4-4-2, 1960, K/C	16.00	24.00	32.00
21161 Steam Loco, Reading, Atlantic, 4-4-2, 1960, K/C	13.00	19.00	26.00

A. F. 4653 0-4-0 Engine, Std., orange-black, brass trim.
Courtesy H. A. Mueller, Continental Hobby House

	G	VG	E
21161 Steam Loco, Reading, Atlantic, 4-4-2, 1960, K/C, "Prestone Car Care Express"	38.00	56.00	75.00
21165 Steam Loco, Erie, Casey Jones, 4-4-0, 1961-65, K/C	12.00	18.00	24.00
21166 Steam Loco, Burlington, Casey Jones, 4-4-0, 1963-64, P/M	12.00	18.00	24.00
21168 Steam Loco, Southern, Casey Jones, 4-4-0, 1961-63, P/M	12.00	18.00	24.00
21205-21205-1 F-9, Boston & Maine, 1961, K/C, priced as set	47.00	70.00	94.00
21206-21206-1 F-9, Santa Fe, 1962, K/C, priced as set	47.00	70.00	94.00
21207-21207-1, F-9, Great Northern, 1963-64, K/C, priced as set	47.00	70.00	94.00
21210 F-9, Burlington, 1961, K/C	39.00	58.00	78.00
21215, 21215-1, F-9, Union Pacific, 1961-62, K/C, priced as set	48.00	71.00	95.00
21551 Alco A, Northern Pacific, 1958, K/C, rare	80.00	120.00	160.00
21561 Alco A, New Haven, 1958, K/C	53.00	79.00	105.00
21573 G.E. Electric, New Haven, with Pantographs, 1958-59, K/C	97.00	147.00	195.00
21720 Alco B, Santa Fe, 1958, K/C, rare	160.00	240.00	320.00
21801 Switcher, C&NW, 1958, K/C	28.00	41.00	55.00
21801-1 Switcher, C&NW, 1958, K/C, Dummy Unit	24.00	35.00	47.00
21808 Switcher, C&NW, 1958, K/C	24.00	35.00	47.00
21813 Switcher, M&SL, 1958, K/C	107.00	161.00	215.00

A. F. 4644 0-4-0 Engine, Std., red, gray, brass trim.
Courtesy H. A. Mueller, Continental Hobby House

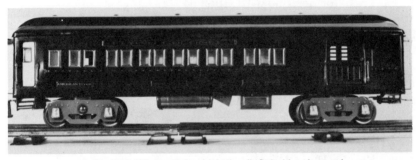

A. F. 4380 "Flying Colonel-Madison", Std., blue, brass trim.
Courtesy H. A. Mueller, Continental Hobby House

	G	VG	E
21831 GP-7, Texas & Pacific, 1958, K/C	125.00	187.00	250.00
21831 GP-7, AFL, 1958, K/C	60.00	90.00	120.00
21902, 21902-1, 21902-2, Alco A-B-A, Santa Fe, 1958, K/C, priced as set	200.00	300.00	400.00
21910, 21910-1, 21910-2, Alco A-B-A, Santa Fe, 1957-58, K/C, priced as set	200.00	300.00	400.00
21918, 21918-1, Switcher, Seaboard, 1958, K/C, priced as set	150.00	225.00	300.00
21920, 21920-1, Alco A-A, Missouri Pacific, 1958, K/C (double motor in 21920), priced as set, rare	187.00	281.00	375.00
21920, 21920-1, Alco A-A, Missouri Pacific, 1963-64, K/C, single motor in 21920, priced as set	97.00	147.00	195.00

	G	VG	E
21922, 21922-1, Alco A-A, Missouri Pacific, 1959-60, K/C, priced as set .	132.00	198.00	265.00
21925/21925-1, Alco A-A, Union Pacific, 1959-60, K/C, rare	167.00	251.00	335.00
21927 Alco A, Santa Fe, 1960-62, K/C	58.00	86.00	115.00
22020 Transformer, 50 Watt, 1957-64	1.00	3.00	5.00
22030 Transformer, 100 watt, 1957-64	1.00	3.00	5.00
22035 Transformer, 175 watt, 1957-64	10.00	15.00	20.00
22040 Transformer, 110 watt, 1957-58	3.00	5.00	7.00
22050 Transformer, 175 watt, 1957-58	7.00	11.00	15.00
22060 Transformer, 175 watt, 1957-58, dual controls	12.00	18.00	25.00
22080 Transformer, 300 watt, 1957-58, dual controls	17.00	26.00	35.00
22090 Transformer, 350 watt, 1959-64, dual controls	20.00	30.00	40.00
23021 Imitation Grass, ½ pound, 1957-60	seven dollars		
23022 Scenery Gravel, 22 ounces, 1956-60	six dollars		
23023 Artificial Coal, ½ pound, 1957-60	six dollars		
23024 Multicolor Wire, 25 foot roll, 1957-64	ten dollars		
23025 Smoke Fluid Cartridges, 12 in box, 1957-60........................	five dollars		
23026 Service Kit, 1957-64	7.00	11.00	15.00
23027 Track Cleaning Fluid, eight ounces, 1957-59	three dollars		
23032 Railroad Equipment Kit, 1960	12.00	18.00	25.00
23249 Tunnel, 11½″, 1957-64	7.00	10.50	14.00
23561 Billboard Horn, similar to 561	10.00	15.00	20.00
23568 Whistling Billboard, 1957-64, similar to 568	10.00	15.00	20.00
23571 Truss Girder Bridge, 1957-64 .	2.00	3.00	4.00
23581 Girder Bridge, lettered "American Flyer", 1957-64	3.00	5.00	7.00
23586 Wayside Station, 1956-59	15.00	22.00	30.00
23589 Passenger and Freight Station, illuminated, 1957-59	15.00	22.00	30.00
23590 Control Tower, illuminated, similar to 590, 1957-59	15.00	22.00	30.00
23596 Water Tank, 1957-58	17.00	26.00	35.00
23598 Talking Station Record, replacement, 1957-59	5.00	7.00	10.00

	G	VG	E
23599 Talking Station Record, replacement, 1957	10.00	15.00	20.00
23600 Crossing Gate with Bell, 1957-62	17.00	26.00	35.00
23750 Trestle Bridge, same as 750 ..	15.00	20.00	30.00
23758 Sam the Semaphore Man, 1957	15.00	22.00	30.00
23759 Bell Danger Signal, 1957-60 ..	10.00	15.00	20.00
23760 Automatic Highway Flasher, 1957-60	3.00	6.00	9.00
23761 Semaphore, two track trips, 1957-64	15.00	22.00	30.00
23769 Revolving Aircraft Beacon, 1957-64	10.00	15.00	20.00
23771 Operating Stockyard Set, 1957-61, similar to 771K	23.00	33.00	45.00
23772 Water Tower, 1957-64, plain tank	12.00	18.00	25.00
23772 As above, checkerboard design on tank	15.00	22.00	30.00
23774 Floodlight Tower, illuminated, 1957-64	10.00	15.00	20.00
23778 Streetlamp Set, 1957-64	6.00	9.00	12.00
23779 Oil Drum Loader, 1958-61, eight oil barrels	45.00	67.00	90.00
23780 Gabe the Lamplighter, 1958-59	50.00	75.00	100.00
23785 Operating Coal Loader, 1957-60	60.00	90.00	120.00
23787 Log Loader, 1957-60	38.00	56.00	75.00
23788 Suburban Station, illuminated, 1958	10.00	15.00	20.00
23789 Station and Baggage-Smasher, illuminated, 1958-59	30.00	45.00	60.00
23791 Cow-On-Track, 1957-59	12.00	18.00	25.00
23796 Sawmill, 1957-64	50.00	75.00	100.00
23830 Piggyback Unloader, 1959-60 .	17.00	26.00	35.00
24003 Box Car, Santa Fe, 1958, K/C	13.00	19.00	27.00
24016 Box Car, MKT, all yellow, 1961, K/C, rare	167.00	250.00	335.00
24016 Box Car, Seaboard, brown, 1958, K/C	24.00	36.00	48.00
24016 Box Car, MKT, yellow sides, 1958, K/C	13.00	19.00	27.00
24019 Box Car, Seaboard, 1958, K/C	24.00	36.00	48.00
24023 Box Car, B&O, dark blue, 1958-59, K/C	24.00	36.00	48.00

A. F. 4392 "President's Special-Army-Navy" Observation, Std., peacock blue, brass trim. Courtesy H. A. Mueller, Continental Hobby House

	G	VG	E
24026 Box Car, Central of Georgia, black, 1957-58, K/C	25.00	37.00	49.00
24029 Box Car, State of Maine, red/white/blue, 1958-60, K/C	30.00	44.00	59.00
24030 Box Car, MKT, yellow, 1960, P/M	16.00	24.00	33.00
24033 Box Car, Missouri Pacific, 1958, K/C	24.00	36.00	48.00
24036 Box Car, New Haven, orange, 1958-60, K/C	30.00	45.00	60.00
24039 Box Car, Rio Grande, white, 1959, K/C	13.00	19.00	27.00
24043 Box Car, Boston & Maine, blue, 1958-60, K/C	24.00	36.00	48.00
24047 Box Car, Great Northern, red, 1959, K/C	63.00	94.00	125.00
24048 Box Car, M.St. L., red, 1959-62, K/C	53.00	79.00	105.00
24052 Box Car, UFGE Bananas, yellow, 1961, P/M	19.00	28.00	38.00
24054 Box Car, Santa Fe, 1962-66, P/M	15.00	22.00	30.00
24056 Box Car, Boston & Maine, blue, 1961, P/M	19.00	28.00	38.00
24057 Box Car, Mounds, white or ivory, 1962, P/M	10.00	15.00	20.00
24058 Box Car, Post, white or ivory, 1963-64, K/C, P/M	10.00	15.00	20.00
24059 Box Car, Boston & Maine, blue, 1963, P/M	45.00	67.00	90.00
24060 Box Car, M St. L, 1963-64, P/M	24.00	36.00	48.00

	G	VG	E
24065 Box Car, New York Central, green, 1960-64, K/C, P/M	24.00	36.00	48.00
24066 Box Car, Louisville & Nashville, blue, 1960, K/C	55.00	82.00	110.00
24067 Box Car, Keystone Camera, orange, 1960, K/C, rare	475.00	702.00	950.00
24068 Box Car, Planters Peanuts, white, 1961, P/M rare	475.00	702.00	950.00
24076 Stock Car, Union Pacific, yellow, 1958-66, K/C, P/M	13.00	19.00	27.00
24077 Stock Car, Northern Pacific, red, 1959-62, K/C, P/M	48.00	71.00	95.00
24103 Gondola, N&W, black, 1958, 1963-64, K/C	7.00	10.50	14.00
24106 Gondola, Pennsylvania, 1960, K/C	5.00	8.00	11.00
24109 Gondola, C&O, black, 1958-60, K/C, pipe load	8.00	12.00	16.00
24110 Gondola, Pennsylvania, 1960, K/C	4.00	6.50	9.00
24113 Gondola, D&H, brown, 1958-59, K/C, Container load	7.00	10.50	14.00
24116 Gondola, Southern, black, 1958-60, K/C	12.00	18.00	24.00
24120 Gondola, Texas & Pacific, green, 1960, P/M	12.00	18.00	24.00
24124 Gondola, Boston & Maine, blue, 1963-64, P/M	7.00	11.00	15.00

A. F. 4341 "Hamiltonian" Pullman, Std., two-tone red, brass trim.
Courtesy H. A. Mueller, Continental Hobby House

	G	VG	E
24125 Gondola, Bethlehem Steel, grey, 1960-65, K/C, P/M	8.00	12.00	16.00
24126 Gondola, Frisco, 1961, P/M ..	24.00	36.00	48.00
24127 Gondola, Monon, grey, 1961, 1963-66, K/C, P/M	7.00	10.50	14.00
24203 Hopper, B&O, black, 1958, 1963-64, K/C, P/M	7.00	11.00	15.00
24206 Hopper, CB&Q, coal load, brown, 1958, K/C	23.00	33.00	45.00
24209 Hopper, Jersey Central, grey, with hatch covers, 1958-60, K/C	17.00	26.00	35.00
24213 Hopper, Wabash, black, 1958-60, K/C	17.00	26.00	35.00
24216 Hopper, Union Pacific, 1958-60, K/C	17.00	26.00	35.00
24219 Hopper, Western Maryland, 1958-59, K/C	23.00	33.00	45.00
24221 Hopper, C&EI, grey, 1959-60, K/C	33.00	49.00	65.00
24222 Hopper, Domino Sugar, yellow, with hatch covers, 1963-64, K/C, P/M rare	45.00	67.00	90.00
24225 Hopper, Santa Fe, red, gravel load, 1960-66, P/M	9.00	13.50	18.00
24230 Hopper, Peabody, 1961-64, K/C, P/M	12.00	18.00	25.00
24309 Tank Car, Gulf, silver, 1958, K/C	7.00	11.00	15.00
24310 Tank Car, Gulf, silver, 1958-60, K/C	13.00	19.00	27.00
24313 Tank Car, Gulf, silver, 1957-60, K/C	13.00	19.00	27.00
24316 Tank Car, Mobilgas, red, 1958-61, 1965-66, K/C, P/M	13.00	19.00	27.00
24319 Tank Car, Penn. Salt, 1958, K/C, rare	112.00	168.00	225.00
24320 Tank Car, Deep Rock, black, 1960, P/M	87.00	131.00	175.00
24321 Tank Car, Deep Rock, black, 1959, K/C	10.00	20.00	30.00
24322 Tank Car, Gulf, silver, 1959, K/C	13.00	19.00	27.00
24323 Tank Car, Bakers, white, 1959-60, K/C	75.00	125.00	150.00

	G	VG	E
24324 Tank Car, Hooker, orange, 1959-60, K/C	25.00	38.00	50.00
24325 Tank Car, Gulf, silver, 1960, K/C	10.00	20.00	30.00
24328 Tank Car, Shell, yellow, 1962-66, P/M	7.00	11.00	15.00
24329 Tank Car, Hooker, orange, 1961, 1963-66, P/M	12.00	18.00	24.00
24330 Tank Car, Baker's Chocolate, white, 1961-62, P/M	25.00	38.00	50.00
24403 Reefer, Illinois Central, orange, 1958, K/C	7.00	10.50	14.00
24409 Reefer, Northern Pacific, orange sides, 1958, K/C	150.00	275.00	300.00
24413 Reefer, ART, orange sides, 1958-60, K/C	23.00	33.00	45.00
24416 Reefer, C&NW, dark green, 1958-59, K/C	150.00	275.00	300.00
24419 Reefer, Canadian National, grey, 1958-59, K/C	58.00	86.00	115.00
24422 Box Car, Great Northern, light green, 1966, P/M	58.00	86.00	115.00
24422 Reefer, Great Northern, light green, 1965-66, P/M	13.00	19.00	26.00
24425 Reefer Bar, red, 1960, K/C	87.00	131.00	175.00
24426 Reefer, Rath Packing, orange sides, 1960-61, K/C	87.00	131.00	175.00
24516 Flat Car, New Haven, Lumber load, 1958-59, K/C	10.00	15.00	20.00
24519 Flat Car, Pennsylvania, depressed center, W.E. spool load, 1958, K/C, rare	100.00	150.00	200.00
24533 Track Cleaning Car, AFL, depressed center, 1957-66, K/C, P/M	10.00	15.00	20.00
24536 Flat Car, Monon, Trailer load, 1958, K/C	11.00	16.00	23.00
24537 Flat Car, New Haven, Pipe load, 1957, K/C	16.00	24.00	32.00
24539 Flat Car, New Haven, Pipe load, 1958-59, 1963-64, K/C, P/M	12.00	18.00	25.00
24540 Flat Car, New Haven, Pipe load, 1960, K/C	12.00	18.00	25.00
24543 Crane Car, Industrial Brownhoist, AFL, 1958, K/C	12.00	18.00	25.00

A. F. 4342 Observation "Hamiltonian", Std., two-tone red, brass trim.
Courtesy H. A. Mueller, Continental Hobby House

A. F. 4340 Pocahontas Club, Std., beige, green, brass trim.
Courtesy H. A. Mueller, Continental Hobby House

	G	VG	E
24546 Work Caboose, AF, 1958-64, K/C	8.00	12.00	16.00
24547 Floodlight, Erie, 1958, K/C ...	102.00	153.00	205.00
24549 Floodlight, Erie, 1958-66, R/C, P/M	11.00	16.00	22.00
24550 Flat Car, Monon, Trailer Load, 1959-64, K/C	11.00	16.00	23.00
24553 Flat Car, Rocket Transport, 1958-60, K/C	12.00	18.00	25.00
24556 Flat Car, Rock Island, wheel transport, 1959, K/C	14.00	21.00	28.00
24557 Flat Car, U.S. Navy, Jeep load, 1959-60, K/C	24.00	36.00	48.00
24558 Flat Car, Canadian Pacific, Christmas tree load, 1959-60, K/C ..	30.00	45.00	60.00

A. F. 4390 "President's Special-West Point", Std., peacock, blue, brass trim.
Courtesy H. A. Mueller, Continental Hobby House

	G	VG	E
24559 Flat Car, New Haven, no load, 1959, K/C	11.00	16.00	22.00
24561 Crane Car, Industrial Brown-hoist, AFL, 1959-66, K/C, P/M	10.00	15.00	20.00
24562 Flat Car, N.Y. Central, no load, 1960, K/C	10.00	15.00	20.00
24566 Flat Car, New Haven, auto transport, 1961-66, P/M	12.00	18.00	25.00
24569 Crane Car, Industrial Brown-hoist, AFL, 1961-66, P/M	10.00	15.00	20.00
24572 Flat Car, U.S. Navy, Jeep load, 1961, P/M	33.00	49.00	65.00
24574 Flat Car, U.S. Air Force, Fuel container load, 1960-61, K/C	19.00	28.00	38.00
24575 Flat Car, National, Milk container load, 1960-66, P/M	9.00	13.50	18.00
24577 Flat Car, Illinois Central, Jet engine container load, 1960-61, 1963-64, K/C, P/M	15.00	22.00	30.00
24578 Flat Car, New Haven, Corvette load, 1962-63, P/M	38.00	56.00	75.00
24579 Flat Car, Illinois Central, multiload, 1960-61, K/C, P/M	10.00	15.00	20.00
24603 Caboose, AFL, red, 1958-59, K/C	3.00	4.50	6.00
24610 Caboose, AFL, red, 1960, K/C	3.00	4.50	6.00
24619 Caboose, bay window, AFL, brown, 1958, K/C	11.00	16.00	23.00
24626 Caboose, AFL, yellow, 1958, K/C	5.00	7.00	10.00

	G	VG	E
24627 Caboose, AFL, red, 1959-60, K/C	3.00	4.50	6.00
24630 Caboose, AFL, red, 1960, K/C	3.00	4.50	6.00
24631 Caboose, AFL, yellow, 1959-61, K/C, P/M	4.00	6.00	8.00
24632 Caboose, AFL, yellow, 1959, K/C	13.00	19.00	26.00
24633 Caboose, bay window, AFL, silver, 1959-62, P/M	8.00	12.50	17.00
24634 Caboose, bay window, AFL, red, 1963-66, P/M	6.00	9.00	12.00
24636 Caboose, AFL, red, 1960-66, P/M	3.00	4.50	6.00
24638 Caboose, Bay Window, AFL, silver, 1962, P/M	9.00	14.00	19.00
24773 Combine, "Columbus" silver 1957-58, 1960-62, K/C, red stripe	23.00	33.00	45.00
24776 Combine, "Columbus", silver, 1959, K/C, orange stripe	23.00	33.00	45.00
24793 Coach, "Jefferson", silver, 1957-58, 1960-62, K/C, red stripe	23.00	33.00	45.00
24813 Vista-Dome, "Hamilton", silver, 1957-58, 1960-62, red stripe	17.00	26.00	35.00
24816 Vista-Dome "Hamilton", silver, 1959, K/C, orange stripe	23.00	33.00	45.00
24833 Observation, "Washington", silver, 1957-58, 1960-62, K/C, red stripe	17.00	26.00	35.00
24836 Observation, "Washington", silver, 1959, K/C, orange stripe	17.00	26.00	35.00
24837 Combine, Union Pacific, yellow/gray, 1959-60, K/C, rare	43.00	63.00	85.00
24838 Coach, Union Pacific, yellow/gray, 1959-60, K/C, rare	43.00	63.00	85.00
24839 Vista-Dome, Union Pacific, yellow, grey, 1959-60, K/C, rare	43.00	63.00	85.00
24840 Observation, Union Pacific, yellow, grey, 1959-60, K/C, rare	43.00	63.00	85.00
24843 Combine, Northern Pacific, green, 1958, K/C	35.00	52.00	70.00
24846 Coach, Northern Pacific, green, 1958, K/C	35.00	52.00	70.00
24849 Vista-Dome, Northern Pacific, green, 1958, K/C	35.00	52.00	70.00

	G	VG	E
24853 Observation, Northern Pacific, green, 1958, K/C	35.00	52.00	70.00
24856 Combine, Missouri Pacific, silver/blue, 1958&1964, K/C rare ...	58.00	86.00	115.00
24856 Same as above, P/M	50.00	75.00	100.00
24859 Coach, Missouri Pacific, silver/blue, 1958, 1963-64, K/C rare	58.00	86.00	115.00
24859 Same as above, P/M	50.00	75.00	100.00
24863 Vista-Dome, Missouri Pacific, silver/blue, 1958, 1963-64, K/C, rare	58.00	86.00	115.00
24863 Same as above, P/M	50.00	75.00	100.00
24866 Observation, Missouri Pacific, silver/blue, 1958, 1963-64, K/C rare .	58.00	86.00	115.00
24866 Same as above, P/M	50.00	75.00	100.00
24867 Combine, AFL, silver, 1958, K/C	30.00	45.00	60.00
24868 Observation, AFL, silver, 1958, K/C	30.00	45.00	60.00
24869 Coach, AFL, silver, 1958, K/C	30.00	45.00	60.00
25003 Log Unloading Car, AFL, log 1958-60, K/C	40.00	60.00	80.00
25016 Lumber Unloading Car, Southern Pacific, Lumber load, 1958-60, K/C	17.00	26.00	35.00
25019 Operating Milk Car, Gilbert, white, 1957-60, K/C, with plastic cans	25.00	38.00	50.00
25025 Coal Dump Car, CB&Q, 1958-60, K/C	23.00	33.00	45.00
25042 Operating Box Car, Erie, brown, 1958, K/C, with aluminum barrels	45.00	67.00	90.00

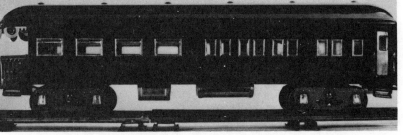

A. F. 4382 "Flying Colonel-Hancock" Observation, Std., blue, brass trim.
Courtesy H. A. Mueller, Continental Hobby House

	G	VG	E
25045 Rocket Launcher, vertical launch, 1958-60, K/C	12.00	18.00	25.00
25046 Rocket Launcher, 45° angle launch, 1960, K/C	14.00	21.00	28.00
25049 Walking Brakeman Car, Rio Grande, white, 1958-60, K/C	38.00	56.00	75.00
25052 Caboose, bay window, AFL, silver, 1960, K/C, rare, "Moving Brakeman"	25.00	38.00	50.00
25057 Exploding Box Car, T.N.T., 1960	24.00	36.00	48.00
25058 Lumber Unloading Car, Southern Pacific, Lumber load, 1961-64, P/M	12.00	18.00	25.00
25059 Rocket Launcher, U.S.A.F., 45° angle launch, 1961-64, P/M	11.00	16.00	22.00
25060 Coal Dump Car, CB&Q, Maroon, 1961-64, K/C	23.00	33.00	45.00
25061 Exploding Box Car, TNT, 1961	24.00	36.00	48.00
25062 Exploding Box Car, Mine carrier, 1962-64, P/M	23.00	33.00	45.00
25071 Tie-Jector Car, AF, tie load, 1961-64, P/M	7.00	11.00	15.00
25081 Box Car, NYC, with Hayjector, light green, 1961-64, P/M	13.00	19.00	27.00
25082 Box Car, New Haven, with Hayjector, orange, 1961-64, P/M	13.00	19.00	27.00
25515 Flat Car, USAF, Rocket Sled load, 1960-63, P/M	23.00	33.00	45.00
26726 Rubber Road Bed, black or gray, ½ straight	.50	.75	1.00

A. F. 4381 "Flying Colonel Adams", Std., blue, brass trim.
Courtesy H. A. Mueller, Continental Hobby House

	G	VG	E
26727 Rubber Road Bed, black or gray, ½ curve	.30	.60	.90
26746 Rubber Roadbed, black or gray, 1957-64, straight	.50	.75	1.00
26747 Rubber Roadbed, black or gray, 1957-64, curve	.30	.60	.90
26749 Bumper, 1957-60, green	2.00	3.00	4.00
26751 Pike Planning Kit, 1957-59 ...	5.00	7.00	10.00
26760 Remote Control Switches (pair, left and right, with controls)	10.00	15.00	20.00
26770 Manual Switches, pair	3.00	6.00	9.00
Buffalo Hunt Gondola, "Buffalo Hunt", green, 1963, P/M	10.00	15.00	20.00
C&N.W.R.Y. (628) Flat Car, C&NWRY, Log load, 1946-53, L/C, K/C, number does not appear on car	9.00	14.00	18.00
Virginian (632) Hopper, Virginian, 1946, L/C	24.00	36.00	48.00
C&NWRY (635) Crane Car, C&NWRY, 1946-49, L/C	15.00	20.00	30.00
Erie (646) Floodlight, Erie, depressed center, 1950-53, LC	12.00	18.00	25.00
Hand Car (742) Handcar, with reversing mechanism	20.00	30.00	40.00
C&NWRY (928) Flatcar, C&NWRY, Log load, 1956-57, K/C, number does not appear on car	9.00	14.00	18.00
Washington FY&PRR (21089), Steam Loco, FY&PRR, Washington, 4-4-0, 1960-61, K/C	68.00	100.00	135.00
Simmons (24420) Reefer, Simmons, Orange, 1958, K/C	200.00	300.00	400.00
Erie (24529) Floodlight, Erie, depressed center, 1958, K/C	12.00	18.00	25.00
New Haven (24564) Flat Car, New Haven, Pipe Load, 1960, P/M	13.00	19.00	26.00
USMC (25056) Detonator Car, USMC, yellow, 1959, K/C	50.00	75.00	100.00
USMC (25056) Rocket Launcher Car, USMC, yellow, 1959, K/C	50.00	75.00	100.00

IVES
by Terry P. Amadon

The grandfather of the toy train industry was certainly Ives. Beginning in 1868, Ives manufactured sixty years worth of such quality toys that they were backed by an unconditional guarantee. Most early Ives showed no marks of identification; however, quite a few old cast iron floor trains, and many later clockwork powerboats exist today to be sought after by collectors. This section will concern itself with Ives production from around 1901 until 1932, when the line was being phased out.

Ives evolved from clockwork motors to be the first to electrify trains. By 1904 they had established 0 gauge as a standard, and embarked on production of trains in the European #1 gauge. They were the only American company to do this, and in the 16 year tenure of this venture produced some of the finest examples of craftsmanship to ever come from the Ives Shops. The cast iron #3239 and #3240 in #gauge are two of the most beautiful center cab electrics to appear in any line.

Although Ives began to manufacture electric trains in 1910, they still continued to make clockwork models for the duration of their existence. Many places did not yet have electricity, so clockworks were the only self-propelled trains they could use. Lack of electricity and slow shipping kept most Ives concentrated on the eastern seaboard, with little going any further than the Mississippi.

Many of the early clockwork cabs and boilers saw duty also as electric engines. Steamer numbers were prefixed with the number 11, so an engine like the grand old #25 became an electric #1125. Center cab numbers were changed more radically. Cabs like #30 became numbers like #3250, while #32 became #3253.

In 1920, Ives phased out #1 ga. to concentrate on #0 and standard ga., and went on to develop some fine standard ga. models.

With smooth-running, simple motors and a patented E-unit superior to those of any competitor, Ives electric trains rode a well-deserved wave of popularity from their beginning until the depression. When, for various reasons, Ives reached rocky ground late in 1929, Lionel and American Flyer happily took advantage of the opportunity to jointly buy Ives out. This procured for them the E-unit which they both had coveted for so long. Soon thereafter, Flyer sold their Ives interest to Lionel, who continued the line through 1932. Occasional pieces were turned out later until all old Ives parts in stock were gone. Then the line was completely discontinued, sadly ending a glorious reign in the field of American toymaking.

Today, due to vintage and usage, most Ives is found at best in 'good' to 'very good' condition, with some appearing to be 'like new'. Few pieces meet the classic definition of 'mint', and these are generally handed down or in the hands of original owners. When sold, these pieces tend to go privately, rather than on the common market. Prices here are those seen on the market, and are not an attempt to establish subjective collector values. For example, the 3220 price here is averaged from the only three I have seen for sale, and is undoubtedly worth somewhat more than its price considering the limited run of that particular piece. Such pieces are difficult to set a value on, because such a value determination is an internal thing to the collector. Ives prices are in many cases very difficult to average because so few of some particular pieces ever turn up to comparatively price. The scarcity of Ives leads to fewer collectors, and helps to keep the prices lower than some comparable pieces in other name lines.

Many collectors are in the train hobby for the pure love of the trains. However, a growing number are coming into it for the love of money they see inherent to the hobby. Hopefully this section will reach out to more of the former than the latter.

Terry Amadon was born and raised in Bucks County, Pennsylvania, and shared with the family a fine running Lionel layout. The trains were sold in a moving sale, leaving a smoldering interest which rekindled later. A relative newcomer to the hobby, and a collector of "anything that runs or can be made to," Mr. Amadon has gradually turned his main interest toward the study and collection of Ives. The pursuit has been a family venture, with family and friends diligently watching yard sales, papers and all other possible avenues for anything of interest. Any questions or items of interest may be directed to Mr. Amadon at the address in the back of the book.

Mr. Amadon is the holder of two Bachelor of Arts degrees from Penn State University and currently resides in State College.

GENERAL NOTES

1.   Engine numbers 00 through 32 are clockwork (windup), as are numbers 66 and 176. Also number 1 gauge locos numbers 40 and 41.

2.   Set prices tend to run less than the sum of the prices of the integral parts of the set, with some notable exceptions, particularly many 1930s sets such as National Limited, Chief, and Black Diamond, for example. Also especially the platinum-plated "Prosperity Special", which commands in the vicinity of $10.000.00.

3.   Heralds. Some cars (mainly numbers 64, 125, and 564) have road heralds on them, and consequently tend to vary in price, generally to unagreed upon parameters. A ballpark range for these is from fifty to a hundred and sixty dollars depending upon condition and desire to possess a particular item. The available heralds are as follows:

On No. 125:

Union Pacific, M.K.&T., Corn Belt Route, Salt Lake Route, Frisco Lines, Wabash R.R., Cotton Belt Route, Star Union Line.

On Nos. 64, 564:

Baltimore & Ohio, Atlantic Coast Line, Chicago & N.W., Rock Island R.R., Sante Fe, Canadian Pacific, Illinois Central, Northern Pacific, Pennsylvania, Lehigh Valley, Star Union, N.Y.C., Burlington Route, Erie R.R., N.Y., N.H.&H.

4.   Wide gauge and standard gauge are the same thing.

5.   Ungauged entries are generally 0 gauge. Number 1 gauge and standard gauge (W) are marked as such.

6.   Although relatively few pieces may be considered in mint, those that are should certainly have the original boxes.

7.   Only set numbers from selected years appear due to time shortage, they give an idea of what pieces went together. More set numbers will be provided next edition.

8.   Reproductions of some pieces, notably the 3245 motor, the number 89 water tower, and the 121 and 122 stations have been made.

9.   Dating by trucks and couplers: Inboard trucks went from before 1900-1909. T-trucks 1910-20. Marklin trucks about 1912-17. Type 4 1918-30. Flat loop couplers before 1900-1910. Hook slot couplers 1904-30. Automatic couplers 1912-30.

	G	VG
0E Set, 1904, Tin loco, tender, 1 baggage, 1 passenger car, eight #111 elevating posts		
00 Loco, 1930, cast, black, smallest clockwork engine	75.00	135.00
0 Loco, 1901, tin, black/red, #1 tender	65.00	110.00
0 Loco, 1902-05, tin, black/red litho, F.E.#1 tender	65.00	110.00
0 Loco, 1930, cast, black/gold litho, F.E.#1 tender	55.00	85.00
0 Loco 1917, cast, black/gold, #11 tender	50.00	75.00
0 Set, 1904, tin loco, tender, 1 passenger car		
0 Set, 1910, #0 loco, #1 tender, #51		
0 Set, 1926, #5 loco, #11 tender, #51		
0 Set, 1914, #2 loco, #1 tender, #51		
0 Set, 1915, #2 loco, #1 tender, #52		
0 Set, 1912, #5 loco, #0 tender, #52		
1 Loco, 1903-29, cast black/gold #11 N.Y.C. tender	43.50	65.50
1 Tender, 1901-12, tin, black, IVES #1, F.E.#1	63.50	95.50
1 Set, 1912, #5 loco, #0 tender, #52		
1 Set, 1919, #5 loco, #11 tender, #52		
1 Set, 1925, #1 loco, #11 tender, #52		
"MANAGER'S SPECIAL"		
1 Set, 1917, #5 loco, #11 tender, #52		
1 Set, 1915, #5 loco, #1 tender, #52		
1 Set, 1904, tin loco, tender, 1 car		
1 Set, 1926, #1 loco, #11 tender, #52		
1 Set, 1914, #5 loco, #1 tender, #52		
1 Set, 1910, #1 loco, #1 tender, #51		
2 Loco, 1912, cast, black/gold, #1 tender		
2 Set, 1910, #2 loco, #1 tender, #50, #51		
2 Set, 1926, #1 loco, #11 tender, #50, #51		
2 Set, 1914, #5 loco, #1 tender, #50, #51		
2 Set, 1904, tin loco, tender, 1 passenger car		
2 Set, 1917, #5 loco, #11 tender, #50, #51		

FOR SET PRICES
SEE
INDIVIDUAL
NUMBERS
AND
GENERAL NOTES
(p. 310).

2 Set, 1915-16, #5 loco, #1 tender, #50, #51

2 Set, 1925, #1 loco, #11 tender, #50, #51

2 Set, 1912, #17 loco, #11 tender, #60, #61

2 Set, 1919, #5 loco, #11 tender, #50, #51

2 Set, 1904, tin loco, tender, 1 baggage car, 1 passenger, eight #111 elevating posts

3 Loco, 1902-09, tin, black/grey, 'CHICAGO FLYER' tender 75.00   125.00

3 Loco, 1911, cast, black/gold, #1 tender 60.00   85.00

3 Set, 1910, #3 loco, #1 tender, #50, #51, #52

3 Set, 1926, #6 loco, #11 tender, #50, #51, #52

3 Set, 1914, #6 loco, #1 tender, #50, #51, #52

3 Set, 1904, tin loco, tender, 2 pass. cars, 1 baggage

3 Set, 1917, #6 loco, #11 tender, #50, #51, #52

3 Set, 1915-16, #6 loco, #1 tender, #50, #51, #52

3 Set, 1925, #6 loco, #11 tender, #50, 51, 52

3 Set, 1912, #6 loco, #0 tender, #50

3 Set, 1919, #6 loco, #1 tender, #50, 51, 52

3 Set, 1904, tin loco, tender, 1 baggage, 2 passenger cars, ten #111 elevating posts

4 Loco, 1910-12, cast, black/gold, #1 tender 55.00   95.00

4 Set, 1910, #4 loco, #1 tender, #50, 51

4 Set, 1926, #1 loco, #1 tender, #50, 51

4 Set, 1914, #11 loco, #11 tender, #550, 551

FOR SET PRICES SEE INDIVIDUAL NUMBERS AND GENERAL NOTES (p. 310).

Ives No. 1 Loco with NO. 11 Tender, 0 ga., black, red.
Courtesy Heinz A. Mueller, Continental Hobby House

	G	VG
4 Set, 1917, #17 loco, #11 tender, #551		
4 Set, 1915-16, #11 loco, #11 tender, #550, 551		
4 Set, 1925, #1 loco, #11 tender, #50, 51		
4 Set, 1912, #6 loco, #0 tender, #50, 51		
4 Set, 1919, #5 loco, #11 tender, #50, 51		
5 Loco, 1915, cast, black/gold, cast drivers, #11 tender	79.00	118.00
5 Loco, 1917-22, cast, black/gold, tin drivers, #11 tender	60.00	95.00
5 Set, 1910, #2 loco, #1 tender, #57, 56		
5 Set, 1917, #5 loco, #11 tender, #57, 56		
5 Set, 1921, #5 loco, #11 tender, #57, 56		
5 Set, 1915-16, #5 loco, #1 tender, #57, 56		
5 Set, 1912, #5 loco, #0 tender, #57, 56		
5 Set, 1919, #5 loco, #11 tender, #54, 56		
5 Set, 1914, #5 loco, #1 tender, #57, 56		
5 Set, 1926, #1 loco, #11 tender, #54, 56		
6 Loco, 1912-27, cast, black/gold, #11 tender	78.00	107.00
6 Set, 1912, #6 loco, #0 tender, #53, 55, 56		
6 Set, 1910, #4 loco, #1 tender, #50, 51		
6 Set, 1927, #6 loco, #11 tender, #53, 55, 56		
6 Set, 1914-16, #6 loco, #1 tender, #53, 55, 56		

FOR SET PRICES
SEE
INDIVIDUAL
NUMBERS
AND
GENERAL NOTES
(p. 310).

Ives No. 2 Loco and No. 6 0-4-0 Windup, 0 ga., black, red.
Courtesy Heinz A. Mueller, Continental Hobby House

Ives No. 5 Loco, No. 11 Tender, 0 ga., black white.
Courtesy Heinz A. Mueller, Continental Hobby House

G   **VG**

6 Set, 1917, #6 loco, #11 tender, #55, 53, 56

6 Set, 1921, 1926, #6 loco, #11 tender, #53, 55, 56

7 Set, 1910, #4 loco, #1 tender, #54, 54, 54, 56

7 Set, 1914, #11 loco, #11 tender, #553, 557

7 Set, 1917, #17 loco, #11 tender, #563, 567

7 Set, 1915-16, #11 loco, #11 tender, #563, 567

7 Set, 1912, #6 loco, #0 tender, #54, 54, 54, 56

8 Set, 1916-17, 1921, 1925-26 #17 loco, #11 tender, #564, 569, 567

8 Set, 1912, #17 loco, #11 tender, #69, 67

8 Set, 1915, #17 loco, #17 tender, #69, 67

FOR SET PRICES
SEE
INDIVIDUAL
NUMBERS
AND
GENERAL NOTES
(p. 310).

314

	G	VG
8 Set, 1914, #17 loco, #11 tender, #69, 67		
8 Set, 1910, #17 loco, #17 tender, #69, 67		
9 Loco, 1922, cast, black, N.Y.C & H.R. tender #25	50.00	75.00
9 Set, 1912-16, #17 loco, #11 tender, #63, 63, 67		
9 Set, 1917, #19 loco, #17 tender, #69, 67		
9 Set, 1910, #17 loco, #17 tender, #64, 64, 67		
10 Loco, 1930, cast, black, clockwork	125.00	175.00
10 Loco, 1931-32, tin, peacock, electric outline, Std. Ga., became LIONEL #10E	195.00	291.00
10 Set, 1910, #17 loco, #11 tender, #68, 65, 64, 67		
10 Set, 1916-17, #19 loco, #17 tender, #64, 63, 67		
10 Set, 1926, #19 loco, #17 tender, #63, 64, 67		
10 Set, 1915, #17 loco, #17 tender, #64, 68, 65, 67		
10 Set, 1925, #19 loco, #17 tender, #63, 64, 67		
10 Set, 1912-14, #17 loco, #11 tender, #68, 65, 64, 67		
10 Set, 1919-21, #19 loco, #17 tender, #64, 63, 67		
11 Loco, 1901-16, cast, black/gold, L.V.E.#11 tender	55.00	85.00
11 Tender, tin, black, IVES #11	34.00	51.00
11 Tender, tin, black, L.V.E. #11	61.00	91.50
11 Set, 1914, #17 loco, #11 tender, #60, 61		
11 Set, 1912, #17 loco, #11 tender, #60		
11 Set, 1916-17, 1919, 1925-26, #17 loco, #11T, #550, 551		
11 Set, 1918, #17 loco, #11T, #550, 551, 552		
11 Set, 1915, #17 loco, #17T, #60, 61		
11 Set, 1904, #11 loco, #11 T, #50, 51		

Ives No. 10 0-4-0 Engine, Lionel Transitional, Std., peacock-black, brass trim.
Courtesy Heinz A. Mueller, Continental Hobby House

Ives No. 11 0-4-0 Wind-up Loco and No. 11 Tender, 0 ga., black, white.
Courtesy Heinz A. Mueller, Continental Hobby House

	G	VG
11E Set, 1904, iron loco, tender, 1 baggage, 1 pass. car. eight #111 elevating posts		
12 Tender, 0	45.00	65.00
12 Set, 1904, #11 loco, #11 T, #50, 51		
12 Set, 1910, #17 loco, #11 T, #60, 61, 62		
12 Set, 1916-17, 1919, 1925-26, #17 loco, #11 T, #550, 551, 552		
12 Set, 1914, #17 loco, #11 T, #60, 61, 62		
12 Set, 1915, #17 loco, #17 T, #60, 61, 62		
12 Set, 1912, #17 loco, #11 T, #60, 61		
13 Set, 1904, #17 loco, #11 T, #50, 51, 51		
13 Set, 1910, 1914, #17 loco, #11 T, #60, 61, 62		
13 Set, 1917, #19 loco, #17 T, #62		
13 Set, 1915-16, #17 loco, #17 T, #60, 61, 62		

FOR SET PRICES
SEE
INDIVIDUAL
NUMBERS
AND
GENERAL NOTES
(p. 310).

316

13 Set, 1912, #17 loco, #11 T, #60, 61, 62

14 Set, 1904, #17 loco, #11 T, #50, 51, 51

14 Set, 1910, 1912, 1914, #17 loco, #11 T, #60, 61, 62

14 Set, 1917, #19 loco, #17 T, #60, 61

14 Set, 1915, #17 loco, #17 T, #60, 61, 62

14 Set, 1916, #19 loco, #17 T, #70, 72

14 Set, 1919, #19 loco, #17 T, #60, 61

15 Set, 1904, #17 loco, #11 T, #60, 61

15 Set, 1910, #17 loco, 11 T, #60, 61, 62, 107 signal

15 Set, 1926, #19 loco, 17 T, #60, 62, 62 'DAY SPECIAL ....

15 Set, 1914, #20 loco, #25 T, #131, 129, 130

15 Set, 1917, #19 loco, #17 T, #60, 61, 62

15 Set, 1915, #20 loco, #25 T, #130, 131, 129

15 Set, 1916, #19 loco, #17 T, #70, 72, 72

15 Set, 1925, #19 loco, #17 T, #70, 72, 72

15 Set, 1912, #20 loco, #25 T, #131, 129, 130

15 Set, 1919, #19 loco, #17 T, #60, 61, 62

16 Set, 1904, #17 loco, #11 T, #60, 61, 62, & 2 flat cars

16 Set, 1910, #20 loco, #17 T, #60, 61, 62

16 Set, 1914, #25 loco, #25 T, #131, 129, 130

16 Set, 1917, #25 loco, #25 T, 130

16 Set, 1915, #25 loco, #25 T, #130, 129

16 Set, 1916, #20 loco, #17 T, #60, 62

16 Set, 1925, #25 loco, #25 T, #131, 129, 130

16 Set, 1925, #20 loco, #17 T, #60, 62

17 Loco, 1901-05, cast, black/gold, embossed boiler bands, #11 tender 60.00 80.00

17 Loco, 1901-05, cast, tin boiler bands, #11 tender 95.00 140.00

17 Loco, 1911-14, cast, black, no brake, L.V.E. #11 tender 60.00 80.00

17 Loco, 1911-18, cast, black, brake, L.V.E.#11 tender 45.00 70.00

17 Loco, 1908, cast, black/gold, red, brake, boiler bands, #11 tender 65.00 85.00

	G	VG
17 Loco, 1911, cast, black/gold, 2 boiler bands, #11 tender	50.00	75.00
17 Loco, 1917, cast, black, 1 boiler band, #11 tender	45.00	65.00
17 Tender, tin, 4 wheels, 0	45.00	68.00
17 Set, 1904, #17 loco, #11 T, #60, 61, 62		
17 Set, 1910, #20 loco, #17 T, #60, 61, 62		
17 Set, 1917, #25 loco, #25 T, #130, 129		
18 Set, 1925, #20 loco, #17 T, #60, 61, 62		
18 Set, 1916, #20 loco, #17 T, #60, 61, 62		
18 Set, 1917, #25 loco, #25 T, #129, 129, 130		
19 Loco, 1916, cast, black/red, brake, #17 tender	125.00	165.00
19 Set, 1914-16, #20 loco, #25 T, #125, 128, 67		
19R set, 1910, #25 loco, #25 T, #128, 128, 67		
19 Set, 1917, #25 loco, #25 T, #128, 67		
19 Set, 1912, #20 loco, #25 T, #125, 128, 67		
20 Loco, 1914, black, has reverse, #25 tender	75.00	110.00
20 Set, 1919-1921, #6 loco, #11 T, #50, 51, 52		
20 Set, 1925, #6 loco, #11 T, #50, 51		
20R Set, 1904, #25 loco, #25 T, #130		
20R Set, 1910, #25 loco, #25 T, #130		
20-192 Boxcar, 1929, yellow/blue; green/red, brass plates	37.50	56.50
20-192 Freight, Std. Ga., Flyer/Ives	206.00	309.00
20-192 Boxcar, Std. Ga., Flyer/Ives .	126.00	189.00
20-193 Cattle, 1929, yellow/red; green/ red	30.00	45.00
20-193 Freight, Std. Ga., Flyer/Ives	206.00	309.00
20-194 Gondola, Std. Ga., Flyer/Ives	20.00	30.00
20-194 Caboose, Std., Ga., Flyer/Ives brass plates	160.50	240.50
20-195 Freight, Std. Ga., Flyer/Ives	206.00	309.00
20-195 Gondola, Std. Ga., Flyer/Ives	73.00	109.00
20-198 Freight, Std., Ga., Flyer/Ives, brass plates	206.00	309.00
20-198 Gondola, Std. Ga., Flyer/Ives, black	218.50	327.50

	G	VG
20-198 Gravel, Std. Ga., Flyer/Ives .	87.50	131.50
21 Loco, 1921, steel, black, clockwork	155.00	285.00
21 Set, 1921, #31 loco, #550, 551		
21R Set, 1910, #25 loco, #25T, #129, 130		
21 Set, 1926, #30 loco, #550, 551		
21 Set, 1916, #30 loco, #550, 551		
21R Set, 1904, #25 loco, #25 T, #130, 129		
21 Set, 1925, #30 loco, #550, 551		
22 Set, 1921, #31 loco, #60, 61, 62		
22 Set, 1925, #31 loco, #70, 72, 73		
22R Set, 1910, #25 loco, #25 T, #129, 130		
22 Set, 1926, #30 loco, #62, 68		
22R Set, 1904, #25 loco, #25 T, #130, 129		
22 Set, 1916, #31 loco, #70, 71, 72		
22 Set, 1927, #32 loco, #60, 62, 68		
23 Set, 1910, #25 loco, #25 T, #131, 129		
23 Set, 1904, #25 loco, #25 T, #131, 129		
23 Set, 1921, #32 loco, #130, 129, 129		
24R Set, 1910, #25 loco, #25 T, #131, 130, 129		
24R Set, 1904, #25 loco, #25 T, #131, 130, 129		
25 Loco, 1904, cast, 3 windows, 6 boiler bands, 2 brakes, L.V.E. #11 ..	317.50	476.50
25 Loco, 1906-11, cast, 2 windows, eccentric rod, L.V.E. #25 tender	95.00	135.00
25 Loco, 1912-14, cast 2 windows 3 boiler bands, #25 tender	85.00	120.00
25 Loco 1911, cast, 3 windows, 4 boiler bands, 4-4-0, #25 tender	95.00	135.00
25 Tender, tin, 4 wheels	100.00	150.00
25 Tender, tin, 8 wheels, L.V.E. #25, N.Y.C. & H.R.	65.00	100.00
26 Loco, 1930, cast, black, clockwork	175.00	225.00
30 Loco, 1924, tin, electric style, green/gold, cast frame	150.00	225.00
30 Loco, 1926, tin, electric style, green/gold, cast frame, dummy headlight	150.00	225.00

Ives No. 17 0-4-0 Wind-up Loco and No. 11 Tender, 0 ga., black red-white.
Courtesy Heinz A. Mueller, Continental Hobby House

	G	VG
30 Set, 1912-16, #25 loco, #25 T, #123, 124, 67		
30R Set, 1910, #25 loco, #25 T, #123, 125, 67		
30R Set, 1904, #25 loco, #25 T, #127, 127, 126		
30 Set, 1917, #25 loco, #25 T, #125, 123, 67		
30 Set, 1930, #00 loco, #11 T, #51, 51 "MOHICAN"		
31 Loco, 1925, clockwork, bell, dummy headlight, cast frame, elec. style	125.00	175.00
31 Set, 1930, #00 loco, #11 T, #50, 51, 51 "SENECA"		
32 Loco, 1925, electric style, bell, dummy headlight, cast frame	125.00	175.00
32 Set, 1930, #10 loco, #11 T, #551, 551 "PEQUOT"		
33 Set, 1930, #176 loco, #12 T, #551, 558 "APACHE"		
34 Set, 1930, #66 loco, #12 T, #53, 54, 56 "SIOUX"		
35 Set, 1930, #176 loco, #12 T, #550, 551, 558 "IROQUOIS"		
36 Set, 1930, #176 loco, #12 T, #563, 564, 567		
37 Set, 1930, #176 loco, #12 T, #551, 558 "MOHAWK"		
38 Set, 1930, #176 loco, #12 T, #551, 558, "BLACKFOOT"		
39 Set, 1930, #26 loco, #550, 551, 558, "OSWEGO"		

Ives No. 40 4-4-0 Loco, black, nickel trim, No. 1 ga.
Courtesy Heinz A. Mueller, Continental Hobby House

Ives No. 41 0-4-0 Wind-up Loco, No. 1 ga., black, red, nickel trim.
Courtesy Heinz A. Mueller, Continental Hobby House

	G	VG
40 Loco, 1904-09, cast, black, 4-4-0, 3 boiler bands, #40 tender, #1 ga.	500.00	750.00
40 Loco, 1910-16, cast, black, 4-4-0, 2 boiler bands, #40 tender, #1 ga.	500.00	750.00
40 Tender, tin, #1 ga.	100.00	150.00
40 Tender, tin, cast ('29, '29), Std. Ga.	100.00	150.00
41 Loco, cast, black, 0-4-0, 3 boiler bands, #40 tender, Std. ga.	500.00	750.00
42 Set, 1904, #40 loco, #40 T, #71		
43 Set, 1904, #40 loco, #40 T, #71, 72		
44 Set, 1904, 1910, #40 loco, #40 T, #70, 71, 72		
45 Set, 1910, #41 loco, #40 T, #75, 77		

	G	VG

46 Set, 1910, #41 loco, #40 T, #76, 76, 75

47 Set, 1910, #41 loco, #40 T, #74, 73, 77, 75

47 Set, 1915, #40 loco, #40 T, #7345, 7950, 7546

47 Set, 1914, #40 loco, #40 T, #71, 72, 72

47 Set, 1912, #40 loco, #40 T, #73, 77, 75

49 Set, 1914, #40 loco, #40 T, #73, 77, 75

49 Set, 1915, #40 loco, #40 T, #71, 72, 72

49 Set, 1912, #40 loco, #40 T, #70, 71, 72

50 Baggage, 1901-03, red or green/ white, painted 175.00 250.00

50 Baggage, 1904-05, white/black, "FAST EXPRESS" 175.00 250.00

50 Baggage, 1906-08, yellow-orange/ red, litho, L.V.E. 125.00 237.50

50 Baggage, 1909, white/green, litho, L.V.E. 75.00 150.00

50 Baggage, 1910-14, yellow-orange/ black, Penn or Ives Lines 60.00 125.00

50 Baggage, 1915-30, red or green/ white, litho, Ives Railway Lines 15.00 37.50

50 Baggage, 1928-30, orange, red, litho, "EXPRESS MAIL" 18.50 29.00

50 Baggage 1930, yellow/black, litho, "EXPRESS MAIL" 22.50 35.00

51 Chair, 1901-03, red or green/white, cast wheels 175.00 250.00

51 Chair, 1901-05, red or green/white, "FAST EXPRESS" 175.00 250.00

51 Chair, 1905-07, litho, "MOHAWK" 175.00 250.00

51 Chair, 1906-08, red, litho, L.V.E. "IROQUOIS", "HIAWATHA" 175.00 250.00

51 Chair, 1909, white/red, L.V.E., "BROOKLYN" 60.00 125.00

51 Chair, 1910-14, Penn or Ives Lines, "NEWARK" 25.00 40.00

51 Chair, 1915-30, white/black, Ives Railway Lines 22.50 37.50

52 Parlor, 1909, white/black, L.V.E., "BUFFALO" 60.00 125.00

52 Parlor, 1910-14, yellow/black, Penn or Ives Lines, "WASHINGTON" 31.50 90.00

Ives 50, 52, 52, 0 ga., yellow, red litho.
Courtesy Heinz A. Mueller, Continental Hobby House

Ives 50, 51, 52, 0 ga., red, green, black, yellow litho.
Courtesy Heinz A. Mueller, Continental Hobby House

	G	VG
52 Parlor, 1915-28, olive, orange/black, Ives Railway Lines	20.00	35.00
52 Parlor, 1928-30, orange, red, yellow, Ives Railway Lines	28.50	29.00
53 Mcdse., 1908-09, wood litho, "FAST FREIGHT"	75.00	150.00
53 Mcdse., 1910-30, white, grey/black litho, "PENNSYLVANIA LINES" .	35.00	75.00
53 Mcdse., 1910-30, white/maroon; white/grey; orange/red; grey/black	15.00	25.00
54 Gravel, 1901-05, green; red/green, painted	75.00	150.00
54 Gravel, 1906, red/white, black frame, litho	25.00	40.00
54 Gravel, 1908, red/black, woodgrain litho	25.00	40.00
54 Gravel, 1911-30, white/green litho	10.00	25.00
54 Gravel, 1911-30, red/grey; grey/red; purple/grey	10.00	15.00
55 Stock, 1910-30, orange/maroon, wood litho, "livestock transportation	15.00	25.00
55 Stock, 1910-30, white/green; white/maroon; grey/maroon; orange/maroon; white/grey	10.00	15.00

Ives 53 Boxcar, 56 Caboose, 0 ga., white, maroon, black litho.
Courtesy Heinz A. Mueller, Continental Hobby House

	G	VG
56 Caboose, 1910-15, white/grey/ maroon, wood litho	35.00	65.00
56 Caboose, 1915-30, red/brown/ black, wood litho	12.50	18.75
56 Caboose, 1915-30, white/maroon/ black; red/brown/black	32.50	78.75
57 Lumber, 1910-30, tan, brown, maroon, black, enamel	10.00	15.00
60 Baggage, 1901-04, red or green/ white, painted	160.00	185.00
60 Baggage, 1905-09, blue, buff, black, brown, red, yellow L.V.E.	125.00	195.00
60 Baggage, 1910-15, yellow, white, red, blue wood litho or steel litho	25.00	45.00
60 Baggage, 1915-28, red/green, maroon, olive, steel litho, 8 wheels	10.00	25.00
60 baggage, 1915-28, olive/yellow, 4 wheels	10.00	25.00
60 Baggage, 1926-30, emerald/orange, 8 wheels, "IVES RAILWAY"	25.00	45.50
61 Pass., 1901-04, red or green/white, painted	160.00	195.00
61 Pass., 1905-09, buff, blue brown, black, yellow litho, "EMPRESS"	125.00	195.00
61 Pass., 1910-15, yellow, blue, white, red, wood litho, "YALE"	60.00	85.00
61 Pass., 1915-28, red/green; maroon; olive, steel litho	10.00	25.00
61 Pass., 1926, emerald/orange, plain litho	10.00	25.00
62 Parlor, 1901-04, red or green/white, painted	160.00	185.00

Ives 60 Express, 61 Chair Car, 62 Parlor Car, 0 ga., red, gray, yellow, black litho.
Courtesy Heinz A. Mueller, Continental Hobby House

Ives 61 Coach, yellow, red, black litho, 0 ga.
Courtesy Heinz A. Mueller, Continental Hobby House

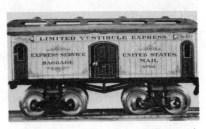

Ives 60 Baggage Car, 0 ga., yellow, red, brown litho.
Courtesy Heinz A. Mueller, Continental Hobby House

Ives 62 Coach, 0 ga., yellow, red, black litho.
Courtesy Heinz A. Mueller, Continental Hobby House

Ives 65 Cattle Car, 0 ga., yellow, gray, brown litho, nickel trim.
Courtesy Heinz A. Mueller, Continental Hobby House

	G	VG
62 Parlor, 1905-09, yellow, blue, red, white litho, "PRINCESS"	125.00	195.00
62 Parlor, 1910-15, buff, blue, red, white, wood litho, "HARVARD", 8 wh.	90.00	125.00
62 Parlor, 1910-15, red; yellow/black, 4 wheel	15.00	28.50
62 Parlor, 1915-28, red, green, maroon, olive, steel litho 8 wh.	10.00	25.00
62 Parlor, 1926, emerald/orange, plain litho	10.00	25.00

Ives 66 Tank Car, 0 ga., orange, black rubber stamp, nickel trim.
Courtesy Heinz A. Mueller, Continental Hobby House

	G	VG
62 Parlor, 1929-30, blue/green, plain litho	10.00	25.00
63 Gravel, 1901-04, cast wheels, painted	125.00	240.00
63 Gravel, 1904-06, blue/grey or tan/brown stripes, litho	115.00	223.00
63 Gravel, 1907-09, buff, brown, wood litho	75.00	125.00
63 Gravel, 1909-15, steel litho, 8 wheels	20.00	35.00
63 Gravel, 1918-26, grey, dark red, 8 wheels, steel litho	15.00	30.00
63 Gravel, 1926-30, grey, dark red, 8 wheels, plain litho	15.00	30.00
64 Mcdse., 1906-09, red/black, dark green roof, litho	138.50	257.50
64 Mcdse. 1910-30 15 or 16 variations, some with 8 wheels, some 4, wood litho, see IVES General Notes		
65 Stock, 1906-07, grey, brown, wood litho	95.00	191.50
65 Stock, 1908-09, white/red, wood litho, 8 wheels	58.50	97.50
65 Stock, 1910-17, orange, plain litho, 8 wheels	20.00	35.00
65 Stock, 1918-30, yellow, orange, plain litho, 8 wheels	12.50	18.75

	G	VG
66 Loco, 1930, cast, black, 0-4-0, brake, clockwork	81.00	121.50
66 Chair, black/red/yellow	84.50	127.00
66 Tank, 1910-15, red/green dome, litho..............................	67.50	125.00
66 Tank, 1916, grey/gold, litho	25.00	52.50
66 Tank, 1917-25, grey/silver dome, litho	15.00	22.50
66 Tank, 1925-28, orange/black dome, litho	10.00	25.00
66 Tank, 1929-30, orange/black dome, litho	17.50	31.50
67 Caboose, 1910-16, white; black/red, wood litho	38.50	57.50
67 Caboose, 1917-25, red/black, wood litho	12.50	18.75
67 Caboose, 1926-30, red/yellow/black, wood litho	15.00	23.50
68 Freight, 1911-12, white/black, wood litho	34.00	51.50
68 Freight, 1917-30, white/black, litho, refrigerated box	61.00	91.50
68 Pass., 1926, emerald/orange, litho, observation	40.00	60.00
68 Pass., 1929-30, blue- green, litho, observation	35.00	52.50

Ives 66 Tank Car, 0 ga., orange, black rubber stamp.
Courtesy Heinz A. Mueller, Continental Hobby House

Ives 67 Caboose, 0 ga., red, grey, brown litho.
Courtesy Heinz A. Mueller, Continental Hobby House

Ives 68 Observation Car, 0 ga., green, red, black, rubber stamp, litho.
Courtesy Heinz A. Mueller, Continental Hobby House

Ives 71 Buffet Car, No. 1 ga., brown, gray, yellow litho.
Courtesy Heinz A. Mueller, Continental Hobby House

	G	VG
69 Lumber, 1910-30, tan, black, brown, maroon, 8 wheels, 3 log chains	10.00	18.75
70 Baggage, 1904-14, yellow/black & green roof, wood litho #1 Ga.	170.00	290.00
70 Baggage, 1925, red/yellow & black trim, 0 Ga.	15.00	30.00
71 Chair, 1925, red/yellow, black, & green trim, 0 Ga.	15.00	30.00
71 Buffet, 1904,10, yellow/black & green roof, wood litho #1 Ga., "ST. LOUIS"	170.00	250.00
71 Buffet, 1911-16, white/green & grey roof, wood litho, #1 Ga.	70.00	140.00
71 Buffet, 1917-20, brown, gold, steel litho, #1 Ga.	70.00	150.00
72 Drawing Room, 1925, red/yellow, black, & Green trim, 0 Ga.	15.00	30.00

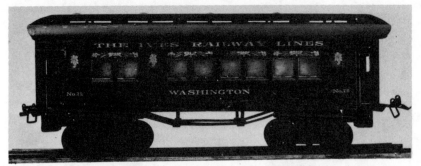

Ives 72 Coach, No. 1 ga., brown, gray, yellow litho.
Courtesy Heinz A. Mueller, Continental Hobby House

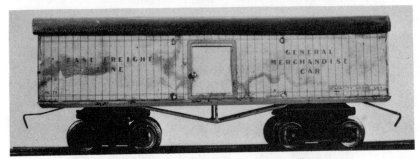

Ives 73 Box Car, No. 1 ga., yellow, green, red litho.
Courtesy Heinz A. Mueller, Continental Hobby House

	G	VG
72 Parlor, 1904-10, yellow/black, wood litho, "SAN FRANCISCO", #1 Ga.	170.00	250.00
72 Parlor, 1911-16, brown/white, wood litho, "CHICAGO", #1 Ga.	170.00	250.00
72 Parlor, 1917-20, brown/yellow, wood litho, "WASHINGTON", #1 Ga.	170.00	250.00
73 Observation, 1925, red/yellow, black, & green trim, 0 Ga.	18.50	28.00
73 Observation, 1917-20, brown/yellow, steel litho, #1 Ga.	137.50	256.00
72 Accessory, 1930, Pole wagon (circus set), Wide Ga.	50.00	100.00
73 Acc., 1930, Pole wagon (circus set), Wide Ga.	50.00	100.00
74 Acc., 1930-32, Animal set (circus set), Wide Ga.	50.00	100.00

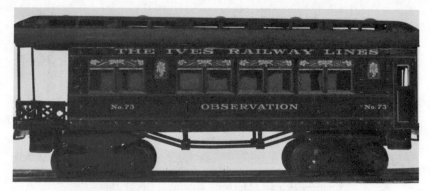

Ives 73 Observation Car, No. 1 ga., brown, gray, yellow litho.
Courtesy Heinz A. Mueller, Continental Hobby House

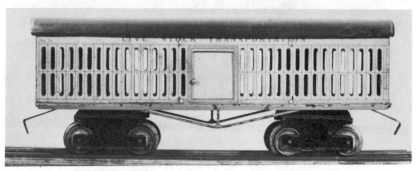

Ives 74 Stock Car, No. 1 ga., yellow, green, red litho.
Courtesy Heinz A. Mueller, Continental Hobby House

	G	VG
75 Acc., 1930-32, Car runways (circus set), Wide Ga.	25.00	50.00
80 Acc., 1906-07, Scenic background panels (3 in set)	45.00	70.00
86 Acc., 1912-30, Telegraph pole	3.00	5.00
87 Acc., 1923-30, Flag pole	8.00	15.00
88 Acc., 1923-30, Lamp bracket	3.00	5.00
89 Acc., 1930, Water tower	125.00	200.00
90 Acc., 1912-27, Small bridge, 0 Ga.	15.00	25.00
90 Acc., 1929, Small bridge, 0 Ga.	15.00	25.00
90 Acc., 1928-29, Automatic drop bridge, 0 Ga.	15.00	35.00
91 Acc., 1912-30, Culvert-style bridge, 0 Ga.	18.50	35.00

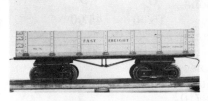

Ives 76 Gondola, No. 1 ga., yellow, red litho.
Courtesy Heinz A. Mueller, Continental
Hobby House

Ives 75 Caboose, No. 1 ga., Yellow, green,
red litho.
Courtesy Heinz A. Mueller, Continental
Hobby House

	G	VG
91-3 Acc., 1912-30, Culvert-style bridge (electric) 0 Ga.	15.00	35.00
92 Acc., 1912-30, Bridge (1923-semaphore signal added) 0 Ga.	25.00	42.50
92-3 Acc., 1912-30, Bridge (electric), 0 Ga.	30.00	65.00
96 Acc., 1929-30, Bridge (1-span with ramps), litho, 0 Ga.	35.00	62.50
97 Acc., 1910-12, Revolving drawbridge (clockwork), 0 Ga.	40.00	95.00
97 Acc., 1929-30, Bridge (3-span with ramps), litho, W Ga.	45.00	65.00
98 Acc., 1912-30, Bridge (1-span with ramps), litho, 0 Ga.	25.00	47.50
98-3 Acc., 1912-30, Bridge (1-span with ramps, electric), litho, 0 Ga.	25.00	50.00
98-1 Acc., 1912-21, Bridge (1-span with ramps, clockwork), litho, #1 Ga.	45.00	75.00
98-1-3 Acc., 1912-21, Bridge (1-span with ramps, electric), litho, #1 Ga. ...	45.00	85.00
99 Acc., 1912-29, Bridge (2-span with ramps, clockwork), litho, 0 Ga.	45.00	95.00
99-3 Acc., 1912-29, Bridge (2-span with ramps, electric), litho 0 Ga.	25.00	75.00
99-1 Acc., 1912-16, Bridge (2-span with ramps, clockwork), litho, #1 Ga.	45.00	95.00
99-1-3 Acc., 1912-16, Bridge (2-span with ramps, electric), litho, #1 Ga. ...	45.00	85.00
99-2-3 Acc., 1923-28, Bridge (2-span with ramps, electric), litho, W Ga. ...	45.00	85.00
100 Acc., 1912-28, Bridge (2 sections, culvert-type, clockwork), 0 Ga.	15.00	35.00

331

	G	VG
100-3 Acc., 1912-28, Bridge (2 sections, culvert-type, electric), 0 Ga.	15.00	45.00
100-1 Acc., 1912-28, Bridge (2 sections, culvert-type, clockwork), #1 Ga.	25.00	50.00
100-1-3 Acc., 1912-28, Bridge (2 sections, culvert-type, electric), #1 Ga.	25.00	55.00
100 Acc., 1930-32, Accessory set (10 pieces)	35.00	65.00
100 Acc., 1930-32, Bridge ramps (Lionel #105), W Ga.	5.00	10.00
101 Acc., 1912-28, Bridge (1-span with ramps), litho, 0 Ga.	15.00	28.50
101-3 Acc., 1912-18, Bridge (1-span with ramps, electric), litho, 0 Ga.	25.00	60.00
101-1 Acc., 1912-16, Bridge (1-span with ramps, clockwork), litho #1 Ga.	20.00	40.00
101-1-3 Acc., 1912-16, Bridge (1-span with ramps, electric), litho, #1 Ga.	25.00	55.00
101 Acc., 1931-32, Single-span bridge with 2 ramps (Lionel #101), W Ga.	15.00	40.00
101-2-3 Acc., 1925-29, Bridge (with semaphore signal), W Ga.	18.50	45.00
102 Acc., 1928, Tunnel	10.00	25.00
102 Acc., 1910-12, Single-span roller-lift drawbridge, 0 Ga.	35.00	70.00
103 Acc., 1910-30, Paper mache tunnel (6.5 inch), 0 Ga.	5.00	10.00
104 Acc., 1910-30, Paper mache tunnel (8.5 inch), 0 Ga.	5.00	10.00
104 Acc., 1931-32, Bridge span (Lionel #101), W Ga.	15.00	40.00
105 Acc., 1910-29, Paper mache tunnel (11 inch)	5.00	10.00
105 Acc., 1931-32, Bridge ramp (Lionel #105), 0 Ga.	5.00	10.00
106 Acc., 1931-32, Single-span bridge with ramps (Lionel #105) W. Ga.	10.00	20.00
106 Acc., 1931-32, Tunnel (14 inch)	8.00	15.00
106E Acc., 1931-32, Tunnel (16 inch)	8.00	15.00
106 Acc., 1910-20, Paper mache tunnel (16 inch)	8.00	15.00
106 Acc., 1929-30, Paper mache tunnel (19 inch), W Ga.	35.00	55.00

332

Ives station, one sliding door, tin litho
Courtesy Mapes Auctioneers & Appraisers

	G	VG
107 Acc., 1929-30, Paper mache tunnel (23 inch), W Ga.	10.00	15.00
107 Acc., 1929-30, Paper mache tunnel (23 inch with highway), W Ga.	50.00	85.00
107 Acc., 1905-19, Signal with check, 0 Ga.	12.50	25.00
107D Acc., 1908-30, Semaphore (2-flag)	20.00	30.00
107S Acc., 1908-30, Semaphore (1-flag)	8.00	15.00
108 Acc., 1911-16, Signal with check, #1 Ga.	10.00	15.00
109 Acc., 1905-22, Platform signal	25.00	50.00
110 Acc., 1904-28, Bumper, 0 Ga.	2.00	4.00
110-1 Acc., 1912-17, Bumper, #1 Ga.	2.00	4.00
110 Acc., 1931-32, Bridge span (Lionel #110), W Ga.	5.00	10.00
111 Ac., 1904-07, Elevating post, 0 Ga.	7.50	13.50
111 Acc., 1912-28, Crossing sign	1.00	2.50
111 Acc., 1929, Crossing sign (Lionel #0-68)	.50	2.00
112 Acc., 1906-32, Track plates, 0 Ga.	.50	1.00
112-1 Acc., 1912-21, Track plates, #1 Ga.	.50	1.00
113 Acc., 1910-28, Station	49.00	73.50

	G	VG
113-3 Acc., 1910-28, Station (illuminated)	60.00	100.00
114 Acc., 1904-23, Station	75.00	150.00
115 Acc., 1904-28, Station	75.00	140.00
116 Acc., 1901-28, Station	85.00	140.00
116-3 Acc., 1926-28, Station (illuminated)	75.00	125.00
117 Acc., 1904-28, Covered platform	40.00	80.00
118 Acc., 1910-12, Covered platform (1 post)	20.00	30.00
119 Acc., 1910-14, Covered platform (2 posts)	25.00	65.00
120 Acc., 1904-16, Covered platform (4 posts, stamped railing)	35.00	65.00
121 Acc., 1910-24, Glass-dome station (6 inch), #1, 0 Ga.	75.00	125.00
122 Acc., 1910-24, Glass-dome platform station, #1 0 Ga.	200.00	450.00
123 Acc., 1910-24, 2-station building with glass dome center #1, 0 Ga. ...	450.00	650.00
123 Lumber, 1925, brown, 8 wheels, 0 Ga.	15.00	22.50
123 Lumber 1929, black or green, 8 wheels, 0 Ga.	15.00	22.50
121 Caboose, 1929, brass plates (Flyer #3211)	15.00	37.50
121 Caboose, 1930, brass plates (Lionel #817)	18.00	40.00
122 Tank, 1929-30, painted (Lionel #815)	30.00	65.00
124 Refrig., 1925-30, white/black, litho	50.00	75.00
125 Mcdse., 1904-09, cream/red & black roof, wood litho, 0 Ga.........	14.50	22.00
125 Mcdse., 1910-17, red or grey/white, wood litho, 0 Ga.	37.50	56.50
125 Mcdse., 1918-30, grey/black, wood litho 0 Ga., for cars with heralds see Ives General Notes, otherwise	25.00	50.00
126 Caboose, 1904-09, grey/red & black roof, wood litho, 0	125.00	237.50
126 Caboose, 1906-09, buff/red & black roof, wood litho, 0	125.00	237.50

334

Ives 124 Refrigerator Car, 0 ga., white, gray, red, blue, black litho.
Courtesy Heinz A. Mueller, Continental Hobby House

Ives 125 Box Car, 0 ga., white, gray, red, black litho.
Courtesy Heinz A. Mueller, Continental Hobby House

Ives 128 Gondola, 0 ga., gray, red, black litho.
Courtesy Heinz A. Mueller, Continental Hobby House

	G	VG
127 Stock, 1904-09, grey/red & black roof, wood litho, 0	125.00	237.50
127 Stock, 1910, grey/green roof, wood litho, 0	125.00	237.50
127 Stock, 1912, grey/white & blue roof, wood litho, 0	30.00	60.00
127 Stock, 1924, yellow/grey roof, wood litho, 0	20.00	30.00
128 Gravel, 1904-09, grey/blue wood litho, 0	15.50	23.50
128 Gravel, 1910-17, green/grey steel litho, 0	15.50	23.50
128 Gravel, 1918-30, grey; maroon/black steel litho, 0	12.50	18.75
129 Observation, 1910-17, green, red, yellow trim, litho, "SARATOGA"	31.50	47.00
129 Pullman, 1904-10, yellow; red; green; grey litho, "PHILADELPHIA"	42.00	63.00
129 Pullman, 1910-17, green, red, yellow trim litho, "SARATOGA"	31.50	47.00

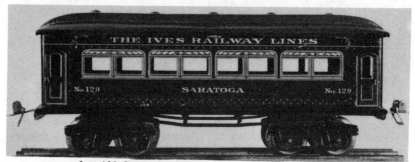

Ives 129 Coach, 0 ga., green, red, yellow litho, nickel trim.
Courtesy Heinz A. Mueller, Continental Hobby House

Ives 130 Coach, 0 ga., green, red, yellow litho, nickel trim.
Courtesy Heinz A. Mueller, Continental Hobby House

Ives 131 Baggage, 0 ga., orange, brown, black litho, nickel trim.
Courtesy Heinz A. Mueller, Continental Hobby House

336

	G	VG
129 Pullman, 1919-25, olive; green; black; red, 0	31.50	47.00
129 Pullman, 1926-30, orange/brown litho, "SARATOGA"	31.50	47.00
130 Pullman, 1904-10, yellow; red; green; grey, L.V.E., Buffet, 0	114.50	172.00
130 Pullman, 1910-17, green red, yellow trim, wood litho, L.V.E., 0 ...	114.50	172.00
130 Pullman, 1919-25, olive, black, red trim, steel litho, "IVES RAILWAY"	37.00	55.00
130 Pullman, 1926-30, orange/brown, plain litho, 0	15.00	22.50
131 Baggage, 1904-10, yellow; green; grey; red litho, 0	114.50	172.00
131 Baggage, 1910-17, green, red, yellow trim, litho, 0	49.00	73.50
131 Baggage, 1926-30, orange/brown, plain litho, 0	15.00	22.50
132 Observation, 1924-25, olive; red/ yellow, steel litho, 0	42.00	63.00
132 Observation, 1926-30, green; blue/red roof, 0	20.00	25.50
133 Parlor, 1928-30, green; blue/red roof, 0	40.00	60.00
134 Observation, 1928-30, green; blue; orange; black, 0	40.00	60.00
135 Parlor, 1926, tan, brass trim, 0, illuminated	44.00	66.00
135 Parlor, 1927, blue, brass trim, 0, illuminated	44.00	66.00

Ives 132 Observation Car, 0 ga., orange, brown, black, yellow litho, nickel.
Courtesy Heinz A. Mueller, Continental Hobby House

Ives 136 Observation, 0 ga., blue, red, brass trim.
Courtesy Heinz A. Mueller, Continental Hobby House

	G	VG
135 Parlor, 1928, orange, brass trim, 0, illuminated	44.00	66.00
135 Parlor, 1929, red/black, brass trim, 0, illuminated	44.00	66.00
135 Parlor, 1930, orange/black; blue/red; red/black, brass trim, 0, illuminated	44.00	66.00
136 Observation, 1926, tan, brass trim, 0, illuminated	44.00	66.00
136 Observation, 1927, blue, brass trim, 0, illuminated	44.00	66.00
136 Observation, 1928, orange, brass trim, 0, illuminated	44.00	66.00
136 Observation, 1929, red/black, brass trim, 0, illuminated	44.00	66.00
136 Observation, 1930, orange/black; blue/red; red/black, brass trim, 0, illuminated	44.00	66.00
140 Pullman, 1926-27, grey, brass trim, 0, illuminated	50.00	85.00
140 Pullman, 1928, black/red, brass trim, "BLACK DIAMOND", 0, illuminated	50.00	85.00
140 Pullman, 1929, green; orange/black; black/red, brass trim, 0, illuminated, "SEAGRAVE SPECIAL".	50.00	85.00
140 Acc., 1910-16, crossing gates, automatic clockwork, 0	18.00	30.00
140-3 Acc., 1910-16, crossing gates, automatic electric, 0	25.00	40.00

Ives 137 Parlor Car, 0 ga., red, black, brass trim.
Courtesy Heinz A. Mueller, Continental Hobby House

Ives 141 Coach, 0 ga., black, red, brass trim.
Courtesy Heinz A. Mueller, Continental
Hobby House

Ives 141 Parlor Car, 0 ga., red, black, brass
trim.
Courtesy Heinz A. Mueller, Continental
Hobby House

Ives 142 Observation Car, 0 ga., red, black,
brass trim.
Courtesy Heinz A. Mueller, Continental
Hobby House

Ives Observation Car, 0 ga., black, red, brass
trim.
Courtesy Heinz A. Mueller, Continental
Hobby House

	G	VG
140 Passenger, 1926, 8 wheels, illuminated, Std.	82.00	123.00
141 Pullman, 1926-27, grey, brass trim, 0, illuminated	65.00	95.00
141 Passenger, 1926, 8 wheels, illuminated Std.	82.50	123.00

	G	VG
141 Pullman, 1928, black/red, brass trim, "BLACK DIAMOND", 0, illuminated	65.00	95.00
141 Pullman, 1929, green; orange/black; black/red, brass trim, illuminated 'SEAGRAVE SPECIAL'	65.00	95.00
142 Pullman, 1926-27, grey, brass trim, 0, illuminated	82.00	123.00
142 Passenger, 1926, 8 wheels, illuminated, Std.		
142 Pullman, 1928, black/red, brass trim, "BLACK DIAMOND", 0, illuminated	50.00	85.00
142 Pullman, 1929, green; orange/black; black/red, brass trim, 0, illuminated, "SEAGRAVE SPECIAL" .	50.00	85.00
145 Acc., 1910-30, turntable (manual), 0	25.00	45.00
146 Acc., 1910-30, turntable (Mechanical), 0	50.00	100.00
171 Buffet, 1925, painted, rubber-stamped, 13″, 8 wheels, Std.	65.00	98.00
172 Parlor, 1925, painted, rubber-stamped, 13″, 8 wheels, Std.	65.00	98.00
173 Observation, 1925, paint, rubber stamp, 13″, 8 wheels, Std.	65.00	98.00
176 Loco, 1930, cast, black, 0-4-0, brake, clockwork, 0	125.00	175.00
180 Club, 1926-27, orange; red; green; grey; blue; yellow, 12 wh., Std.	75.00	125.00
180 Club, 1927-28, orange; red; green; grey; blue; yellow, 12 wh., Std.	75.00	125.00
181 Parlor, 1926-27, orange; red; green; grey; blue; yellow, 12 wh., Std.	75.00	125.00
181 Parlor, 1927-28, orange; red; green; grey; blue; yellow, 12 wh., Std.	75.00	125.00
181 Buffet, 1912-20, dark green/grey roof, steel litho, #1 Ga.	147.00	220.50
182 Observation, 1926-27, orange; red; green; grey; blue; yellow, 12 wh., Std.	75.00	125.00
182 Drawing Room, 1912-20, dark green/grey roof, steel litho, #1 Ga...	147.00	220.00
183 Observation, 1912-20, dark green/grey roof, steel litho, #1 Ga.	197.00	220.50

Ives 176 0-4-0 Wind-up Loco, tender, black, red.
Courtesy Heinz A. Mueller, Continental Hobby House

Ives 180 Club Car, Std, green, gold, brass trim.
Courtesy Heinz A. Mueller, Continental Hobby House

Ives 181 Parlor Car, Std., green, gold, brass trim.
Courtesy Heinz A. Mueller, Continental Hobby House

	G	VG
184 Buffet, 1921-30, green; red; brown; grey; blue; tan; orange, 8 wh., Std. Ga.	65.00	95.00
184-3 Buffet, 1925-30, green; red; brown; grey; blue; tan; orange, 8 wh., Std. Ga., illuminated	56.00	84.00
185 Parlor, 1921-30, green; red; brown; grey; blue; tan; orange; maroon, 8 wh., Std. Ga.	65.00	95.00

341

Ives 181 Baggage-Parlor Car, No. 1 ga., green, red, gold, rubber stamp.
Courtesy Heinz A. Mueller, Continental Hobby House

Ives 182 Coach, No. 1 ga., green, red, gold rubber stamp.
Courtesy Heinz A. Mueller, Continental Hobby House

Ives 182 Observation Car, Std., green, gold, brass trim.
Courtesy Heinz A. Mueller, Continental Hobby House

Ives 183 Observation Car, No. 1 ga., green, red, gold rubber-stamped.
Courtesy Heinz A. Mueller, Continental Hobby House

Ives 184 Club Car, Std., red, black, brass trim.
Courtesy Heinz A. Mueller, Continental Hobby House

	G	VG
186 Observation, 1921-30, green; red; brown; grey; blue; tan; orange, 8 wh., Std. Ga.	65.00	95.00
186-3 Observation, 1925-30, green; red; brown; grey; blue; tan; orange, 8 wh., Std. Ga., illuminated	56.00	84.00
187 Truck Car, green, 12 wh., Std. Ga.	276.00	414.00
187-3 Passenger Car, white, 4 wh., Std. Ga.	166.00	249.00

Ives 185 Parlor Car, Std. ga., orange, black, brass trim.
Courtesy Heinz A. Mueller, Continental Hobby House

Ives 186 Observation Car, Std. ga., orange, black, brass trim.
Courtesy Heinz A. Mueller, Continental Hobby House

Ives 187 Buffet Car, Std., green, red, rubber-stamped.
Courtesy Heinz A. Mueller, Continental Hobby House

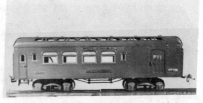

Ives 187 Club Car, Std., green, gold, brass trim.
Courtesy Heinz A. Mueller, Continental Hobby House

Ives 187-1 Buffet Car, Std., white, gold, rubber-stamped, nickel trim.
Courtesy Heinz A. Mueller, Continental Hobby House

	G	VG
187 Club, 1921-28, green; grey; red; blue, 8 wh., Std. Ga.	60.00	95.00
187-1 Club, 1921-22, green; grey; red; blue, 8 wh., Std. Ga.	60.00	95.00
187-3 Club, 1923-25, green; grey; red; blue, 8 wh., Std. Ga.	166.00	249.00

Ives 187-3 Buffet Car, Std., orange, black rubber-stamped, nickel trim.
Courtesy Heinz A. Mueller, Continental Hobby House

Ives 188 Parlor Car, Std., green, gold, brass trim.
Courtesy Heinz A. Mueller, Continental Hobby House

	G	VG
188 Parlor, 1921-26, green or grey, 8 wh., Std. Ga.	60.00	95.00
188 Parlor, 1926-28, green or grey, 8 wh., brass plates, illuminated, Std. Ga.	90.00	125.00
188-1 Parlor, 1921-22, green; grey, 8 wh., Std. Ga	60.00	95.00
188 Truck Car, green, 12 wh., Std. Ga.	276.00	414.00
188-3 Passenger Car, white, 4 wh., Std. Ga.	166.00	249.00
189 Truck Car, white, 4 wh., Std. Ga.	276.00	414.00
189 Observation, 1926-27, green; red; grey; blue, 8 wh. Std. Ga.	60.00	95.00
189 Observation, 1926-28, green; red; grey; blue, brass plates, illuminated, Std. Ga.	90.00	125.00
189-1 Observation, 1921-22, green; red; grey; blue, Std. Ga.	75.00	110.00
189-3 Observation, 1923-25, green; red; grey; blue, Std. Ga.	166.00	249.00

	G	VG
191 Tank, 1921-28, orange; green; yellow, 8 wh., Std. Ga.	65.00	110.00
190-20 Tank, 1929, brass plates, 8 wh. (Flyer), Std. Ga.....................	72.50	115.00
190 Tank, 1930, brass plates, 8 wh. (Lionel), Std. Ga...................	200.00	400.00
191 Coke, 1921-30, black; maroon; brown; blue, 8 wh., Std. Ga.	75.00	150.00
192 Mcdse., 1921-23, green; blue, litho, 8 wh., Std. Ga.	182.00	273.00
192 Mcdse., 1924-28, brown; orange; white, litho, 8 wh., Std. Ga.	40.00	60.00
192-20 Mcdse., 1929, yellow/blue; green/red, litho, 8 wh., (Flyer), Std. Ga.	195.00	250.00
192 Mcdse., 1930, yellow/blue, litho 8 wh., (Lionel), Std. Ga.	62.50	90.00
193 Stock, 1921-23, grey; orange, 8 wh., Std. Ga......................	78.50	117.50
193 Stock, 1924-28, brown, 8 wh., Std. Ga.	65.00	95.00
193-20 Stock, 1929, brass plates, 8 wh., (Flyer), Std. Ga....................	65.00	95.00
193 Stock, 1930, brass plates, 8 wh., (Lionel), Std. Ga...................	100.00	250.00
194 Coal, 1921-30, grey; black; maroon, litho, 8 wh., Std. Ga.	100.00	200.00

Ives 188-1 Parlor Car, Std., white, gold rubber stamp, nickel trim.
Courtesy Heinz A. Mueller, Continental Hobby House

Ives 188-3 Parlor Car, Std., orange, black rubber-stamped, nickel trim.
Courtesy Heinz A. Mueller, Continental Hobby House

Ives 189 4-4-0 Loco and Tender, black, gold.
Courtesy Heinz A. Mueller, Continental Hobby House

Ives 189 Observation Car, Std., green, gold, brass trim.
Courtesy Heinz A. Mueller, Continental Hobby House

Ives 189 Observation Car, Std., green, red rubber-stamped, nickel trim.
Courtesy Heinz A. Mueller, Continental Hobby House

Ives 189 Observation Car, Std., brass trim.
Courtesy Heinz A. Mueller, Continental Hobby House

	G	VG
195-20 Freight, 1930, brass plates, (Lionel)	202.00	303.00
195 Caboose, 1921-23, maroon, litho, 8 wh., Std. Ga.	75.00	150.00
195 Caboose, 1924-28, red, litho, 8 wh., Std. Ga.	75.00	150.00

Ives 189-1 Observation Car, Std., white, gold rubber-stamped, nickel trim.
Courtesy Heinz A. Mueller, Continental Hobby House

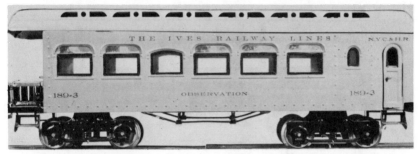
Ives 189-3 Observation Car, Std., orange, black rubber-stamped, nickel trim.
Courtesy Heinz A. Mueller, Continental Hobby House

Ives Tank Car, Std., brown, black.
Courtesy Heinz A. Mueller, Continental Hobby House

	G	VG
195-20 Caboose, 1929, red, brass plates, litho, 8 wh., (Flyer), Std. GA.	85.00	170.00
195 Caboose, 1930, red, brass plates, litho, 8 wh., (Lionel), Std. Ga.	75.00	112.00
196 Flat, 1921-25, olive; dark green, 8 wh., Std. Ga.	40.00	60.00
196 Flat, 1926, orange, 8 wh., Std. Ga.	40.00	60.00

347

Ives 190 "Texas Oil" Tank Car, Std., orange, gray, black, brass trim.
Courtesy Heinz A. Mueller, Continental Hobby House

Ives 191 Coke Car, Std., green, black, brass trim.
Courtesy Heinz A. Mueller, Continental Hobby House

Ives 192 Box Car, Lionel Transition, Std., yellow, green, brass trim.
Courtesy Heinz A. Mueller, Continental Hobby House

Ives 192 Refrigerator Car, Std., brown, black, rubber-stamped.
Courtesy Heinz A. Mueller, Continental Hobby House

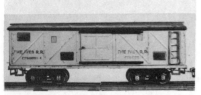

Ives 192 Circus Box Car, Std., yellow, red, black, brass trim.
Courtesy Heinz A. Mueller, Continental Hobby House

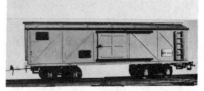

Ives 192 Box Car, American Flyer transitional, Std., beige, blue, brass trim.
Courtesy Heinz A. Mueller, Continental Hobby House

Ives 193 Circus Car Std., yellow, red, black, nickel and brass trim.
Courtesy Heinz A. Mueller, Continental Hobby House

Ives 193 Stock Car, Std., green, black.
Courtesy Heinz A. Mueller, Continental
Hobby House

Ives 194 Hopper, Std., black, red, nickel trim.
Courtesy Heinz A. Mueller, Continental
Hobby House

Ives 195 Caboose, Std., red, green.
Courtesy Heinz A. Mueller, Continental Hobby House

	G	VG
196 Flat, 1922, "HARMONY CREAMERY", Special, 8 wh., Std. Ga.		
196 Freight, Std. Ga.	250.00	400.00
196 Cage Flat, 1928, circus car with hippos in cage, Std. Ga.	300.00	500.00

349

Ives 195 Caboose, Std., brown, black, white.
Courtesy Heinz A. Mueller, Continental Hobby House

Ives 195 Caboose, American Flyer transitional, Std., two-tone red, brass trim.
Courtesy Heinz A. Mueller, Continental Hobby House

	G	VG
197 Lumber, 1928-29, green; orange, 8 wh., Std. Ga.	110.00	165.00
197 Lumber, 1930, green, 8 wh. (Lionel #211), Std. Ga.	202.00	303.00
198-20 Gravel, 1929, black, brass plates, 8 wh., (Flyer), Std. Ga.	125.00	200.00
198 Gravel, 1930, black; maroon, brass plates, 8 wh., (Lionel), Std. Ga.	202.00	303.00
199 Derrick, 1929-30, blue/maroon, brass plates, 8 wh., Std. Ga.	250.00	325.00
200 Acc., 1910-14, power house (battery cover), litho	100.00	200.00

Ives 196C Circus Flat Car, Std., yellow, green, red, nickel, brass trim.
Courtesy Heinz A. Mueller, Continental Hobby House

Ives 198 Gondola, American Flyer transitional, Std., green, brass trim.
Courtesy Heinz A. Mueller, Continental Hobby House

Ives 198 Gondola, Lionel transitional, Std., maroon, black, brass trim.
Courtesy Heinz A. Mueller, Continental Hobby House

	G	VG
200 Acc., 1923-28, freight station, litho, (#220 in 1929)	25.00	60.00
201 Acc., 1910-14, power house, litho	125.00	250.00
201 Acc., 1923-28, passenger station, litho, (#221 in 1929)	35.00	75.00
201-3 Acc., 1923-28, passenger station, litho, 2-#88 lamp brackets	35.00	75.00
202 Acc., 1910-11, power house, litho	125.00	250.00
202 Acc., 1912-14, rotary transformer	5.00	15.00
203 Acc., 1912-14, power house, litho (2 transformers)	125.00	250.00
203-214 Acc., 1912-30, transformers .	3.00	4.50
215 Acc., 1923-30, crossing gate, litho (manual), 0	12.50	18.00
216 Acc., 1923-26, crossing gate, litho (manual), with sign, 0	13.50	20.00

351

Ives 241 Club Car, Std., black, red, brass trim.
Courtesy Heinz A. Mueller, Continental Hobby House

Ives 242 Parlor Car, Std., black, red, brass trim.
Courtesy Heinz A. Mueller, Continental Hobby House

Ives 243 Observation Car, Std., black, red, brass trim.
Courtesy Heinz A. Mueller, Continental Hobby House

Ives 247 Club Car, Std., black, red, yellow, gold decal, brass trim.
Courtesy Heinz A. Mueller, Continental Hobby House

Ives 246 Dining Car, Std., orange, black, yellow.
Courtesy Heinz A. Mueller, Continental Hobby House

	G	VG
225 Acc., 1929-30, station, illuminated, Lionel #137	40.00	85.00
226 Acc., 1929-30, station, illuminated, Lionel #136	35.00	75.00
228 Acc., 1929-30, covered platform	18.50	38.00
230 Acc., 1929-30, station, illuminated, Lionel #124	40.00	95.00
230-3x Acc., 1929-30, station, illuminated (set with #228)	63.00	130.00

Ives 247 Club Car, Std., orange, black, yellow, brass trim.
Courtesy Heinz A. Mueller, Continental Hobby House

Ives 248 Pullman, Std., black, red, yellow, gold decal, brass trim.
Courtesy Heinz A. Mueller, Continental Hobby House

	G	VG
230-3XX 1920-30 Station, illuminated set with (2) #228	75.00	140.00
241 Club, 1928-29, painted, illuminated, brass plates, Std.	500.00	1000.00
242 Parlor, 1928-29, painted, illuminated, brass plates, Std.	500.00	1000.00
243 Observation, 1928-29, paint, illuminated, brass plates, Std.	500.00	1000.00
246 Dining Car, 1930, paint, illuminated, brass plates, 12 wh., Std.	500.00	1000.00
247 Club, 1930, paint illuminated, brass plates, 12 wheels, Std.	400.00	750.00
248 Chair, 1930, paint, illuminated, brass plates, 12 wheels, Std.	500.00	1000.00
249 Observation, 1930, paint, illuminated brass plates, 12 wh., Std.	500.00	1000.00
250 Acc., 1929-30, house, Lionel #184	17.00	40.00
251 Acc., 1929-30, house, illuminated, Lionel #189	45.00	95.00

353

Ives 248 Pullman, Std., orange, black, yellow.
Courtesy Heinz A. Mueller, Continental Hobby House

Ives 249 Observation Car, Std., orange, black, yellow.
Courtesy Heinz A. Mueller, Continental Hobby House

	G	VG
252 Acc., 1929-30, house, illuminated, Lionel #191	45.00	95.00
257 Loco, 1931, steel, cast frame, tender tank, Lionel #257	125.00	200.00
258 Loco, 1931-32, steel, cast frame, tender tank, Lionel #258	125.00	200.00
306 Acc., lamp post (12" with fluted shade)	15.00	30.00
310 Acc., signal	10.00	15.00
330 Acc., automatic block semaphore .	15.00	30.00
331 Acc., double light target, Std.	15.00	30.00
331-0 Acc., double light target, 0	15.00	30.00
332 Acc., bell crossing signal, Std.	15.00	30.00
332-0 Acc., bell crossing signal, 0	15.00	30.00

Ives 249 Observation Car, Std., black, red, yellow, gold decal, brass trim.
Courtesy Heinz A. Mueller, Continental Hobby House

Ives 332 Railway Mail, Std., peacock, green, orange, brass trim.
Courtesy Heinz A. Mueller, Continental Hobby House

Ives 258 2-4-0 Loco and Tender, 0 ga., black, orange stripe, brass trim.
Courtesy Heinz A. Mueller, Continental Hobby House

332 Baggage, 1932, peacock/orange, brass plates, illuminated, Std.	35.00	75.00
332 Acc., automatic bell signal, Std. . .	15.00	30.00
332-0 Acc., automatic bell signal-0 . . .	15.00	30.00
333 Acc., bell and banjo signal, Std. . .	15.00	30.00
333 Acc., bell and banjo signal, 0	15.00	30.00
338 Acc., bridge approach signal	15.00	30.00
339 Pullman, 1932, peacock/orange, brass plates, illuminated, Std.	35.00	75.00
341 Observation, 1932, peacock/ orange, brass plates, illuminated Std.	35.00	75.00
400 Set, 1917, #1100 loco, #11 T, #550, 551		
400R Set, 1921, #1122 R, #25 T, #141, 141, 142 'SEAGRAVE SPECIAL DELUXE'		
400 Set, 1919, #1100 loco, #11 T, #550, 551		
401 Set, 1919, #1116 loco, #11 T, #550, 551, 552		
401 Set, 1925, #19 loco, #17 T, #60, 68		
402 Set, 1925, #19 loco, #17 T, #60, 61, 68		

Ives 332 Railway Mail, Lionel Transitional, Std., peacock, orange, brass trim.
Courtesy Heinz A. Mueller, Continental Hobby House

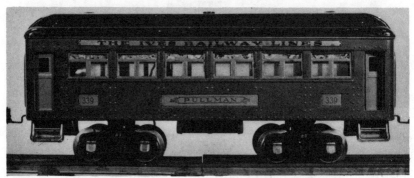

Ives 339 Pullman, Std., peacock, green, orange, brass trim.
Courtesy Heinz A. Mueller, Continental Hobby House

Ives 339 Pullman, Std., peacock, orange, brass and nickel trim.
Courtesy Heinz A. Mueller, Continental Hobby House

403 Set, 1919, #1118 1 co, #25 T, #130,
129, 129
416 Set, 1928, Ives Village #3260 loco,
#62, 68 plus #103, 107, 221, 111, 215, 87,
308, (6) #86

FOR SET PRICES
SEE
INDIVIDUAL
NUMBERS
AND
GENERAL NOTES (p. 310).

417 Loco, cast, black/red, 4-4-0, 8 wh.
tender 125.00   250.00

479 Set, 1928, #3260 loco, #63, 70,
'SUBURBAN FREIGHT'

480 Set, 1928, #3260 loco, #62, 68,
'BLUE COMET EXPRESS'

481 Set, 1928, #3260 loco, #133, 134,
'ORIOLE LIMITED'

482 Set, 1928, #3261 loco, #133, 133,
134, 'SOUTHERN SPECIAL'

483 Set, 1928, #3255 loco, #63, 64, 69,
70, 'COMMERCE FREIGHT'

483R Set, 1928, #3255 loco, #63, 64, 69,
70, auto reverse

484 Set, 1928, #3255 loco, #135, 135,
136, 'RED HAWK SPECIAL'

484R Set, 1928, same, auto reverse

485 Set, 1928, #1122 loco, #25 T, #125,
128, 67, 'MIDWEST FAST FREIGHT'

485R Set, 1928, same, auto reverse

486 Set, 1928, #1122 loco, #25 T, #135,
135, 136, 'MAJOR H.O.D. SEA-
GRAVE SPECIAL'

486R Set, 1928, same, auto reverse

487 Set, 1928, #3257 loco, #141, 141,
142, 'DIXIE FLYER'

487R Set, 1928, same, auto reverse

488 Set, 1928, #1122 loco, #25 T, #141,
141, 142, 'CASCADE LIMITED'

488R Set, 1928, same, auto reverse

489 Set, 1928, #1122 loco, #25 T, #141,
141, 142, 'BLACK DIAMOND JUN-
IOR'

489R Set, 1928, same, auto reverse

490 Set, 1928, #1122 loco, #25 T, #123,
124, 125, 127, 128, 122, 121, 'UNIVER-
SAL FAST FREIGHT JUNIOR'

490R Set, 1928, same, auto reverse

500 Set, 1926, #3258 loco, #551, 552

500 Set, 1924, #3250 loco, #551, 550

500 Set, 1927, #3258 loco, #551, 552,
'GREEN MOUNTAIN EXPRESS'

500 Set, 1919, #3250 loco, #550, 551

500 Set, 1925, #3251 loco, #60, 62

FOR SET PRICES
SEE
INDIVIDUAL
NUMBERS
AND
GENERAL NOTES
(p. 310).

357

Ives 341 Observation Car, Lionel Transitional, Std, peacock, orange, brass trim. Courtesy Heinz A. Mueller, Continental Hobby House

Ives 341 Observation Car, Std., peacock, green, orange. Courtesy Heinz A. Mueller, Continental Hobby House

Ives 417 4-4-0 Steam, 8-Wheel Tender, 0 ga., black, red, orange.
Courtesy Heinz A. Mueller, Continental Hobby House

501 Set, 1919, 1924, #3251 loco, #550, 551, 552

501 Set, 1925, #3252 loco, #60, 68

501 Set, 1924, #3251 loco, #60, 61, 62

501 Set, 1926, #3251 loco, #61, 68, 'RED ARROW'

502 Set, 1926, #3252 loco, #60, 62-3, 68-3 'MANAGER' SPECIAL'

502 Set, 1925, #3254 loco, #60, 61, 68

502 Set, 1927, #3259 loco, #551, 552, 568 White Owl

502 Set, 1919, 1924, #3252 loco, #60, 61 61

503 Set, 1919, #3253 loco, #60, 61, 62

503 Set, 1927, #3255 loco, #135, 135, 136, 'IVES LIMITED'

503R Set, 1927, same, auto reverse

503 Set, 1926, #3254 loco, #135, 135, 136, 'IVES LIMITED'

504 Set, 1919, #3253 loco, #130, 129, 129

FOR SET PRICES
SEE
INDIVIDUAL
NUMBERS
AND
GENERAL NOTES
(p. 310).

358

	G	VG
504 Set, 1925, #3255R loco, #129, 132		
504R Set, 1925, #3255R loco, #130, 129, 132		
504R Set, 1926, #3255 loco, #130, 129, 132, 'FORT ORANGE'		
504 Set, 1924, #3253 loco, #130, 129, 132 (illuminated cars)		
504R Set, 1926, #3255 loco, #131, 129, 132		
505 Set, 1924, 1925, #3250 loco, #50, 51		
506 Set, 1924, 1925, #3250 loco, #53, 56		
507 Set, 1926, #3257 loco, #140, 140, 141 'GREYHOUND'		
507R Set, 1926, same, auto reverse		
508 Set, 1926, #3255 loco, #130, 132, 'GREEN MOUNTAIN EXPRESS'		
510 Set, 1924, 1925, #3251 loco, #63, 64, 67		
510 Set, 1926, #3251 loco, #63, 64, 67, 'MERCHANT'S DISPATCH'		
510 Set 1927, #3252 loco, #63, 64, 67, 'MERCHANT'S DISPATCH'		
511 Set, 1924, 1925, #3252 loco, #63, 64, 66, 67		
516 Set, 1924, 1925, #3253 loco, #125, 127, 128, 67		
516 Set, 1926, #3255 loco, #127, 128, 125, 67, 'FAST FREIGHT'		
550 Baggage, 1915, red/yellow/black, wood litho, 4 wh., 0	22.50	34.00
550 Baggage, 1916-25, olive/orange/yellow, wood litho, 4 wh., 0	12.50	18.00
550 Baggage, 1926-28, olive/orange, litho, 4 wh., 0	15.50	23.50
550 Baggage, 1915, white/red/black, litho, 4 wh., 0	25.00	40.00
550 Baggage, 1929, green/black, litho, 4 wh., 0	15.50	23.50
550 Baggage 1930, buff/blue, litho, 4 wh., 0	25.00	40.00
551 Chair, 1915, red/yellow/black, wood litho, 4 wh., 0	22.50	34.00

Ives 551 Chair Car and 550 Mail Car, blue yellow, orange litho.
Courtesy Heinz A. Mueller, Continental Hobby House

Ives 550 Baggage, 0 ga., white, green, black litho.
Courtesy Heinz A. Mueller, Continental Hobby House

Ives 551 Coach, 0 ga., red, green, black, yellow litho.
Courtesy Heinz A. Mueller, Continental Hobby House

Ives 552 Parlor Car, 0 ga., red, green, black, yellow litho.
Courtesy Heinz A. Mueller, Continental Hobby House

Ives 552 Parlor Car, 0 ga., gray, maroon, black, gold litho.
Courtesy Heinz A. Mueller, Continental Hobby House

Ives 558 Observation Car, 552 Parlor Car, 0 ga., blue, yellow, orange litho.
Courtesy Heinz A. Mueller, Continental Hobby House

360

	G	VG
551 Chair, 1916-25, olive/orange/ black, steel litho, 4 wh., 0	12.50	19.00
551 Chair, 1926-28, olive/orange, litho, 4 wh., 0	15.00	23.50
551 Chair, 1928, white/red/gold black, litho, 4 wh., 0	25.00	45.00
551 Chair, 1930, blue/buff/black/ white, litho, 4 wh., 0	25.00	45.00
552 Parlor, 1916-25, olive/orange/ yellow, steel litho, 4 wh., 0	12.50	19.00
552 Parlor, 1926-28, olive/orange/ black, litho, 4 wh., 0	15.00	23.00
552 Parlor, 1928, white/red/gold/ black, litho, 4 wh., 0	25.00	45.00
552 Parlor, 1929, green/black, litho, 4 wh., 0	15.50	23.50
552 Parlor, 1930, buff/green/black, litho, 4 wh., 0	25.00	45.00
558 Observation, 1928, white/red/ gold/black, litho, 4 wh., 0	25.00	40.00
558 Observation, 1929, green/black, litho, 4 wh., 0	19.50	32.00
558 Observation, 1930, blue/buff/ white, litho, 4 wh., 0	25.00	45.00
558 Observation, 1930, buff/green/ black, litho, 4 wh., 0	19.50	32.00
562 Caboose, 1930, red, brass trim, 4 wh., 0	25.00	45.00
563 Gondola, 1915-16, green/grey, steel litho, 4 wh., 0	17.50	28.50
563 Gondola, 1917-30, grey/maroon, steel litho, 4 wh., 0	15.00	24.00
564 Box, 1915-30, yellow; orange; red, wood litho, 4 wh., 0	18.50	28.00
565 Stock, 1915-17, orange/silver, litho, 4 wh., 0	23.50	32.50
565 Stock, 1917-30, yellow; white/ black, wood litho, 4 wh., 0	15.00	25.00
566 Tank, 1915-17, grey/gold, litho, 4 wh., 0	11.50	18.00
566 Tank, 1917-28, grey; orange/ black, litho, 4 wh., 0	9.00	13.50
567 Caboose, 1915-28, red/white/ black, wood litho, 4 wh., 0	15.00	30.00

361

	G	VG
567 Caboose, 1929, 1930, red/white/ black, litho, 4 wh., 0	9.00	13.50
569 Lumber, 1915-28, black, painted, 4 wh., 0	11.50	15.00
570 Set, 1930, #3258 loco, #552, 558, 'YANKEE CLIPPER'		
571 Set, 1930, #3258 loco, #564, 63, 562, 'COUNTRY FREIGHT'		
572 Set, 1930, #1125 loco, #17 T, #550, 552, 558, 'BLUE VAGABOND'		
572R Set, 1930, same, auto reverse		
572F Set, 1930, #1125 loco, #17 T, #554, 562, 63, 'TRADER'S FAST FREIGHT'		
573 Set, 1930, #3261 loco, #133, 133, 134, 'KNICKERBOCKER'		
573R Set, 1930, same, auto reverse		
574 Set, 1930, #3255 loco, #135, 135, 136, 'PATRIOT'		
574R Set, 1930, same, auto reverse		
575 Set, 1930, #1122 loco, #25 T, #121, 125, 128, 'MIDWEST FAST FREIGHT'		
575R Set, 1930, same, auto reverse		
576 Set, 1930, #1122 loco, #25 T, #135, 135, 136, 'COMMODORE VANDER-BILT'		
576R Set, 1930, same, auto reverse		
577 Set, 1930, #3257 loco, #141, 141, 142, 'COLUMBIAN'		
577R Set, 1930, same, auto reverse		
579 Set, 1930, #1122 loco, #25 T, #141, 141, 142, 'BLACK DIAMOND'		
579R Set, 1930, same, auto reverse		
590 Set, 1930, #1122 loco, #25 T, #123, 124, 125, 127, 128, 122, 121, 'UNIVER-SAL FAST FREIGHT'		
590R Set, 1930, same, auto reverse		
600 Acc., 1926, electric arc light (single)	13.00	27.50
601 Acc., 1926, electric arc light (double)	15.00	29.00
610 Pullman, 1931-32, olive, window inserts, 8 wh. illuminated, 0	35.00	58.50
610 Set, 1924, #3251 loco, #550, 552		

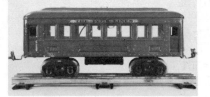

Ives 610 Coach, 0 ga., green, maroon, nickel trim.
Courtesy Heinz A. Mueller, Continental Hobby House

Ives 612 Observation Car, 0 ga., green, maroon, brass, nickel trim.
Courtesy Heinz A. Mueller, Continental Hobby House

	G	VG
610 Set, 1925, #3251 loco, #550, 552 (includes #201, 103, 107S)		
610 Set, 1926, #3251 loco, #550, 552 (includes #201, 103, 107S) 'JOY TOWN'		
611 Set, 1926, #3252 loco, #60, 62, 68 (includes #201, 107, 215, 111, 103, (6)#86)		
611 Set, 1927, #3252 loco, #60, 62, 68 (includes #201, 107D, 215, 111, 103, (6)#86), 'WONDERVILLE'		
611 Set, 1924, #3252 loco, #70, 72, 72, (includes #201, 215, 103, 107, (6)#86)		
611 Set, 1925, #3252 loco, #70, 72, 72 (includes #201, 107D, 215, 111, 103, (6)#86)		
612 Observation, 1931-32, olive, window inserts, illuminated, 8 wh., 0 ...	35.00	58.00
612 Set, 1926, #3255 loco, #130, 129, 132 (includes #114, 600, 111, 310, 103, (6)#86)		
612 Set, 1915-16, #3253 loco, #130, 129, 129 (includes #600, 310, 103, 111, 114, (6)#86)		
612 Set, 1925, #3253 loco, #130, 129, 129 (includes #114, 600, 111, 310, 103, (6)#86)		
620 Set, 1925, 1926, #1 loco, #11 T, #50, 51 (includes #107S, 89, 201		
620 Set, 1924, #1 loco, #11 T, #50, 51		
620 Set, 1927, #1 loco, #11 T, #50, 51 (includes #107S, 89, 201), 'PLEASANTVILLE'		

FOR SET PRICES SEE INDIVIDUAL NUMBERS AND GENERAL NOTES (p. 310).

363

621 Set, 1924, #6 loco, #11 T, #50, 51, 52 (includes #215, 107S, 201, 103)
621 Set, 1925, #6 loco, #11 T, #50, 51, 52 (includes #107S, 201)
639 Set, 1930, #176 loco, #12 T, #551, 551 (includes #221, 103, 107D, 215, 111, (5)#86), 'TRIBAL VILLAGE'
690 Set, 1924, #3235 loco, #171, 173
691 Set, 1927, #3235 loco, #184, 186, 'RED ARROW'
691 Set, 1924, #3235 loco, #171, 173 (illuminated)
691 Set, 1925, #3235 loco, #184, 186
691R Set, 1925, same, auto reverse
691 Set, 1926, #3235 loco, #184, 186, 'FIFTH AVENUE SPECIAL'
691R Set, 1926, same, auto reverse
692 Set, 1925, #3236 loco, #184, 185, 186
692R Set, 1925, same, auto reverse
692 Set, 1926, #3236 loco, #184, 185, 186, 'NIGHT HAWK'
692R Set, 1926, same, auto reverse
700 Set, 1921, #3241 loco, #184, 185
700 Set, 1924, #3241 loco, # 185,3, 186,3
701 Set, 1921, #3241 loco, #184, 185, 185
701 Set, 1924, #3241 loco, #184-3, 185-3, 186-3
701 Set, 1925, #3241 loco, #184, 185, 186
701 Set, 1926, #3242 loco, #184, 185, 186 'NEW YORKER'
701R Set, 1926, same, auto reverse
702 Set, 1921, #3242 loco, #187, 189
703 Set, 1921, #3242 loco, #187, 188, 189
703 Set, 1924, #3242 loco, #187-3, 188-3, 189-3
703 Set, 1925, #3242 Loco, #187, 188, 189
703R Set, 1925, same, auto reverse
703 Set, 1926, #3237 loco, #187, 188, 189 'TRANSCONTINENTAL LIMITED'

FOR SET PRICES SEE INDIVIDUAL NUMBERS AND GENERAL NOTES (p. 310).

703 Set, 1926, same, auto reverse
704 Set, 1921, #3243 Loco, #187-1, 188-1, 189-1
704 Set, 1924, #3243 loco, #187-3, 188-3, 189-3
704 Set, 1925, #3243 loco, 180, 181, 182
704R Set, 1925, same, auto reverse
704 Set, 1926, #3243 loco, #180, 181, 182, 'DELUXE SPECIAL'
704R Set, 1926, same, auto reverse
705 Set, 1921, #1132 loco, #40 T, #184, 185, 185

FOR SET PRICES
SEE
INDIVIDUAL
NUMBERS
AND
GENERAL NOTES
(p. 310).

705 Set, 1924, #1132 loco, #40 T, #184-3, 185-3, 186-3
705R Set, 1924, same, auto reverse
705 Set, 1925, #1132 loco, #40 T, #184, 185, 186
705R Set, 1925, same, auto reverse
705 Set, 1926, #1132 loco, #40 T, #191, 192, 195, 'IVES NIGHT FREIGHT'
705R Set, 1926, same, auto reverse
705 Set, 1927, #1134 loco, #40 T, #184, 185, 186, 'CAPITOL LIMITED'
706 Set, 1925, #3243 loco, #187-3, 189-3
706R Set, 1925, same, auto reverse
706 Set, 1926, #3243 loco, #187, 189, 'BANKER'S SPECIAL'
706R Set, 1926, same, auto reverse
707 Set, 1927, #1134 loco, #40 T, #187, 188, 189, 'CAPITOL CITY SPECIAL'
710 Set, 1921, #1132 loco, #40 T, #191, 192, 195
710 Set, 1924, 1925, #1132 loco, #40 T, #191, 192, 195
710R Set, 1924, 1925, same, auto reverse
710 Set, 1926, #1132 loco, #40 T, #184, 185, 186, 'CANNONBALL EXPRESS'
710R Set, 1926, same, auto reverse
710 Set, 1927, #1134 loco, #40 T, #184, 185, 186, 'CAPITOL LIMITED'
710R Set, 1927, same, auto reverse
711 Set, 1926, #3242 loco, #196, 195, 'NUMBER SEVEN ELEVEN'
711 Set, 1924, 1925, #3241 loco, #196, 195
712 Set, 1924, #3241 loco, #196, 191, 192, 195
712 Set, 1925, #3221 loco, #196, 192 195
712 Set, 1927, #1134 loco, #40 T, #190, 191, 192, 193, 194, 195, 196, 'UNIVERSAL FAST FREIGHT'
713 Set, 1924, 1925, #3242 loco, #196, 196, 191, 192, 193, 195

FOR SET PRICES
SEE
INDIVIDUAL
NUMBERS
AND
GENERAL NOTES
(p. 310).

Ives 809 Coach, 809 Inter-urban, 0 ga., green, yellow, red litho.
Courtesy Heinz A. Mueller, Continental Hobby House

714R Set, 1927, #1134R loco, #40 T, #190, 191, 192, 193, 194, 195, 196 (includes #115, 116-3, 106, 216, 301, 332, 99-2-3, (3)#307, (28)#86), 'PARK CITY SET'

800 Trolley, 1910-13, yellow;red/ black, litho, c/w	350.00	700.00
801 Trolley, 1910-13, yellow; red; brown, litho, c/w	350.00	700.00
805 Trail Car, 1912-15, red; white; blue; yellow; green, for #809 trolley	125.00	200.00
809 Trolley, 1912-15, red; white; blue; yellow; green, spoke wheels, electric	400.00	800.00
810 Trolley, 1910-12, red; white; blue; yellow; green, spoke wheels, electric	400.00	800.00

1000 Set, 1928, #1134 loco, #40 T, #241, 242, 243, 'PROSPERITY SPECIAL'
1000R Set, 1928, same, auto reverse
1070 Set, 1928, #1134 loco, #40 T, #192C, 193C, 196C, 196C, 171 (includes #72, 73, 74, 75), 'IVES RAILWAY CIRCUS'
1071 Set, 1930, #3236 loco, #185, 186, 'TIGER'
1071R Set, 1930, same, auto reverse
1072 Set, 1930, #3236 loco, #198, 195, 'LOCAL FREIGHT'
1072R Set, 1930, same, auto reverse
1073 Set, 1930, #3242 loco, #184, 185, 186, 'SKYLINER'
1073R Set, 1930, same, auto reverse

367

Ives No. 1100 0-4-0 Loco and F. E. No. 1 Tender, 0 ga., black, red.
Courtesy Heinz A. Mueller, Continental Hobby House

1075 Set, 1930, #1134 loco,#40 T, #192, 198, 195, 'MERCHANT'S FAST FREIGHT'

1075R Set, 1930, same, auto reverse

1076 Set, 1930, #1134 loco, #40 T, #184, 185, 186, 'WESTERNER'

1076R Set, 1930, same, auto reverse

1078 Set, 1930, #3245 loco, #247, 248 248, 249, 'CHIEF'

1077R Set, 1930, same, auto reverse

1078 Set, 1930, #3245 loco, #247, 248, 249, 'OLYMPIAN'

1079 Set, 1930, #1124 loco, #40 T, #247, 246, 249, 'NATIONAL LIMITED'

1079R Set, 1930, same, auto reverse

1080 Set, 1928, #3236 loco, #185, 186, 'CADET EXPRESS'

1080R Set, 1928, same, auto reverse

1081 Set, 1928, #3236 loco, #198, 195, 'LOCAL FREIGHT'

1081R Set, 1928, same, auto reverse

1082 Set, 1928, #3236 loco, #184, 185, 186, 'INTERSTATE LIMITED'

1082R Set, 1928, same, auto reverse

1083 Set, 1928, #3242 loco, #198, 192, 197, 195, 'LUMBERJACK'

1083R Set, 1928, same, auto reverse

1084 Set, 1928, #3242 loco, #184, 185, 186, 'CARDINAL SPECIAL'

1084R Set, 1928, same, auto reverse

FOR SET PRICES SEE INDIVIDUAL NUMBERS AND GENERAL NOTES (p. 310).

	G	VG
1085 Set, 1928, #1134 loco, #40 T, #192, 198, 195, 'MERCHANT'S FAST FREIGHT		
1085R Set, 1928, same, auto reverse		
1086 Set, 1928, #1134 loco, #40 T, #184, 185, 186, 'WESTERNER'		
1086R Set, 1928, same, auto reverse		
1087 Set, 1928, #3237 loco, #244, 245, 246, 'NORTHERN LIMITED'		
1088 Set, 1928, #3245 loco, #241, 242, 243, 'OLYMPIAN'		
1088R Set, 1928, same, auto reverse		
1089 Set, 1928, #1134 loco, #40 T, #241, 242, 243, 'BLACK DIAMOND EXPRESS'		
1089R Set, 1928, same, auto reverse		
1090 Set, 1928, #1134 loco, #40 T, #190, 196, 192, 197, 198, 193, 195, 'UNIVERSAL FAST FREIGHT'		
1090R Set, 1928, same, auto reverse		
1091 Set, 1930, #1134 loco, #40 T, #198, 190, 192, 197, 195, 'DOMESTIC FREIGHT'		
1091R Set, 1930, same, auto reverse		
1100 Loco, 1910-13, cast, black/red/gold, 2-2-0, #1 tender, 0 Ga.	75.00	115.00
1100 Loco, 1914-23, cast, black/red/gold, 0-4-0, #11 tender, 0	75.00	115.00
1102 Set, 1912, 1915, #1100 loco, #11 T, #50, 51		
1102x Set, 1912, 1915, #3200 loco, #50, 51		
1102F Set, 1912, #1100 loco, #11 T, #57, 56		
1102 Set, 1917, #1100 loco, #11 T, #551		
1102 Set, 1914, #1100 loco, #1 T, #50, 51		
1102x Set, 1914, #3200 loco. #50, 51		
1102F Set, 1914, #1100 loco, #1 T, #57, 56		
1105 Set, 1910, #1100 loco, #11 T, #50, 51, 52		
1105 Set, 1912, 1915, #1117 loco, #11 T, #550, 551, 552		

Ives 1117, 1118 0-4-0 Locos, 0 ga., black, gold.
Courtesy Heinz A. Mueller, Continental Hobby House

Ives 1122 4-4-2 Loco with Tender, 0 ga., red, brass trim.
Courtesy Heinz A. Mueller, Continental Hobby House

Ives 1125 0-4-0 Loco and Tender, 0 ga., blue, gold.
Courtesy Heinz A. Mueller, Continental Hobby House

1105x Set, 1912, 1915, #3217 loco, #550, 551, 552

1105F Set, 1912, #1117 loco, #11 T, #554, 556, 557

1105 Set, 1917, #1116 loco, #11 T, #550, 552

1105x Set, 1917, #3216 loco, #550, 552

1105 Set, 1914, #1117 loco, #11 T, #550, 551, 552

1105x Set, 1914, #3217 loco, #550, 551, 552

1105F Set, 1914, #1117 loco, #11 T, #554, 556, 557

FOR SET PRICES
SEE
INDIVIDUAL
NUMBERS
AND
GENERAL NOTES
(p. 310).

Ives 1125 4-4-0 Loco and No. 25 Tender, 0 ga., black, red, yellow.
Courtesy Heinz A. Mueller, Continental Hobby House

FOR SET PRICES
SEE
INDIVIDUAL
NUMBERS
AND
GENERAL NOTES
(p. 310).

	G	VG
1112 Set, 1917, #1116 loco, #11 T, #550, 551, 552		
1112x Set, 1917, #3216 loco, #550, 551, 552		
1113 Set, 1917, #1118 loco, #17 T, #61		
1114 Set, 1912, 1914, #1118 loco, #11 T, #60, 61, 62		
1114x Set, 1912, 1914, 1915, #3218 loco, #60, 61, 62		
1114F Set, 1912, 1914, #1118 loco, #11 T, #63, 64, 67		
1114 Set, 1917, #1118 loco, #17 T, #60, 61		
1114x Set, 1917, #3218 loco, #60, 61		
1114 Set, 1915, #1118 loco, #17 T, #60, 61, 62		
1114 Set, 1910, #17 loco, #17 T, #60, 61		
1115 Set, 1910, #1118 loco, #11 T, #60, 61, 62		
1115 Set, 1912, 1914, 1915, #1125 loco, #25 T, #130, 129, 131		
1115x Set, 1912, 1914, 1915, #3238 loco, #131, 129 130		
1115F Set, 1912, #1125 loco, #25 T, #127, 67		
1115 Set, 1917, #1118 loco, #17 T, #60, 61, 62		
1115x Set, 1917, #3218 loco, #60, 61, 62		
1115F Set, 1914, #1125 loco, #25 T, #125, 127, 67		
1116 Loco, 1916-18, cast, black/red/ gold, 0-4-0, #11 tender 0	100.00	150.00

371

Ives 1129 2-4-2 Loco and No. 40 Tender, No. 1 ga., black, red.
Courtesy Heinz A. Mueller, Continental Hobby House

	G	VG
1117 Loco, 1910-18, cast, black/red/ gold, 0-4-0, #11 tender 0	95.00	145.00
1118 Loco, 1910-25, cast, black, tin bands, 0-4-0, #17 tender, 0	50.00	75.00
1120 Loco, 1916, black, 0-4-0, #1117 or #25 tender, 0	115.00	145.00
1120 Loco, 1928, black/gold, 4-4-0, #25 tender, 0	150.00	250.00
1122Loco, 1928-30, black, copper trim, 4-4-2, cast #25 tender with coal load, 0	175.00	250.00
1125 Loco, 1910-16, black/gold, 4-4-0, tin boiler bands, #25 tender, 0	195.00	250.00
1125 Loco, 1930, black;blue, 0-4-0, #17 tender, 0	100.00	150.00
1126 Set, 1910, #1125 loco, #25 T, #129, 130, 131		
1126 Set, 1917, #1125 loco, #25 T, #130		
1127 Set, 1910, #3238 loco, #129, 130, 131		
1127 Set, 1917, #1125 loco, #25 T, #130, 129		
1127x Set, 1917, #3238 loco, #130, 129		
1128 Set, 1917, #1125 loco, #25 T, #130, 129, 129		
1128x Set, 1917, #3238 loco, #130, 129 129		
1129 Loco, 1915-20, cast, black, hand rails, 2-4-2, #40 tender, #1	648.00	900.00
1130 Set, 1912, #3239 loco, #70, 71, 72		
1130 Set, 1915, #1129 loco, #40 T, #71, 72, 72		
1130 Set, 1914, #3239 loco, #71, 72, 72		

Ives 1132 0-4-0 Loco and Tender, Std., nickel trim.
Courtesy Heinz A. Mueller, Continental Hobby House

Ives 1132R 0-4-0 Loco, Std., and Tender, black, white, nickel trim.
Courtesy Heinz A. Mueller, Continental Hobby House

Ives 1134 R "President Washington" 4-4-0 Loco with Tender, Std., green, red, gold rubber-stamped.
Courtesy Heinz A. Mueller, Continental Hobby House

Ives 1134 4-4-2 Loco, Std., with Tender, black, brass trim.
Courtesy Heinz A. Mueller, Continental Hobby House

	G	VG
1130x Set, 1915, #3239 loco, #71, 72, 72		
1130x Set, 1917, #3239 loco, #71, 72		
1131x Set, 1917, #3239 loco, #71, 72, 73		
1132 Loco, 1925, steel, black/red, 0-4-0, manual reverse, Std. ga.	250.00	600.00
1134 Loco, 1927, black;olive, 4-4-0, #40 tender, 'PRESIDENT WASHINGTON', Std. ga.	525.00	775.00
1134 Loco, 1929, black, 4-4-2, IVES/FLYER	545.00	818.00
1140 Set, 1912, #3240 loco, #181, 182, 183		
1140 Set, 1914, #3240 loco, #181, 182, 183		
1140 Set, 1915, #1129 loco, #40 T, #181, 182, 183		
1140x Set, 1915, #3240 loco, #181, 182, 183		
1140 Set, 1917, #1129 loco, #40 T, #181, 183		
1141 Set, 1917, #1129 loco, #40 T, #181, 182, 183		
1145 Set, 1917, #3240 loco, #181, 182, 183		
1150 Set, 1917, #1129 loco, #40 T, #7345, 7546		
1151 Set, 1917, #1129 loco, #40 T, #7849, 7648, 7546		
1152 Set, 1917, #1129 loco, #40 T, #7648, 7446, 7345, 7546		
1501 Loco, 1932, steel, red, 0-4-0, #1502 tender (Lionel #257) 0	35.00	80.00
1502 Tender, 1931-32, steel, red, 4 wh., 0	25.00	35.00
1504 Coach, 1931-32, black/yellow/red/green, 0	27.50	40.00
1504 Pullman, 1931-32, red/blue, 0 . .	7.50	10.00
1506 Loco, 1931-32, steel, black/red, bell, brake, c/w, #1507 tender	35.00	52.50
1507 Tender, 1932, steel, black, 4 wh., 0	15.00	23.50
1512 Gondola, 1931-32, blue, 4 wh., litho,0	13.50	19.00

Ives 1651 0-4-0 Engine, 0 ga., red, yellow, black, brass trim.
Courtesy Heinz A. Mueller, Continental Hobby House

Ives 1661E 2-4-0 Steam, 0 ga., black, red, copper trim.
Courtesy Heinz A. Mueller, Continental Hobby House

	G	VG
1513 Cattle, 1931-32, various colors, 4 wh. litho, 0	15.00	27.50
1514 Mcdse. 1931-32 yellow/blue 4 wh. litho 0	8.00	12.00
1515 Tank 1931-32 aluminum brass & copper trim 4 wh. litho 0	8.00	12.00
1517 Caboose 1931-32 red/brown 4 wh. litho 0	8.00	12.00
1614 Set 1931 #257 loco, #257 T, #610, 610, 610, 612		
1651 Loco 1932 steel yellow/blue;red/ maroon box electric	95.00	150.00
1661 Loco 1932 steel black/red 2-4-0 #1661 tender 0	65.00	80.00
1661 Tender 1932 black 4 wh. 0	15.00	20.00
1663 Loco 1931 black cast frame 2-4-2 0	75.00	125.00

Ives 1679 Box Car, 0 ga., yellow, blue, brown, black litho.
Courtesy Heinz A. Mueller, Continental Hobby House

Ives 1680 Tank Car, 0 ga., silver, black, brass trim.
Courtesy Heinz A. Mueller, Continental Hobby House

Ives 1690 Coach, 0 ga., two-tone red, yellow, black, brass trim.
Courtesy Heinz A. Mueller, Continental Hobby House

	G	VG
1677 Gondola 1931-32 8 wh. litho 0 .	8.00	12.00
1678 Cattle 1931-32 8 wh. litho 0	8.00	12.00
1679 Box 1931-32 yellow/blue/buff 8 wh. litho 0	7.00	10.50

Ives 1682 Caboose, 0 ga., red, brown, yellow, black litho.
Courtesy Heinz A. Mueller, Continental Hobby House

Ives 1691 Observation Car, 0 ga., two-tone red, yellow, black, brass trim.
Courtesy Heinz A. Mueller, Continental Hobby House

Ives 1694 4-4-4 Engine, 0 ga., gray, maroon, brass trim.
Courtesy Heinz A. Mueller, Continental Hobby House

	G	VG
1680 Tank 1931-32 aluminum 8 wh. litho 0	7.00	10.50
1682 Caboose 1931-32 red/brown litho 8 wh. 0	7.00	10.50
1690 Coach 1932 red/cream 8 wh. litho 0	10.00	15.00

Ives 1695 Coach, 0 ga., gray, maroon, beige windows rubber stamp, brass trim.
Courtesy Heinz A. Mueller, Continental Hobby House

Ives 1695 Baggage Car, 0 ga., gray, maroon, beige windows, rubber stamp, brass trim.
Courtesy Heinz A. Mueller, Continental Hobby House

Ives 1697 Observation Car, 0 ga., gray, maroon, beige windows, rubber-stamped, brass trim.
Courtesy Heinz A. Mueller, Continental Hobby House

Ives 1707 Gondola, 0 ga., yellow, brown, black litho.
Courtesy Heinz A. Mueller, Continental Hobby House

Ives 1708 Reefer, 0 ga., two-tone green, brown, black litho.
Courtesy Heinz A. Mueller, Continental Hobby House

Ives 1709 Box Car, 0 ga., two-tone green, orange, black litho, nickel trim.
Courtesy Heinz A. Mueller, Continental Hobby House

	G	VG
1691 Observation 1932 red/cream 8 wh. litho 0	10.00	15.00
1694 Loco 1932 grey/maroon 4-4-4 box cab electric 0		
1695 Pullman 1932 beige/maroon 12 wh. illuminated 0	Value	Rare

The only set of this I saw was something like 4255.00.

	G	VG
1696 Baggage 1932 beige/maroon 12 wh. illuminated 0		
1697 Observation 1932 beige/maroon 12 wh. illuminated 0	Rare	
1707 Gondola 1932 8 wh. litho 0	20.00	40.00
1708 Cattle 1932 8 wh. litho front & rear ladders 0	20.00	40.00
1709 Box 1932 8 wh. litho 0	20.00	40.00
1712 Caboose 1932 red front & rear ladders litho 8 wh. 0	20.00	40.00
1760 Loco 1931 steel Lionel #384 #1760 tender Std.	200.00	300.00
1760 Tender 1931 steel copper trim 8 wh. Std.	65.00	95.00
1764 Loco 1932 electric type Std.	200.00	300.00
1766 Coach brown/maroon/yellow Std.	60.00	90.00
1767 Baggage brown/maroon yellow Std.	60.00	90.00
1770 Loco 1932 2-4-2 Lionel #390 Std.	200.00	300.00
1768 Observation brown/maroon/ yellow Std.	60.00	90.00
1771 Lumber 1932 brakes nickel stakes Std.	95.00	143.00
1772 Gondola 1932 peacock brakes Std.	95.00	143.00
1773 Cattle 1932 sliding doors Std. .	105.00	150.00
1774 Box 1932 yellow/orange Std. . .	105.00	150.00
1775 Tank 1932 white/black Std. . . .	105.00	150.00
1776 Coal 1932 red coal load adjustable bottom Std.	100.00	145.00

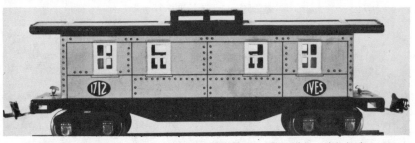

Ives 1712 Caboose, 0 ga., orange, maroon, black, yellow litho, nickel trim.
Courtesy Heinz A. Mueller, Continental Hobby House

Ives 1764E 4-4-4 Engine, Std., brown, maroon, brass trim.
Courtesy Heinz A. Mueller, Continental Hobby House

Ives 1766 Coach, Std., brown, maroon, yellow, brass trim.
Courtesy Heinz A. Mueller, Continental Hobby House

Ives 1767 Baggage Car, Std., maroon, yellow, brass trim.
Courtesy Heinz A. Mueller, Continental Hobby House

Ives 1768 Observation Car, Std., brown,

Ives 1771 Lumber Car, Lionel Trans., Std., green, nickel trim.
Courtesy Heinz A. Mueller, Continental Hobby House

Ives 1772 Gondola, Lionel Transitional, Std., green, brass, red trim.
Courtesy Heinz A. Mueller, Continental Hobby House

Ives 1770-E 2-4-2 Loco with Tender, Std., black, orange stripe, brass and copper trim.
Courtesy Heinz A. Mueller, Continental Hobby House

Ives 1777 Caboose, Std., green, red, black, brass trim.
Courtesy Heinz A. Mueller, Continental Hobby House

Ives 1811 Pullman, 1812 Observation, 1813 Baggage, 0 ga., green, orange, yellow, black litho.
Courtesy Heinz A. Mueller, Continental Hobby House

	G	VG
1777 Caboose 1932 red/green brass trim illuminated Std.	95.00	143.00
1778 Refrig. 1932 white/green swinging doors Std.	95.00	143.00
1779 Derrick 1932 litho automatic operation Std.	135.00	210.00
1810 Loco 1931-32 blue; orange box cab electric 0	45.00	65.00

	G	VG
1811 Pullman 1931-32 blue; orange litho 4 wh. O	13.50	20.00
1812 Observation 1931-32 blue; orange litho 4 wh. O	13.50	20.00
1813 Baggage 1931-32 blue; orange litho 4 wh. O	13.50	20.00
1867 Acc. 1981 signal tower	100.00	150.00
1868 Acc. 1931 suburban villa	15.00	40.00
1869 Acc. 1931 Colonial house	35.00	70.00
1870 Acc. 1931 cottage	15.00	35.00
1871 Acc. 1931 suburban station	50.00	125.00
1872 Acc. 1931 way station	25.00	60.00
1873 Acc. 1931 city station	75.00	150.00
1875 Acc. 1931 freight shed.........	75.00	150.00
1876 Acc. 1931 power house	40.00	100.00
1878 Acc. 1931 crossing gate 0 ga. ...	15.00	30.00
1879 Acc. 1931 crossing gate Std.	15.00	30.00
1880 Acc. 1931 flashing signal......	15.00	30.00
1881 Acc. 1931 traffic light	15.00	30.00
1883 Acc. 1931 crossing bell	20.00	40.00
1885 Acc. 1931 target signal Std. ...	35.00	65.00
1886 Acc. 1931 target signal 0 ga. ..	35.00	65.00
1901 Acc. 1931 panel board.........	20.00	45.00
1906 Acc. 1931 freight station set ...	50.00	75.00
3200 Loco 1910 cast olive open wheels electric style 0	150.00	350.00
3200 Loco 1914 cast black/gold electric style 0	65.00	105.00
3200 Loco 1911 cast black embossed lettering 0	110.00	145.00
3216 Loco 1917 cast grey integral pilots headlight 0	112.00	150.00
3217 Loco 1912-16 cast maroon; red/ gold separate pilots 0	112.00	150.00
3218 Loco 1910-17 cast maroon headlight letters embossed or stamp.....	135.00	160.00
3220 Loco 1916 cast black/red headlight separate pilot 0	95.00	135.00
3235 Loco 1924-27 steel brown/gold brass plates Std.	100.00	125.00
3235R Loco 1925-27 steel brown/gold brass plates Std.	100.00	125.00

Ives 3218 0-4-0 Engine, 3216 0-4-0 Engine, 0 ga., black and white.
Courtesy Heinz A. Mueller, Continental Hobby House

Ives 3235-R, 0-4-0 Engine, Std., red, black, gold, brass trim.
Courtesy Heinz A. Mueller, Continental Hobby House

Ives 3236 0-4-0 Engine, Std., orange, brass trim.
Continental Hobby House

	G	VG
3236 Loco 1925-30 brown (became Lionel #8 in '29, '30) Std.	100.00	135.00
3236R Loco 1925-30 same, auto reverse...........................	105.00	140.00
3237 Loco 1926-30 black brass plates Std................................	300.00	475.00
3237R Loco 1926-30 same, auto reverse...........................	325.00	485.00
3238 Loco 1912-17 black/red cast headlight lettering embossed or stamp lettered 0	225.00	285.00
3239 Loco 1913-20 cast electric style #1 gauge	535.00	750.00
3240 Loco 1912-20 cast electric style brass trim #1 gauge	850.00	1075.00
3241 Loco 1921-25 red; maroon electric style Std.	135.00	225.00
3241R Loco 1924-25 olive auto reverse Std................................	145.00	250.00

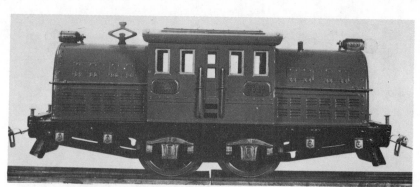

Ives 3237 0-4-0 Loco, green, brass trim.
Courtesy Heinz A. Mueller, Continental Hobby House

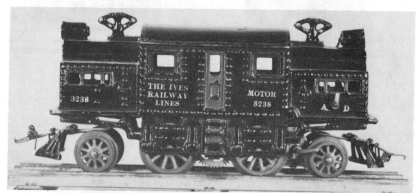

Ives 3238 2-4-2 Electric Engine, 0 ga., black, red, rubber-stamped.
Courtesy Heinz A. Mueller, Continental Hobby House

Ives 3239 0-4-4-0 No. 1 ga., black, red, small letters.
Courtesy Heinz A. Mueller, Continental Hobby House

Ives 3239 0-4-4-0 Engine, No. 1 ga., black, red, large letters.
Courtesy Heinz A. Mueller, Continental Hobby House

IVes 3240 0-4-4-0 No. 1 ga., gray, black, red.
Courtesy Heinz A. Mueller, Continental Hobby House

Ives 3241R, 0-4-0 Std., red, black, brass trim.
Courtesy Heinz A. Mueller, Continental Hobby House

385

Ives 3242 0-4-0 Engine, Std., black, brass trim.
Courtesy Heinz A. Mueller, Continental Hobby House

Ives 3242R, 0-4-0 Engine, Std., green, black, brass trim.
Courtesy Heinz A. Mueller, Continental Hobby House

Ives 3243 4-4-4 Electric Engine, Std., white, gold rubber-stamped, nickel trim.
Courtesy Heinz A. Mueller, Continental Hobby House

Ives 3243R 4-4-4 Electric Engine, Std., orange, black, rubber-stamped, nickel trim.
Courtesy Heinz A. Mueller, Continental Hobby House

Ives 3245R 4-4-4 Electric Engine, Std., black, orange, brass trim.
Courtesy Heinz A. Mueller, Continental Hobby House

Ives 3253 0-4-0 0 ga., orange, black rubber-stamped, brass trim.
Courtesy Heinz A. Mueller, Continental Hobby House

Ives 3253 0-4-0 Engine, green, white.
Courtesy Heinz A. Mueller, Continental
Hobby House

Ives 3254 0-4-0 Engine, 0 ga., maroon, black,
brass trim.
Courtesy Heinz A. Mueller, Continental
Hobby House

Ives 3255 0-4-0 Engine, 0 ga., blue, red, brass
trim, stamped frame.
Courtesy Heinz A. Mueller, Continental
Hobby House

Ives 3257 0-4-0 Engine, 0 ga., green, brass
trim.
Courtesy Heinz A. Mueller, Continental
Hobby House

Ives 3258 0-4-0 Engine, 0 ga., green, maroon,
black, gold, litho, brass trim.
Courtesy Heinz A. Mueller, Continental
Hobby House

Ives 3259 0-4-0 Engine, 0 ga., gray, maroon,
black, gold, litho.
Courtesy Heinz A. Mueller, Continental
Hobby House

Ives 3261 0-4-0 Engine, orange, black, brass trim, 0 ga.,
Courtesy Heinz A. Mueller, Continental Hobby House

	G	VG
3242 Loco 1921-30 green; orange/ black manual reverse Std.	175.00	250.00
3242R Loco 1926-30 same, auto reverse	185.00	275.00
3243 Loco 1921-27 green; orange; red 4-4-0 electric style Std.	250.00	375.00
3243R Loco 1924-27 orange/black brass plates Std.	250.00	375.00
3245 Loco 1928 short cab manual reverse Std.	675.00	800.00
3245R Loco 1928 short cab auto reverse Std.	675.00	800.00
3245 Loco 1929-30 long cab manual reverse Std.	750.00	1500.00
3245R Loco 1929-30 long cab auto reverse Std.	750.00	1500.00
3250 Loco 1919-24 brown; red bell 0 gauge	45.00	65.00
3250 Loco 1924-27 red bell, headlight 0	45.00	65.00
3251 Loco 1919-27 green; red hand-rails electric style 0	45.00	65.00
3252 Loco 1919-24 maroon; green manual reverse stamp lettered 0	45.00	65.00
3252 Loco 1924-25 maroon; green manual reverse brass plates 0	55.00	75.00
3253 Loco 1919-27 olive, maroon head-light 0 gauge	75.00	125.00
3254 Loco 1925-28 red brass plates manual reverse headlight	50.00	75.00
3255 Loco 1926-30 red; blue brass plates steel frame headlight 0	109.00	163.50
3255R Loco 1926-30 orange cast frame brass plates headlight 0	85.00	145.00
3257 Loco 1926-30 red; grey brass plates manual reverse 2 headlights 0 ga.	205.00	295.00
3257R Loco 1927-30 grey brass plates manual reverse 2 headlights 'OLY-PIAN'	225.00	300.00
3258 Loco 1928-30 green/gold box cab litho or brass plates 0	55.00	95.00
3259 Loco 1927-29 white; maroon manual reverse headlight 0	65.00	105.00

Ives 64387 Box Car, 0 ga., yellow, gray, black, red litho, nickel trim.
Courtesy Heinz A. Mueller, Continental Hobby House

Ives 0-4-0 Loco with "No. 1" Tender, 0 ga., black, white.
Courtesy Heinz A. Mueller, Continental Hobby House

Ives 0-4-0 Wind-up Loco, 0 ga., black, red, copper trim.
Courtesy Heinz A. Mueller, Continental Hobby House

Ives 4-4-0 Loco, black, red, with "N.Y.C. & H.R." Tender (front trucks missing in photo).
Courtesy Heinz A. Mueller, Continental Hobby House

Ives Coach, cast iron, "Limited Vestibule Express", black gold.
Courtesy Heinz A. Mueller, Continental Hobby House

Ives Lumber Car, 8-Wheel, 0 ga., brown, black.
Courtesy Heinz A. Mueller, Continental Hobby House

	G	VG
3260 Loco 1929-30 blue-green headlight litho 0 ga.	80.00	120.00
3261 Loco 1929-30 peacock; olive headlight litho 0	80.00	120.00
7345 Mcdse. 1915-20 steel litho spring doors #1 ga........................	120.00	180.00
7446 Stock 1915-20 litho #1 ga.	150.00	225.00

Ives Station, calendar in window reads "Tues. Aug 2", green, brown litho.
Courtesy Heinz A. Mueller, Continental Hobby House

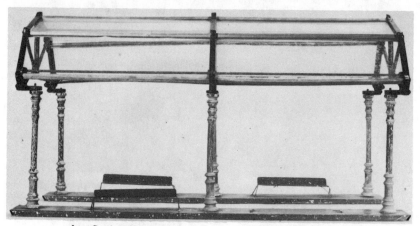

Ives Station, Glass Dome, Std., green, gray.
Courtesy Heinz A. Mueller, Continental Hobby House

	G	VG
7546 Caboose 1915-20 red/silver litho #1 ga.	67.00	108.50
7648 Hopper 1915-20 maroon; black litho #1 ga.	140.00	210.00
7849 Tank 1915-20 black litho #1 ga.	140.00	210.00
7950 Coke 1915-20 black; maroon litho #1 ga.	93.50	140.00
3016 Set 1932 #1694 Loco, #1695, 1696, 1697		
17882 Cattle orange; green; black; red litho 'D&L TRANSPORTATION		

Ives Box Car, cast iron, "Union Line", black, gold.
Courtesy Heinz A. Mueller, Continental Hobby House

Ives 703 Train Set, and Ives accessories
Courtesy PB Eighty-Four New York

Ives 29 Observation Car
Courtesy Amadon Family Collection

AFTERWORD
by Terry Amadon

The shadows were already lengthening when I took on the responsibility of doing this section, so invariably some things have been short-changed or forgotten. Some set numbers or variations which could have been included may not have made it. However, this section is certainly more than a general overview; nearly every Ives item number has been represented by at least one variation. It should be here noted that many of the Herald cars have numbers on them which are railroad markings, not Ives numbers. Most other Ives made after 1903 has an Ives number on it somewhere, unless the stamping has worn off.

Many Ives collectors also are interested in the two big German manufacturers, Maerklin and Bing, both of whom made trains similar to much of the Ives. All three companies made high quality trains which are still desirable so many years later. There are several references available on the market to familiarize the interested party with Maerklin products; of Bing, however, less is generally known as most of the files and records in Germany pertaining to Bing were destroyed during the war.

Were there more time before publication, I would have been tempted to try to put together a Bing section for the book, also. If anyone has any questions or information they wish to share pertaining to Bing or Ives, I would be happy to receive correspondence at my address at the back of the book.

In any event, I hope that this section has proven at least a little informative and useful, and that some of the enthusiasm I have for the subject has been conveyed. So, until next time. . .

Ives 1125 Loco, circa 1930
Courtesy Amadon Family Collection

Top: Ives 30 Pony Express Set, probably 1930.
Bottom: Ives 6 Loco, 11 Tender, 50 & 52 Cars.
Courtesy Amadon Family Collection

Ives 60, 61 cars with 4 wheels, 89 water tower in background.
Courtesy Amadon Family Collection

Top: 114 Station, 115 Station; Bottom: Two 114 Stations.
Courtesy Amadon Family Collection

Ives 1125 (1930)
Courtesy McManus Collection

3 versions of 1100 Loco, early, middle, late.
Courtesy Amadon Family Collection

Two variations of 1118 Loco
Courtesy Amadon Family Collection

547R Ives Patriot Set (1930), 3255, 135, 135, 136
Courtesy Amadon Family Collection

Ives 257 Loco, 1663 Tender beneath 89 Water Tower.
Courtesy Amadon Family Collection

Early Ives, before numbering began.
Courtesy McManus Collection

Ives 3255
Courtesy Amadon Family Collection

Ives 3254
Courtesy Amadon Family Collection

Ives 3253   Courtesy Amadon Family Collection

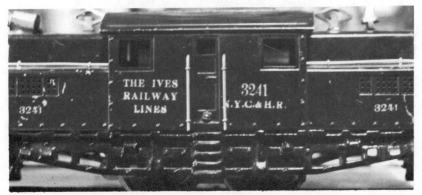
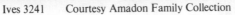

Ives 3241   Courtesy Amadon Family Collection

Ives 3238   Courtesy Amadon Family Collection

Ives 3218
Courtesy Amadon Family Collection

Ives 3217
Courtesy Amadon Family Collection

Early Ives 3250
Courtesy Amadon
Family Collection

Ives 3251
Courtesy Amadon
Family Collection

Ives 3252
Courtesy Amadon
Family Collection

Ives 3200, smallest
electric style.
Courtesy Amadon
Family Collection

1930 Commodore Vanderbilt Set, 1122 Loco, 25T, 135, 135, 136 Cars.
Courtesy Amadon Family Collection

Ives 3216 in front of 115 Freight Station.
Courtesy Amadon Family Collection

Ives 25 Loco and Tender (1911)
Courtesy Amadon Family Collection

Ives 1100   Courtesy Amadon Family Collection

Ives 130 Limited Vestibule Express
Courtesy Amadon Family Collection

Ives 129 Limited Vestibule Express
Courtesy Amadon Family Collection

Ives 1118
Courtesy Amadon Family Collection

Ives 131 Limited Vestibule Express
Courtesy Amadon Family Collection

Ives 550, 552 (early)   Courtesy Amadon Family Collection

Ives 3220
Courtesy Amadon Family Collection

Ives 3238, black with grey roof.   Courtesy Amadon Family Collection

DORFAN

Dorfan produced trains for only ten years, from 1924-1933, but during that time was one of the Big Four of American Train-making, along with Ives, Lionel and American Flyer.

Dorfan's origins go back to Nuremburg, Germany, and the toy trains firm of Jos. Kraus & Co. Kraus used "Fandor" as its trademark, reading either "J.K.Co. Fandor" or "Kraus Fandor J.K. Co. N."

Two cousins of Kraus, Julius and Milton Forcheimer, worked with the firm from before WWI untill 1923, Julius involved in production and Milton with sales. Also working at Fandor at the time was John C. Koerber, who had previously designed many of Bing's trains, and then moved over to Fandor to fulfill the same function. In 1923, after considerable planning, the three men moved to the U.S., where they became American citizens. Dorfan, simply a reversal of Fandor, was born in 1924, at 137 Jackson Street in Newark, where it remained till the end. Milton Forcheimer was President, and his brother Julius the Vice-President and Treasurer.

Dorfan's first engines were mechanical, but one represented a considerable innovation, one of the many to be devised by the firm; it was die-cast, the first ever made in America. By 1925, the company brought out its first electric model, the "Electric Constructive Locomotive". This was lettered "51", but was sold as Nos. 255 and 260, the latter a more deluxe version with a headlight and brass handrails. These engines represented another innovation by Dorfan, as they were the first practical construction set in the field. Other companies' reaction to the die-casting was similar to the original reaction to Fulton's steamboat, but as Julius Forcheimer once recalled. "Twelve years later they were all using it."

These were not all of Dorfan's innovations. Louis H Hertz constructed a list of "firsts" by Dorfan that were then copied by other companies. This list does not include innovations that were used only by Dorfan:

> First die-cast locomotive bodies
> First easily assembled locomotive construction sets
> First upright lamp post
> First switchboard or "Panel Board"
> First lacquered lithographed cars
> First sets to build both locomotive and motor from same parts
> First double-track 0-gauge working hopper car

First to have inserted window frames in passenger cars
(inserted from outside of car)

First to make drive wheels and axles removeable as one
unit

First automatic circuit breaker

First die-cast trucks

First die-cast car wheels

First ball-bearing locomotive

First 0-gauge derrick car

First die-cast steam-outline electric locomotive

First remotely controled train-stop signals

First directional remote control for locomotives

First steam-type locomotives with separate polished metal
domes and stacks

First model position-light signals

First model signal bridge

First remote control uncoupler

However, despite the company's originality and the quality of its product, the stock market crash of 1929 and the events subsequent were fatal to the company. In its heyday, Dorfan employed about 150 people. By 1934 the firm was listed in a business directory as having twelve male employees and eighteen female. Since these figures were probably given in 1933, the actual total in 1934 may have been even lower, as by then all production had stopped. Because of the huge backlog, however, sales continued into 1938, when the company finally faded into history.

(Much of the above information comes from articles by noted toys authority Louis H. Hertz in the 12/38, 1/39 and 3/49 issues of The Model Craftsman magazine)

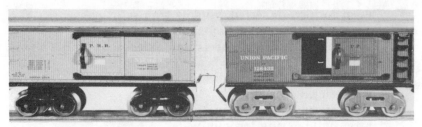

Dorfan 517953, 126432 Box Cars, 0 ga., orange, brown, green, black.
Courtesy Heinz A. Mueller Continental Hobby House

Dorfan "Boston" Coach, 0 ga., red, brass trim.
Courtesy Heinz A. Mueller Continental Hobby House

Dorfan Observation Car, 0 ga., red, brass trim, people in windows.
Courtesy Heinz A. Mueller Continental Hobby House

Dorfan "Boston" Coach and Observation cars, 0 ga., maroon, yellow, brass trim.
Courtesy Heinz A. Mueller, Continental Hobby House

Dorfan 0-4-0 Engine, Std., orange, green, brass trim.
Courtesy Heinz A. Mueller Continental Hobby House

	G	VG	M
DORFAN 5 Caboose, Std. Ga., brown, yellow, green black litho	51.00	76.50	102.00
DORFAN 51 0-4-0 Engine, 0 Ga., Green, Yellow	50.00	75.00	100.00
DORFAN 52 Engine, Green	110.00	165.00	220.00
DORFAN 53 0-4-0 Engine, 0 Ga., Peacock, Yellow, Brass trim	100.00	200.00	300.00
DORFAN 53 0-4-0 Engine, 0 Ga., Green, Maroon	100.00	200.00	300.00
DORFAN 53 0-4-0 Engine, 0 ga., Red	100.00	200.00	300.00
DORFAN 54 0-4-0 Engine, Green 0 Ga.	100.00	200.00	300.00
DORFAN 54 0-4-0 Engine, 0 Ga., Silver, Gray, Brass trim	100.00	200.00	300.00

Dorfan 51 0-4-0 Engine, 0 ga., green, yellow.
Courtesy Heinz A. Mueller
Continental Hobby House

Dorfan 53 0-4-0 Engine, 0 ga., peacock,
yellow, brass trim.
Courtesy Heinz A. Mueller
Continental Hobby House

Dorfan 53 0-4-0 Engine, 0 ga., green, maroon.
Courtesy Heinz A. Mueller
Continental Hobby House

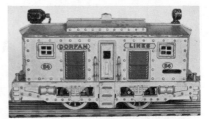

Dorfan 54 0-4-0 Engine, 0 ga., silver, gray,
brass trim.
Courtesy Heinz A. Mueller
Continental Hobby House

Dorfan 492 Baggage, 0 ga., green, maroon,
brass trim.
Courtesy Heinz A. Mueller, Continental
Hobby House

Dorfan 493 "Seattle" Coach, 0 ga., green,
maroon, brass trim.

	G	VG	M
DORFAN 54 0-4-0 Engine, Silver Blue, 0 Ga.	100.00	200.00	300.00
DORFAN 55 0-4-0 Engine, 0 Ga., Black or Red	100.00	200.00	300.00
DORFAN 70 Automatic Electric Crane	500.00	750.00	1000.00

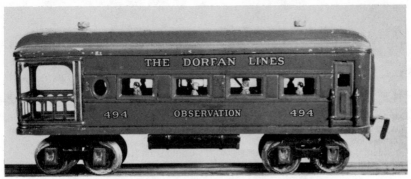

Dorfan 494 Observation, 0 ga., green, maroon, brass trim.
Courtesy Heinz A. Mueller Continental Hobby House

Dorfan 610 Derrick, 486751 Caboose, green, red, Caboose red, orange, yellow litho, nickel trim.
Courtesy Heinz A. Mueller Continental Hobby House

Doran 771 "San Francisco" Passenger Car.,
Std., green, black, red, nickel trim.
Courtesy Heinz A. Mueller
Continental Hobby House

Dorfan 770 Baggage Car, Std., green, black,
red, nickel trim.
Courtesy Heinz A. Mueller
Continental Hobby House

411

Dorfan 772 "Washington" Coach, Std., yellow, red, brass, nickel trim.
Courtesy Heinz A. Mueller
Continental Hobby House

Dorfan 773 Observation, Std., crackle green, black, red, nickel and brass trim.
Courtesy Heinz A. Mueller
Continental Hobby House

Dorfan 789 "Mountain Brook" Coach, Std., maroon, yellow.
Courtesy Heinz A. Mueller
Continental Hobby House

Dorfan 790 "Pleasant View" Coach, Std., maroon, yellow.
Courtesy Heinz A. Mueller
Continental Hobby House

	G	VG	M
DORFAN 160 Tender, 0 Ga.	15.00	35.00	50.00
DORFAN 410 Bridge, 0 Ga.	15.00	20.00	30.00
DORFAN 492 Baggage, 0 Ga., Green Maroon, Brass trim	30.00	50.00	75.00
DORFAN 493 "Seattle" Coach, 0 Ga., Green, Maroon, Brass trim	20.00	30.00	50.00
DORFAN 493 "Seattle" Coach, 0 Ga., Peacock	45.00	67.50	90.00
DORFAN 494 Observation, 0 Ga., Green, Maroon, Brass trim	30.00	30.00	50.00
DORFAN 496 Passenger, Red or Silver Blue	20.00	40.00	60.00
DORFAN 497 Observation, Red or Silver Blue	20.00	40.00	60.00
DORFAN 498 Passenger, Red or Brown	20.00	40.00	60.00
DORFAN 499 Observation, Red or Brown	20.00	40.00	60.00

	G	VG	M
DORFAN 600 Gondola, Narrow Gauge	8.00	12.00	16.00
DORFAN 601 Boxcar, Narrow Gauge	10.00	15.00	20.00
DORFAN 604 Tank Car, Narrow Gauge	10.00	15.00	20.00
DORFAN 605 Hopper, Narrow Gauge	10.00	15.00	20.00
DORFAN 607 Caboose, Narrow Gauge	8.00	12.00	16.00
DORFAN 609 Lumber Car, Narrow Gauge	10.00	15.00	20.00
DORFAN 610 Derrick, Narrow Gauge	20.00	40.00	60.00
DORFAN 770 Baggage Car, Std. Ga., Green, Black, Red, Nickel trim	100.00	200.00	300.00
DORFAN 771 "San Francisco" Passenger Car, Std. Ga., Green, Black, Red, Nickel trim	200.00	300.00	400.00
DORFAN 771 Coach, Orange, Black, with people in windows	100.00	200.00	300.00
DORFAN 772 "Washington" Coach, Std. Ga., Yellow, Red, Brass and Nickel trim	100.00	200.00	300.00
DORFAN 772 Coach, Std. Ga., Brown and Green Crackle	100.00	200.00	300.00
DORFAN 772 Coach, Std. Ga., Blue and Yellow	100.00	200.00	300.00
DORFAN 773 Observation, Std. Ga., Crackle Green, Black, Red, Nickel and Brass trim	200.00	300.00	400.00
DORFAN 773 Observation, Orange, Black, with people in windows	62.50	93.75	125.00
DORFAN 789 "Mountain Brook" Coach, Std. Ga., Maroon, Yellow	100.00	200.00	300.00
DORFAN 789 Coach, Std. Ga., Orange, Green	100.00	200.00	300.00
DORFAN 789 "Mountain Brook" Coach, Green, Light brown	80.00	120.00	160.00
DORFAN 789 "Mountain Brook" Coach, Black, Red	100.00	150.00	200.00
DORFAN 790 "Pleasant View" Coach, Std., Ga., Maroon, Yellow	70.00	105.00	140.00
DORFAN 800 Gondola, Wide Gauge	20.00	40.00	60.00
DORFAN 801 Boxcar, Wide Gauge	25.00	50.00	75.00
DORFAN 804 Tank Car, Wide Gauge	25.00	50.00	75.00

Dorfan 14048 Gondola, 11201 Hopper, 0 ga., gray, yellow litho, nickel trim.
Courtesy Heinz A. Mueller Continental Hobby House

Dorfan S182999 Box and L.R.C.X.84 Tank Car, 0 ga., red, yellow black litho.
Courtesy Heinz A. Mueller Continental Hobby House

Dorfan 0-4-0 Steam Loco and Tender, 0 ga., maroon, yellow, brass, nickel trim.
Courtesy Heinz A. Mueller Continental Hobby House

Dorfan 0-4-0 Steam Loco and Tender, 0 ga., red, yellow, brass trim.
Courtesy Heinz A. Mueller Continental Hobby House

Dorfan 0-4-0 Steam Loco, Wind-up and Tender, 0 ga., black, maroon, yellow, brass trim.
Courtesy Heinz A. Mueller Continental Hobby House

	G	VG	M
DORFAN 805 Hopper, Wide Gauge .	50.00	75.00	100.00
DORFAN 806 Caboose, Wide Gauge	20.00	40.00	60.00
DORFAN 809 Lumber Car, Wide Gauge	20.00	40.00	60.00
DORFAN 1201 Car, Gray litho	100.00	150.00	200.00
DORFAN 3919 Engine, Orange, Wide Gauge, 0-4-0	200.00	400.00	600.00
DORFAN 3920 Engine, Red, Wide Gauge, 0-4-0	200.00	400.00	600.00
DORFAN 3930 Electric loco, 4-4-4 ..	500.00	750.00	1000.00
DORFAN 3931 Electric loco, 4-4-4, Wide Gauge, Green	500.00	750.00	1000.00
DORFAN 3931 Electric loco, 4-4-4, Wide Gauge, Black	500.00	750.00	1000.00
DORFAN 5402 "Washington" Coach, 0 Ga., Red, Black, Yellow	50.00	75.00	100.00
DORFAN 11201 Hopper, Gray, 0 Ga.	15.00	22.50	30.00
DORFAN 14048 Gondola, 0 Ga., Yellow litho, nickel trim	20.00	40.00	60.00
DORFAN #21499 Santa Fe box car, black/red/green/brown/brass trim litho	185.00	277.50	370.00
DORFAN 126432 Box Car, 0 Ga., Green, Black	20.00	40.00	60.00
DORFAN #234561 Gondola, orange/ black	185.00	277.50	370.00
DORFAN #29325 Tank car, robin egg blue/red/black/white	185.00	277.50	370.00
DORFAN #486751 Caboose, brown/ green/red/yellow/black	185.00	277.50	370.00

Dorfan 0-4-0 Wind-'up, 4-wheel tender, 5402 "Washington" Coach, 0 ga., red, black, yellow.
Courtesy Heinz A. Mueller Continental Hobby House

Dorfan 0-4-0 Loco, Wind-up, 160 Tender, Pullman, 0 ga., black, red, yellow.
Courtesy Heinz A. Mueller Continental Hobby House

	G	VG	M
DORFAN 517953 Box Car, 0 Ga., Orange, Brown	20.00	40.00	60.00
DORFAN Atlanta Pullman, Red ...	17.50	26.50	35.00
DORFAN "Boston" Coach, 0 Ga., Maroon, Yellow, Brass trim, also Red/Yellow	20.00	40.00	60.00
DORFAN "Boston" Coach, 0 Ga., Red, Brass trim, also Silver Gray/ Red, Blue/Yellow	20.00	40.00	60.00
DORFAN "Boston" Observation Car, 0 Ga., Maroon, Yellow, Brass trim, also Red/Yellow	20.00	40.00	60.00
DORFAN "Boston" Coach, Peacock	44.00	66.00	88.00
DORFAN "Boston" Pullman, 0 Ga., Red	32.00	48.00	64.00
DORFAN Box Car, S182999, 0 Ga., Yellow, black litho	20.00	40.00	60.00
DORFAN Champion 100 watt transformer	3.00	4.50	6.00
DORFAN Chicago coach, green w/ brass window inserts	45.00	67.50	90.00
DORFAN Chicago Pullman	72.00	108.00	144.00

	G	VG	M
DORFAN Gondola, orange/black/ litho — Std.	35.00	52.50	70.00
DORFAN Gondola, yellow/litho.	40.50	60.50	81.00
DORFAN Lumber car, 8 wheel	99.00	148.50	198.00
DORFAN Observation, green with brass windows	45.00	67.50	90.00
DORFAN Observation Car, 0 Ga., Red, Brass trim, people in windows	20.00	40.00	60.00
DORFAN Observation, red/yellow .	43.00	64.50	86.00
DORFAN Observation car, peacock/ red/black	19.00	28.50	38.00
DORFAN Observation, peacock w/ people and lights	45.00	67.50	90.00
DORFAN 0-4-0 Engine, Std. Ga., Orange, Green, Brass trim	200.00	300.00	400.00
DORFAN 0-4-0 Steam Loco and Tender, 0 Ga., Maroon, Yellow, Brass, Nickel trim	100.00	200.00	300.00
DORFAN 0-4-0 Steam Loco and Tender, 0 Ga., Red, Yellow, Brass trim	100.00	200.00	300.00
DORFAN 0-4-0 Steam Loco, Windup, and Tender, 0 Ga., Black, Maroon, Yellow, Brass trim	50.00	75.00	125.00
DORFAN 0-4-0 Windup Loco, 4-wheel tender, Black, Red, 0 Ga.	50.00	75.00	125.00
DORFAN 0-4-0 Loco, Windup, Black	50.00	75.00	125.00
DORFAN Pullman, Peacock, Red, Black	20.00	30.00	40.00
DORFAN Pullman, Yellow, Red litho, 0 Ga.	20.00	30.00	40.00
DORFAN "Seattle" Coach, 0 Ga., Red, Brass trim	20.00	30.00	40.00
DORFAN "Seattle" Coach, Red, Yellow	20.00	30.00	40.00
DORFAN "Seattle" Pullman, Red ..	20.00	30.00	40.00
DORFAN Tank Car, Indian Refining Co., Reddish Brown litho, 0 Ga., early	22.00	50.00	75.00
DORFAN Tank Car, L.R.C.X.84, Red, Black litho, 0 Ga.	20.00	50.00	75.00
DORFAN Tank car, robin egg blue/ maroon/litho. brass trim	127.50	191.50	255.00
DORFAN Tank car, robin egg blue .	120.00	180.00	240.00

Dorfan "Seattle" Coach, 0 ga., red, brass trim.
Courtesy Heinz A. Mueller Continental Hobby House

	G	VG	M
DORFAN Tender, 6 wheel, crackle black/yellow	96.00	144.00	192.00
DORFAN Transformer, 50 watt	1.50	2.50	3.00
DORFAN Trestle bridge	15.00	22.50	30.00
DORFAN Litho. tunnel with cows, horse and wagon, car, house, trees and mountains — 0	6.00	9.00	12.00
DORFAN Electric loco 0-4-0	180.00	270.00	360.00
DORFAN Loco 0-4-0	197.00	295.50	394.00
DORFAN Super Dorfan set - engine, lumber car, 2 cars, and caboose	800.00	1200.00	1600.00
DORFAN Washington pullman	72.00	108.00	144.00
DORFAN Washington coach, green w/brass windows	45.00	67.50	90.00

Following are excerpts from the Dorfan Modern Electric Train Catalog of 1930.

DORFAN SPECIAL No. 215 (Green)

FAST FREIGHT No. 252

No. 252 — Freight Train—Complete with Dorfan die cast take apart engine No. 51 with headlight and brass hand rails. One gondola No. 600; one tank car No. 604 and one caboose No. 606. Track terminal, eight pieces curved track and two pieces straight track. Length of train, 28 inches. Shipping weight, 7 pounds. Packed in individual box.
Retail price, each **$8.50**

SCENIC LIMITED No. 254 (Brown)

STEAM-TYPE LOCOMOTIVE No. 55 (Black or Red)
Reversible. With 6-wheel tender. Triple action piston rods. Headlight in front of boiler. A most powerful engine. Length, 13¼ inches. Shipping weight, 2½ pounds. Retail price, each **$9.50**

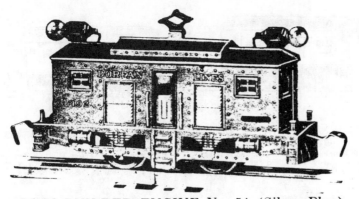

LOCO-BUILDER ENGINE No. 54 (Silver Blue)

Reversible. This is the dandiest engine of its type ever put on the market. With its rich brass trimmings, silver colored finish, headlights at each end, and pennant holders at front and rear platforms, it has an outstanding eye appeal. Swift, powerful, flashing action. Length of engine, 9¾ inches. Shipping weight, 2¾ pounds.
Retail price, each **$8.95**
No. 54-RC—Distance Remote Control. Retail price, each **$13.45**

CHAMPION LIMITED No. 890 (Orange)

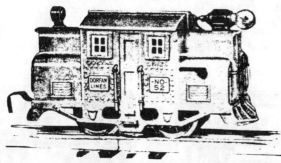

LOCO-BUILDER ENGINE No. 52 (Red)

Reversible. Electric headlight and brass hand rails. A most powerful engine for its size. Length, 7¼ inches. Shipping weight, 2½ pounds. Retail price, each **$5.95**

LOCO-BUILDER ENGINE No. 51 (Green)

Not Reversible. Otherwise same as No. 52. Length, 7¼ inches. Shipping weight, 2 pounds 6 ounces. Retail price, each **$4.95**

PASSENGER CAR No. 498
(Red or Brown)
Single trucks, inserted window frames.
A very sturdy built car at its price.
Retail price,
each **$1.00**

OBSERVATION CAR No. 499
(Red or Brown)
Single trucks, inserted window frames,
observation brass platform.
Retail price, each **$1.15**

LOCO-BUILDER ENGINE No. 3930 (Green or Black)
Reversible. Six ball bearings and 12 wheels—4 big driving wheels and
8 trailer wheels. Electric headlights front and rear. Brass hand rails.
A beautifully proportioned engine. Length, 14½ inches.
Shipping weight, 7 pounds. Retail price, each **$24.25**

No. 3930-RC—Distance Remote Control. Retail price, each $30.75

PASSENGER CAR No. 496
(Red or Silver Blue)
Double trucks. Duco finish. Illuminated.
Brass hand rails and passengers.
Length, 9 inches. Shipping weight, 1
pound 5 ounces.
Retail price, each **$3.20**

OBSERVATION CAR No. 497
(Red or Silver Blue)
Double trucks. Duco finish. Illuminated.
With passengers. Length, 8¼ inches.
Shipping weight, 1 pound 5 ounces.
Retail price,
each **$3.70**

LOCO-BUILDER ENGINE No. 3920 (Red)

Reversible. Six ball bearings, 2 headlights, brass trimming. A very sturdy built engine for rough usage. Length, 13 inches. Shipping weight, 6 pounds 4 ounces. Retail price, each **$16.75**

No. 3920-RC—**Distance Remote Control.** Retail price, each $23.25

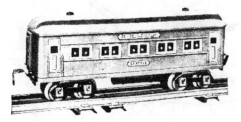

PASSENGER CAR No. 493 (Green)
Narrow Gauge

Double trucks. Die-cast wheels. Journal boxes. Illuminated. Passenger at every seat. Length, $9\frac{1}{2}$ inches. Shipping weight, $1\frac{1}{2}$ pounds.
Retail price, each **$3.95**

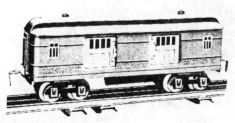

BAGGAGE CAR No. 492 (Green)
Narrow Gauge

Die-cast wheels. Double trucks. Journal boxes, sliding doors. Illuminated. Length, $9\frac{1}{2}$ inches. Shipping weight, $1\frac{1}{2}$ pounds.
Retail price, each **$3.70**

DORFAN SPRING-WIND TRAIN No. 135

No. 135—One of the finest mechanical train outfits on the market at the price. Includes die cast steam type engine No. 155 with tender; two lithographed pullman cars No. 355. Engine black and cars finished in a combination of red and yellow. One lithographed tunnel No. 310 in beautiful colors; one warning signal No. 340; four pieces curved track and two pieces straight track. Length of train, 20 inches. Shipping weight, 4½ pounds.
Retail price, each   **$2.50**

DERRICK CAR No. 610
Narrow Gauge
Double truck. Derrick can be swung to right or left and hook raised and lowered. Length, 7½ inches. Shipping weight, ¾ pound.
Retail price, each   **$2.25**

LOCO-BUILDER ENGINE No. 53 (Green)
Heavy Duty, Reversible. Headlights at each end. Brass rails. 5 ball bearings..Length, 9½ inches. Shipping weight, 3 pounds 4 ounces. Retail price, each   **$9.50**
No. 53-RC—**Distance Remote Control.** Retail price, each $14.00

DORFAN ELECTRIC SWITCHES

Heavy Gauge Steel, Insulated with Bakelite

No. 485—Narrow Gauge.
Retail price, per pair   **$3.75**

No. 885—Wide Gauge.
Retail price, per pair   **$5.50**

No. 485L—Narrow Gauge—Illuminated.
Retail price, per pair   **$5.50**

No. 885L—Wide Gauge—Illuminated.
Retail price, per pair   **$6.85**

The illuminated switch flashes green light when switch is open and a red light when closed.

No. 886LRC—Wide Gauge "Remote Control." Illuminated Switches. These switches may be controlled from any distance. Controlling means included.
Retail price, per pair   **$12.00**

DORFAN CROSSOVERS

No. 475 — Narrow Gauge — Heavy gauge steel with rigid center piece.
Retail price, each   **$1.30**

DORFAN STRAIGHT ELECTRIC TRACK

No. 450—Narrow Gauge—10¼ inches long, 1⅜ inches wide.
Retail price, each **$.20**

No. 850—Wide Gauge—14 inches long, 2¼ inches wide.
Retail price, each **$.30**

DORFAN CURVED ELECTRIC TRACK

No. 460—Narrow Gauge—11 inches long, 1⅜ inches wide.
Retail price, each **$.20**

No. 860—Wide Gauge—16 inches long, 2¼ inches wide.
Retail price, each **$.30**

Standard Packing of Track—
10 Pieces to a Box

TRACK TERMINAL

No. 403—Narrow Gauge.
Retail price, each **$.25**

No. 404—Wide Gauge.
Retail price, each **$.25**

Standard Packing—6 to a box

TRACK BINDERS

No. 465—Fit both narrow gauge and wide gauge tracks. Sold in dozen lots only.
Retail price, per dozen **$.30**

No. 875—Wide Gauge—Very sturdy construction.
Retail price, each **$1.50**

426

No. 442

DORFAN TRANSFORMER No. 442

For 110-volt, 60-cycle alternating current. 50-watt capacity. 5 steps, ranging from 5½ to 10½ volts. Two outlet connections. Air cooled. Strong metal case. Cord 6⅛ feet long. Must NOT be used with Direct Current. Shipping weight, 3 pounds 6 ounces.
Retail price, each **$3.50**

No. 443

DORFAN TRANSFORMER No. 443

For 110-volt, 60-cycle alternating current. 100-watt capacity. 6 steps of ¾ volts each. Range 5½ to 23 volts. Four outlet connections. Die-cast, air-cooled housing. Must NOT be used with Direct Current. Guaranteed. Shipping weight, 5 pounds 4 ounces.
Retail price, each **$6.50**

No. 310

DORFAN TUNNEL No. 310

For small mechanical trains. Length, 7½ inches. Height, 5 inches. Width, 5 inches. Shipping weight, 11 ounces.
Retail price, each **$.50**

TUNNEL No. 319

Made of durable composition in one piece. Embossed and decorated in colors. Length, 8¼ inches. Width, 8 inches. Height, 8 inches.
Retail price, each **$1.50**

No. 319

STATION No. 424

Small metal station, 5 by 7½ inches. Shipping weight, 10 oz.
Retail price,
each $1.00

STATION No. 426

Three-story building, resembling brick. Electrically lighted. Covered platform; clock dial; arcade. Height, 9½ inches, with 12½ inches base. Shipping weight, 3 pounds, 4 ounces.
Retail price, each $4.85

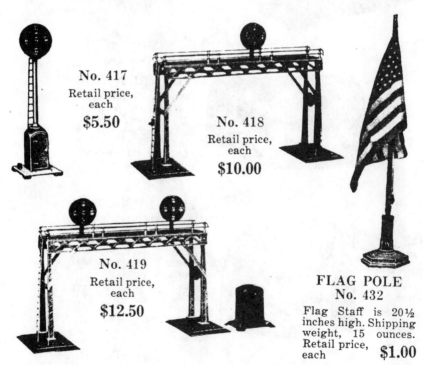

No. 417
Retail price,
each
$5.50

No. 418
Retail price,
each
$10.00

No. 419
Retail price,
each
$12.50

FLAG POLE
No. 432
Flag Staff is 20½ inches high. Shipping weight, 15 ounces.
Retail price,
each $1.00

These are the latest models of modern, up-to-date signals. The arm of the old type of semaphore is replaced by electric bulbs, as used today in modern railway signaling. Two indications, stop and go, are operated from a switchbox. Very simple hookup, as all wires are on plugs, which will be inserted in receptacles. By switching the switch to the stop position, the bulbs will light horizontal, and the train comes to a stop and will wait there till the switch is set for clear track which is indicated by bulbs lighted vertically. Train will proceed and will continue to run till signal will be set again for stop. Very solid construction, no automatic devices which will go out of order. A pleasing and interesting addition to any train outfit.

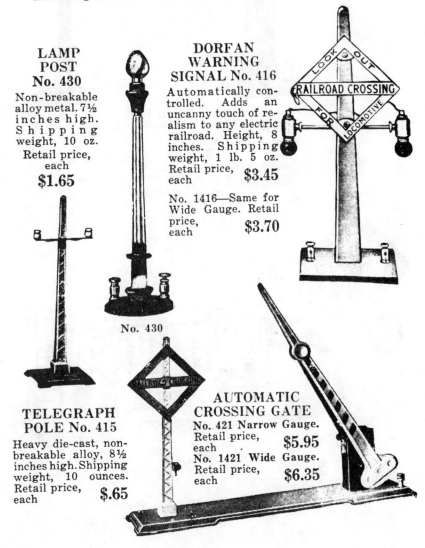

LAMP POST No. 430

Non-breakable alloy metal. 7½ inches high. Shipping weight, 10 oz.
Retail price, each
$1.65

No. 430

DORFAN WARNING SIGNAL No. 416

Automatically controlled. Adds an uncanny touch of realism to any electric railroad. Height, 8 inches. Shipping weight, 1 lb. 5 oz.
Retail price, each **$3.45**

No. 1416—Same for Wide Gauge. Retail price, each **$3.70**

TELEGRAPH POLE No. 415

Heavy die-cast, non-breakable alloy, 8½ inches high. Shipping weight, 10 ounces.
Retail price, each **$.65**

AUTOMATIC CROSSING GATE

No. 421 Narrow Gauge.
Retail price, each **$5.95**
No. 1421 Wide Gauge.
Retail price, each **$6.35**

429

BOULEVARD LIGHT No. 420

Die cast. Drop style. Height, 7 inches. Shipping weight 10 ounces.

Retail price, each

$1.65

BLOCK SIGNAL SET No. 401

Narrow Gauge. When trains approach this signal, the red light flashes on, and the train comes to a stop. It doesn't start up again until you switch the light in the signal post back to green. Set consists of Block Signal 6 inches high, switch box, 2 track terminals, 2 insulation plates and necessary wire for hook up. Shipping weight, 1 pound. Retail price, **each**   **$4.95**

No. 1401—Same set for Wide Gauge. Retail price, each   **$5.20**

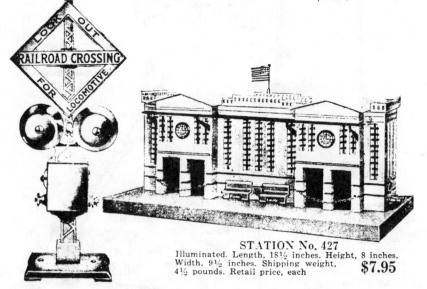

STATION No. 427

Illuminated. Length, 18½ inches. Height, 8 inches. Width, 9¼ inches. Shipping weight, 4½ pounds. Retail price, each   **$7.95**

BELL RINGING WARNING SIGNAL No. 406

This signal operates in the same manner as No. 416, as shown on page 13, the use of a bell in place of lights. Height, 8½ inches. Shipping weight, 1½ lbs. Retail price, each   **$4.20**

No. 1406—Same for Wide Gauge. Retail price, each   **$4.50**

430

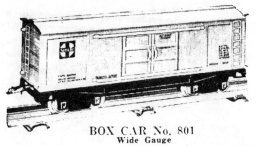

BOX CAR No. 801
Wide Gauge
Length, 15½ inches. Shipping weight, 3½ lbs. **$4.75**
Retail price, each

BOX CAR No. 601
Narrow Gauge
Length, 7½ inches. Shipping weight, 12 oz. **$1.00**
Retail price, each

COAL CAR No. 805
Wide Gauge
Length, 15½ inches. Shipping weight, **$4.75**
3 lbs. 4 oz. Retail price, each

COAL CAR No. 605
Narrow Gauge
Length, 7½ inches. Shipping weight, 12 oz. **$1.00**
Retail price, each

OIL TANK CAR No. 801
Wide Gauge
Length, 7½ inches. Shipping weight, 12 oz. **$4.75**
Retail price, each

OIL TANK CAR No. 601
Narrow Gauge
Length, 7½ inches. Shipping weight, 10 oz. **$1.00**
Retail price, each

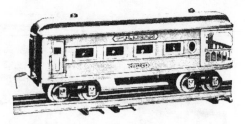

OBSERVATION CAR No. 494 (Green)
Narrow Gauge

Double trucks. Die-cast wheels. Illuminated. Passenger at every seat. Platform enclosed with brass railing and lighted. Length, 9½ inches. Shipping weight, 1½ pounds.
Retail price, each **$3.95**

GONDOLA CAR No. 800
Wide Gauge

Length, 15½ inches. Shipping weight, 2½ lbs.
Retail price, each **$3.75**

GONDOLA CAR No. 600
Narrow Gauge

Length, 7½ inches. Shipping weight, 10 oz.
Retail price, each **$1.00**

CABOOSE CAR No. 806
Wide Gauge

Length, 15½ inches. Shipping weight, 3 lbs. 5 oz. Retail price, each **$5.25**

CABOOSE CAR No. 607
Narrow Gauge

Length, 7½ inches. Shipping weight, 12 oz.
Retail price, each **$1.00**

DORFAN AUTOMATIC CIRCUIT BREAKER No. 446

The Dorfan Automatic Circuit Breaker shuts off the electric current when a short circuit occurs in operating Toy Electric Trains. The current remains off until the cause of the short circuit is removed. The Dorfan Automatic Circuit Breaker makes it possible for the very young child to play with Electric Toy Trains without any fear of what might happen if the train should jump the track. It makes Dorfan the World's Safest Toy Railway. Dealers are now able to run electric trains in their show windows with absolute safety.

The Dorfan Automatic Circuit Breakers is the cheapest kind of Transformer insurance. This modern improvement should be included in every sale of an Electric Train. PLAY SAFE—use the Dorfan Automatic Circuit Breaker No. 446.

Retail price, each   **$2.65**

Originated
by the
Dorfan
Engineers

Makes
Dorfan the
World's
Safest
Miniature
Railroad

PATENT APPLIED FOR

433

No. 70

This miniature crane is the most interesting mechanism to a boy, next to the Dorfan Engine. It operates just as perfectly as a big crane. The horizontal arm can be revolved continuously in a complete circle and can be reversed. The lifting hook can be raised or lowered. 20 inches high, 19 inches wide; two gear-shift levers; start-stop-reverse; double clutch and worm gear; solid die cast construction. Electric motor controlled; finished in a beautiful combination of colors. Illustration approximately one-fifth actual size. Packed in individual box. Net weight, 11 pounds. Shipping weight, approximately 25 pounds. Shipped completely assembled, ready for operation. Retail price, each **$19.50**

TOOTSIETOY

TOOTSIETOY began as Dowst and Company in 1876, publishing a trade paper, The National Laundry Journal. It later began to manufacture laundry supplies, and in 1893, when Charles O. Dowst saw a linotype machine at the Columbian Exposition, he secured one, and in time began to turn out non-laundry items, such as toys and novelties, as well. Sometime before 1921 the company produced its first train set, and though Tootsietoy was known mainly for its vehicles, its trains remained popular, and a number of new sets were produced as the years went on. The company is still in business.

Tootsietoy 1088 Refrigerator Car, 1094 Oil Tank Car.

	G	VG	M
(TTF) Tootsie toy flyer	2.50	4.00	5.00
(TTF) U.S. mail car	2.50	4.00	5.00
(186) Fast freight loco, black	4.00	6.00	8.00
(186) Fast freight NYC tender, black	4.00	6.00	8.00
(186) Fast freight Cracker Jack box car, orange	4.00	6.00	8.00
(690) Union Pacific loco	4.50	7.00	9.00
(960A) Union Pacific diesel loco, yellow/silver	4.00	6.00	8.00
(1086) Penn. Loco, gray	4.00	6.00	8.00
(1086) Penn. Loco, gold	2.00	3.00	4.00
(1086) Penn. Loco, copper	4.00	6.00	8.00
(1088) Refrigerator car	2.50	3.75	5.00
(1089) Box car, Southern Fruit Growers on side	1.50	2.25	3.00
(1091) Stock car, Pioneer Stock Shippers on side	2.50	4.00	5.00
(1091) Stock car	2.00	3.00	4.00
(1093) Milk tank car	2.50	3.75	5.00

Tootsietoy 1086 Pennsylvania Loco

	G	VG	M
(1094) Oil tank car	3.00	4.50	6.00
(1101) Baggage car	2.00	3.00	4.00
(1102) Pullman	2.00	3.00	4.00
(1103) Observation car	2.00	3.00	3.50
(1875) Shell Oil tank car	4.00	6.00	8.00
(1956) Erie tanker, die cast wheels ..	3.00	4.50	6.00
(4620) Loco, 2-6-0, black	4.00	6.00	8.00
(4620) Loco 2-6-0, red	3.00	4.50	6.00
(4621) #221 tender, black	3.00	4.50	6.00
(4623) Pullman coach, yellow	3.00	4.50	6.00
(4623) Pullman coach, red	3.00	4.50	6.00
(4623) Pullman coach, blue	3.00	4.50	6.00
(4623) Pullman coach, green with sliding doors	4.00	6.00	8.00
(4624) Gondola car, D.B. & CO., black	2.50	4.00	5.00
(4697) Caboose, red	3.00	4.50	6.00
(4697) Caboose, gray/blue	3.00	4.50	6.00
(4697) Caboose	1.50	2.00	2.50
(5435) Penn. passenger train loco ...	4.00	6.00	8.00
(9804) NYC caboose, red	4.00	6.00	8.00
(9804) NYC caboose	2.00	3.00	4.00
(9853) Tanker car, black rubber tires	2.00	3.00	4.00
(22001) Penn. coal car, gray/black ..	4.00	6.00	8.00
(22001) Penn. coal car	2.00	3.00	4.00
(23030) Box car, green	4.00	6.00	8.00
(122390) A.T. & S.F. Stock Car	2.00	3.00	4.00

UNIQUE
by Richard L. MacNary

UNIQUE trains were manufactured by Unique Art Manufacturing Company of Newark, NJ. According to some of their WW II ads, they had been making toys since 1916. Their first mechanical (clock-work) trains were introduced in 1949. Electric trains soon followed. With pressure from both the Louis Marx Company and Korean War material shortages, the complete Unique operation seems to have folded about 1952. Most of their train items carried no numbers but the pieces are easy to identify. All items are somewhat rare but most are not too desirable. As in the Marx section, unknown catalog numbers that are not marked on the car are in parenthesis. All cars have 4 wheels.

	G	VG	M
(100) Box car, 7½" tin, silver with red lettering "Unique Lines" and "3509"	5.00	7.00	10.00
(101) Hopper Car, 7½" tin, orange, with red inside, with black lettering "Unique Lines"	5.00	7.00	10.00

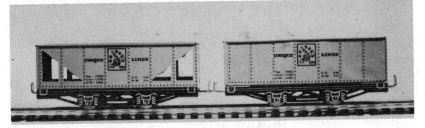

Unique 101 Hopper Car and High Side Gondola
Photo Courtesy Richard MacNary

Unique 102(b) and 102(a) Passenger Cars.
Photo Courtesy Richard MacNary

	G	VG	M
(—) High Side Gondola, 7½" tin, same as (101) but without punched out sides (and harder to find)	10.00	20.00	30.00
(102) (a) Passenger Car, 9" tin, blue body with silver roof, with white and black lettering "Pullman" and "CITY OF JOPLIN".......................	30.00	45.00	60.00
(102) (b) Passenger Car, same as above but marked "GARDEN CITY"	30.00	45.00	60.00
(105) (a) Caboose, 7½" tin, red with yellow lettering "Unique Lines" and Alfred E. Neuman types looking out windows	5.00	7.00	10.00
(105) (b) Caboose, same as above but with swing-out "Benny the Brakeman" on the rear platform.........	10.00	15.00	20.00
(107) Cattle Car, 7½" tin, red with yellow roof, marked "Unique Lines". How did the cows get their heads through the slats?	10.00	15.00	20.00
(109) (a) Circus Car, 7½" tin, mostly red with yellow roof, marked "*Jewel T Circus*", ELEPHANT in center panel	20.00	30.00	40.00
(109) (b) Circus Car, 7½" tin, same as above marked "*Jewel T Circus*" but with TIGER in center panel	20.00	30.00	40.00
(109) (c) Circus Car, 7½" tin, similar to (109) (a) above but *open top*, marked "*Unique U Circus*", ELEPHANT in center panel. Rare	30.00	50.00	80.00
(109) (d) Circus Car, 7½" tin, similar to (109) (b) above but *open top*, marked "*Unique U Circus*", TIGER in center panel. Rare	30.00	50.00	80.00
742 Engine, 10" tin, multicolored but mostly gray with 7½" tin tender, marked "Unique Lines" in red. Clock work.............................	15.00	20.00	25.00
1950(a) Engine, 10" tin, multicolored but mostly blue with 7½" tin tender marked "Unique Lines" in white. Electric with reverse and headlite ..	15.00	20.00	25.00

438

Unique 105(a) and 105(b) Cabooses
Photo Courtesy Richard MacNary

Unique 107 Cattle Car and 100 Box Car
Photo Courtesy Richard MacNary

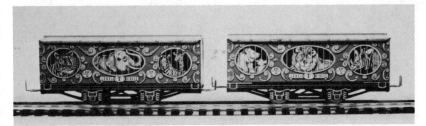

Unique 109(a) and 109(b) "Jewel T Circus" Cars
Photo Courtesy Richard MacNary

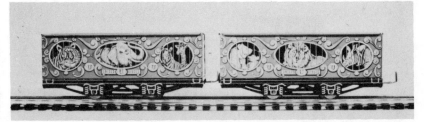

Unique 109(c) and 109(d) "Unique U Circus" Cars
Photo Courtesy Richard MacNary

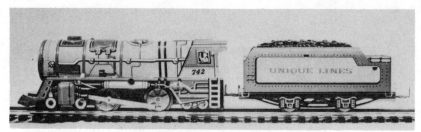

Unique 742 Engine & Tender, clockwork.
Photo Courtesy Richard MacNary

Unique 1950(a) Engine & Tender, electric with headlight.
Photo Courtesy Richard MacNary

2000 "Rock Island" Powered "A" unit
Photo Courtesy Richard MacNary

Unique Control Tower with complete handle and transformer.
Photo Courtesy Richard MacNary

440

	G	VG	M
1950(b) Engine, 10″ tin, same as 1950(a) but no headlite, no reverse ..	15.00	20.00	25.00
2000 Engine, diesel, 14″ tin, comes powered "A" and dummy "A", multi-colored but mostly maroon, marked "Rock Island". Very ugly toy train.	10.00	20.00	30.00
(—)(a) Control Tower, two story, tin litho, mostly cream with green roof (some have reverse button), control handle almost always broken, 3″ × 2″ × 4″.	2.00	4.00	6.00
(—)(b) Control Tower, same as above but with *complete* control handle. DON'T TRY TO TURN HANDLE OR IT WILL END UP LIKE (a).	15.00	20.00	25.00

MISCELLANEOUS

	G	VG	M
A.C. GILBERT Erector Hudson Engine and Tender	800.00	1200.00	1600.00
ARCOR RUBBER TOY CO. #649 Engine (see Auburn 529)	10.00	12.50	15.00
ATOMIC train, tin, 4″ long	1.50	2.50	3.00

AUBURN RUBBER (Also Aub-Rub'r) was founded in 1913, in Auburn, Indiana as the Double Fabric Tire Corporation, making auto tubes and tires for Model T Fords, etc. Its first toys, five soldiers, were produced in 1935. Within a few years it also made train sets, with at least two sold before World War II began. After the war, making of toys, including trains, resumed, again in rubber. By the 1950s vinyl was also being used, and was eventually employed exclusively. In 1960 the toys portion of Auburn transferred to the town of Deming, New Mexico, where it remained until it went out of business in 1969.

	No	Price	Found
No. 325 Train Set - contents unknown, pre-WW II			
No. 525 Train Set, vinyl, in 1958 catalog, loco-tender, coal car, gondola, caboose, three trainmen	20.00	25.00	30.00
No 529 Train Set, in 1953 catalog, made of rubber, loco 9½″ long, red/silver or black/silver, dump car 6″ long either green/black or red/black, gondola 6″ long, red or black, caboose 5″ long, red. Marked ARCOR Safe Play Toys, though apparently Auburn	20.00	30.00	35.00
No. 577 Train Set, Loco-tender gray, 10½″ long, tender marked "999", dump car 5″ long, black/orange, caboose 4⅜″ long, red, pre-War, possibly post-War as well (pre-War included 3 gondolas)	20.00	30.00	40.00
No. 599 Diesel Locomotive, vinyl, in 1958 catalog, not sold with other cars	6.00	8.00	10.00
No. 649 loco - part of 529 Train Set			

	G	**VG**	**M**
No. 922 Western Train Set, vinyl, Loco 8″ long, black, red wheels, tender 5½″ long, green, passenger car 6½″ long, pink/gold, circa mid or late 1950s	15.00	20.00	25.00
No. 945 Army Train Set, in 1958 catalog, loco, two flat cars, two jeeps, two cannon, 2 soldiers	No	Price	Found
No. 965 Union Station Set. Same as 525 set.			
No. 999 Loco and tender from 577 set.			
AVERY Traction Engine, 4½″	65.00	97.50	130.00

Auburn 525 Train Set.
Courtesy Mr. & Mrs. Stacy Feller

Auburn 529 Set
Courtesy Mr. & Mrs. Stacy Feller

Auburn 599
Courtesy Mr. & Mrs. Stacy Feller

Auburn 577 Set   Courtesy Mr. & Mrs. Stacy Feller

Auburn 922 Western Train Set   Courtesy Mr. & Mrs. Stacy Feller

444

BARCLAY Mfg. Co. was in business in New Jersey from 1923 or 1924 till 1971. It was producing trains by the early 1930s at least, and continued until it closed down, although its primary toys were soldiers and vehicles.

Barclay's "5 Car Freight Train Set", circa 1932-4.
Photo by Bill Kaufman. Courtesy Evelyn Besser

Barclay Loco 335, Tender 336, Passenger Car 337

	G	VG	M
No. 59? Loco 0-6-0 and tender, in 1931 catalog	3.00	4.50	6.00
No 60? Mail and Baggage Car, in 1931 catalog	2.00	3.00	4.00
No. 61? Passenger Coach, in 1931 catalog	2.00	3.00	4.00
No 62? Box Car, in 1931 catalog	2.00	3.00	4.00
No. 63? Coal Car, in 1931 catalog ..	2.00	3.00	4.00
No 64? Oil Tank Car, in 1931 catalog	2.00	3.00	4.00
No. 65? Caboose, in 1931 catalog ...	2.00	3.00	4.00
No. 335 Loco, 0-4-0	2.00	3.00	4.00
No. 336 Tender	1.50	2.25	3.00
No. 337 Passenger Car	1.50	2.25	3.00
No. 550 "5 Car Freight Train Set", in 1931 catalog	15.00	22.50	30.00

	G	VG	M
No. ? "Passenger Train Set", Loco-tender, Passenger Coach, Mail and Baggage Car, in 1931 catalog	10.00	15.00	20.00
BEGGS Loco #1, brass and painted tin, lead wheels, paper litho on cardboard Coach, with tin roof and ends, lead wheels	400.00	600.00	800.00
BLISS "Nickel Plate Line Railroad #295" set, loco 7" long, tender, two coaches, litho paper on wood	230.00	345.00	460.00
Box car with moving doors, "Merchants Dispatch"	16.00	24.00	32.00
Box car #38, small, white rubber tires	2.00	3.00	4.00
Caboose #40, small, white rubber tires	2.00	3.00	4.00
Caboose, cast iron 3½" with 2 passenger cars............................	14.00	21.00	28.00
CARLISLE & FINCH Electric Railway Streetcar, brass wood and tin ..	1250.00	1875.00	2500.00
CARLISLE & FINCH 0-4-0 Mining Loco	500.00	750.00	1000.00
CARLISLE & FINCH Passenger Train Set, "P.R.R." loco, 131 Tender, two brass-sided Passenger Cars with wooden floors	700.00	1050.00	1400.00
Carved wooden and paper litho. train, Penn. RR	9.00	13.50	18.00
Tin mechanical "Casey Jr. Disneyland Express" plastic loco, 12" long	14.50	22.00	29.00
CASS LIMITED Wooden train set - loco, tank car, flat car, caboose	24.00	36.00	48.00
(976) Cast iron coal car	11.00	16.50	22.00
Cast iron train (3 pcs.) 14" long	19.00	28.50	38.00
Cast metal train on pedestal, 4" long	4.00	6.00	8.00
Circus car, tin and wood with litho paper animals	46.00	69.00	92.00
(122) CONCORD TOY CO. STREAMLINE FLYER Paper Train set - engine that rolls, station, crossing signal, baggage truck, baggage & people	9.00	13.50	18.00
CONVERSE Loco, tender, box car, tin litho	70.00	105.00	140.00

	G	VG	M
CORCOR Train - engine, tender, box car, caboose, 5″ long (1940)	171.00	256.50	342.00
CRITERION PRODUCTS Caboose, Playland RR #22-14, 3″ long	2.50	4.00	5.00
DAYTON "HILLCLIMBER" Engine, 20″ long, 2-4-0	50.00	75.00	100.00
DAYTON "HILLCLIMBER" Engine and tender, 27″ long, 2-4-0	62.00	93.00	124.00
DAYTON "HILLCLIMBER" Engine 2-4-2, 17″ long	60.00	90.00	120.00
DAYTON "Hillclimber" Loco and Tender, 20″ long, painted pressed steel and wood, friction	90.00	135.00	180.00
DAYTON "Hillclimber" Loco "150" and Tender, painted wood and pressed steel, friction, 19″ long	225.00	337.50	450.00
DAYTON Steel Streetcar, yellow with red roof	90.00	135.00	180.00
DENT Loco, "999", Tender, three passenger cars, nickel-plated cast iron, 13″ long	110.00	165.00	220.00
DENT Loco "999", 4-4-0, Tender, Flat Car, woody, pressed steel and cast iron, circa 1890s	90.00	135.00	180.00
DENT Loco and two Passenger Cars, early, 38″ long, cast iron	75.00	112.50	150.00
DENT Passenger Train Set, loco, tender, four cars, cast iron	60.00	90.00	120.00

DOEPKE was located in Rossmoyne, Ohio, and was in business from the end of World War II until the late 1950s. Most of its toys were highly detailed, authorized replicas of vehicles. Its "Yardbird" set of rideable trains was produced as early as 1956.

Because it is rare, few prices have surfaced. However, two handcars were sold in 1984. One, with a base about 6″ smaller than the other sold in restored condition for $275. The larger was offered, in good condition, for $350.

	G	VG	M
Dump car, cast iron, 6½″ long	7.00	10.50	14.00
"Elephant car" & "Greatest show on earth" cars with elephant, cast iron	500.00	750.00	1000.00
Engine, coal car and passenger car, tin 23″ long (early)	100.00	150.00	200.00

ALL ABOAR-R-R-RD FOR PROFITS!
on the sensational *NEW, IMPROVED*

YARDBIRD

FOR 1957

Here's the big-enough-to-ride railroad that steals the show in any display — and steals the heart of every boy and girl who sees it! Designed for children from 3 years up, the all-metal, chain-driven handcar responds to a touch from the littlest railroader in the crew, yet it's rugged enough for Dad to ride. The Yardbird fits any level space, indoors or out, that's at least 12 feet square. Kids are wild about the Yardbird because it's more fun than anything in the world. Parents are just as tickled at the way a Yardbird builds muscles, the wonderful way it keeps youngsters happy hour after hour, while it keeps them safely at home. Dealers are happier than anybody at the way the fast-moving Yardbird sells and sells and sells!

YARDBIRD, No. 2024, includes: Handcar, 27¾" long, 11½" wide. Track, 40', assembles into 8 5-ft. sections making 12' diameter circle. Pack: 2 cartons, KD. 1, 30" x 11⅛" x 7½". 1, 4½" x 3½" x 65". Assembly instructions included. Total weight, 79 lbs. Retail, $39.95. West, $44.95.*

TRAIN LEAVING ON THIS TRACK FOR TOP PROFITS!

The crack Super-Yardbird Streamliner is roaring along a through track to big profits in any dealer's books! Powered with a husky gasoline engine or a powerful electric motor, the real-as-life Super-Yardbird is a dream come true for any youngster — the one big, significant plaything in any young life. Even though it's the newest thing on wheels, dealers have already discovered that the Super-Yardbird makes a smash display and packs a terrific sales wallop. High-profit first sales are followed by sale after sale, year after year, of all the wonderful Yardbird accessory equipment. Better climb aboard!

YARDVILLE STATION No. 2043
Here's the central passenger terminal of the Yardbird R.R.
— and what backyard railroad is complete without a station?
Anywhere a Yardbird Railroad runs, there's always a crowd
of eager young passengers waiting for a ride — this hand-
some station will accommodate them in style! Sturdily made
of wood, bolted construction, with Duron roof. Painted red,
green, blue, yellow and white. 55" high, 48" wide. Pack:
KD, I carton, 54" x 19" x 1½". Weight, 25 lbs. Retail, $15.95.

COWCATCHER No. 2044
A real safety measure that adds a further touch of realism.
For Super-Yardbird Streamliners only; made of heavy gauge
steel, welded, attaches to front and rear trucks. Available
on order only, installed at the factory. Weight, 3 lbs. Retail,
$9.95 pair.

CROSSING SIGN No. 2040
A big, real-as-life crossing sign that really makes 'em Stop,
Look and Listen! Easily moved from place to place, wherever
the traffic is heaviest. Strong wood construction. White
Duron crossarms with black lettering. Stop sign bar, black
with bright red warning discs. 50" high. Pack: KD, I carton,
25" x 4" x 2½". Weight, 4 lbs. Retail, $3.95.

FLATCAR STAKE BODY No. 2036
Sturdy hardwood sides that fit onto Flatcar, converting it to
a hard-working, freight-hauling gondola car. Easily lifted off
when the dispatcher schedules a passenger run. Bright red
and natural wood finish. 28" x 12½" x 4". Pack: I carton,
4" x 2" x 29½". Weight, 2½ lbs. Retail, $4.95.

ROAD SIGN SET No. 2042
He can't build a railroad without some interruption to backyard highway traffic — and these road signs are just what the
traffic laws specify! They're also an excellent lesson in good
safety practices. Same shape as standard highway signs,
with the same yellow background and black lettering. Posts
and bases wood, signboards Duron. Fully painted for weather-
proofing. Sold only in sets of four, as shown. Each 32" high.
Pack: KD, I carton, 22½" x 9½" x 1½". Weight, 5 lbs.
Retail, $4.95.

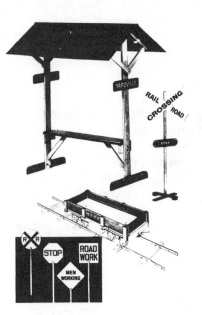

SUGGESTED DELUXE PACKAGE LAYOUT...

1— No. 2027—Super-Yard. bird Streamliner	$225.00
1— No. 2033 Handcar	22.95
2— No. 2025 — Flatcars @ 15.95	31.90
1— No. 2036—Stake body	4.95
1— No. 2029—8-section track package	18.95
1— No. 2030 — 4-section track package	11.95
1— No. 2035 — Half Track package	4.95
3— No. 2032 — Left hand switches @ 14.95	44.85
2— No. 2031 — Right hand switches @ 14.95	29.90
1— No. 2034 — Crossing	9.95
1— No. 2043 — Station	15.95
1— No. 2040—R.R. Crossing Sign	3.95
1— No. 2042—Road Signs (set of 4)	4.95
Total	$430.20

THE CHAS. WM. DOEPKE MANUFACTURING CO.
Rossmoyne, Ohio

	G	VG	M
Engine, tender, 2 flat cars, cast iron, 20″ long	80.00	120.00	160.00
Engine, tender, 3 flat cars, cast iron, 23″ long	30.00	45.00	60.00
Engine, tender and 1 car, 13¼″ long	10.00	15.00	20.00
Cast iron train - engine and passenger car, 8″ long	8.00	12.00	16.00
Engine, cast iron, 8″ long (early) ...	6.00	9.00	12.00
Engine, cast iron, 8 wheels with cow catcher, bell	40.00	60.00	80.00
Engine, tall stack, cast iron, 4 wheels (early)	30.00	45.00	60.00
Engine and coal car, cast iron PRR & CO. 14″ long	30.00	45.00	60.00
Engine, iron and tin, decorated, 12″ long	40.00	60.00	80.00
Engine, tin, with 2 passenger cars #1858	46.00	69.00	92.00
Engine, tin and wood friction, 12″ long	60.00	90.00	120.00
Engine friction and coal tender, 15″ long	45.00	67.50	90.00
Flat car, cast iron, MCRR 9″ long ..	5.00	7.50	10.00
Flat car, pressed steel, 7½″ long	3.00	4.50	6.00
Flat car, tin plate, small, with steel wheels and axle....................	1.50	2.50	3.00
FUTUREMATIC STREAMLINER Wind-up train (3 sections) 11″	4.00	6.00	8.00
GEORGE BROWN tin train set, 22″ long, "NY Elevated RR", circa 1875	1000.00	1500.00	2000.00
GEORGE BROWN "Union" Loco, painted tin, circa 1875	500.00	750.00	1000.00
Hand car, tin and wood, operated by 2 peg wood figures, 3½″ long (circa 1900)	110.00	165.00	220.00
HILLCLIMBER Loco and tender, pressed steel friction	143.00	214.50	286.00
HILLCLIMBER Tin friction drive loco and coal car, 22½″	24.00	36.00	48.00
HOGE MFG. CO. Union Pacific streamline coach, sheet brass, 3 piece unit	300.00	450.00	600.00
HOGE MFG. CO. Burlington Zephr streamline coach, 5 rail, autom. bell	300.00	450.00	600.00

Hubley Loco, Tender, two Skiddoo Passenger Cars, cast iron, c. 1915.
Courtesy Mapes Auctioneers & Appraisers

Hubley Overland Railroad
Courtesy Lloyd Ralston

	G	VG	M
HUBLEY loco, tender, two skiddoo passenger cars, circa 1915	25.00	37.50	50.00
HUBLEY Overhead Railroad, cast iron, pressed steel, clockwork, 31″ × 15″ high, loco, tender, coach, sold in October, 1981 at Lloyd Ralston in generally very good condition for $6300.00			
KENTON No. 999 Empire State Express, cast iron and brass floor loco, tender and two cars	550.00	825.00	1100.00
KENTON Engine, 9″ long, and two 9¼″ long Cattle Cars, cast iron, no tender	125.00	187.50	250.00

451

"Pullman Railplane"
Photo by Bill Kaufman   Courtesy Good Old Days Store

	G	VG	M
KENTON Loco, Tender and three cars, cast iron	60.00	90.00	120.00
KENTON Loco, Tender, Pullman car, cast iron	25.00	37.50	50.00
KENTON Passenger Set, "70" Loco and Tender, "705 Blackwater" Passenger car, "704 Overbrook" Baggage and Passenger Car, electroplated cast iron, 15½" long	150.00	225.00	300.00
KEYSTONE #6400 Loco, 27" long	26.00	39.00	52.00
KEYSTONE Backyard Train set, 4 pieces, 8" long (1930)	138.00	207.00	276.00
KEYSTONE Riding toy engine, 26" long	40.00	60.00	80.00
KEYSTONE R.R. Train with engine, coal car and Pullman	200.00	300.00	400.00
KINGSBURY Floor pull toy loco, 2 wheels with ringing bell	6.00	9.00	12.00
KINGSBURY Tin friction engine and tender, red/gold, 17" long (early)	80.00	120.00	160.00
KINGSBURY Loco and Tender, 17" long, friction floor runner	80.00	120.00	160.00
Loco, cast iron, with 2 cast iron car marked Michigan Central Railroad	54.00	81.00	108.00
Loco, cast iron, Penn. R.R., and Tender, 13"	20.00	30.00	40.00
Loco, cast iron, Penn. R.R. coal car, and open car	23.00	34.50	46.00
Loco, cast iron, with coal car and passenger car, 17½"	20.00	30.00	40.00
Loco, cast iron, with engineer in cab waving, coal car, two passenger cars	38.00	57.00	76.00
Loco, cast iron, Penn. R.R., coal car and two passenger cars, 28½" long	30.00	45.00	60.00

	G	VG	M
Loco, tin friction, and coal car, iron wheels, 24"	60.00	90.00	120.00
Loco and Tender, Wood, Paper and Tin Litho, 14" long, two 13" gondolas, rubber-stamped lettering	600.00	900.00	1200.00

MANOIL began production of slush lead toys in 1934, and was located in New York City until 1940, when it moved to Waverly, New York, where it remained until it went out of business about 1954. Manoil basically produced toy soldiers and vehicles, but in 1941 or 1942 designed a military train that never reached production because of the War. However, the molds have survived (one of them actually made up by a collector years later, as only the plaster casting for one of the cars had been produced), and are in the hands of Ron Eccles, who sells the set for $40.00 (see leading collectors and dealers). The train consisted of a locomotive, marked "41-42", a tender marked "USA" and "41-43" with a Manoil "M" marking, a flat car marked "US" carrying two airplanes and a flat car carrying a tank.

	G	VG	M
MITCH TOY Diesel loco	2.00	3.00	4.00
Mechanical NYC 3 piece train, litho. tin and pressed steel engine, tender and car, 18" long	9.00	13.50	18.00
OVERLAND Flyer Train	29.00	43.50	58.00
Cast iron passenger car with stencils and numbers, 13"	16.00	24.00	32.00
Cast iron passenger car with stenciling and numbers, 14¾"	20.00	30.00	40.00
Cast iron "America" passenger coach, 7" long	3.00	4.50	6.00
Cast iron passenger coach, 13" long	32.00	48.00	64.00
Tin passenger car, 6" long	20.00	30.00	40.00
Pedal train, sheet metal, like railroad engine "Casey Jones, The Cannonball Express" 33½" long	26.00	39.00	52.00
PLAYLAND #22-14 Railroad caboose, small, die cast body and wheels	2.00	3.00	4.00
PLAYSKOOL "Sleep-Dolly-Sleep" Pullman car	40.00	60.00	80.00
PRATT & LETCHWORTH Cast iron and pressed steel cars, 23" long	26.00	39.00	52.00

Manoil Army Train
Photo by Terry Sells

Kenton Loco, Tender and Pullman, cast iron.
Courtesy Mapes Auctioneers & Appraisers

PRATT & LETCHWORTH "Wagner Buffet Vestibule" car, cast iron, 14½" long	G	VG	M
	130.00	195.00	260.00
Pull toy small engine (early)	34.00	51.00	68.00
Pull toy tin engine, coal car and 2 passenger cars, 22½" long, engine stenciled "Apollo"	200.00	300.00	400.00

	G	VG	M
Pullman K.T. & N. RR passenger cars, small (1935)	2.00	3.00	4.00
Pullman railplane, 8¼″ long (circa 1939)	40.00	60.00	80.00
RANGER FAST FREIGHT-RANGER STEEL PRODUCTS Wind-up tin plate engine with tender, flat car, caboose key and freight station, small size (circa 1940)	4.00	6.00	8.00
RANGER loco, wind-up, small tin plate	1.00	1.50	2.00
REPUBLIC Steel street car, yellow with green trim and red roof 16″ long (circa 1926)	80.00	120.00	160.00
REVELL #3550 Union Pacific switcher (1956) HO	7.00	10.50	14.00
REVELL #4011 Pacific Fruit Express box car, HO	2.00	3.00	4.00
REVELL #4020 Union Pacific stock car, HO	3.00	4.50	6.00
REVELL #4041 Great Northern Box car, HO	2.50	4.00	5.00
REVELL #4042 Norfolk and Western hopper car with load, HO	2.00	3.00	4.00
REVELL #4050 NYC low side gondola with load, HO	2.00	3.00	4.00
REVELL #4060 Union Pacific caboose, HO	2.50	4.00	5.00
ROCKET Train set - painted tin engine, tender and 2 cars	540.00	810.00	1080.00
SCHIEBEL "HILLCLIMBER" Engine 2-4-0 friction motor and tender, iron driving wheels, 25″ long	64.00	96.00	128.00
SCHIEBEL "HILLCLIMBER" "Rapid Transit" trolley, navy blue with red roof, friction motor, 21″ long	110.00	165.00	220.00
SCHOENHUT Railroad Station with ticket and telegraph office	75.00	100.00	150.00
Station, "Central Station", tin	166.00	249.00	332.00
Station, "Central Station", large painted tin with awnings and accessories	400.00	600.00	800.00

Stevens Big 6 loco, tender, gondola, circa 1885, 18" long.
Courtesy Mapes Auctioneers & Appraisers

	G	VG	M
"NRA" steam engine and #991 tender, tin	54.00	81.00	108.00
Steam engine, cast iron, 8¾" long	8.00	12.00	16.00
Steam engine, cast iron, 9¼" long	15.00	22.50	30.00
Stock car, cast iron, 11" long	26.00	39.00	52.00
STEVENS Big 6 loco, tender, gondola, circa 1885, 18" long	130.00	195.00	260.00
Talking station	10.00	15.00	20.00
#39 Tank car, small, white rubber tires	2.00	3.00	4.00
Tin Train - engine, coal car and passenger car	166.00	249.00	332.00
Tin 3 pc. Train set wind-up, 20" long, wooden wheels (1930)	14.50	22.00	29.00
Tin train, litho., 17" long	5.00	7.50	10.00
Tin litho. small pull train	12.00	18.00	24.00
Tin friction trolley car (1900)	99.00	148.50	198.00
Cast iron horse drawn trolley, small (circa 1905-10)	40.00	60.00	80.00
Tin friction drive trolley car, 13" long	34.00	51.00	68.00
Tin friction trolley, painted	16.00	24.00	32.00
Tin "City Hall Park" trolley, (early) 15" × 5"	166.00	249.00	332.00
Tin "Broadway 270" trolley	99.00	148.50	198.00
"Public Service 365" trolley car, tin	99.00	148.50	198.00
Tin friction drive "Pay As You Enter" trolley, 22" long	37.50	56.50	75.00
Trolley, friction toy (1900)	74.00	111.00	148.00

"Union" Loco, painted tin, circa 1875.
Courtesy PB Eighty-Four New York

"Velo-King" No. 67 pedal loco.
Courtesy PB Eighty-Four New York

	G	VG	M
#206 Universal Choo Choo solid wood loco in natural finish with red painted wheels and stenciling of engineer and name (1930)	16.00	24.00	32.00
"Velo-King" No. 67, circa 1880 pedal train	250.00	375.00	500.00
"Victor" steam engine, tender and one passenger car, 11″ long	10.00	15.00	20.00
VOLTAMP 2100 Loco and tender, No. 2 gauge	750.00	1125.00	1500.00
WEEDEN "Dart" alcohol-burning loco "1887"	300.00	450.00	600.00
WEEDEN "Dart 1887" Live Steam Loco, Tender, "I.& A.R.R.", Coach, "City of New Bedford"	375.00	525.00	750.00
WILKENS Coal car, 9″ long	40.00	60.00	80.00
WILKENS Engine, tender and two cars, 36½″	34.00	51.00	68.00
WILKENS Cast iron engine, tender and 2 cars	60.00	90.00	120.00
WILKENS loco, tender, passenger car, baggage car, 30″ long, cast iron, early	20.00	30.00	40.00

458

Voltamp 2100 Loco and tender, No. 2 gauge
T. W. Sefton collection

Weeden "Dart" alcohol burning loco, "1887".
Courtesy Mapes Auctioneers & Appraisers

	G	VG	M
WILKENS Loco, coal car and passenger car, 36″ long	200.00	300.00	400.00
WILKENS NYC & Hudson River Baggage and smoking car	36.00	54.00	72.00
WILKENS NYC & Hudson River Passenger car	36.00	54.00	72.00
WILKENS NYC & Hudson River Pullman car	30.00	45.00	60.00
WILKENS Oil tank car, 13½″	30.00	45.00	60.00

459

Wilkens Loco, tender, passenger car, baggage car (not shown), 30" long.
Courtesy Mapes Auctioneers & Appraisers

Wilkens NYC & Hudson River Baggage and smoking car, cast iron, 18" long.
Courtesy Mapes Auctioneers & Appraisers

	G	VG	M
"The Winner" electric tin train engine and 2 cars, orange and green, tin station houses transformer	130.00	195.00	260.00
WOLVERINE Streamline railway, tin litho. pull toy, 17"	19.00	28.50	38.00
Wood and metal loco with cow catcher, friction	26.00	39.00	52.00
Wooden train with engine, tender, open freight car, tanker car and caboose	66.00	99.00	132.00
WYANDOTTE Low side gondola car	1.50	2.50	3.00

Wilkens NY Central & Hudson River Pullman car, 18" long.
Courtesy Mapes Auctioneers & Appraisers

Wilkens NYC and Hudson River Passenger car, 18" long
Courtesy Mapes Auctioneers & Appraisers

AUCTIONEERS

These are established firms experienced in disposing of large collections of toys by auction.

Sotheby's
   1334 York Ave.
   New York, N.Y. 10021
   (212)606-7000

Heinz A. Mueller
   Continental Auctions
   P.O. Box 193
   Sheboygan, Wisconsin 53081

Lloyd W. Ralston
   447 Stratfield Road
   Fairfield, Connecticut 06432
   (203) 366-3399

Mapes Auctioneers & Appraisers
   1600 Vestal Parkway West
   Vestal, New York 13850
   (607) 754-9193

Ted Maurer
   1931 N. Charlotte Street
   Pottstown, Pennsylvania
   (215) 323-1573

Gene Harris Antique Center
   P.O. Box 476- 203 So. 18th Ave.
   Marshalltown, Iowa 50158
   (515) 752-0600

Butterfield & Butterfield
   1244 Sutter Street
San Francisco, California 94109
   (415) 673-1362

Kruse Auctioneers
   Kruse Building
   Auburn, Indiana 46706
   (219) 925-5401

LEADING COLLECTORS AND DEALERS

(It is suggested that, when writing to any of the following, you enclose a stamped, self-addressed envelope.)

THOMAS W. SEFTON - Standard Gauge and BUDDY L
San Diego Trust & Savings Bank
Box 1871
San Diego, California

GERALD C. WAGNER - Old Toy Trains, especially foreign
4455 Hermosa Way
San Diego, California 92103

RICHARD MACNARY - MARX trains, dimestore lead soldiers, toys made during WW II
4727 Alpine Drive
Lilburn, Georgia 30247

STEVEN HINTZE
572 Broad Ave.
Leonia, New Jersey 07605

HERMAN & FLORENCE LOTSTEIN - Trains of all kinds
Cook's Antique Flea Market
Rt. 29, Lambertville, New Jersey

THE TRAIN COLLECTORS ASSOCIATION
National Business Office
Box 248
Strasburg, Pennsylvania 17579

CONTINENTAL HOBBY HOUSE - Trains of all types
P.O. Box 193
Sheboygan, Wisconsin 53081

FRANK L. FERRARA
102 Teaneck Road
Ridgefield Park, N.J. 07660

TERRY P. AMADON - IVES trains
410 W. Foster Ave.
State College, Pa. 16801

JAN RECHENBERG - buys and trades all trains
Golden Spike International
1700 Grand Concourse
Bronx, New York 10457
(212) 294-1614

RON ECCLES - Manoil Army Train and lead figures and vehicles. from original molds
  902 Summer Street
  Burlington, Iowa 52601

BILL LANGO - Barclay, etc., toys from original molds, for train accessories
  127 74th Street
  North Bergen, New Jersey 07047

FRANK CAMILERI - Lionel, Flyer, HO, N Gauge, bought, sold, repaired
  10 Front Street
  East Rockaway, New York 11518

MADISON HARDWARE COMPANY-New and old trains, repairs
  105 East 23rd St.
  New York, New York